Law of Mass Communications: Freedom and Control of Print and Broadcast Media

Law of Mass Communications: Freedom and Control of Print and Broadcast Media

Contributors

Elo Ibagere et al.

AURIS
Reference

www.aurisreference.com

Law of Mass Communications: Freedom and Control of Print and Broadcast Media

Contributors: Elo Ibagere et al.

Published by Auris Reference Limited

www.aurisreference.com

United Kingdom

Printed in 2017 for Sale in the Indian Subcontinent

Law of Mass Communications: Freedom and Control of Print and Broadcast Media

ISBN: 978-1-78154-735-9

British Library Cataloguing in Publication Data
A CIP record for this book is available from the British Library

Printed in the United Kingdom

Exclusively distributed by CBS Publishers & Distributors Pvt. Ltd.

Sales & Distribution Rights only for India, Pakistan, Bangladesh, Sri Lanka, Nepal and Bhutan.This book is not to be sold outside these territories.

Contents

List of Abbreviations .... *vii*

List of Contributors .... *ix*

Preface .... *xi*

Chapter 1 **The Mass Media, the Law and National Security: The Nigerian Perspective** **1**

Elo Ibagere

Chapter 2 **The Diversity Policy Model and Assessment of the Policy Debates and Challenges of (Media) Diversity** **9**

Kim P. McCann

Chapter 3 **The Media Representations of Police Image Research Notes on the Hong Kong's Occupy Movement** **25**

Wayne W. L. Chan

Chapter 4 **Health Reporting in Print Media in Lebanon: Evidence, Quality and Role in Informing Policymaking** **51**

Fadi El-Jardali, Lama Bou Karroum , Lamya Bawab , Ola Kdouh, Farah ElSayed , Hala Rachidi, Malak Makki

Chapter 5 **Criminal Risk, Media Representation and Role of the Criminal Law Culture** **79**

Mario Caterini

Chapter 6 **Modeling the Adoption of Innovations in the Presence of Geographic and Media Influences** **99**

Jameson L. Toole, Meeyoung Cha, Marta C. Gonza´lez

Chapter 7 **Act Clxxxv Of 2010 on Media Services and Mass Communication** **119**

Citations **273**

Index **275**

List of Abbreviations

CSC	Civil Servant Cooperative
CSOs	Civil Society Organizations
DMA	Designated Market Area
DI	Diversity Index
EMR	Eastern Mediterranean Region
ITV	Independent Television
IRB	Institutional Review Board
MOPH	Ministry of Public Health
NSSF	National Social Security Fund
NTA	Nigerian Television Authority
PDP	Peoples Democratic Party
SSS	State Security Services
SI	Susceptible - infected
WAI	War against Indiscipline

List of Contributors

Elo Ibagere
Department of Theatre Arts, Delta State University, Abraka, Nigeria

Kim P. McCann
Saginaw Valley State University, Midland, MI, USA

Wayne W. L. Chan
The Open University of Hong Kong, Hong Kong

Fadi El-Jardali
Department of Health Management and Policy, American University of Beirut, Riad El Solh, Beirut, Lebanon
Knowledge to Policy (K2P) Center, Faculty of Health Sciences, American University of Beirut, Riad El Solh, Beirut, Lebanon
Center for Systematic Reviews on Health Policy and Systems Research (SPARK), American University of Beirut, Riad El Solh, Beirut, Lebanon
Research, Advocacy and Public Policy-making Program, Issam Fares Institute for Public Policy and International Affairs, American University of Beirut, Riad El Solh, Beirut, Lebanon
Department of Clinical Epidemiology and Biostatistics, McMaster University, Hamilton, Ontario, Canada

Lama Bou Karroum
Department of Health Management and Policy, American University of Beirut, Riad El Solh, Beirut, Lebanon

Lamya Bawab
Department of Health Management and Policy, American University of Beirut, Riad El Solh, Beirut, Lebanon

Ola Kdouh
Department of Health Management and Policy, American University of Beirut, Riad El Solh, Beirut, Lebanon

Farah ElSayed
Department of Health Management and Policy, American University of Beirut, Riad El Solh, Beirut, Lebanon

Hala Rachidi
Department of Health Management and Policy, American University of Beirut, Riad El Solh, Beirut, Lebanon

Malak Makki
Assafir newspaper, Beirut, Lebanon

Mario Caterini
University of Calabria, Rende, Italy

Jameson L. Toole
Engineering Systems Division, Massachusetts Institute of Technology, Cambridge, Massachusetts, United States of America

Meeyoung Cha
Graduate School of Culture Technology, Korea Advanced Institute of Science and Technology, Daejeon, Korea

Marta C. Gonza´lez
Department of Civil and Environmental Engineering, Massachusetts Institute of Technology, Cambridge, Massachusetts, United States of America

Preface

Mass communication is the study of how people and entities relay information through mass media to large segments of the population at the same time. The text Law of Mass Communications: Freedom and Control of Print and Broadcast Media includes substantial material involving new media, as technological changes affect traditional patterns of both communication and governance. First chapter employs the analytical method to examine the set out issues against the backdrop of the feeling that one views the mass media and law as complementary sectors that could impinge on each other in the facilitation of the operations of other sectors of the polity. Second chapter investigates the diversity policy within a broad context of legal, political, economic, and sociocultural grounds. The aim of third chapter is to investigate the media images of police role in one singular period of Hong Kong's occupy movement. Fourth chapter aims at exploring the role of media in informing health policies in Lebanon, identifying the factors influencing health reporting and investigating the role of evidence in health journalism and the quality of health reporting. Fifth chapter discusses about the media's redundant emphasis on risks and the elitist specious creation of collective worries, in particular with relation to the criminal phenomenon, presenting the results of criminological researches that validate the empirical demonstration of the media representation's artificiality of criminal risk. In sixth chapter, we update and unify traditional models of information spread and technology adoption to more accurately reflect the novel economic and social environments in which spreading now occurs. Last chapter focuses on Act CLXXXV of 2010 on media services and mass communication.

Chapter 1

THE MASS MEDIA, THE LAW AND NATIONAL SECURITY: THE NIGERIAN PERSPECTIVE

Elo Ibagere

Department of Theatre Arts, Delta State University, Abraka, Nigeria

ABSTRACT

The issue of national security is a fundamental issue in national and international discourses. It is in recognition of this fact that this paper explores the Nigerian perspective of how the operations of the mass media and the law may encroach into each other's domain as well as the implication of such encroachment to national security. The paper employs the analytical method to examine the set out issues against the backdrop of the feeling that one views the mass media and law as complementary sectors that could impinge on each other in the facilitation of the operations of other sectors of the polity. The operation of law affects and influences the way the mass media functions. In the same vein, the operations of the mass media equally affect and influence the operation of law in certain fundamental ways. Having examined the issue in focus, it argues that there is no notable conflict between the operation of the mass media and the law. It concludes by recommending that if recourses are made to the grundnorm of the country (that is the constitution), it would be discovered that the media would operate without any conflict or hindrance and any gatekeeper who violates the law can be punished.

INTRODUCTION

The mass media, by their pre-eminent position in national life, affect other sectors in national development. They are also affected and influenced in their functions by the operations of other sectors. It is against the backdrop of this feeling that one views the mass media and law as complementary sectors that impinge on each other in the facilitation of the operations of other sectors of the polity. The operation of law affects and influences the way the mass media function. In the same vein, the operations of the mass media equally affect and influence the operation of law in certain fundamental ways.

The concern of this paper is the issue of national security – a very fundamental issue in national discourse. The question is, how do the mass media function towards enhancing national security? It is the assumption a priori that both sectors function to ensure national security. But in carrying out their respective functions, they encroach into each other's domain and cause hiccups or dislocation to the system of the other. This paper, therefore, intends to examine this encroachment as well as the resultant dislocations, for the purpose of better understanding of how both sectors function. It may also be necessary to proffer solutions to the problem of interference, with the aim of ensuring better functioning in order for the realization of national security. However, it would also be necessary to, first, establish what is meant by the mass media, how they function as well as what the law is and how it affects the functions of the mass media.

THE MASS MEDIA

Several scholars have variously described the mass media as gadgets used to effect mass communication. For example, Defleur and Dennis (1981) define the mass media as "devices for moving messages across distance or time to accomplish mass communication." The issue of application of the term "mass media" to technical devices is crucial to the understanding of the concept. In fact, the general acknowledgment of this conceptual fact of the mass media has resulted in the terse submission of Uyo (1987) that the mass media, being gadgets used to effect mass communication cannot be practiced. According to him, it amounts to sheer "verbicide" to refer to anyone as a "media practitioner", because one cannot practice gadgets. He likens the pejorative use of this term to such unthinkable expressions as a "teacher practicing blackboard" or "a doctor practicing stethoscope." Thus, those involved in the operations of the mass media are gatekeepers who are responsible for the purveyance of information in the mass communication process. They are, therefore part of the mass media.

THE LAW

The law has been conceived in several ways, depending on each scholar's perspective. Aigbovo (2000), list some of these definitions as follows:

Carl Liewellyn: What officials do about disputes.

John Austin: A command from a political superior to a political inferior backed up with sanctions for its violations.

Oliver Wendel Holmes: The prophecies of what the courts will do.

Sir Edward Coke: Perfection of reasoning.

Hans Kelsen: The primary norm which stipulates the sanctions.

These definitions somewhat show the practical aspects of law in the sense that they focus on the operation of law. This has culminated in the emergence of various schools of thought representing the different groups of scholars who view law from the same perspective. Thus, we have positive law school, natural law school and utilitarian law school.

However, whether any particular definition falls within a particular school does not fall within the purview of this paper. The concern is how law operates within the confines of a civilized environment. Generally, the common definition of law which encompasses the various definitions so enumerated is that it is a body of rules enacted to guide human conduct in any particular society. By this definition, the various bye-laws in the states, the various codes guiding professional practices of professional bodies including the National Broadcasting Code and even the Mass Communication Policy are all parts of the law, because they are all made to regulate conduct at different levels. But a close look at the various definition by scholars as stated above would reveal a kind of conformity with how the law has operated in Nigeria at various times. For example, the law under military regimes conforms to John Austin's definition.

It has been stated that the concern of this paper is how the operation of the mass media and the law encroach into each other's domain as well as the implication of such encroachment to national security. It was also stated that national security is a fundamental issue in national discourse. For a proper understanding, then, of the focus of this paper, it becomes expedient to briefly define the term national security.

National Security

There is the erroneous equation of national security with territorial security. Nigeria today can boast of territorial security in the sense that it is fully protected against its neighbours who cannot dream of attacking Nigeria on their own. Such a move would be suicidal. But the country cannot place its national security on the same pedestal as its territorial security. Ekoko (2004) has classified the definitions of national security into two broad groups. "The first is the military / strategic concept of security and the second (is), non-strategic socio-economic" Quoting the Encyclopaedia of the Social Sciences, he eventually defines security as "the ability of a nation to protect its internal values from external threat" (13). It is in the light of this definition that AI-

Mashat (1985) in Ekoko (2000) submits that national security transcends territorial defence and should focus on the physical, social and psychological quality of life of a society and its members, both in the domestic setting and within the larger regional and global setting.

From the foregoing, it is clear that the main index of national security is the maintenance of values within territorial boundaries. This is more meaningful in view of the current emphasis on global security whereby it is virtually impossible for one nation to attack another just to satisfy an expansionist tendency. Thus, today, national security functions to safeguard the internal working systems of a nation. This does not mean disregard for military security. National security may involve and include the military strategies. But that has to do more with external aggression. We are more concerned here with socio-economic indices as more relevant to our existence. The pertinent question then is: what are those values which should be protected to ensure national security? Values are in close affinity with norms, since values dictate the norms that ensure such values. Norms are guided by rules which determine human conduct. In the quest to control human conduct within the bounds of civilization, nations have made constitutions.

A constitution, therefore, is the grundnorm of a country, because it is the supreme law. And any law enacted which is inconsistent with any provision of the constitution becomes null and void to the extent of its inconsistency. But the constitution may not fully cover every aspect of life. Hence, there are other sources of law made to guide citizens. Other sources of law in Nigeria include legislations, customary law, received English law, judicial precedents and so on. From time to time, policies are enacted and various bodies established to continuously remind us to fall into line in the protection of values. For example, the first attempt at a conscious and organized social change took place in 1984 during the General Muhammadu Buhari's regime, with the establishment of the War against Indiscipline (WAI). Various practices which were inimical to civilized conduct were classified as acts of indiscipline. There was therefore, the establishment of values which every Nigerian was expected to cherish. Some of these are queuing, rather than rushing, patriotism, fairness and justice. The Babangida regime replaced WAI with the Mass Mobilization for Social and Economic Recovery (MAMSER), with virtually the same focus as WAI. If the values of WAI and MAMSER can be religiously protected, then there would be a measure of national security. It must be noted that national security depends on the country's leadership. The lesson from Africa indicates that the greatest threat to national security emanates from the various countries' rulers, who have constituted themselves into a band of brigands inexorably focused on the wanton plunder of the continent's vast natural wealth. Soyinka

(2007) rightly notes: The theme of power is one that remains too pertinent to a continent which having freed itself from colonial tyranny still finds itself obliged to contend with a renewed colonization from within.

New leaders have colonized the populace they are expected to lead. This has resulted in the systematic impoverishment of the populace by those who seize power through the barrel of the gun or massive electoral fraud backed by fullscale thuggery. This lamentable plunder of Africa by its profligate leaders is aptly captured by Wilmot (2007) who notes that politicians, the higher military and police and their cronies have taken hold of the wealth of their nations and divided it among themselves. Using Nigeria as an example, Wilmot continues, "you can always tell when rich Nigerians land in a European airport" (2007).

In Nigeria, corruption, which has become a venerated way of life, continues to result in crises as people have become disenchanted with the socio-political system. This phenomenon includes reward of cronies with juicy appointments by politicians. These appointments are hardly on merit. This has resulted in inequitable distribution of resources with the populace developing a serious apathy to the electoral system. The inequitable distribution of resources has led to violent agitations, part of which has turned the Niger Delta region of the country into a cauldron of violence and kidnappings. In all this, the mass media have the duty to function appropriately (yet within the confines of law). The media often find themselves in a dilemma regarding the performance of their duty as it should be performed as well as performing such duty in such a way that would not offend the law. So how does the operation of the mass media and the operation of law conflict with each other in pursuance of the attainment of national security. And what are the implications of such a clash, for national security? These questions can only be answered through an examination of the operations of both sectors.

THE MASS MEDIA AND THE LAW

The mass media function in various ways. However,the mass media's basic function has to do with what Harold Lasswell defines as communication. That is, to tell people, who says what in the society, to Whom, When and How. In carrying out this basic function, the mass media perform various tasks that have been classified into four functions by Wright (1960) and cited in Akindele and Lamidi (2001). These are:

- surveillance ,
- correlation of facts of the environment,
- transmission of heritage, and
- entertainment.

The surveillance function involves mass media operators having to nose into the nooks and crannies of the society to fish out information that is of interest to the people. In correlation, the media act to mediate even the taste of the people because they interpret the information so gathered by sifting and discarding what may not be in the interest of the people before purveying such information to them. By such interpretation, they help to create values (for culture), which are then transmitted from generation to generation.

The three functions of the mass media, explained above, if closely examined, would reveal the role of the media in fostering national security. First, by effective surveillance of the environment, the mass media would unveil those areas, individuals or entities that may likely constitute a breach of national security. Secondly, by correlation, the mass media assist other agencies to interpret the information so gathered about the environment and contribute in the utilization of such information to take steps to remedy any breach of national security or foster the perpetuation of practices that enhance national security. Thirdly, by transmission of culture, the media enhance the entrenchment of those norms, the defence of which constitutes national security.

On the other hand, the law contributes to the perpetration of national security by ensuring that values are respected and protected. This it does by the creation of norms which guide human conduct. It must seek to punish any breach of values that may threaten national security. It must be noted that national security is about people whose minds need to be geared towards the defence of values that enhance their collective dignity, that would make them secure from external aggression. The result of such a situation is development. The sacrosanct areas of law in this regard, are those that concern the dignity of man which, if fully protected, would enhance peace and progress in a nation. By this is meant chapter four of the Nigerian constitution (1999), which is on fundamental rights. The chapter encapsulates sections 33-46. The most relevant of these sections to this paper, is section 39 –the Right to Freedom of Expression and the Press. Sub – section I of this section states that: Every person shall be entitled to freedom of expression, including freedom to hold opinions and to receive and impart ideas and information without interference. The operation of the mass media is provided for by this section. And it is in the performance of their functions that the media collide with the law. It should be noted that subsection 3 of the section (39) provides for enactments that seek to punish aberrant use of the freedom so given in sub-section I.

It has already been stated that the law exists to regulate conduct. There are thus, laws guiding the conduct of mass media men in the course of their duties. At times the regulation of conduct might run counter to the diligent performance of the stated functions of the media, especially where the operation of law takes the form of the definition of John Austin. Mass media operators are expected to operate within the confines of the laws guiding their operations without prejudice to section 39 of the 1999 constitution. Some of these laws include libel (encompassing seditious and blasphemous libel), breach of confidence, copyright, contempt of court, leaking of official secrets, invasion of privacy and so on.

The operators of the mass media, including journalists, producers, newscasters, editors and so on, are expected to know their limitations in order to avoid offending the law. The areas of most conflict between the media and the law are libel, invasion of privacy and disclosure of official secrets. At times gatekeepers experience a situation where they are between the call of duty and the need for "national security". This is the kind of security equated with the safety of the interests of a political superior. The dilemma here is whether to publish or broadcast information that is detrimental to the interest of the superior and jeopardize his job and personal security, or falsify the information or ignore it and keep his job. This becomes crucial by virtue of the kind of leadership this country has had. National security appears to be the protection of government officials. And in pursuance of the realization of this security, media men are forbidden from purveying information that is at variance with the interests of those in power. This colonial view informed the colonial enactment entitled: The Seditious Offences Bill of 1909, which aimed at punishing "publications that were designed to inflame an excitable and ignorant populace" (Mytton 1983 in Ibagere 1996). This was sequel to the comment of a colonial official that, press liberty was a "dangerous instrument in the hands of semi-civilized negroes" (Adeseye and Ibagere 1999).

But there have not been many significant cases of libel. Nor have there been cases of invasion of privacy or breach of confidence because the codes of practice also regulate the conduct of gatekeepers in specific terms. This indicates that the mass media have been working in partnership with the law to ensure national security, peace and progress. However, the rule of law continues to be abused by those in power. Here a schism exists between the law and the mass media. If the rule of law is allowed to prevail, cases involving any breach of the law should proceed to the court where the judiciary performs its function of interpreting the law. By the rule of law we mean the three principles enunciated by A.V. Dicey (cited in Atsegbua 1997). These are:

- The absolute supremacy or predominance of regular law as opposed to the influence of wide uncontrolled discretionary powers … A man may be punished for a breach of the law and nothing else.
- It means equality before the law or the equal subjection of all classes

of persons to the ordinary law of the land as administered by ordinary courts.

- The rule of law may be used as a formula for expressing the fact that laws of the constitution, the rules which in foreign countries naturally form part of a constitution code are not the source but consequences or the right of the individual as defined and enforced by the regular courts.

It is pertinent to note that the mass media have somewhat operated against the background of these principles. And within this context, bearing cognizance of the separation of powers, any breach of the law by any person should be a matter before the judiciary. It is also necessary to state that any abuse of the rule of law is itself, not just detrimental but also a serious threat to national security in the sense that it violates one of the cardinal values constituting national security. When there is any publication or broadcast of any material which is calculated to embarrass or injure another or the government, then such media personnel constitute themselves into an entity that is detrimental to national security. However, in a zealous pursuance of the need for effective surveillance, media operators might inadvertently venture into areas whereby so doing would constitute a breach of the law. This was the case in 1984 when Tunde Thompson and Nduka Irabor, both of The Guardian were arrested and charged for publishing facts regarded by government as official secrets. Despite the brilliant argument by their lawyer, Chief Rotimi Williams as to the validity of their action, the government was not convinced and they were jailed for one year.

Media men can also compromise national security when they become unduly protective of those who own such media. Of course, it should be noted that most private media organizations are owned by politicians who use such media to enhance their political fortunes. In a bid to protect their owners' interests, the mass media could engage in acts that are inimical to national security. Such was the case in the years after independence. According to Omu (1996), in Popoola (2002), "the Action Group crisis of 1962, the census crisis of 1963-04 and the Federal Election of 1964 and its aftermath – the newspaper press provided a remarkable example of overzealous and irresponsible partisanship and recklessness." Today, media organizations with affiliation to some politicians go down to despicable depths in defence of these politicians, no matter their excesses. This is why Herbert J. Altschull (1984) in Severin and Tankard (1988) concludes that "the news media are agents of the people who exercise political and economic power." To him, then, an independent press cannot exist. Thus, the media do not serve the people's interest. For example, Benin City, the capital of Edo State remains the best planned city in the country by virtue of its network of roads. But there was virtually no road in Benin between 1999 and 2007 when Lucky Igbinedion ruled the state as the roads remained neglected. Despite the deplorable state of Benin roads, one keeps being buffeted daily on Independent Television (ITV) with the purported billions of naira the government continued to spend on road maintenance in the city. It is instructive to note that ITV is owned by the Edo State Governor's father who is a stalwart of the Governor's party – the Peoples Democratic Party (PDP). In such a situation the media cannot be said to be enhancing national security, having abandoned the ethics of gate-keeping. Rather they are seen as contributing to the security adversity of the state.

But it is not this unethical abdication of responsibility by the media or their contravention of the law that constitutes the most serious threat to national security. Rather, it is the corrupt minds of leaders whose acts negate all that should enhance national security. Having engaged in socio-political transgressions, they seek to protect their interests. And depending on the extent of their power, they punish such media men who may be unfortunate to venture into revealing such transgressions. Such punishment is usually to deter and scare away any other recalcitrant gatekeeper who may want to engage in such a venture. And such punishment is usually severe and without recourse to the rule of law. During the regime of General Sani Abacha, the Judiciary was emasculated. In 1994, the State Security (Detention of Persons) (Amendment) Decree, 14 was promulgated. This decree which was a carryover of Decree 2 of 1984 from the Buhari regime through Babangida to Abacha was amended to include a clause ousting the power of any court of law to issue a writ of Hebeas Corpus. "Thus no court of law in the country could ask that a person detained under Decree 2 of 1984 should be produced in court nor could the lawfulness of such detention be questioned" (Ibagere 2002). The promulgation of the decree could have been informed by the Minere Amakiri Saga of 1973. Amakiri, then the Nigerian Observer correspondent in Port Harcourt was flogged and locked up in a disused toilet by the Aide de Camp to the then Military governor of Rivers State, Diette-Spiff, for daring to publish the ultimatum by Rivers State teachers to the governor that they would go on strike if their demands were not met. Amakiri had, thereafter, gone to court where he was awarded the sum of N10, 000 as damages. The Abacha regime, perhaps to forestall legal victory for anybody so dehumanized, had to amend Decree 2 which had already empowered the government to detain anybody without charge, to include an ouster clause that emasculated the judiciary.

Failure to compromise standards and work in the selfish interests of politicians could be fatal to the mass media gatekeeper as could be revealed by what happened to Vincent Maduka during the Shagari regime. The then ruling party had determined to use the mass media to further its selfish interests.

To concretize the plan, Vincent Maduka, then career Director General of the Nigerian Television Authority (NTA), was relieved of his position and replaced with, Walter Ofonagoro, a History lecturer and party loyalist. The action of the Shagari government had negated section 21 of the 1979 constitution which he (Shagari) had sworn to defend. The section states that: the press, radio, television and other agencies of the mass media shall at all times be free to uphold the fundamental objectives contained in this chapter and uphold the responsibility and accountability of the Government to the people.

It is therefore not much the mass media that violate the law as those who are expected to protect and execute it. During the military administration of General Abacha, a Decree 43 setting up a Newspapers Registration Board was enacted. It specified that each newspaper must register with the Board with the sum of N250, 000 and this registration must be renewed every year. The Guardian challenged the legality of this decree at a Lagos High Court. The court ruled in the newspaper's favour. According to Babatunde Olugboji (1997):

Government appeared to have conceded defeat when it did not appeal against the ruling. But about a year later, the Board advised news organizations to register with it or face sanctions as spelt out in the decree. In 1996, the Board published a "last reminder" warning newspapers to comply "in their own interest."

It is clear from the above that the court is usually relegated to an inconsequential back seat as those who are expected to uphold the rule of law turn apostates and become violators of it. The above is a clear case of insolent display of contempt for the court. There are other cases of violations. For example, there is no provision in law for surrogate arrest. But in 1997, when the editorial staff of Tell magazine were being hunted by men of the State Security Services (SSS), the siblings of those staff were arrested in their place when they were not found at home. This culminated in an action by the family of Nosa Igiebor whose wife and child were arrested when he could not be found. Yet the government cherished this development, just so that interests of highly-placed officials of government would be protected.

It is clear therefore, that the area of conflict between the media and the law is not interference but the abuse of the rule of law. This development threatens the existence of the media and is capable of rendering them ineffective.

Implications for National Security

From the foregoing, it is clear that it is not the encroachment of law into the domain of mass media that has grave implications for national security. Neither is the encroachment of the mass media into the precincts of law as epitomized in violation that is the problem. The actual problem in the relation of both sectors lies with the despotic use of power and in the unbridled manipulation of the law to protect selfish primordial interests. This is why laws have been made with individuals in mind. The Buhari, Babangida and Abacha regimes made laws specifically to punish media organizations which published information that was not favourable to them. This development known as ad hominem law is repugnant to natural justice and good conscience.

The consequences of this unhealthy development are grave for national security. When a nation's values no longer constitute the grounds for which norms are created, and aberrations become cherished norms, such a nation is sitting on a keg of gun powder with fire approaching. National security would experience the most serious threat in such a despicable situation. The most serious threat of disintegration was noticed during the regimes of Babangida and Abacha. The threat was this immense because both regimes institutionalized corruption, crime and other aberrant conduct that supplanted cherished values necessary to enhance national security.

Today, the discontent in virtually all sectors and geopolitical areas in the country, leading to the dislocation of social life with the concomitant enthronement of various crimes such as kidnapping of foreign oil workers and robbery, vivifies the failure to effectively protect those values that should ensure our national security. It is therefore crucial now that the mass media and law should make concerted, coherent and focused effort towards ensuring national security. It is erroneous to believe that the operations of the mass media which may, at times, offend the law constitute the most serious threat to national security. The real threat is the unjust manipulation of the law to serve selfish sectional interests of a few corrupt individuals.

CONCLUSION AND RECOMMENDATION

The paper set out to explore the relationship between the mass media and the law. It focused on how the operation of the mass media impinges on the law and how the law is manipulated to encroach on media operations. These issues were examined including their implications for national security. Having examined the issue in focus, it is concluded that there is no notable conflict between the operation of the mass media and the law. If we have recourse to the grundnorm of the country (that is the constitution), it would be discovered that the media would operate without any conflict or hindrance and any gatekeeper who violates the law can be punished. But because those who hold and operate the apparatus of power sinfully manipulate the law to serve their interests, the mass media become seen as acting to negate national security which is equated with their personal safety. There can never be any threat to national security from the mass media if the country's leadership defend our national values and seek to establish an egalitarian society that is just and fair to everyone.

Based on the foregoing, it would be safe to recommend that mass media men should contribute to the enhancement of national security by carrying out their duties against the backdrop of law and ethics. The law must be upheld at all times. Lawyers must defend the rule of law and uphold the integrity of the judiciary. They should not be part of the design to conduct a trial of those engaged in the legitimate performance of their duties. Those in the judiciary should refuse to adjudicate in matters that negate the rule of law. They should also repudiate laws that are inimical to human dignity. Mass media gatekeepers should carry out their duties with the following guidelines in mind:

- Purvey information with respect for human dignity. Such respect connotes the defence of national values.
- Information dissemination should be done without malice against a perceived enemy, such that the intention is to embarrass the person.
- The major aim of information dissemination should be to inform the people better and improve their lot.
- Gatekeepers must have a sense of national security and seek to improve on it at all times. Thus, whatever does not enhance the perpetration or perpetuation of our established values should be discarded.
- Gatekeepers must abide by the rule of law as well as the established ethics guiding their profession.
- All laws that hinder the performance of the duty of gatekeeper should be repudiated.

It is however fitting to end this piece by quoting the maxim of Pope Gringory XVI which says: but if the truth causes a scandal, then let a scandal arise than the truth is abandoned. So go ahead, publish and broadcast it if it is the truth.

REFERENCES

1. Adeseye F, Ibagere E 1999. Communication and Man: A Theoretical Base for the Student. Akure: Ola-Olu Enterprises.
2. Aigbovo O 2000. Introduction to Nigerian Legal System. Akure: Sylva Publishers Ltd.
3. Akindele R, Lamidi K 2001. Fundamentals of Mass Communication. Ibadan: Adalef Communications.
4. Atsegbua L 1997. Administrative Law: An Introductory Text. Benin City:

New Era Publications.

5. The Constitution of the Federal Republic of Nigeria 1979. Lagos: Federal Government of Nigeria.
6. The Constitution of the Federal Republic of Nigeria 1999. Abuja: Federal Government of Nigeria.
7. Defleur ML, Dennis EE 1981. Understanding Mass Communication. Boston: Houghton Mifflin.
8. Ekoko AE 2004. Boundaries and National Security. Paper presented at the 6th Inaugural Lecture of Delta State University, Abraka, December 2004.
9. Ibagere E 1996. The socio-political paradigm in Nigerian mass media studies. In: Crowther E Ojo, Elo Ibagere (Eds.): Communication: A Book of Readings. Warri: Tonand Klass Communication Ltd., pp. 96-105.
10. Ibagere E 2002. The mass media in the Nigerian democratization process: The assessment of a paradigm and the paradigm of assessment. The Parnassus: University of Uyo Journal of Cultural Research, 1(1): 63-75.
11. Olugboji B 1997. Suppression of the Press in Nigeria. Lagos: Constitutional Rights Project.
12. Popoola I S 2002. Nigeria's fourth republic in search of identity: A commentary in political communication. Humanities Review Journal, 2(1): 22-29.
13. Soyinka W 2007. Of Power (Interventions V). Ibadan: Bookcraft.
14. Uyo O A 1987. Mass Communication Media: Classifications and Characteristics. New York: Civiletis International.
15. Wilmot P 2007. Nigeria: The Nightmare Scenario (Interventions VI). Ibadan: Bookcraft.

Chapter 2

THE DIVERSITY POLICY MODEL AND ASSESSMENT OF THE POLICY DEBATES AND CHALLENGES OF (MEDIA) DIVERSITY

Kim P. McCann

Saginaw Valley State University, Midland, MI, USA

ABSTRACT

Diversity is a central policy goal in achieving democracy, which has guided the Federal Communications Commission's action in media ownership regulation. Although the role of diversity in sustaining democracy is presumable, the diversity principle and regulatory concepts applied to communications policy seem far from reaching a practical consensus. Among the regulatory challenges to achieving diversity goals are controversy on a theoretical level, inconsistent measurement, the interplay of conflicting public interest motivations, and the changes in the media system. This article investigates the diversity policy within a broad context of legal, political, economic, and sociocultural grounds: It proposes an integrative policy model that offers a platform for the analysis of the policy implications and decisions, analyzes the existing policy imposed to achieve diversity goals, and suggests alternative ways of responding to current regulatory challenges for strengthening policymaking.

INTRODUCTION

Diversity is a central policy goal in achieving democracy, which has guided the Federal Communications Commission's (FCC) action in media regulation (see Report and Order and Notice of Proposed Rulemaking, 2003; Report and Order and Order on Reconsideration, 2008). Although the role of diversity in sustaining democracy is presumable, the diversity principle and regulatory concepts applied to communications policy seem far from reaching a practical consensus. Among the regulatory challenges to achieving diversity goals are controversy on a theoretical level, inconsistent measurement, the interplay of conflicting public interest motivations, and the changes in the media system.

Critics, for example, have indicated that policies designed to promote diversity are contradictory due to the FCC's imprecision in defining its regulatory concepts and the limitations of diversity measurement (see Candeub, 2008; Hill, 2006; Ho & Quinn, 2009). An increasingly politicized policymaking process itself, struggling over ideological conflict (see Braman, 2003; Napoli, 2008; Napoli & Gillis, 2006), is also another problem associated with diversity policy. The transformed media environment due to technological developments and media convergence has eliminated much of the legal validity of the scarcity concept that has served as a fundamental justification for the FCC's public interest standard in broadcast regulation. The marketplace of ideas that has replaced the scarcity rationale, and served a primary justification for ownership regulation is now under critical scrutiny due to its contradictory effects on diversity. Growing judicial skepticism about the FCC's economic antitrust-based decision in formulating the logic of public interest has opposed to the long-standing presumed link between ownership diversity and content diversity (see *Schurz Communications, Incorporated v. FCC and the United States of America*, 1992; *Lutheran Church-Missouri Synod v. FCC*, 1998).

The discussion above reflects the conceptual, legal, and regulatory challenges the FCC confronts for the promotion of pluralism and diversity. In response to the issue highlighted, this article investigates the diversity policy within a broad context of legal, political, economic, and sociocultural grounds: It (a) proposes a policy model that offers a platform for the analysis of the policy implications and decisions, (b) analyzes the existing policy imposed to achieve diversity goals, and (c) addresses regulatory challenges. Derived from an overview of the analysis, it (d) suggests alternative ways of responding to current regulatory challenges for strengthening policymaking. The proposed policy model is integrative, self-reflexive, and procedural in its nature, which provides several benefits: First, it reconciles the perceived theoretical and ideological schism in formulating the public interest, as it combines the benefits of economic development with social unity in fulfilling democracy. Second, it is flexible in responding to the current policy condition because the self-reflexive mechanism corrects and renews the ongoing policy system. Finally, it offers the grounds for communication research contributing to the policy process for its procedural step essentially involves various contextual analyses that in turn demands communication resources and research. See Figure 1 for the proposed model.

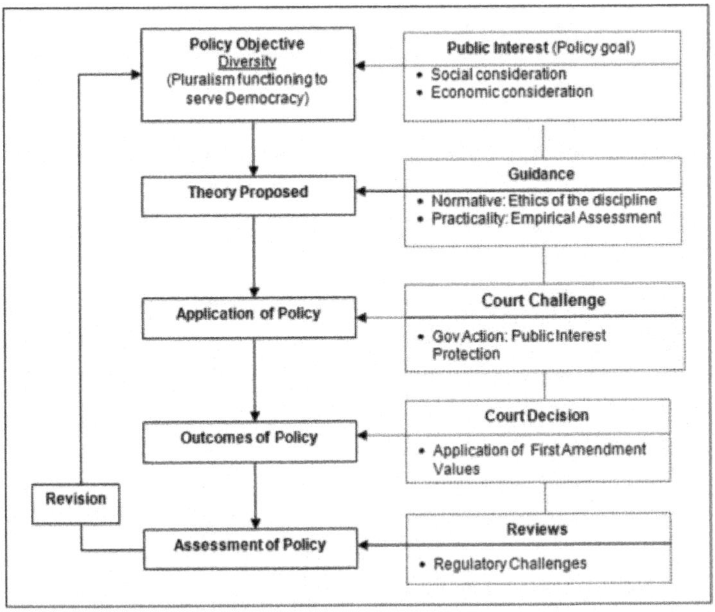

Figure 1: Media diversity policy paradigm.

The Policy Objective: The Public Interest Standard

One major challenge in the development of diversity policy stems from the competing principles of the public interest. The FCC's interpretation of the public interest mandate means achieving competition, diversity, and localism (Report and Order and Notice of Proposed Rulemaking, 2003; Report and Order on Reconsideration, 2008). Alas, these concepts are elusive, and difficult to measure. There is considerable conceptual overlap between localism and diversity, which makes it difficult to distinguish localism from diversity. More importantly, not all these values fit into the existing policy framework due to its deficiency in social and political evaluative criteria. While competition lends itself to the existing economic analysis, diversity and localism do not (Ho & Quinn, 2009). As history tells us, the failure of diversity policy is often a result of the FCC's vague definition of regulatory concepts of diversity, closely tied to the public interest standard.

Establishing the Public Interest Standard: Political, Social, and Economic Values

Media and communications policy is made for the *benefit of the public*. The public, according to John Dewey, is a social creation that is not biased toward government administrative goals nor individual freedom, but the product that reflects consequences of *social, political, and economic considerations* we all share (see also Aufderheid, 1999; Van Cuilenburg & McQuail, 2003, for the dimensions of the public interest). Although the public interest may take various forms, depending on what current national policy emphasizes and how a legal system operates in a society, the general components of public interest should encompass these three considerations, necessary for guiding media and communications policy.

The criteria defining political values are associated with the function of democracy, ensured by the adoption of the First Amendment: Pluralism and diversity are political goals, concerned with whether diverse ownership and content would cultivate informed citizenry for their meaningful participation in democratic public life.

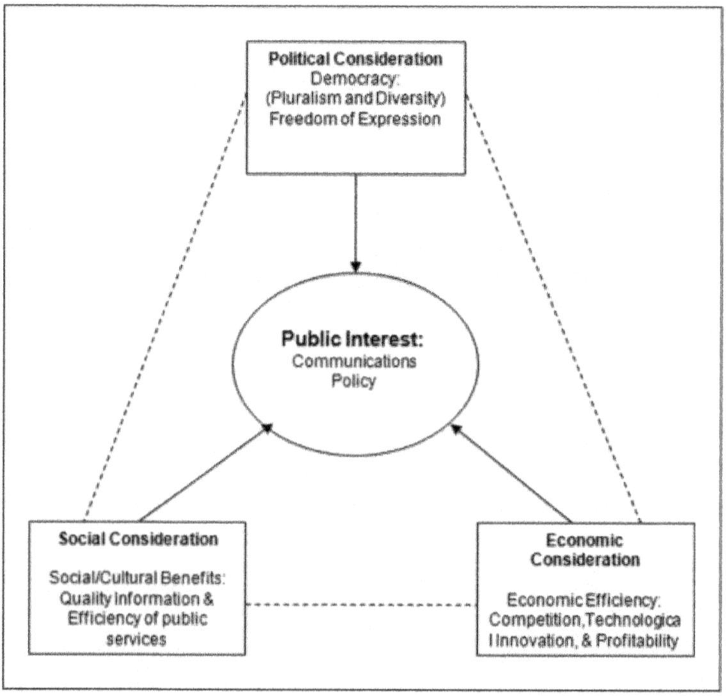

Figure 2: Dimensions of the public interest and media institution.

Diversity Policy Objective: Pluralism to Serve Democracy

Social values relate to the social impact of media content in terms of cultural and social benefits; under this consideration, diversity concerns whether diverse viewpoints in media content foster socially desirable outcomes for the public needs. Economic values relate to the economic efficiency of technology, competition, and profits; under this consideration, diversity concerns whether diverse competition and media outlets provides an access for citizens' participatory democracy. Economic values, however, are more effective in facilitating pluralism than diversity. Understood by and large, the political premise of freedom of expression, such as democracy, has been enforced through the economic consideration of effective competition as well the social consideration of critical and substantive media content. Discerning the complementary function of the public interest is thus desirable for approving particular communication services and improving the policies while avoiding a potential political conflict, fueled by following the narrow logic in competing principles (see Figure 2).

Diversity as political pluralism is to achieve democracy. By creating diverse sources, and ideas (i.e., pluralism) through an open communication system (i.e., public sphere or marketplace), it attempts to facilitate genuine public debate by participation of well-informed citizens (i.e., democracy). Within this framing, diversity policymaking starts from stating a clear policy objective that is, "creating pluralism to serve democracy." The critical relationship between media and democracy in a society has often been debated, primarily due to the presumption that media exercises a critical public role in cultivating citizenship. Whether citizens take an active role in making a democratic decision largely hinges on the responsibility of media in a self-governing system. This raises a diversity inquiry into whether the current media system functions as a source of guidance for citizens' participation and deliberation in democracy, which ultimately guides the FCC's implementation of the public interest standard for the diversity policy.

THEORY PROPOSED: GUIDANCE TO THE POLICYMAKING

The Integrative Theory: Political Outcomes in Economic and Social Contexts

Two major approaches to diversity revolve around the economic and social values of media's democratic performance: Each conceptualizes media diversity within separate domains and proposes divergent ways of envisioning audiences, namely, "citizens" and "consumers," respectively. Responding to such division, many critics have suggested the need for conceptual clarification in the study of communications policy (e.g., Braman, 2003; Entman & Wildman, 1992; Giddens, 2000; Meehan, 1981; Mullender, 2000; Streeter,

1990; Vick, 2006). Braman (2003), for example, pointed out that the failure of issue-oriented policy analysis is due to certain theoretical propositions that oversimplify contradictions and complexities of the negotiation held by policymakers. In a similar vein, Entman and Wildman (1992) criticized the lack of constructive discussion between the market economics and social value schools of thoughts and unwillingness to learn from the other's approach.

The proposed theory responds to the need for developing an analytical framework for diversity policy that involves the wider intellectual frames consistent to the public interest standard, and discerning complementary functions of social and economic goal in achieving political goal, democracy. Social and economic theories share common goals in the specific context of media regulation, such as pursuing liberty, pluralism, and diversity, although they differ in their preferred means of achieving these goals. The effort in conceptual clarification of the diversity principle, thus, should examine common goals as well as contentious issues developed from social and economic standpoints on the diversity policy.

Economic Approach: Empirical Claim and Efficiency of Competition

The economic approach has its roots in market liberalism, dubbed the market economics. It maintains that the media should carry content that most appeals to consumers, and success of media performance is primarily measured by market behavior (see Candeub, 2008; Croteau & Hoynes, 2006; Miller, 2011; Shelanski, 2006). Entrenched in laissez-faire economics, the market economics proposes the benefits of the free market, advancing the neutral role of government due to its distrust of government. The market is more responsible to consumers than the state, thus can enhance consumer choices (Vick, 2006). By establishing a free market line, the economic approach legitimatized deregulation policy (see Candeub, 2008; Curran, 2000;Hopkins, 1996; Vick, 2006). To that extent, the market theory offers an assumption that pluralism and diversity will flourish within a free marketplace.

The economic concept of market liberalism has been widely applied in the courts and ownership regulations, dubbed the marketplace of ideas metaphor. Accordingly, the marketplace of ideas has served as the theoretical underpinning of the diversity principle in the United States (seeCandeub, 2008; Curran, 2000; Hopkins, 1996; Napoli, 1999; Vick, 2006) as it was introduced by Justice Holmes (1919) in his dissenting opinion in *Abrams v. United States*. The metaphor suggests that the best policy can be made out of the "competition of extensively various ideas" in an unregulated market, well reflected in the FCC's assumption that ensuring *antagonistic sources*would be instrumental to achieving diverse viewpoints for audiences.

In policy and juridical circumstances, empirical evidence takes an important role in justifying FCC's regulatory efforts. Economic analysis is inherently quantitative, and thus can estimate the causal mechanism involved in the issue by either proving or disproving the theory. Such an empirical assessment functions to narrow down a general claim of diversity to testable outcomes, and accordingly can generate pragmatic alternatives to the market reality. Historically, economic analysis has a large role to play in policymaking.

However, the empirical analyses of the economic approach alone do not effectively capture the democratic values associated with media content (i.e., diverse viewpoint cultivating citizenship). Although mass media policy has used various methods to serve the policy interests of market efficiency and democratic issues (Shelanski, 2006), democratic values within the economic approach have often been defined as pluralism satisfying popular demands rather than diversity. Moreover, the FCC has failed to provide substantial evidence to prove the nexus between liberalizing media markets and preserving deliberative democratic values. Consumers' ideas are often the opposite of the diverse intellectual activity and politically informed public body the marketplace of ideas suggests, as they tend to eschew challenging established notions (seeCurran, 2000; Entman & Wildman, 1992). This illustrates the limitation of market economics in offering appropriate insights into diversity policy goals, and the need for incorporating a social approach to the diversity principle and policy development.

Social Approach: Moral Claim and the Media Content in Cultivating Deliberative Democracy

The social-based theory, in general, pursues statism, egalitarian, and deliberative democracy (seeBaker, 2007; Croteau & Hoyne, 2006; Curran, 2000; Entman & Wildman, 1992; Giddens, 2000; Mullender, 2000; Vick, 2006). Statism finds expression in the advocacy of government intervention for enhancing social values and protecting the public interest against the private market power. It purports that unregulated private market power is socially detrimental, and can be a threat to democracy, diversity, and freedom of expression; thus, it does not identify market efficiency as a primary goal of media policy (see Giddens, 2000; Mullender, 2000; Vick, 2006). Concerned with the inequality of market power, social advocates would argue that the decentralization of media ownership, for its own sake, should be a political goal (e.g., Baker, 2005, 2009; Croteau, 2003; McChesney, 1997, 1999). However, they also view the ownership restrictions relying on economic mechanism of antitrust law as failure in terms of connecting to any quantifiable social and political goals (see Candeub, 2008). With an emphasis on deliberative democracy, promoting diversity is seen as facilitating an informed public discussion of important issues and rational-critical debates (see Shelanski, 2006). To achieve such goals, it underlines the media's obligation to pursue social goals as public resources over their professed organizational goals. Hence, diversity is assessed in terms of whether the media facilitate critical independent thought among citizens, information quality, and the social/cultural order in society, and whether policy can effectively help the media provide different viewpoints. Because of assuring citizens' informed judgments about public issues, the social approach meets the requirement for deliberative democratic values of media content vital to achieve diversity. Unfortunately though, social values are often dismissed as externalities by market economics proponents because they are not easily quantifiable (see Baker, 2009;Entman & Wildman, 1992).

APPLICATION OF THE POLICY: GOVERNMENT ACTION AND COURT CHALLENGES

The application to policy involves not only government regulations on behalf of the public interest, but also court challenges and judicial decisions about the constitutionality of proposed rules. The constitutionality of the rules and regulations, in this way, hinges on the government's logic to justify the public interest. The following briefly provides regulatory concepts of diversity defined by the FCC to increase the understanding of how the FCC uses them, and second examines the imposition of the regulations rules and the FCC's justifications for them.

Concepts of Diversity Defined by the FCC

The FCC defined diversity as five distinctive yet interrelated concepts, namely, viewpoint, program, outlet, source, and minority and women ownership diversity (FCC, 2011; Report and Order and Notice of Proposed Rulemaking, 2003): Viewpoint diversity refers to the availability of media content reflecting a variety of perspectives; Program diversity refers to a variety of programming formats and content; Outlet diversity means that, in a given market, there are multiple independently owned firms; Source diversity refers to the availability of media content from a variety of content producers; Minority and female ownership diversity refers to encouraging minority and female ownership (Report and Order and Notice of Proposed Rulemaking, 2003, para 19-42). The first two concern content diversity while the later three concern ownership diversity. Insisting on the presumed link between ownership diversity and content diversity, the FCC has attempted to create viewpoint and program diversity through outlet, source, and workforce diversity. This explains that the FCC regulatory concepts center primarily on competition of ownership to achieve diversity goals.

Content Control: Fairness Doctrine–Political Viewpoints

In spite of the First Amendment conflict, the content of broadcasting has been subject to censorship due to its legally distinctive nature; broadcasting can reach the general public and broadcasters are public trustees for the public. A primary example is the fairness doctrine, mostly linked to viewpoint diversity. The fairness doctrine reflects the public interest rationale for content restriction, allowing government supervision of broadcasters' programming, mandating more diverse programming, and particularly political viewpoints (see "In Re Application of Great Lakes," 1929). The fairness doctrine-based content restriction was validated and constituted by firm establishment of the scarcity rationale in *Red Lion Broadcasting Co. v. FCC* **(1969)**. Nonetheless, faced with First Amendment challenges, the public interest demand for media delivering diverse viewpoints does not seem applicable to an increasingly competitive economic environment. Accordingly, with its opinion in Syracuse Peace Councils in 1986, the FCC refused to enforce the fairness doctrine, and formally abolished it in 1987.

Ownership Regulations: Economic Analysis of Antitrust Law

The FCC's efforts to achieve diversity goals have focused heavily on ownership structure, largely guided by the economic principles of antitrust law (see Connolly & Kwerel, 2007; Ho & Quinn, 2009). The ownership regulations involve the three areas: ownership of outlet (outlet diversity), ownership of programming (source diversity), and ownership of workforce within the distribution system (minority and female ownership diversity).

From the cross-ownership rules to cross-media limit: Outlet and viewpoint diversity

The FCC adheres to the presumption that outlet diversity is the most reliable means of promoting viewpoint diversity (Report and Order and Notice of Proposed Rulemaking, 2003). To preserve outlet diversity, the FCC has imposed various cross-ownership rules to prevent common ownership within the same market (e.g., newspapers–broadcaster cross-ownership and the television–radio cross-ownership). The public interest rationale for these rules was to protect the availability of viewpoint diversity, pertinent to editorial content, to local communities, closely linked to localism. Yet, the newspaper–broadcast cross-ownership rule was substantially relaxed and the television–radio cross-ownership rule was entirely eliminated (retained now due to a failure of justifying the new rules), based on the FCC's adoption of the cross-media limits in 2002. The Commission explained that there is no substantial record that indicates that the cross-ownership limits significantly protect a diversity of viewpoints (or localism) in those media (Report and Order and Notice of Proposed Rulemaking, 2003; Report and Order and Order on Reconsideration, 2008).

When the commission fist proposed the newspaper–broadcast cross-ownership rule it was challenged in *FCC v. National Citizens Committee for Broadcasting* **(1978)**. The court, however, held the validity of the challenged regulations, accepting the difficulty of defining and measuring viewpoint diversity (436 U.S. 793-815). Although it was conceded that the rulemaking record was inconclusive in establishing the connection between ownership limits and viewpoint diversity, the court recognized the need for qualitative judgment on defining an elusive concept of viewpoint diversity. Nevertheless, the court began to take seriously the connection between them in the *Prometheus Radio Project v. FCC*, in which the court criticized the FCC's use of the DI to measure viewpoint diversity, and remanded it (Dissent by Chef Judge Scirica).

Fin/syn rules: Source and program/viewpoint diversity

The FCC's ownership regulation to ensure content diversity is also concerned with the ownership of program producers (i.e., source diversity). Based on the belief that increasing independent program suppliers furthers program and viewpoint diversity, the FCC imposed Financial Interest and Syndication rules (fin/syn). The fin/syn rules were originally adopted in 1970 to restrict the three established networks (ABC, CBS, and NBC) from owning monetary rights in syndicated programs while encouraging the bargaining power and profitability of independent program suppliers (see Review of the Syndication and Financial Interest Rules, 1995; Rosencrans, 1990). The public interest rationale for the fin-syn rules is to limit the networks' control over television programming and thereby encourage the development of a diversity program through diverse and antagonistic sources of program services (Review of the Syndication and Financial Interest Rules, 1995).

Notably, the rules have received substantial criticism. Along with changes in the media market, the networks, restricted from the syndication market, seemed unable to compete with the cable and video companies in terms of the price offered. The independent producers have tended to purchase inexpensive products from domestic syndicators rather than producing innovative and diverse television content. As a result, in 1983, the FCC proposed eliminating much of the fin/syn rules fueled by a deregulation climate. In 1991, after receiving extensive comments and conducting a hearing, the FCC relaxed certain aspects of the fin/syn, yet retained the revised fin/syn rules. On appeal, however, the 1991 decision was overturned by the United States Court of Appeals for the Seventh Circuit due to the failure of proving the nexus between the modified rules and diversity goals (Review of the Syndication and Financial Interest Rules, 1995). In*Schurz Communications, Incorporated v. FCC* **(1992)**, Judge Posner criticized the logic of the public interest built on the FCC's long-standing economic antitrust foreclosures applied for enhancing diversity, and struck down the revised fin/syn rules.

EEO rules: Workforce diversity and viewpoint diversity

The Equal Employment of Opportunity rules (EEO) are an obvious example of the FCC's effort to create diverse viewpoints or programming through the ownership of the workforce within the distribution system. The EEO rules were designed to ensure that minority groups (racial, ethnicity, and gender based) have a fair chance of being employed in electronic media services to foster diversity in programming. Yet, in *Lutheran Church-Missouri Synod v. FCC* **(1998)** the D.C. Circuit court criticized the FCC's logic of formulating the race-based rules, and rejected the FCC's ruling against the church. According to the court, the FCC did not clarify what exactly constitutes diversity of programming, and thus failed to establish a connection between the minority ownership and viewpoint diversity.

OUTCOMES: COURT DECISIONS AND FIRST AMENDMENT VALUES

Scarcity Rationale: Constraint on Media Voices for Socially Desirable Media Content

The legal question, raised by the court challenges, involves the validity of the primary justification for media regulations, which lends itself to different applications of First Amendment values to the diversity policy. It addresses the significant challenges in regulatory justification for achieving diversity goals. The scarcity rationale is the primarily legal justification for broadcast regulations, allowing government intervention to promote the First Amendment values for *the public* (see Krattenmaker & Powe, 1999; Spitzer 1989). The court imposed a legal presumption of distinctive treatments for different communications media for First Amendment purposes (476 U.S. 496), drawing on "the social impact of the media content." Democracy (i.e., diversity) is, thus, achieved through an adoption of the legal framework based on the normative principle that demands diverse programming or "socially desirable content," equally applicable to all "citizens."

However, the constitutional significance of the scarcity rationale was widely attacked during the convergence era that legitimatized deregulation policy. The blurring media services, due to technological innovation and digitalization, goes beyond the ability of the broadcast model that is confined to single media legislation. In this way, it seems impossible for the Supreme Court to apply a distinctive legal framework to First Amendment issues, evidenced when the Supreme Court expressed doubts about continued reliance on scarcity, and the minimal control of government over broadcast programming in *Turner Broadcasting v. FCC* **(1994)**. Consequently, the diversity goals envisioning social values and deliberative democracy, enforced within broadcasting, have been greatly undermined.

The Marketplace of Ideas: Constraint on Government Actions for a Robust Competition

While the changing media landscape eliminated much of the scarcity in broadcast regulations, the marketplace of ideas has been a prominent guiding metaphor for ownership decisions. It has been primarily used for justifying economic antitrust laws, drawn upon the value of efficient market, responsive to the public needs. Democracy is thus achieved through the First Amendment purpose that protects *a robust competition of multitude of media voices* against the government intervention, which in turn meets *the public needs*. Nevertheless, the courts threw the validity of the marketplace of ideas into doubt, calling into question a mere economic authorship over media structure with little regard to its connection to democratic values of content diversity, particularly viewpoint diversity (e.g., *Schurz, Lutheran Church, Time Warner*, and *Prometheus*cases). With an undercurrent of the demand for substantial proof to justify ownership rules, the courts discredited the marketplace of ideas. The question raised about the continued validity of the regulatory justifications addresses the critical demands for reframing the existing policy framework for an adequate implementation of the policy.

ASSESSMENT OF POLICY: REVIEWS AND REGULATORY CHALLENGES

Section 202 (h) of the Telecommunication Act of 1996 allows the Commission to periodically review its ownership rules (except the national television ownership limit) and determine whether any of such rules are necessary in the public interest as the result of competition (Report and Order and Order on

Reconsideration, 2008). The reviews of 1998, 2002 Biennial and 2006 and 2010 Quadrennial involve important policy issues of (a) the deregulatory climate governing the marketplace ideas, (b) the challenges in defining regulatory concepts in terms of competition, diversity, and localism, and (c) the limitation of the entire range of existing economic regulation to further diversity.

Deregulation Policy and Value of Monopoly

The FCC's decisions within the 2002 Biennial and 2006 and 2010 Quadrennial Review Orders reflect their profound consideration of diversity at the local level or localism, and the increased provision of the benefits of common ownership. In 2002 Biennial Review and Order, the Commission significantly relaxed the cross-ownership limits with an adoption of the cross-media limits, derived from the Diversity Index (DI). In completing the 2006 Quadrennial Regulatory Review, the FCC further relaxed the 32-year-old ban on newspaper/broadcast ownership rules within the television market (Report and Order and Order on Reconsideration, 2008). The rules ban not only certain newspaper/broadcast cross-ownership combinations in the top 20 markets, but generally will apply to all other markets (Report and Order and Order on Reconsideration, 2008).

The ownership decisions, contained in 2002 and 2006 Orders, are based on the FCC's belief that the cross-ownership actually produces localism rather than harms competition; the newspaper-owned television stations tend to produce local news and public affairs programming (Report and Order and Order on Reconsideration, 2008, para. 15). The FCC's consideration of the benefits of common ownership is also based on the assumption that the technological advancements support the operation of mainstream media companies delivering news and information to their local communicates (see Report and Order and Notice of Proposed Rulemaking, 2003;Report and Order and Order on Reconsideration, 2008). The growing number of media outlets for news and information, and entertainment today provides more choices via nontraditional modes of media, such as cable, satellite television, digital transmission, and the Internet (Report and Order and Notice of Proposed Rulemaking, 2003; Report and Order and Order on Reconsideration, 2008).

The FCC's significant liberalization of the media ownership was not a simple modification of the rules, but rather a significant change in media structure, which allows substantial concentration in the national and local television markets. The ownership decisions encompass the benefits of a free market, provisioned by values of monopoly in creating multiple media outlets or voices for consumers. In fact, the significant teleological advancements have fully developed economic sectors around electronic media and telecommunications since the 1970s, leading to vertical integration of the previously separated communication industry, known as convergence (seeMcQuail & Siune, 1998; Miller, 2011; Vick, 2006). With increased provisions of economic viability of communication services, the value of monopoly has been reconsidered. The market liberalists and economists advanced the benefit of monopoly and contrived competition among corporate media, necessary for increasing national compatibility within globalized market.

Nevertheless, the commonly expressed concern raised by critics indicates a gradual decline of the public accountability of media and rational debates among citizens (see Miller, 2011). Today's highly competitive media system with increased news outlets hasn't yielded a sufficient amount of public issues and diverse news (see Entman, 2003; Miller, 2011). One of major caveats is that more outlets produced by new media do not necessarily offer new media content when "broadcast TV programs are recycled for cable channels, and newspaper and cable news content is repackaged for the internet, and so on." (Croteau, D. Federal Communications Commission Broadcast Ownership En Banc. Virginia, 27 February 2003.http://transition.fcc.gov/ownership/enbanc022703_docs/Croteau.pdf) Relevant research also indicated that media diversity has declined where scarcity has been more present after the passage of the Telecommunication act of 1996, in broadcasting and local media (e.g., Croteau, 2003; Einstein, 2004). The decline of space for new programs and for public services and the creation of polarized online discussions were also true in spite of a multichannel environment (seeCampbell, Martin, & Fabos, 2012; Dahlberg, 2007).

Defining Regulatory Concepts

In the 1998 Biennial Review, the cross-ownership limits of cable and broadcasting were vacated by the D.C. Circuit due to the FCC's inability to precisely define what constitutes a voice for diversity. For the constitutionality of the proposed ownership rules, the Commission used the DI (Report and Order and Notice of Proposed Rulemaking, 2003) to measure viewpoint diversity at the local market. The DI was designed to measure viewpoint diversity by giving insight into consumers' reported preferences for their media sources of information and news (see*Prometheus*). It weighs the market share of various media outlets in local media markets for antitrust purposes. Nevertheless, the DI does not directly measure, nor sufficiently measure viewpoint diversity. With its economic scheme, it measures the number of participants rather than to coherently measure viewpoint diversity (see Candeub, 2008; Hill, 2006). The court found that DI is not clearly linked to viewpoint diversity, citing in its remands that the Commission irrationally assigned outlets of the same media-type equal market shares, and inconsistently derived the cross-media limits from its DI results (*Prometheus*). On the issue remanded by the Third Court in *Prometheus*, the FCC commissioned the empirical research, namely, the Media Ownership Study that informed the 2006 Quadrennial Review of the ownership policies. Yet, the broad and inconsistent definition of local and localism renders contradictory results from the research, making its application questionable. The definition of local identified by the FCC was based on a Designated Market Area (DMA) as determined by Nielsen Media Research, which has boundaries of geographically distinctive television viewing areas. For example, the FCC's previous research conducted by Alexander and Brown (2004) established the necessarily condition for measuring localism where viewpoints or local stores take place within DMA. In contrast, under the Media Ownership Study of 2006, localism does not appear to be precisely delineated from DMA, expending from geographically bounded definition of local within state to a broader one across state (e.g., Milyo, 2007). Furthermore, a broad definition of localism resulted in inconsistency in defining the local content and news. According to the FCC, localism is broadly defined as the level of responsiveness of a station to the needs of its local communities and local news and quality. Given such a definition, any story would be considered a local content. The inconsistency of defining local content is apparent when Milyo's (2007) study included sports and weather in the component of local news, which has been excluded in the FCC's previous research (e.g., Alexander & Brown, 2004). Of course, a broad definition of local and localism inevitably overestimates the local content. More importantly, what makes the FCC's research unsustainable is that only a few studies respond to the intention of the court's demand for precisely defining viewpoint diversity. For instance, Milyo's (2007) study appears to be the only one performing content analysis that directly measures local content and the political slant of local television news among the others of the Media Ownership Study.

Limitation of Economic Regulation for Democratic Values

The use of the DI to measure viewpoint diversity and inconsistency of measuring localism indicate the FCC's inability or unwillingness to define viewpoint diversity. It also explains the FCC's assumption that viewpoint diversity could be empirically established by a justification for economic effects-based competition policy. Approached empirically though, the existing economic analysis is not effective to measure political or democratic values of viewpoint diversity. As Baker (2009)noted, the problem with viewpoint measurement is its reliance on what is easy to measure rather than what is important. Similarly, Entman and Wildman (1992) argued that democratic values of media diversity do not seem to render economic analysis. Along with scholarly criticism, growing judicial skepticism about viewpoint diversity clearly points out an inclusiveness of the entire range of the existing economic regulations to further democratic values of diversity. In retrospect, the FCC would continually confront difficulty in making its regulation constitutional in the future unless it provides substantial empirical backing for the presumption that diversity of ownership is an essential proxy for content diversity or viewpoint diversity.

REVISION

Policy Objectives: Government Responsiveness to the Major Problem

The policy analysis in the previous sections addresses insufficient government responsiveness to the major problem with the unpredictable impact of a new media landscape on the marketplace. Instead of balancing the potentially negative effect of ownership concentration on diversity against the economic viability of struggling media outlets, the policy tends to leave out the democratic value of diversity, insofar as the assessment of diversity has relied on the economic impact of the marketplace. In opposition to the democratic purpose of antitrust law, its economic analysis has provided justification for significant relaxation of ownership.

Although the First Amendment principles for unprecedented media convergence inherently value the liberalization of ownership undermining the traditional regulatory rationale, it is important to recognize the courts' shifting concern from the structure of the communication market to the content of communication, and government is responsible to that content contributing to democracy (see Krattenmaker & Powe, 1995). With this regard, two possible responses the FCC could make to the given regulatory challenges are (a) developing a more sophisticated and rigorous measure of viewpoint diversity, aimed at democratic values, and (b) diversity of ownership as a separate political goal from viewpoint diversity.

Metrics of Viewpoint Diversity: Input of Communication Research into the Policy

The regulatory challenges address the need for empirical evidence about viewpoint diversity, yet existing quantifiable measures lack in accounting variables that influence outcomes of viewpoint diversity. More critically, a substantial effort to increase analytical resources has been degraded in spite of increasingly evidence-driven policymaking demanded by current law (see Napoli, 2008). The perceived gap between the FCC's rationale for economic regulations and judicial interpretation of First Amendment values of diversity addresses the need for a collaborate effort of policymakers, legal, and communication scholars in answering the constitutional questions and capitalizing the norms for an empirical assessment of diversity. Indeed, the input of communication research into the policymaking is valuable in responding to the courts' increased requirement for convincing empirical justification for viewpoint diversity. A number of scholars provide the value of communication research that provides informational inputs to policymaking (e.g., Braman, 2003; Napoli, 1999).

To develop a more sophisticated and meaningful metrics of viewpoint diversity, diversity inquires should entail the complementary functions of (a) deliberative democracy that ensures substantive ideas and information for cultivating informed citizenry and (b) participatory democracy that encourages citizens' engagement in the democratic process. The norms for assessing viewpoint diversity thus encompass the inquiry into how media democratic system affects informed citizenry, and in turn how citizens' widespread habit of media use affects their democratic decisions. Such metrics of viewpoint should be drawn from a collective understanding of normative and empirical inferences developed and contextualized within and across economic and social disciplines that propose reasons for value-laden inquires as well as statistical analysis, respectively.

Normative and Empirical Inferences

Unlike the critical social approach that challenges the uncritical acceptance of empirical findings and proposes an unquantifiable nature of social values with its normative approach, social scientists have empirically or statistically measured "social values" with its positive approach. Inversely, statistical analysis quantified by the market economics is not necessarily drawn from positive inferences, as its conceptual root is grounded in Marxist's critical perspective that proposes normative social justice based on class analysis. Moreover, contemporary economic approaches have imposed a critical role of government to attain the desired democratic needs, which is opposed to the classical market approach (see Van Cuilenburg & McQuail, 2003).

Understanding such complexity of theoretical and methodological propositions in terms of democracy, developed within and across the social and economic field, is important to avoid theoretical schism and ideological conflict that often hinders developing a comprehensive and schematic assessment of diversity. In other words, two democratic values of diversity, such as deliberative and participatory democracy, should be explained from the interdisciplinary interplay between normative and empirical inquires developed across a variety of disciplines without generalization of each approach.

Deliberative democracy: Political diversity reflected in media content

The FCC's definition of viewpoint diversity and various approaches to it have involved these two democratic values stated above. Traditionally, as reflected in *Red Lion*, and enforced through the fairness doctrine, viewpoint diversity would measure "political endorsement." Later, as stated byHundt (1996), the measure of viewpoint diversity involves "editorial perspective" or editorial content. Most recently, the FCC in the 2003 Report and Order states that viewpoint diversity is most easily measured through "news and public affairs programming," concerning political ideas and information necessary to guide the cultivation of rational deliberation between citizens. These tell that the norms of viewpoint diversity underline deliberative democratic values represented in media content, which affects the robustness of democratic participation of citizens by increasing political knowledge or ideological viewpoints. Under this direction, many researchers have developed variables relevant to political endorsement, and editorial perspectives and positions in news and public affairs programming in measuring viewpoint diversity (e.g., Entman, 1989;Halavais, 2007; Ho & Quinn, 2009; Miller, Goldenberg, & Erbring, 1979). The variables that involve such deliberative democratic values of viewpoint diversity are

- Newspaper or broadcast content based on political endorsements
- Counts of time and space allotted to political candidates in broadcast.
- Political content (liberal vs. conservative positions) of news articles offered by newspaper editors and broadcasters
- Word frequencies in editorials and news article

Viewpoint diversity reflecting deliberative democracy is critical to cultivate well-informed citizenry; thus, their participation in democracy is accountable. The scholarly criticism questioning the reliability of viewpoint diversity stems from the deficiency of critical social values of deliberative democracy in its measurement, which is closely linked to the methodological flaw of the DI that measured the number of participants in a market (number of media outlet) rather than substantive viewpoints. Continual efforts in capitalizing and advancing norms for deliberative democratic values of viewpoint diversity are critical to empirically assessing the social benefits of media content.

Participatory democratic values: Survey of citizens and use of media

Viewpoint diversity extends its definition to participatory democracy that accentuates the citizens' participation in their democratic public life. Technological advances have greatly increased citizens' active participation in public issues and democratic decisions through an interactive medium, namely, the Internet. The emphasis of participatory democratic values of viewpoint diversity inherently involves audience research, such as surveying citizens or ethnographic inquiries into citizen's information processing through various mediums. The norms for viewpoint diversity in this approach involve access for civic engagement in democratic decision via news and information served by various media outlets (see Braman, 2007; Horwitz, 2005; Waldfogel, 2007). The citizens' right to receive a diverse range of ideas through guaranteed access has been understood as a more encompassing notion of the freedom of communication system and is a central principle of diversity.

It is, however, important to note that the market approach to participatory democracy has measured viewpoint diversity based on media reflection of public demands with little regard to how their demands fulfill democratic ideals. However, the public demands are not necessarily equivalent to the public needs in their democratic decisions. Emphasized earlier, the literature supports that audiences' demands are popular rather than intellectually diverse. Thus, measuring political dimension of viewpoint diversity in participatory democracy should entail the inquiry into whether citizens' response to or use of media information (i.e., citizens' participation) through various mediums (i.e., access offered by media outlets) affects their public or democratic decisions. Considerable research in the communication field has addressed this diversity inquiry (e.g., Braman, 2007; Dalton, Beck, & Huckfildt, 1998; Gunther, 1992; Horwitz, 2005; Napoli, 2007; Waldfogel, 2007). The variables that potentially measure such participatory democratic function are

- Citizen's public competence or knowledge that affects civic engagement in political issue and public decision
- Citizens' education level that affects information processing in terms of political issue
- Cultural or demographic aspect, including racial, gender, and age background that affect their participation in political issue and
- How these variables affect their particular use of mediums and its relevance to democratic decisions.

Diversity of Ownership as a Separate Goal from Viewpoint Diversity

Developing objective and meaningful metrics of viewpoint diversity is necessary and should be a primary goal in academic research because such an effort has its own intellectual rigor. But, particularly, in times of increased judicial skepticism about viewpoint diversity and empirical justifications for regulations, the FCC inevitably faces methodological challenges. Even if more rigorous and advanced methodologies of viewpoint are developed within and across various disciplines, ongoing debate on its conceptual elusiveness and subjectivity is more likely to exist as a result of the contradictory effects of the economic antitrust law on diversity. Dealing in a practical manner, there seems no greater chance that the FCC would satisfy the court's critical demand for objective and scientific proof for establishing the connection between ownership diversity and viewpoint diversity, thereby continually hindering the government responsiveness to media's democratic performance. If this is the case, an alternative way of countering such struggle in regulations is setting diversity of ownership as a separate goal from viewpoint diversity. Put differently, the FCC may simply make ownership diversity by itself as a political goal (consideration reflected in the 2002 Biennial Review). Enforcement of antitrust law, in this way, is preserving democratic values of not content diversity but ownership diversity in a First Amendment principle.

The proposition of decentralizing ownership is not a new concern. Grounded in normative concern, numerous media scholars have addressed the danger of ownership concentration. For example, McChesney (1997, 1999) proposed reform of media structure to affirm the democratic function of media. He argues that concentrated corporate control is detrimental to any notion of participatory democracy, yet the First Amendment has provided an exclusive shield for corporate media. Croteau (2003, Croteau & Hoynes, 2006) addressed the potential danger of corporate media power that undermined democracies deemed in the public interest, thus the relaxation of ownership would reduce diversity in terms of quantity and quality. Baker (2009) also provided reasons for decentralized ownership regardless of the contradictory effect of antitrust law on viewpoint diversity. The commonly expressed concerns, addressed by these scholars are that concentration of ownership

- would reduce quality diversity, journalism, cultural pluralism in commercial media content;
- would hinder informed public participation or distribution of citizens' voices with the democratic public sphere;
- would undermine democratic value of egalitarian premise in sharing

political power;

- would lead to demagogic political power, failing to serve watchdog function.

Implementing diversity of ownership as a separate political goal from viewpoint diversity would avoid burdensome scrutiny as a result of its content neutral restriction. This approach, while encouraging government responsiveness to media democracy, may also be less competing against the courts' interpretation of the First Amendment values than approving its connection to viewpoint diversity.

CONCLUSION

Media diversity is central to democracy, through which the First Amendment is expressed and promoted by specific policies. In the goal of greater precision of the diversity principles, and of implications and decisions of the diversity policy, this article proposed an alternative policy model, acknowledging the social, economic, and political schisms in fulfilling the goal of media diversity. The policy model attempted to establish the policy objective that is, creating pluralism of outlets, ownership, and choices of people to serve democracy, such as diversity of media content to cultivate citizenship. The predicable connection between pluralism and diversity, in this way, should not be overlooked. The theoretical underpinning of media diversity proposed in the article entailed the wider intellectual frames consistent to the public interest. With the analysis of the integrative function of market economics and social values of media diversity and desirable outcomes on their own, it attempted to avoid oversimplification of complexities existing in the concept of media diversity. Clearly while the empirical analysis of the economic approach can be appropriate to measuring the pluralistic value of competition, the critical analysis of the social approach is equally important to assess the democratic value of media content that can cultivate intellectual activity and politically informed public body.

The application of diversity policy involves judicial decisions about the constitutionality of proposed rules and regulations. The clarification of regulatory concepts of media diversity was attempted to understand the FCC's logic to justify the public interest for preserving the competition of outlets and ownership, and diversity of content (i.e., viewpoint diversity). The major regulatory challenge the FCC has faced was the failure to establish the substantial connection between competition and diversity closely connected to localism. The improvement of the FCC's use of the DI to measure viewpoint diversity is thus critical to justify the public interest rationale. Two regulatory justifications historically used for achieving diversity goals were the scarcity rationale and the marketplace of ideas, each of which renders different applications of legal framework to First Amendment issues. The shift from the scarcity rationale to the marketplace ideas due to the changing media landscape consequently undermined social values of media content while justifying economic antitrust laws designed to protect ownership competition. Hence, the continued validity of the marketplace of idea for promoting viewpoint diversity is largely questionable.

The critical analysis of the FCC's periodical review of the ownership rules and regulations raised important policy issues, such as the continual decline of media diversity fueled by deregulation, the challenges in defining regulatory concepts, left poorly defined, and the limitation of an entire range of existing economic regulations for promoting democratic values of viewpoint diversity. The potential revision of the existing policies precisely responding to these problems is a key factor in effective policymaking. For that reason, the article suggested developing a rigorous assessment for measuring viewpoint diversity strengthened by entailing the complementary function of deliberative and participatory democracy to ensure substantive and critical content for rational deliberation, public participation, and citizen empowerment rather than diversity policies serving as mere rhetorical tools for justifying market motivation of corporate media. With the increased attention to the current media ownership, which is heavily concentrated, the article finally suggested implementing diversity ownership as a separate political goal from viewpoint diversity. This attempt may eschew the recurring problem of equating competition of ownership with diversity of media content.

AUTHOR BIOGRAPHY

Kim P. McCann is an adjunct professor at Saginaw Valley State University. She has taught at Bowling Green State University and completed an appointment of visiting assistant professor at Northern Illinois University. She joined the Donald McGannon Communication Research at Fordham University as a visiting research fellow.

REFERENCES

1. Abrams v. United State, 250 U.S. 616 (1991).
2. Alexander P. J., Brown K. (2004, July). Do local owners deliver more localism? Some evidence from local broadcast news (Federal Communications Commission Working Paper).
3. Aufderheid P. (1999). Communication policy and the public interest: The Telecommunications Act of 1996. New York, NY: Guilford.

4. Baker C. E. (2005). Media structure, ownership policy, and the First Amendment. Southern California Law Review, 78, 733-762.
5. Baker C. E. (2007). Media concentration and democracy: Why ownership matters. Cambridge, UK: Cambridge University Press.
6. Baker C. E. (2009). Viewpoint diversity and media ownership. Federal Communication Law Journal, 61, 651-671.
7. Berresford J. W. (2005). The scarcity rationale for regulating traditional broadcasting: An idea whose time has passed (Federal Communications Commission Media Bureau Staff Research Paper No. 2005–2).
8. Braman S. (2003). The long view. In Braman S. (Ed.), Communication researchers and policy-making (pp. 11-31). Cambridge, MA: MIT Press.
9. Braman S. (2007). The limits of diversity. In Napoli P. M. (Ed.), Media diversity and localism: Meaning and metrics (pp. 139-150). Mahwah, NJ: Lawrence Erlbaum.
10. Campbell R., Martin C. R., Fabos B. (2012). Media and culture: An introduction to mass communication (8th ed.). Boston, MA: Bedford/St.Martin's.
11. Candeub A. (2008). Media ownership regulation, the First Amendment, and democracy's future. University of California, Davis Law Review, 41, 1547-1611.
12. Connolly M., Kwerel E. (2007). Economics at the Federal Communications Commission: 2006–2007. Review of Industrial Organization, 31, 107-120.
13. Croteau D. (2003). Federal Communications Commission Broadcast Ownership EN BANC. Retrieved from http://www.fcc.gov/Speeches/Hundt/spreh617.txt
14. Croteau D., Hoynes W. (Eds.). (2006). The business of media: Corporate media and the public interest. Thousand Oaks, CA: Pine Forge.
15. Curran J. (2000). Rethinking media and democracy. In Curran J., Gurevitch M. (Eds.), Mass media and society (pp. 120-135). London, England: Edward Arnold.
16. Dahlberg L. (2007). Rethinking the fragmentation of the cyberpublic: From consensus to contestation. New Media & Society, 9, 827-846. Abstract/FREE
17. Dalton R. J., Beck P. A., Huckfeldt R. (1998). Parisian cues and media information flows in the 1992 presidential election. American Political Science Review, 92, 111-126.
18. Einstein M. (2004). Media diversity: Economic, ownership, and the FCC.

Mahwah, NJ: Lawrence Erlbaum.

19. Entman R. M. (1989). Democracy without citizens: Media and the decay of American politics. New York, NY: Oxford University Press.
20. Entman R. M. (2003). Putting the First Amendment in its place: Enhancing American democracy through the press. In Braman S. (Eds.), Communication researchers and policy-making (pp. 461-479). Cambridge, MA: MIT Press.
21. Entman R. M., Wildman S. S. (1992). Reconciling economic and non-economic perspectives on media policy: Transcending "the marketplace of ideas." Journal of Communication, 42, 5-19.
22. Federal Communications Commission v. National Citizens Committee, 436 U.S. 775 (1978).
23. Federal Communications Commission. (2011). Before the Federal Communications Commission (Washington, D.C. 20554). Retrieved from http://www.fcc.gov/document/fcc-releases-notice-proposed-rulemaking-media-ownership-rules.
24. Giddens A. (2000). The third way and its critics. Malden, MA: Polity Press.
25. Gunther A. C. (1992). Biased press or biased public? Attitudes toward media coverage of social groups. Public Opinion Quarterly, 56, 147-167. Abstract/FREE
26. Halavais A. (2007). Convergence of newspaper election coverage: 1992 to 2000. In Napoli P. M. (Ed.), Media diversity and localism: Meaning and metrics (pp. 97-112). Mahwah, NJ: Lawrence Erlbaum.
27. Hill B. C. (2006). Measuring media market diversity: Concentration, importance, and pluralsim. Federal Communication Law Journal, 58, 169-194.
28. Ho D. E., Quinn K. M. (2009). Viewpoint diversity and media consolidation: An empirical study. Stanford Law Review, 61, 781-868.
29. Holmes O. W. (1919). Dissent, Abrams v. United States (250 U.S. 616).
30. Hopkins W. W. (1996). The Supreme Court defines the marketplace of ideas. Mass Communication Quarterly, 73, 40-52.
31. Horwitz R. B. (2005). On media concentration and the diversity question. The Information Society, 21, 181-204.
32. Hundt L. (1996, March 28). Speech by Reed Hundt, Chairman (To the American Bar Association). Retrieved from http://www.fcc.gov/Speeches/Hundt/spreh617.txt
33. In re application of Great Lakes Broadcasting Co. FRC Docket 4900, 3

F.R.C. Ann.Rep. 32 (1929).

34. Krattenmaker T. G., Powe L. A. (1995). Converging First Amendment principles for converging communications media. Yale Law Journal, 104, 1719-1741.
35. Lutheran Church-Missouri Synod v. FCC. 141 F.3d 344, 349 (D.C. Cir.1998).
36. McChesney R. W. (1997). The corporate media and the threat to democracy. New York, NY: Seven Stories Press.
37. McChesney R. W. (1999). Rich media and poor democracy: Communication politics in dubious times. New York, NY: The New York Press.
38. McQuail D., Siune K. (Eds.). (1998). Media policy: Convergence, concentration and commerce. London, England: SAGE.
39. Meehan E. J. (1981). Reasoned argument in social science: Linking research to policy. Westport, CT: Greenwood.
40. Miller A. H., Goldenberg E. N., Erbring L. (1979). Type-set politics: Impact of newspapers on public confidence. The American Political Science Review, 73, 844-845.
41. Miller V. (2011). Understanding digital culture. Los Angeles, CA: SAGE.
42. Milyo J. (2007). The effects of cross-ownership on the local content and political slant of local telvision news. Federal Communications Commission Media Ownership Study.
43. Mullender R. (2000). Theorizing the third way: Qualified consequentialism, the proportionality principle, and new social democracy. Journal of Law and Society, 27, 493-516.
44. Napoli P. M. (1999). Deconstructing the diversity principle. Journal of Communication, 49, 7-34.
45. Napoli P. M. (Ed.). (2007). Media diversity and localism: Meaning and metrics. Mahwah, NJ: Lawrence Erlbaum.
46. Napoli P. M. (2008). Paradoxes of media policy analysis: Implications for public interest media regulation (Donald McGannon Communication Research Center). Retrieved from http://fordham.bepress.com/mcgannon_working_papers/17/
47. Napoli P. M., Gillis N. (2006). Reaccessing the potential contribution of communication research to communication policy: The case of media ownership. Journal of Broadcasting & Electronic Media, 50, 671-691.
48. Prometheus Radio Project v. Federal Communications Commission, 373 F.3d 372.

49. Red Lion Broadcasting Co. v. FCC, 395 U.S. 367 (1969).
50. Report and Order and Notice of Proposed Rulemaking. (2003). In the matter of 2002 biennial regulatory review, FCC 03–127.
51. Report and Order and Order on Reconsideration. (2008). In the matter of 2006 Quadrennial Regulatory Review, FCC 07–216.
52. Review of the Syndication and Financial Interest Rules. FCC 95–144 (1995).
53. Rosencrans S. (1990). The questionable validity of the network syndication and financial interest rules in the present media environment. Federal Communication Law Journal, 43, 65-77.
54. Schurz Communications, Incorporated v. Federal Communications Commission and the United States of America. 982 F.2d. (7th Cir. 1992).
55. Shelanski H. A. (2006). Antitrust law as mass media regulation: Can merger standards protect the public interest? California Law Review, 94, 371-421.
56. Spitzer M. L. (1989). The constitutionality of licensing, broadcasters. New York University Law Review, 64, 990-1071.
57. Streeter T. (1990). Beyond freedom of speech and the public interest: The relevance of critical legal studies to communications policy. Journal of communication, 40, 43-63.
58. Turner Broadcasting v. FCC, 512 U.S. 622 (1994).
59. Van Cuilenburg J., McQuail D. (2003). Media policy paradigm shifts. Towards a new communications policy paradigm. European Journal of Communication, 18, 181-207.
60. Vick D. W. (2006). Regulatory convergence? Legal Studies, 26, 26-64.
61. Waldfogel J. (2007). Should we regulate media ownership? In Napoli P. M. (Eds.), Media diversity and localism: Meaning and metrics (pp. 139-150). Mahwah, NJ: Lawrence Erlbaum.

Chapter 3

THE MEDIA REPRESENTATIONS OF POLICE IMAGE RESEARCH NOTES ON THE HONG KONG'S OCCUPY MOVEMENT

Wayne W. L. Chan

The Open University of Hong Kong, Hong Kong

ABSTRACT

The Hong Kong Police Force has undergone one of its biggest challenges in the Occupy Movement that emerged in the last year. Despite the sheer complexity of the police roles, we know little about its representations in the media coverage, and even less about the extent to which the imagery impacts of police acting as peacekeepers would have been made upon the images of police acting as crime fighters. Against this background, this empirical research aims to investigate the police image and its relation to the police's specifically categorized duties in Hong Kong. The content analysis of local newspaper accounts is used as the research method. It is found that there would be generally negative media representations of police in the order-maintenance work whereas the police images in the crime-fighting duties could still remain positive. The reasons for these findings and their implications for the conceptions of the police role are discussed.

INTRODUCTION

According to the Basic Law, which is Hong Kong's mini-constitution negotiated between China and Britain for the governance of Hong Kong after the handover in 1997, universal suffrage for electing Hong Kong's governor, namely the chief executive, would be introduced in 2017. In 2014, the details of the elective arrangements for 2017 were being formulated. In particular, the power of nominating candidates is to be given to an Election Committee, which mainly comprises a small number of social elites. The opposition therefore demanded to bypass the Election Committee and called for a civil nomination of candidates for the chief executive. Some major oppositional figures announced that if this demand was not met, they would call for an "Occupy Central" struggle, in which the "Central" is generally referring to the core business district, and the "Occupy Central" suggests that the opposition would attempt to bring Hong Kong's financial and commercial activities to a standstill if a more democratic universal suffrage in terms of the civil nomination could not be introduced. However, the Central Government of China took the elective arrangements for the chief executive to be a sovereignty issue and refused to the civic nomination.

In the autumn of 2014, the Occupy Movement materialized and a 79-day-long protest occurred, sometimes dubbed as the "Umbrella Revolution" by the foreign media. Revolution or not, it indeed very much constituted an insurrection, with violent clashes with the police occurring on many occasions. The police initially attempted to prevent the occupation of the area around government headquarters with teargas but failed. Meanwhile, the occupiers paralyzed several major traffic arteries in the heartlands of Hong Kong. The government then changed tactics and allowed the occupation to continue, letting it to cause as much damage as possible to the daily life of the traveling public. This tactic worked and eventually sentiment among probably the majority of the public turned against the occupiers, and the police was finally able to restore normality.

It is against this politicalized background that the current research is taking place. It should be further noted that the Occupy Movement has polarized Hong Kong society so much that the occupiers and the police supporters incessantly argued with each other. The police were somewhat caught in a dilemmatic position. In view of this, this research aims to investigate the representations of police image in the media coverage during the Occupy Movement. In particular, given that politicalized context of Hong Kong, this study asks, what are the media representations of police as a peacekeeper? Simultaneously, what are the media images of police as a crime fighter? More important, what are the possible dynamics between the police image in the media coverage and its relation to the police's specifically categorized duties?

LITERATURE REVIEW

The importance of a distinction between crime-fighting (hereafter, law enforcement and crime fighting are used interchangeably) and order-maintenance (hereafter, order maintenance and peacekeeping are also used interchangeably) functions of the police has long been discussed in the police studies. Baton (1964) has nominally distinguished "law enforcers" (detectives) from "peace officers" (patrolmen). Wilson (1968) has proposed the classic policing styles by focusing on such a distinction. In particular, a "legalistic style" of policing would emphasize the enforcement of law dealing with various offences whereas a "watchman style" of police activities would treat order maintenance as the primary police function. More specifically, Wilson (1969) has pointed out the fundamental difference between the law enforcers and peacekeepers in this way:The difference between order maintenance and law enforcement is not simply the difference between "little stuff" and "real crime" or between misdemeanors and felonies. *The distinction is fundamental to the police role, for two functions involve quite dissimilar police actions and judgments* . . . Handling a disorderly situation requires the officer to make a judgment about what constitutes an appropriate standard of behavior; law enforcement requires him only to compare a person's behavior with a clear legal standard. Murder or theft is defined; unambiguously, by statutes; public peace is not. (p. 131, emphasis added)

Although these distinctions are the important typologies that help account for various police practices, they do not resolve the complexity of police roles and the dynamics between crime-fighting and order-maintenance functions of the police in a particular social context.

Considering the complexity of police roles and functions, Manning (1977, 2005, 2010) goes much further by discussing the "impossible" mandate of the police. It has been argued that the traditional role of police as law enforcer serves to promote a neutral and apolitical conception of policing, concealing the fact that the police are politically defined and function as an instrument of political system (Manning, 1977). Seen in this view, the "crime-fighting" police work is nothing more than managing an apolitical appearance of the politicalized police roles. Thinking along the same line, Bittner (2004) has outlined several ways by which the imagery management of a depoliticized police role as crime fighter or law enforcer was conducted. For instance, the knowledge about criminal law is necessarily incorporated into the police training, and the enforcement of criminal law is highly emphasized in the career development of a police organization.

Derived from the above theory, this study presupposes that the police would be equipped with the "impossible" mandate when performing order-maintenance duties. However, it presupposes that the police would be equipped with a relatively "possible" mandate when acting as crime fighters. As also argued in Robert Reiner's (2000) *The Politics of the Police*,If policing is an inherently political activity, it does not follow that it usually appears as such. Policing may be inescapably political, but it need not be politicalized, that is, the centre of overt political controversy over its manner, tactics, or mode of operation and organization. Like riding a bike, policing is the sort of activity that is thought about mainly when the wheel comes off. When things are

running smoothly it tends to be a socially invisible, undiscussed routine. (p. 9)
Simply put, from Wilson (1969) to Manning (1977) and then to Reiner (2000), the police's crime-fighting work could be understood as "possible" because it is equipped with the more clearly legal standard, and more important, the impression management of a depoliticized role like "a bike running smoothly." In a similar vein, the police's order-maintenance work would be "impossible" because the public peace could not be easily defined, or more precisely, the policing of it would be doomed to be politically defined, thus being vulnerably subject to the overt political controversy like "a bike with the wheel coming off."

In this study, what is new is that I will address the complexity and diversity of police roles by focusing a special dimension of the imagery projection of police activities; that is, the media representations of the police image. In particular, a number of hypotheses are postulated in this study:

- **Hypothesis 1:** There would tend to be a positive police image represented in the media when the police perform crime-fighting duties.
- **Hypothesis 2:** There would tend to be a negative police image represented in the media when the police conduct order-maintenance work.
- **Hypothesis 3:** In a highly politicized context, the overall representation of police image would tend to be negative.

In Hypothesis 3, the highly politicized context is referring to Hong Kong's Occupy Movement as mentioned in the "Introduction" section. This is because the policing of Occupy Movement is a case in point of what Thacher (2001) called "a high degree of value pluralism" for the police activities.

Finally, a few words about the theoretical and practical significance of this study should be added. Theoretically, the media representations of police image have long been regarded as a major source of popular perceptions of crime and policing (Cavender, 2004; Mawby, 2012;Wu, Sun, & Smith, 2011). Specifically, the conservatives claim that the media accounts of crime and policing would tend to subvert the authority of law enforcers (e.g., Surette, 2007). However, the liberals believe that the media representations of crime and control would tend to exaggerate the seriousness of crime and then result in a legitimatization of authoritarian policing, or in Reiner's (2003) term, a reproduction of "police fetishism." However, neither the conservative view nor the liberal thought has ignored the dimension of "impossible police mandate"; that is, the media accounts of the order-maintenance police work are by and large left underdeveloped. Therefore, this is a gap that the current study aims to fill in. Taken together, this study is attempting to reconcile the media representations of police image by placing the policing of crime on an equal footing with the policing of order maintenance.

Practically, the Hong Kong Police Force has received compliments of the "Asia's Finest" and even the "World Finest" not long after the handover in 1997. However, in recent years, Hong Kong's police image seems to be badly influenced by their handling of public order events. For example, the police force was accused by an official U.S. report of turning to aggressive and abusive tactics on protests ("Police Chief Rejects Claims," 2013), and was criticized for making a political arrest of the social activists ("Police Chief Defends Activist's Arrest," 2013). As such, it is not a wonder that when the police force was being named as runner-up for the Best Public Image Award in the government's civil service awards held in 2013, some stakeholders had strong opinions about it ("Police Chief Defends Force's," 2013). Against this background, the current research is an empirical investigation that can contribute to our latest understanding of the police images in post-handover Hong Kong.

In summary, to the best of my knowledge, this research is the first-of-its-kind analysis of police image in Hong Kong. The result of this research would not only throw light on academic discussion about the "impossible" mandate for the police, but also on policy making for advancing police image. In the modern society like Hong Kong, this would be of profound importance because policing is as much a matter of symbolism as substance (Reiner, 2003), and the legitimation of policing involves a careful construction and reconstruction of police image (Mawby, 2002).

RESEARCH METHOD

The content analysis of local newspaper accounts had covered a whole period of the "Hong Kong's Occupy Movement," dating from September 29 to December 15 in 2014. Specifically, the investigation period covered a total of 79 days. The data were collected from the three major local newspapers: (a) *Oriental Daily*, (b) *Apple Daily*, and (c) *Ming Pao*. The reason for selecting the above newspapers was that they are all the major newspapers with high circulation, having coverage of a wide variety of social strata in Hong Kong. Simply put, the selection was suggesting that the media representations of police image are representative and influential.

The researcher had collected the above-mentioned three newspapers in the duration of Occupy Movement. As such, a total of 237 copies of newspapers were collected (3 newspapers × 79 days). After that, there were two major types of investigation derived from the research questions. The first type was the content analysis of police image and its relation to the order-maintenance duties. The second one was the content analysis of police image and its relation to the crime-fighting duties.

In the first type of investigation, the data collection was focused on collecting news items of relevance to the police's order-maintenance duties. In the above-mentioned 237 copies of newspapers, the researcher would first use the search engine of *wisenews* to identify the relevant news items by using three pairs of dual keywords, including "police and crime," "police and steal," and "police and robbery." In the second type of investigation, the data collection was focused on colleting news items of relevance to the police's crime-fighting duties. Also, in the above-mentioned 237 copies of newspapers, the researcher would use*wisenews* to identify the relevant news items by using another three pairs of dual keywords, including "police and order," "police and demonstration," and "police and protest."

In all the collected news items, the researcher had gone further to conduct a systematic analysis by classifying each news item along the parameters of positive, negative, neutral police image, or if necessary, unclassified item. Crosschecking and moderation of the classification would be done to ensure the reliability of data analysis. Specifically, a codebook was compiled to serve two purposes. One was to allow the researcher to judge whether or not a news item is of relevance to the police's order-maintenance and crime-fighting duties. The second purpose was to allow the researcher to judge whether the relevant news item is fitting into a positive, negative, neutral, or unclassified protocol.

Finally, the classified data could be statistically analyzed to investigate whether there was a general tendency of the negative representations of police image in relation to the police's order-maintenance duties. Also, by a statistical analysis of the data, researcher would attempt to investigate whether there was a general tendency of positive representations of police image in relation to the police's crime-fighting duties.

DATA REPORTING AND ANALYSIS

The researcher intensively collected the relevant news items on every single day in the duration of Occupy Movement. A total of 1,769 news items were collected. Among them, there are a total of 883 relevant news items. More specifically, in the crime-fighting aspect, the number of relevant news items, which were sorted out by using the dual keywords of "police and crime," is 166. The number of news items derived from the dual keywords of "police and robbery" is 43. Finally, those being generated by the dual keywords of "police and steal" is 84. As a result, a total of 293 news items of relevance to the police's crime-fighting work were collected.

However, concerning the police's order-maintenance work, the number of relevant news items, which were sorted out by using the dual keywords of "police and order," is 173. The number of news items developed from the dual keywords of "police and demonstration" is 336. Finally, those being searched by the dual keywords of "police and protest" is 81. In summary, a total of 590 news items of relevance to the police's order-maintenance duties were collected.

After the data collection, all the relevant news items were classified into four categories: (a) showing positive police image, (b) showing negative police image, (c) showing neutral police image, and (d) unclassified items. The results are tabulated in Table 1.

Table 1: The Classification of News Items

Dual keywords	Positive images	Negative images	Neutral images	Unclassified items	Total number of news items
Police and crime	115 (69.3%)	18 (10.8%)	4 (2.4%)	29 (17.5%)	166 (100%)
Police and steal	48 (57.2%)	6 (7.1%)	30 (35.7%)	0 (0%)	84 (100%)
Police and robbery	19 (44.2%)	12 (27.9%)	7 (16.3%)	5 (11.6%)	43 (100%)
Police and order	34 (19.7%)	103 (59.5%)	20 (11.6%)	16 (9.2%)	173 (100%)
Police and demonstration	62 (18.5%)	208 (61.9%)	51 (15.2%)	15 (4.4%)	336 (100%)
Police and protest	20 (24.7%)	41 (50.6%)	18 (22.2%)	2 (2.5%)	81 (100%)

From the above collected data, what this study would call a "police image index" is then created with the purpose of showing the overall representations of police image when the police performed crime-fighting and order-maintenance duties, respectively. Analytically, the police image index for crime-fighting duties was generated by a summation of the relevant news items derived from the three sets of dual keywords, that is, "police and crime," "police and robbery," and "police and steal." Similarly, the police image index for order-maintenance duties was generated by a statistical addition of the relevant news items derived from another three sets of dual keywords, that is, "police and order," "police and demonstration," and "police and protest." After adding up all the news items with positive, negative, neutral, and unclassified police images, the figures are shown in Table 2.

Table 2: The Police Image Index

Police image index	Positive images	Negative images	Neutral images	Unclassified items	Total number of news items
Police image index (corresponding to crime-fighting duties)	182 (62.1%)	36 (12.3%)	41 (14.0%)	34 (11.6%)	293 (100%)
Police image index (corresponding to order-maintenance duties)	116 (19.7%)	352 (59.7%)	89 (15.1%)	33 (5.5%)	590 (100%)
Overall representations of police image index	298 (33.7%)	388 (43.9%)	130 (14.7%)	67 (7.7%)	883 (100%)

From the collected data, we can basically confirm the two fundamental hypotheses in this study: First, the media representation of police image tended to be positive when the police were handling the crime-fighting duties, as shown in Table 2, with a majority of 62.1% of the news items indicating positive police image. Second, the media representation of police image tended to be negative when the police were performing the order-maintenance duties, as also shown in Table 2 with a majority of 59.7% of the news items showing negative police image. Finally, it is worth noting that in the duration of Hong Kong's Occupy Movement, the overall representation of police image in the newspaper accounts tended to be negative in a relative term of 43.9% news items. However, simultaneously, there were 33.7% news items showing positive police image during that time. This suggests that the police image was not necessarily turning into the negative one by a landslide during a politicalized period. The reasons for these findings will be discussed in the subsequent section.

DISCUSSION

The above findings are to be mainly discussed in threefold. First, it is about the implications for the police image derived from the police's crime-fighting duties. Second, it concerns the police image related to the police's order-maintenance work. Finally, the overall representation of police image and its theoretical implications are discussed.

As regards to how the police image tends to be positive when performing crime-fighting duties, there are a number of important reasons outlined as below:

- The positive representations of police image are largely due to the news reporting that described the police dealing with the crime efficiently and effectively.
- A large number of news items were the reporting of court cases. In these kinds of new items, the police were more than often portrayed as an able law enforcement agency, which could successfully bring the criminals to justice.
- The news reporting always mentioned that the citizens showed their support of the police dealing with the criminals.

Concerning the negative representations of police image, it is worth pointing out that the political inclination of local media has played a significant role in explaining the formulation of negative police image. In this research, the three selected newspapers were (a) *Oriental Daily*, (b) *Apple Daily*, and (c) *Ming Pao*. Simply put, in terms of political inclination, the*Oriental Daily* could be delineated as pro-establishment media, whereas the *Apple Daily*could be perceived as pro-democracy newspaper. In between the two, the *Ming Pao*somewhat remained to be politically neutral with the objective editorial for news reporting. As such, according to various political standings of the newspaper account, there are three particular sets of reasons for understanding the negative representations of police image during the Occupy Movement:

- In the *Oriental Daily*, the editorial explicitly criticized the Occupy Movement. In particular, the demonstrators were very often portrayed as those who were uncontrollable. At best, the demonstrators were reported to be unwilling to cooperate with the police; at worst, the demonstrators were reported to be challenging the police authority. According to the coding guideline in this research, all these news items suggested the police's incapability in their order-maintenance duties, thus being classified as showing the negative police images.
- In the *Apple Daily*, the editorial explicitly showed support to the Occupy Movement. In particular, the police were always portrayed as those whose action were violating human rights, constituting unfair treatment to the demonstrators, and even breaching the rule of law. It is also noteworthy that the police were frequently accused of being the political tool of government, no matter the Hong Kong Government or the Central Government of China, during the Occupy Movement. All these news items were therefore classified as representing the negative police image.
- In the *Ming Pao*, the editorial tended to stay neutral. In its news reporting, the Occupy Movement was being neither criticized nor supported. However, the police images were being largely represented as negative. This was partly due to the fact that even the neutral reporting of the serious clash between the police and demonstrators were in itself showing the negative police image, in the sense that the police were unable to perform their order-maintenance work. In addition, seven police officers who were alleged to beat up one of the demonstrators in the Occupy Movement were widely and intensively reported. Regardless of whether the allegation is true, the news reporting of this instance had conjured up many negative representations of police images.

Last but not the least, as shown in the Table 2, the overall representations of positive police image counted up to 33.7% whereas the summation of negative images was 43.9%. In view of the figures, the police image during the Occupy Movement could be confirmed as neither positive nor negative by a landslide. This has several important implications. Most important, the overall media representations of police image would somewhat fail to reflect an inclination of the real police image, given that the police image is not closely associated with the major distinction of police role between peacekeeper and law enforcer. Methodically, the measurement of an overall media representation of police images could be even misleading, in case that it was conducted during a special period that there were no any major kind of either public order event or criminal activities. Therefore, it is worth noting that the representations of police image and their associations with the police roles and functions are sort of a monolithic bloc. In such as much politicalized context as in the Hong Kong's Occupy Movement, it is not surprising to observe that the negative images, corresponding to the police's order-maintenance works, added up to the high level of 59.7% (as indicated in Table 2). However, it should be remarkable to find that thc positivc imagcs, corresponding to the police's crime-fighting duties, also stayed at the high level of 62.1% (as also indicated in Table 2). In other words, this suggests that however negative the police image of handling controversial public order event is, it has very little bearing on the police image of fighting crime.

Theoretically, the significances of this study are twofold. Concerning the media representations of police image and their relation to crime, despite the conservative view that the media accounts would tend to subvert the police authority, this study is showing an opposite tendency that in the newspaper accounts, the police are much more likely to gain the public support, secure the legitimacy, and display both the efficiency and effectiveness of police action when performing crime-fighting duties. In this aspect, Reiner's (2003) "police fetishism" is still under the auspices of the media representation. What is innovative in this study is that this sort of "police fetishism" could be established when the police were caught in exceptionally politicalized circumstances, like the Occupy Movement in Hong Kong. Thinking along this line, another significance of this study is concerned about the "possible" and "impossible" police mandates (Manning, 1977, 2005, 2010). As informed by the literature, the so-called "possible" police mandate, no matter in the name of crime fighter or in terms of "police fetishism," is to serve the purpose of concealing the fact that policing is an inherently political activity. However, this study shows that a successful portray of the police as crime fighters would not necessarily function to legitimize the "impossible" police mandate, thus de-politicalizing the police role as a governmental tool for "peacekeeping" for various political reasons. The opposite is also true; that is, a highly politicized depiction of the police as "peacekeepers" would not be destined to deal a blow to the "possible" mandate for crime fighting. Taken together, the conception of police role is much more dynamic than we are informed by the previous literature in police studies, at least we can now understand that the "possible" and "impossible" police mandates are not mutually exclusive in the media representation.

CONCLUSIVE REMARKS

The current study on the conception of police role should not be conclusive, especially when we observe the dynamic coexistence of "possible" and "impossible" police mandate. In view of this, the present research could be further developed along several dimensions in the near future. In particular, the qualitative methodology could be adopted to conduct some specific types of content analysis. Based on the quantitative results, this research confirmed that the positive police images were frequently represented in the news reports on crime fighting. However, we know little about the perceptions of police role in some specific types of crime, for example, the offences with sexual elements or serious violence. Similarly, we know even less about the ideological reflections of police action in managing mass demonstrations staged by various political groups, for example, the pan-democrats versus pro-establishment camp in Hong Kong.

By and large, the media representations of police image have profound symbolic significance, in the sense that they are an integral part of "the presentation of society as governed by the rule of law" (Reiner, 2000, p. 138). From Hong Kong's perspective, a longitudinally comparative study on the media representations of Hong Kong's police image between the colonial and post-handover era would deserve our scholarly effort. From an international point of view, a comparative study on the media representations of Hong Kong's police image with the ones in other Asian cities would also be worth an intellectual consideration. In summary, the present study has been designated to investigate the media images of police role in one singular period of Hong Kong's Occupy Movement. The future directions could be moving toward different times and places.

REFERENCES

1. Baton, M. (1964). The policeman in the community. New York, NY: Basic Books.
2. Bittner, E. (2004). Florence nightingale in pursuit of Willie Sutton: A theory of the police. In J. Jacoby (Eds.), Classics of criminology (pp. 458-467). Long Grove, IL: Waveland Press.
3. Cavender, G. (2004). Media and crime policy. Punishment & Society, 6, 335-348.
4. Manning, P. (1977). Police work: The social organization of policing. Cambridge, MA: MIT Press.
5. Manning, P. (2005). The police: Mandate, strategies, and appearances. In T. Newburn (Eds.), Policing: Key readings (pp. 191- 214). Devon, UK:

Willan.

6. Manning, P. (2010). Democratic policing in a changing world. Boulder, MA: Paradigm.
7. Mawby, R. (2002). Policing images: Policing, communication and legitimacy. Devon, UK: Willan.
8. Mawby, R. (2012). "Crisis? What crisis?" Some research-based reflections on police-press relations. Policing: A Journal of Policy and Practice, 6, 272-280.
9. Police chief defends activist's arrest. (2013, May 10). South China Morning Post.
10. Police chief defends force's public image prize. (2013, September 8). South China Morning Post.
11. Police chief rejects claims of harder line on protests. (2013, April 21). South China Morning Post.
12. Reiner, R. (2000). The politics of the police. Oxford, UK: Oxford University Press.
13. Reiner, R. (2003). Policing and the media. In T. Newburn (Eds.), Handbook of policing (pp. 313-335). Devon, UK: Willan.
14. Surette, R. (2007). Media, crime, and criminal justice: Images, realities, and policies. Belmont, CA: Wadsworth.
15. Thacher, D. (2001). Policing is not a treatment: Alternative to the medical model of police research. Journal of Research in Crime & Delinquency, 38, 387-415
16. Wilson, J. (1968). Varieties of police behavior: The management of law and order in eight communities. Cambridge, MA: Harvard University Press.
17. Wilson, J. (1969). What makes a better policeman. Atlantic Monthly, 3, 129-134.
18. Wu, Y., Sun, I., & Smith, B. (2011). Race, immigration, and policing: Chinese immigrants' satisfaction with police. Justice Quarterly, 28, 745-774.

Chapter 4

HEALTH REPORTING IN PRINT MEDIA IN LEBANON: EVIDENCE, QUALITY AND ROLE IN INFORMING POLICYMAKING

Fadi El-Jardali[1,2,3,4,5], Lama Bou Karroum[1] , Lamya Bawab[1] , Ola Kdouh[1], Farah ElSayed[1] , Hala Rachidi[1] , Malak Makki[6]

[1]Department of Health Management and Policy, American University of Beirut, Riad El Solh, Beirut, Lebanon

[2]Knowledge to Policy (K2P) Center, Faculty of Health Sciences, American University of Beirut, Riad El Solh, Beirut, Lebanon

[3]Center for Systematic Reviews on Health Policy and Systems Research (SPARK), American University of Beirut, Riad El Solh, Beirut, Lebanon

[4]Research, Advocacy and Public Policy-making Program, Issam Fares Institute for Public Policy and International Affairs, American University of Beirut, Riad El Solh, Beirut, Lebanon

[5]Department of Clinical Epidemiology and Biostatistics, McMaster University, Hamilton, Ontario, Canada, [6]Assafir newspaper, Beirut, Lebanon

ABSTRACT

Background

Media plays a vital role in shaping public policies and opinions through disseminating health-related information. This study aims at exploring the role of media in informing health policies in Lebanon, identifying the factors influencing health reporting and investigating the role of evidence in health journalism and the quality of health reporting. It also identifies strategies to enhance the use of evidence in health journalism and improve the quality of health reporting.

Methods

Media analysis was conducted to assess the way media reports on health-related issues and the quality of reporting using a quality assessment tool.

Semi-structured interviews were also conducted with 27 journalists, researchers and policymakers to explore their perception on the role of media in health policymaking and the factors influencing health reporting. In addition, a validation workshop was conducted.

Results

Out of 1,279 health-related news articles identified, 318 articles used certain type of evidence to report health issues 39.8% of which relied on experts' opinions as their source of evidence while only 5.9% referenced peer-reviewed research studies. The quality of health reporting was judged to be low based on a quality assessment tool consisting of a set of ten criteria. Journalists raised concerns about issues impeding them from referring to evidence. Journalists also reported difficulties with the investigative health journalism. Policymakers and researchers viewed media as an important tool for evidence-informed health policies, however, serious concerns were voiced in terms of the current practice and capacities.

Conclusion

Our study provides a structured reflection on the role of media and the factors that influence health reporting including context-specific strategies that would enhance the quality and promote the use of evidence in health reporting. In the light of the political changes in many Middle Eastern countries, findings from this study can contribute to redefining the role of media in strengthening health systems.

INTRODUCTION

Media is an important source of health-related information for the public, policymakers and health professionals. It can influence individuals' health behaviors, prompt policymakers to make decisions to promote health and disseminate health research results to the medical and science community [1–4].

Media plays a vital role in shaping public policies through influencing the different stages of the policymaking process [5]. The Kingdon model (1984) considers the mass media to play a crucial role in opening a policy window where interest groups pinpoint problems, advocate for solutions, and exert pressure on the government to respond [6–8]. However, media's influence can go beyond agenda-setting; it can influence the whole policy process [9], by speeding up or slowing down the process through highlighting some issues of policymaking more than others [10]. Moreover, through media, policies can be evaluated and policymakers can be held accountable for their decisions [9].

Media can be the conduit that links the public, the civil society and researchers to policymakers. Civil Society Organizations (CSOs) and researchers can use media to promote issues to the forefront of policymakers' agenda [7, 8]. Furthermore, the media can be used as a strategy to engage the public and the different stakeholders in policy development and implementation. Public engagement in policy development and implementation encourage participative democracy, transparency and accountability [11].

Media can also be a tool to promote evidence-informed policymaking and bridge the existing "know-do" gap through disseminating research results to policymakers and the public [12]. Evidence in the policymaking process consists of information derived from research, feedback from projects and programs, views of the public such as CSOs, expert opinion [13], in addition to experiences from other countries, reports conducted by academic, research and public institutions, international organizations or consultancy companies. However recent studies showed that misreporting evidence provides the public and policymakers with inadequate information, leading to misguided health choices and inappropriate health policies [14–18]. Literature suggests many factors hindering the dissemination and the accurate reporting of health research in the media. These factors include journalists' lack of time, limited publishable time, lack of science background, difficulties in understanding jargons, complexities of health issues, commercial pressures and problems with finding and using resources [17, 19, 20]. Researchers also worry about the inaccuracy and sensationalism of their work by the media [21–23].

In the Eastern Mediterranean Region (EMR), reporting research evidence in the media is scarce. Newspaper articles in this region are among the lowest in using or describing health systems research and policy dialogues [24]. A study conducted in 12 countries from the EMR showed that researchers considered the media, including newspaper articles, as a strong strategy for promoting the use of evidence in policymaking [25]. Furthermore, policymakers from the EMR reported that the media exerted a strong influence on the health policymaking process in the region [26].

The Lebanese Context

To the best of our knowledge, few studies explored the quality of health reporting in media and the use of evidence in health journalism in the EMR and none in Lebanon. This study explores the quality of health reporting and the use of evidence in health journalism and policymaking in Lebanon. Lebanon is a Low and Middle Income Country (LMIC) in the EMR, where sectarianism plays a major role in the political life. The political parties, represented in the

Parliament and in the cabinet, are mainly sectarian-based parties that have a great impact on the political system [27]. Sectarian-based parties also have great influence on the media in Lebanon where most of media outlets including newspapers, televisions and radios are owned by these parties [28]. There are over 20 daily newspapers in Lebanon published in Arabic, English and French which are provided in web versions as well as in print form.

In Lebanon, the health care system is characterized by the multiplicity of financing intermediaries including the NSSF that cover the formal sector of employees, the Civil Servant Cooperative (CSC) that covers civil servants, four military schemes that cover the uniformed armed forces, in addition to the private insurance and the Ministry of Public Health (MOPH) [29]. In addition, Lebanon still lacks a social insurance system that provides health coverage for elderly and workers after retirement and still suffers from weak capacities of public institutions. The study aims to 1) explore the nature of media coverage of health stories and evidence, 2) assess the quality of health reporting, 3) understand the role of media in health policymaking, 4) identify the factors influencing health reporting and 5) identify strategies to enhance the use of evidence in health journalism. Findings from this study will help designing strategies that would enhance the quality of health reporting. Study findings will also inform efforts aiming at strengthening the role of the media in communicating research results to the public and policymakers and in setting policymakers' agenda in Lebanon and other LMICs in the EMR.

METHODS

The study employed a mix of quantitative and qualitative research design. Data was collected from two sources: 1) media review and 2) key informant interviews and then validated in an interactive workshop.

Media Review

Newspaper articles were analyzed to investigate the role of evidence in health journalism, the way newspaper articles are reporting health stories and evidence and the quality of this reporting. Articles reviewed for this study included articles from Arabic, English and French newspapers (tabloid and broadsheet) published in Lebanon that tackled health-related topics issued between January 2012 and December 2013. The newspaper articles were obtained from the archive databases of the Syndicate of Hospitals and the Ministry of Public Health (MOPH). These two databases are the most comprehensive databases for health-related newspaper articles in Lebanon. They comprise a complete set of health-related articles that appear in all Arabic, English and French newspapers published in Lebanon.

In order to assess the way newspaper articles are reporting research evidence and the quality of the reporting, each article was reviewed and information was extracted onto a coding form developed using Excel spreadsheet. The coding form was adapted from Bubela & Caulfield (2004), Woloshin & Shwartz (2002), Robinson et al. (2013) and Teixeira et al. (2002) [15, 16,30; 31]. The section for coding general information of the reviewed articles (S1 Coding Form) was adapted from Bubela & Caulfield (2004). This section mainly identifies author's name, title and date of publication, key topics and nature of headlines (whether optimistic, pessimistic or neutral) [15, 31]. The nature of the headline whether it is optimistic, pessimistic or neutral refers to whether the story reported is a positive (good news), negative (bad news) or neutral story. For example, the headline "Flawed health care system leaves 2 million people at risk" is considered to be pessimistic in that it reports on bad news while the headline "Medical tourism in Lebanon on rise" is considered as optimistic. Headline such as "Medial conference about gastrointestinal system in Nabatieh" and "Conference on low back pain" is considered to be neutral. Exploring whether the media reports on optimistic (good news) versus pessimistic (bad news) stories is important to understand the world of the media and what makes a story newsworthy for journalists. The criteria for judging the quality of health news articles (S2 Coding Form) were mostly adapted from the quality assessment tool used by Robinson et al. (2013) [30]. Framing the problem criterion was adapted from Bubela & Caulfield (2004) [15] and the criterion for reporting on limitations was adapted from Woloshin & Shwartz (2002) [16]. The form was first piloted on 100 newspaper articles by two independent reviewers and slightly modified to ensure validity and reliability of the tool.

The first section of the coding form identified general information of the article (S1 Coding Form). The second section consisted of the quality assessment tool (S2 Coding Form). The quality of the articles was assessed using a set of ten criteria. The first criterion of the quality assessment tool was about the use of evidence. If the first criterion was met the assessment continues by scoring the criteria, if not the assessment stops. In this study, evidence is defined as information derived from research papers, expert opinions, studies, reports and other sources that support (and give proof to/ back up) what the author is reporting in the article. Articles that did not use any evidence included those that reported health-related events such as awareness and health campaigns, health episodes, and seminars. The remaining nine criteria were scored using 0 and 1 grading system to quantify whether the criteria were met or not, except for the "type of evidence used" criteria where articles were classified into three categories A, B or C depending on the type of evidence used and graded 2, 1, and 0 respectively (Table 1). For newspaper articles, falling under categories A and B, information was retrieved and evaluated against the next four criteria. A grade of 1 was given if the article met each of the following criteria: mentioning the title of the study, the author(s)' name(s), the organization with which the authors are affiliated and the journal title or conference from which the evidence was retrieved. For the remaining four criteria, information was claimed from articles that fell under category A. Research studies, from which the evidence was used in the articles, were retrieved and evaluated against the last four criteria (again assigning a grade of 1 if the criterion was met): location of the research, reporting on limitations of the study, framing the problem and consistency with the findings of the cited study. After evaluating each newspaper article against the set of criteria, the articles that used evidence were given a score over a total of 10. The mean of these scores was then calculated using SPSS version 21.

Table 1. Category A, B and C classification

Category	Grade	Type of evidence
A	2	Peer-reviewed research studies including:
		- Systematic reviews
		- Randomized controlled trials
B	1	Expert opinions that refer to their own knowledge and experience
		Official or policy documents (laws and decrees)
		Grey literature:
		- Reports from public entities (ministries, government agencies,
		- parliamentary committees etc.)
		- Reports from Non-Governmental Organizations (NGOs), Civil Society Organizations (CSOs) and international organizations
C	0	Articles not providing source for the evidence

doi:10.1371/journal.pone.0136435.t001

doi:10.1371/journal.pone.0136435.t001

The coding and the scoring were conducted independently by two members of the research team. Disagreements between the two reviewers were solved by discussion. A third reviewer was consulted when agreement could not be reached.

Key Informant Interviews

Key informants interviews aimed at understanding the role of media in health policymaking, identifying the factors influencing health reporting and identifying strategies to enhance the use of evidence in health journalism. Participants were purposively selected based on a sampling frame. The "journalists" category consisted of journalists including reporters, editors-in-chief and section editors involved in reporting health news in print media. The "policymakers" category included senior and middle level policymakers engaged in health policymaking such as officials from the MOPH, members of the parliamentary health committee, and members of health professional associations (including the Order of Pharmacists, Syndicate of Hospitals, Order of Physicians, Order of Nurses, and the National Social Security Fund (NSSF)). The "researchers" category included researchers conducting health research. Additional participants were identified via a respondent-driven technique whereby interviewees suggested potential key informants who could provide additional information. Key informants identified were approached through a targeted email or a phone call explaining the purpose of the study and its benefits. Of the 35 key informants approached, 27 accepted to be interviewed including 9 journalists, 9 policymakers and 9 researchers. Interviews took place from February till March 2014. Semi-structured face-to-face interviews were conducted and lasted between 45 and 60 minutes. The interviews were transcribed verbatim. Arabic transcripts were translated to English then back-translated to Arabic to ensure the accuracy of the translation process. The participants had diverse backgrounds and experiences to ensure diversity and comprehensiveness of claims.

Three different interview tools were used with each of the journalists, policymakers and researchers (S1 Interview Tool). The Crewe & Young (2002) framework for understanding research-policy links was used as a guide for developing the interview tools. The framework aggregates issues around four areas: *The political context, the evidence, links and external influences* [32]. The interview tools were piloted with one journalist, one policymaker, and one researcher. They covered the following main topics: role of media in policymaking and public opinion, factors influencing health reporting, factors influencing the use of evidence in health journalism, role of evidence in health journalism, quality of health reporting, and strategies to improve the quality of health reporting and to incorporate evidence into health journalism.

Validation Workshop

An interactive workshop was conducted to validate the findings and receive feedback and insights from the participants. The workshop included 10 journalists that report on health issues from various Lebanese newspapers, news websites, radio and Television. Journalists participating from newspapers were also interviewed during the key informant interviews. The findings of the media review were presented during the workshop where the research team asked the participants' feedback on what are the factors that affected the quality of the reporting and why there is low proportion of news articles reporting on evidence. They also deliberated on the outcome of the interview findings and discussed the role of media in health policymaking and presented recommendations and strategies to enhance the use of evidence in health reporting. Field notes were taken during the workshop. Field notes were then compared with the thematic analysis of the interviews so information is added or validated where appropriate.

Ethical Considerations

The Institutional Review Board (IRB) at the American University of Beirut granted ethics approval for the study. Interviewees were contacted over the phone or via email to request their participation. Upon their approval and prior to data collection, written informed consent was collected. Interviews were audio-recorded upon request; two interviewees refused to be tape-recorded so their responses were recorded by extensive note-taking. Interviews took place in the interviewees' workplace based on their requests. The interviews were conducted in Arabic or English depending on the interviewee's preference. The interview transcripts were anonymous and recordings were immediately destroyed following transcription. All transcripts were reviewed and validated by three members of the research team.

Data Analysis

Qualitative thematic analysis of the interviews was conducted. The responses of all informants were coded using an Excel spreadsheet. Open coding was conducted for each of the three participant categories. The responses were segregated into sections that relate similar concepts. Thereafter, research members discussed and cross-checked the emerging concepts. This was followed by axial coding whereby concepts were organized into themes and subthemes that reflect the study's objectives. Data was obtained from both the media review and the key informant interviews to ensure data triangulation. This helped ensure completeness of data collected through the use of different data sources for the same study [33]. The findings from the media review and key informant interviews were further validated through the workshop.

RESULTS

Findings are presented in two parts. The first part consists of the findings of the media review. The second part presents interview findings on the nature of health journalism, quality of health journalism, the influence of media and research on health policymaking and strategies to enhance the use of evidence in health journalism.

I. Results from the Media Review

A total of 1,279 newspaper articles reporting health issues were reviewed. The agreement between reviewers was 81%. Seven key health topics recurred in the retrieved articles (Fig 1). The most repeated topic was *health care financing*, reporting the MOPH's and NSSF's inability to reimburse hospitals for their claims, this topic appeared at least once every month in 2012 and several times at the end of 2013. The second most recurrent topic was *poor medical care services*, which involved news about patients' death, admission, safety and medical errors and appeared every other month throughout the study period. The *drug abuse* and *universal health coverage* subjects appeared at the end of 2013. Whereas, the delay of the implementation of the smoking ban law (*law no. 174)* topic emerged in the newspapers starting March 2013 until the end of the year 27 times. Other topics that appeared were *social insurance system* as a plan under study and *disabled people's rights*. Although these topics recurred frequently, single incidents were reported at their occurrence and were rarely followed up.

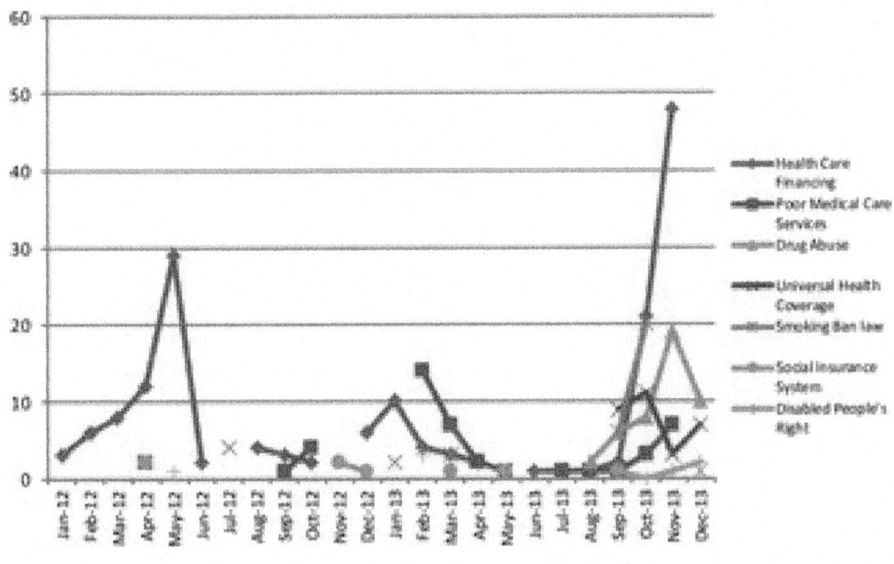

Figure 1: Most recurring topics monthly appearance.

doi:10.1371/journal.pone.0136435.g001

Out of 1,279 articles, 625 (48.8%) incurred optimistic claims, reporting news that implemented more favorable events to the reader, such as opening new clinics and hospital units, fundraisings, awareness campaigns and others. Whereas, 485 (37.9%) incurred pessimistic claims related to less favorable events in Lebanon such as medical errors, deaths and financial crisis. The remaining articles reported either claims that were neutral or articles that had both pessimistic and optimistic claims.

The majority of articles (75%) detailed health-related events and did not use evidence, while only a quarter was informative articles that relied on evidence (Fig 2).

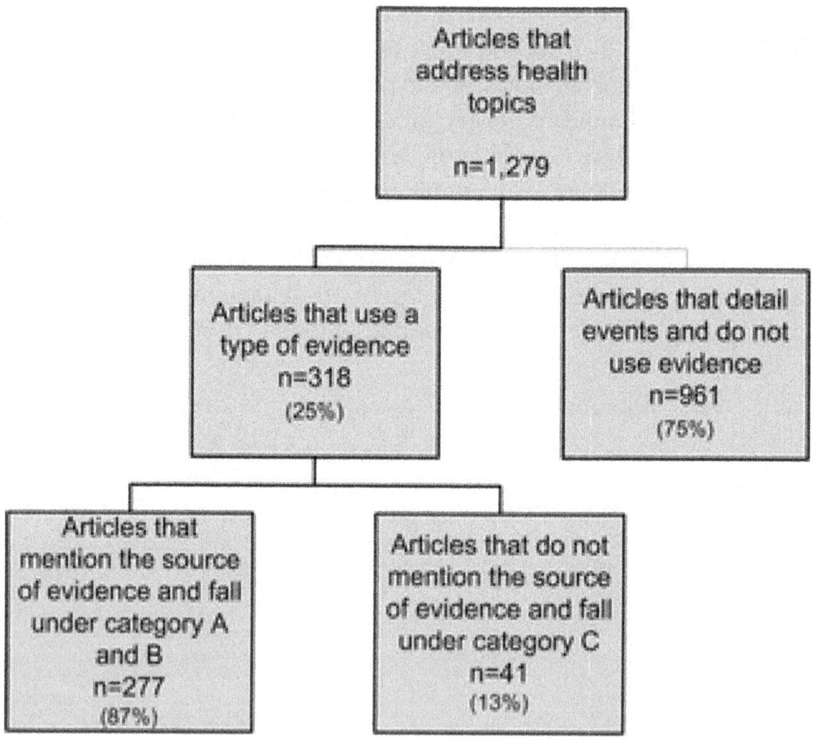

Figure 2: Evidence use in newspaper articles.

doi:10.1371/journal.pone.0136435.g002

The 277 newspaper articles that mentioned the source of evidence were grouped into ten different categories based on the source of evidence (Fig 3). These articles might have used more than one source of evidence resulting in a total of 304 sources used in the 272 newspaper articles using evidence. The source that journalists mostly relied on was expert opinion, which was used 121 times (39.8%) out of the total 304 sources. The second commonly used source for health reporting was studies and reports conducted by public entities, which was used 72 (23.6%) times. These were followed by official or policy documents (14.8%), peer-reviewed studies and studies from academic institutions (7.8%) (Fig 3).

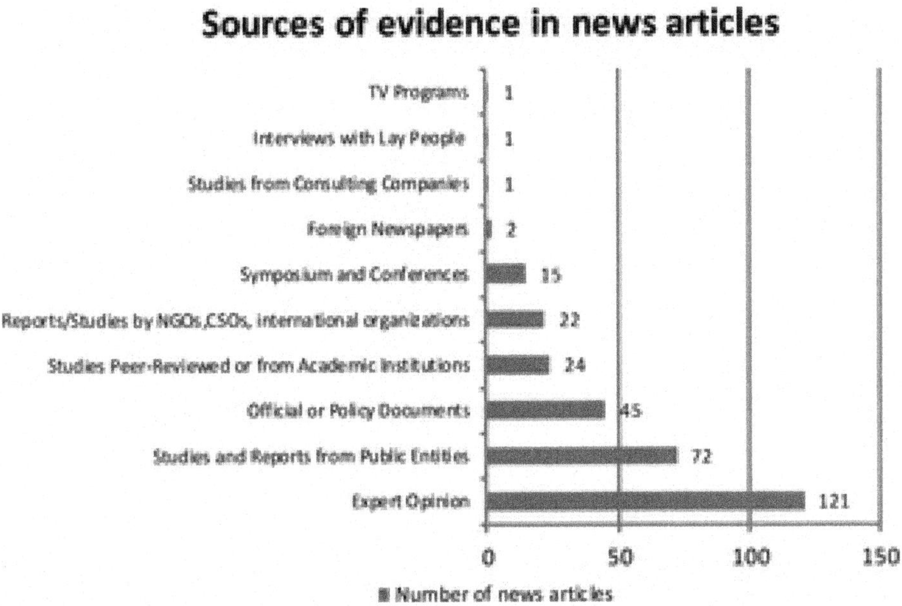

Figure 3: Sources of evidence in news articles.

doi:10.1371/journal.pone.0136435.g003

Quality of Newspaper Articles Reporting Evidence.

Assessment of the quality of the 318 newspaper articles using evidence resulted in an average quality score of 2.68 (± 1.29) out of a maximum score of 10, with scores ranging from 0 to 8.

Articles mostly used evidence of category B (81.8%) followed by category C (12.9%) then A (5.3%) (Fig 4). From the 277 articles under categories A and B, 81 (29.2%) stated the journal which published the study, such as the International Journal of Public Health or the New England Journal of Medicine, or the conference that discussed the evidence, such as the ESMO 2012 conference. Out of the articles under categories A and B, 21 (7.6%) mentioned the name of the author of the study, whereas 119 (42.9%) articles included the organization that the study or the author was affiliated to and two (0.7%) articles mentioned the title of the study. From the 17 articles under category A, that are peer-reviewed or from academic institutions, such as the American University of Beirut or the Lebanese University, 13 articles were consistent with the original study reporting the exact information present in the original study and fifteen reported evidence neutrally as it was reported in the original study without framing the problem into a positive or negative claim.

All 17 articles mentioned the location of the research, but none reported on the limitations of the study they referred to.

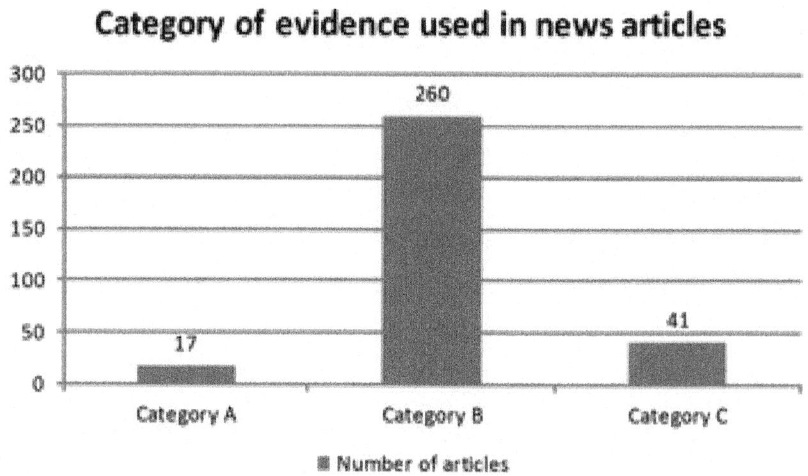

Figure 4: Category of evidence used in newspaper articles.

doi:10.1371/journal.pone.0136435.g004

II. Results from the Key Informant Interviews

Thematic analysis identified five main themes: nature of health journalism, factors affecting quality of health journalism, evidence use in health journalism,the influence of media and research on health policymaking and strategies to enhance the use of evidence in policymaking.

Nature of Health Journalism

Most journalists emphasized that health is not a priority in Lebanon, and that health journalism is still not well-established, as evident by the lack of daily health sections in the newspapers. One journalist attributed the lack of interest in health journalism to the overall culture. The need for the media to direct its attention more frequently to health issues was mentioned by a number of policymakers.

"The problem isn't from policymakers as to why health is not a priority, it's everyone.Media doesn't shed a spotlight on such issues; it doesn't place it on its first pages.Researchers don't think that these issues should reach the people; they think it's hard for people to understand."- A journalist

Interviews with journalists identified four types of health journalism in Lebanon. The first type is related to reporting health research; it is usually disease-oriented and has the goal of educating the public. The second type is related to covering health events including conferences, campaigns and health days. The third type of health journalism is related to covering topics about the health system, whereby journalists use research evidence to back up claims or evaluate the situation. The fourth type of health journalism is investigative journalism, whereby journalists follow up on news and investigate its accuracy, such as news related to the spread of low quality vaccines in the Lebanese market. Most journalists reported several difficulties with the investigative type of health journalism. They reported feeling threatened when working on investigative reports and that they preferred to cover neutral issues instead. As one journalist mentioned:

"Sometimes, I feel threatened because I have heard stories, particularly with journalists engaged in investigative journalism where they were exposed to harm for investigating a certain health issue and promoting political action and attempting to provoke changes in policies"

Most journalists expressed their tendency to report on humanitarian issues, such as violence against women, death due to some disease or the MOPH inability to provide medicine to the less fortunate. The main factors that reportedly influenced journalists' choice of topics included the timeliness of the topic and journalists' preferences for and curiosity about certain topics. Most journalists, in both the interviews and the workshop, also highlighted the influence of public relations and advertisement including those by pharmaceutical companies on their choice of topics. At the same time, they all ensured that they stayed away from advertising and promoting products in their reports.

"A large chunk of media has an advertisement rather than an informative attribute."- A journalist

Most respondents, including journalists, agreed that journalists report news according to the public's interests and benefits in order to get high ratings. They also perceived that people are interested in humanitarian news, as previously mentioned, and tabloids rather than health topics and research evidence.

Factors Affecting Quality of Health Reporting

There are several shortcomings in the quality of health reporting in Lebanon. Almost all journalists disclosed that they judge the credibility of a source of health information based on the source's professional title, such as whether the source is a physician or a ministry official. This finding was also confirmed in the workshop. Only one journalist mentioned peer-reviewed journals as a trustworthy source of health information.

Main factors affecting quality of health reporting included time and competition among journalists. In the workshop, lack of time was mentioned as a major barrier to constrain journalists from reporting on scientific research evidence. Most journalists admitted that competition and reporting on a scoop might force them to publish articles before being able to get the full information on the news, which in turn might have contributed to policymakers' and researchers' loss of trust in the credibility of media. Journalists further justified that they can publish more information after they get the initial news out.

"If I know about something and I need to write it on the same day, I won't be able to get all the facts, because if someone else picks it up [repots on the scoop], there will be no point in my writing about it the next day."- A journalist

The majority of policymakers and researchers also added that journalists' inaccuracy in reporting is affecting the quality of health journalism. They stated that the media should intensify its role as an accountability tool for information, especially since people have a tendency to take media reports as facts without further inquiry or examination.

"The public is affected by the media and tends to believe falsely reported news"—A policymaker

One main issue that most respondents from all three categories agreed on was that media does not follow-up on news that it has previously reported on.

"The media never follows up [on news] even if it brings up important issues"- A policymaker

Another issue that almost all respondents in the interviews and the workshop agreed on is journalists' lack of specialization in health journalism. Although some of the interviewed journalists had backgrounds in science such as biology, medical laboratory and medicine, still none were specialized in health journalism.

Evidence use in Health Journalism

Most respondents agreed that media does not rely on evidence. This might be due, according to one researcher and one journalist, to the fact that the concept of evidence use and its importance in reporting is still lacking in Lebanon. However, journalists acknowledged the importance of evidence-informed health journalism and of incorporating it into their work routine in order to make their reports more reliable and comprehensive.

"Time is definitely an issue, but I do it [access and read research] anyway because I care about scientific reporting. I incorporate it into my work routine. It is something important and offers something to the reader and gets us readers as well."- A journalist

Almost all journalists in the interviews and the workshop preferred interviewing experts to reading research. They explained that they preferred to talk to the researchers and have them explain in brief the aim and results of the study. This was attributed to time limitations, having to work in more than one section and the complexity of research language, which was perceived by some of the journalists as being dry, boring and difficult to translate and simplify to the reader. Many reporters were not aware of the availability of research databases and all save one journalist expressed an intention to access research. Additionally, journalists in the workshop acknowledged that they do not have the skills or institutional capacity to access databases.

"I usually access information through personal relationships with doctors who inform me of recent health issues and discoveries. It is even better when the doctor or researcher conveys the information in the language in which I write in."- A journalist

Moreover, most of the journalists and one researcher indicated that journalists prefer the use of international rather than local evidence, acknowledging the fact that local research is scarce.

Media and Research Influence on Health Policymaking

Most journalists agreed that they should be involved throughout the stages of the policymaking process. In the workshop, journalists agreed on the influential role that they may play in the process. However, they acknowledged that extensive and ongoing coverage of health policymaking is difficult to achieve due to time restrictions. Additionally, journalists reported that they felt discouraged from reporting on health policymaking. They explained that they were notified of decisions after a policy is made or implemented mainly because of their limited interaction with policymakers.

"No one discusses policy issues beforehand. We rarely know what's going on during [policy] development. Usually, policies are be already implemented then you go and cover it"- A journalist

Further contributing to their feeling of discouragement is journalists' perception that their health-related reports have limited implications on policy actions.

"I feel like whatever I report or cover, it does not get results. It's like working for nothing. We see no real change in policies and we feel like we are not heard"- A journalist

Some journalists also mentioned that their inability to measure the impact of their news reports on policymaking was mainly due to the long term nature of this impact and the complexity of such measurement. Additionally, even if evaluation were conducted it would strictly be based on opinions and impressions rather than on evidence.

"It is difficult to measure that [impact]. You can gauge the response of officials by their feedback. It's hard to tell that this is a result of your story"- A journalist

Moreover, most respondents and journalists from the workshop acknowledged the influential role research can play in informing policymaking, which has yet to be realized in Lebanon. Researchers attributed the gap in the uptake of research to the misalignment of research priorities with those of policymakers. Researchers' main focus is on publishing research studies in academically valued peer-reviewed journals rather than on disseminating research to policymakers and stakeholders.

"Publishing in peer-reviewed journals, that's great for our personal and professional development, but it's not effective in policymaking"—A researcher

Most journalists and researchers and one policymaker alluded to the unstructured nature of the policymaking process in Lebanon. According to them, policy decisions arise as a reaction to surfacing health issues and not as a product of careful planning and agenda setting.

"*Policymaking comes as a reaction, not something that is pre-planned or part of an agenda that is being monitored or worked on regularly*"—A researcher

Most journalists and researchers agreed that policymakers are primarily concerned with politics rather than policies rendering them unresponsive to evidence and media reports. Moreover, these respondents perceived policymaking as governed by political and religious interests rather than evidence.

"*Policymakers [in Lebanon] are not technocrats, they are politicized. So they tend to address those issues on an ad-hoc basis. They are reactive and only respond to things when they reach crisis proportions*"—A journalist

Policymakers and researchers ascribed media's narrow impact on policy actions to journalists' insufficient coverage of health policy issues and their lack of follow up. They also alluded to the absence of systematic framework enabling media to consistently link researchers and policymakers. As one policymaker stated:

"Not once did the media in Lebanon alert me to something useful in my domain as in something that would help me make pertinent decisions"

Strategies to enhance the use of Evidence in Health Journalism

Three main strategies to improve the quality of health reporting and the use of evidence in health journalism and policymaking were identified from the key informant interviews and the validation workshop. These strategies are: a) specialization of journalists in health reporting, b) research dissemination through media outlets, academic institutions, journalists' education and research briefs, and c) forming a platform as a link between media, policymakers and researchers.

The first strategy identified by respondents to enhance the use of evidence in health journalism is the "specialization of journalists into health reporting".

All respondents agreed on the need for qualified and specialized health journalists, as a means for promoting the use of evidence in reporting.

"We need specialized journalists and specialized publications. Anyone who wants to report on the health sector should have the knowledge and specialty to do so. Media specialized in health can play a role in making research reach policymakers"—A policymaker

Specialization may contribute to establishing health sections within newspapers, which exclusively report health news, and qualifies journalists in health reporting. Some researchers and journalists from the workshop also suggested incorporating health into the curriculum of media specialties. Respondents perceived that such specialization could enhance media's access to research evidence as well as its understanding and accurate reporting, which could then be channeled into policies.

In addition, as a first step towards specialization, most researchers stressed the importance of training journalists who are currently practicing health reporting. This can be done through educating them on the importance of research evidence as well as providing them with the means to access reliable evidence through databases and interpreting research findings. Most journalists agreed on the importance of training, while keeping in mind their time limitations for such trainings.

The second strategy is "research dissemination to media". According to most researchers and journalists, academic institutions play an important role in disseminating research to media particularly through university media offices. These offices can attract attention to particular issues and promote public's awareness of critical health and policy matters. However, some researchers mentioned that institutions do not consider communication with media as a priority, which is reflected in the deficiency of funding media offices and the poor attempts researchers make to reach out to the media.

"The media office in our faculty hasn't been as responsive as I would have liked them to be and there might be different reasons for that. I think the values

and the priorities of the people in charge and what they are concerned with in terms of image, are from my point of view distorted"- A researcher

Another suggestion by most of the journalists and researchers is the need for simplified research formats to render research evidence more accessible to journalists and facilitate its use in health reporting. Most journalists, in the interviews and at the workshop, expressed their preference for brief summaries of research that include quantified results, take home messages, public health significance and do not dwell on methodology and technicalities. Journalists preferred research summaries written in a contextualized manner using the same language in which journalists write their reports. They also stressed on the importance of delivering research briefs in a timely manner.

"I want a summary of the results, the main take home ideas and numbers. It should be framed in a way that relates to the health benefits of the reader and does not dwell on methods and technicalities"- A journalist

The third strategy is "forming a platform". Respondents collectively emphasized that in order for the media to achieve a positive influence on the public and policymaking, it necessitates a well-established network that facilitates communication between journalists, policymakers, and researchers. According to most researchers and journalists, such networks can bridge the gap between the media and the research worlds, promote the use of evidence in health journalism and improve the quality of health reporting.

Connections between researchers and policymakers can also reportedly help establish ongoing dialogues and align researchers' priorities with those of policymakers. Moreover, some researchers viewed their contact with policymakers as an opportunity to contextualize their research findings.

"If research is to feed into policy, the researcher must understand the needs of the policymakers and their intents to change, or have a good knowledge of the context and try to bring in through research new ways to influence policies"- A researcher

DISCUSSION

The study findings suggest that the timeliness of a story, the preferences of the journalists and their curiosity about certain issues influence the newsworthiness of a story. The nature of the news claim, whether pessimistic or optimistic, has a lesser influence since optimistic stories were almost equally reported as the pessimistic ones. This contradicts with the findings of previous studies that showed that journalists tend to report bad news which might be appealing to the readers. For example, a study conducted by Bartlett et al. (2002) showed that pessimistic news are more likely to be reported than optimistic news [34].

Our study also pointed out the limited follow-up on news by the journalists and the difficulties in practicing investigative journalism. This is supported by the findings of the media review that shows that single incidents were rarely followed up.

Quality of Health Reporting

Results from the media review, the key informant interviews, and the validation workshop confirmed the low quality of health reporting and the limited use of evidence in health reporting. Respondents reported that evidence is not often used in media, which affects the quality of reporting. Interview findings suggest many factors behind this limited use of evidence which include time constraints, the complexity of research language, competition, lack of specialization in health journalism, the limited skills and institutional capacity to access databases and the scarcity of local research. This claim was further supported by the limited number of news articles that use evidence and the low quality of reporting obtained from the media analysis. The media analysis showed that the low quality of health reporting is mainly attributed to the failure of journalists to report on the limitations of the studies and to mention the source of evidence, the title of the study and the author's name. Another main reason behind the low quality of health reporting is the reliance on expert opinion as the main source of evidence in health reporting. Expert opinions were found, by the media analysis, to be the most frequently used source of evidence in health reporting, while the use of peer-reviewed studies was found to be scarce, yet again affecting the quality of reporting. Similarly, Albaek (2011) reported that the use of expert opinions as a source of evidence in journalism is on the rise [35]. This may be attributed to journalists' perception of research as dry and boring, in addition to difficulties and time limitations to access, understand and translate research studies. Similar findings were reported by Voss (2002), Larsson et al., (2003) and Ashorkhani et al., (2012) linking difficulties in evidence based health reporting to time pressures and the rigid nature of evidence [17,19,20]. The limited use of evidence in health reporting was also found in two international health information television programs as reported in Korownyk et al. (2014). Around half of the recommendations lacked evidence or are contradicted by evidence [36]. Robinson et al (2013) indicated that the higher the level of evidence used in health reporting the higher the quality of the newspaper article [30].

Lack of Specialized Health Journalists

One major finding was the lack of health-specialized journalists as well as the lack of sections dedicated to health in newspapers in Lebanon. Respondents from the interviews showed the need for specialized health journalists, as a means for enhancing the quality of reporting and promoting the use of evidence in reporting which could then be channeled into policies. The lack of specialized journalism was also linked to low quality of health reporting in Iran [17]. Similarly, a study from Australia found higher quality of stories written by specialized health journalists compared to those written by non-specialists in the same media outlet [37].

Media and Health Policymaking

The interviews findings highlighted the limited interactions between policymakers and journalist which have led to discouragement of journalist from reporting on health policymaking. In addition, policymakers and researchers expressed their lack of trust in the credibility and accuracy of media reporting. This lack of trust in health journalism was also established in other studies whereby media was found to be incapable of conveying research messages accurately to the public [18, 38]. Other reported barriers impeding the interaction between journalists from one side and policymakers and researchers from other side include poor communication skills of researchers and lack of alignment of priorities between these groups. These findings were supported in other studies from the EMR, whereby the policymakers mainly rely on politics and opinions rather than on evidence and researchers' main incentives were primarily to publish in peer reviewed journals [25, 26, 38]. Moreover, the misalignment between media and researchers' priorities highlighted in this study was also revealed in a study from Canada, where journalists were found to rely on researchers to help them interpret events, and researchers are rarely available and have little patience when it comes to giving explanations to journalists [39].

This study has highlighted concerns from policymakers, journalists and researchers of the limited impact of the media on policymaking. This is in line with findings from Cook et al. (1983), where media is capable to inform the public but not to generate policy action [2]. Moreover, a recent print media analysis in LMICs, including Lebanon, concluded that the climate for evidence-based policymaking in those countries is still premature [24].

Strategies to enhance the use of Evidence in Health Journalism

This study identifies three main strategies to improve the quality of health reporting and the use of evidence in health journalism based on the findings of the key informant interviews and the validation workshop. These strategies are specialization of journalists in health reporting, research dissemination through media outlets, academic institutions, journalists' education and research briefs, and forming a platform as a link between media, policymakers and researchers.

Study findings on strategies to enhance the use of evidence in health journalism concur with the findings of Oxman et al. (2009) that suggests strategies to ameliorate to role of media in engaging the public in evidence-informed policymaking [11]. One of the strategies identified by the respondents is to simplify the research format presented to the media, which comes in line with literature highlighting the importance of media releases in facilitating access of journalists to evidence [11,17]. Journalists interviewed conceptualized their preferred format of the research summary as brief, simple and result-oriented. Developing summaries with policy recommendations for decisions-makers was also found to be a facilitator to the use of research evidence in health policymaking in a study from the EMR [39]. Another suggestion was to educate and train health journalists on the importance and use of evidence. A study by Schwitzer et al. (2005) revealed the effectiveness of educating journalists to facilitate evidence based health reporting [40]. In their study Oxman et al. (2009) found that training journalist enhanced the accuracy and hence the quality of health reporting [11]. Moreover, all stakeholders interviewed emphasized the need to establish networks to govern the ongoing interaction and dialogue amongst them. Literature shows that such an interaction increases the chances of mediating research to policymakers for promoting evidence-informed policymaking [41–43]. A qualitative study identified building relationships between researchers and journalists as an effective strategy for the cultivation of an environment supporting evidence based health reporting [44].

Strengths and Limitations

This study has several strengths. First, the study is the first of its kind in the EMR to explore the quality of health reporting in media and the use of evidence in health journalism and policymaking. Second, the study employed data triangulation to ensure completeness and comprehensiveness of the data collected from both the media review and the key informant interviews, in addition to data validation by conducting a workshop. Third, the key informant interviews involved a diverse sample of journalists, researchers and policymakers with various backgrounds, which helped provide in depth views on the use of evidence in health reporting. Finally, the study provides strategies that can be used to guide future action in the EMR and in LMICs for promoting evidence use in health reporting and policymaking.

This study has a few limitations. First, data for the media review was only collected from print media thus health news articles published online via news websites or social media, and health news broadcasted on television were not assessed. However we can assume that print media can be representative of the other sources of evidence since the findings were validated by the workshop that was attended by journalist from all media means (print, television, radio, news websites). Second, 9 of the 16 journalists approached accepted to be interviewed which means we did not capture all the journalists. However, we believe that those journalists have fully represented the experiences and perception of this category of participants and we have reached data saturation. Third, social desirability bias is a second limitation that might have influenced interview responses. Respondents may have provided the answers they considered desirable by the investigators. However, it can be safely assumed that the results are not overly inflated as findings were cross-checked with those from the media review and the workshop. Finally, recall bias might be one of the limitations. However, recall bias had minimal influence on study results since findings were validated by the media review and the validation workshop.

Implications for Policy and Practice

In light of the changes in the EMR and the transition towards democratic systems, findings from this study can contribute to the efforts of strengthening and redefining the role of media in this region. Media can play a greater role in informing the public, advocating for policy changes and impacting public policymaking especially during this period as new political systems are being built in the region. Media can empower citizens groups and promote community participation in policymaking as well as in planning and monitoring health services. Findings from this study can also help provide ways for moving forward for improving the use of evidence in health journalism mainly by focusing on strengthening the relationship between journalists, researchers and policymakers and building the capacity of journalists in evidence-based health reporting. This will reinforce the role of the media in the EMR, and increase its reliability as a source of research evidence to be able to influence policy and policymaking, while strengthening its role as an accountability tool.

CONCLUSION

This study sheds the light on the lack of appropriate use of research evidence in health journalism, the low quality of health reporting in newspaper articles and the lack of specialization in health journalism in Lebanon. The gap between the media and research world is still wide. Journalists reported many factors hindering the use of research evidence in health reports mainly time constraints and the complexity of research language and the lack of specialization in health journalism. Policymakers also showed concerns regarding the limited role of media in influencing the public and policymakers' decisions. This study suggests strategies that can improve the use of evidence in health reporting. The findings of this study would also contribute to designing context-specific knowledge translation strategies that would enhance the role of media in channeling evidence into policies.

ACKNOWLEDGMENTS

We would like to thank Nour Ataya for providing comments on the draft.

AUTHOR CONTRIBUTIONS

Conceived and designed the experiments: FJ LBK MM. Performed the experiments: LBK LB OK FS HR. Analyzed the data: FJ LBK LB OK FS HR. Wrote the paper: FJ LBK LB OK FS HR.

REFERENCES

1. Yanovitzky I, Bennett C (1999) Media attention, institutional response, and health behavior change the case of drunk driving, 1978–1996. CommunicationResearch26:429–53.doi:10.1177/009365099026004004
2. Cook FL, Tyler TR, Goetz EG, Gordon MT, Protess D, Leff DR et al. (1983) Media and agenda setting: Effects on the public, interest group leaders, policy makers, and policy. The Public Opinion Quarterly 47: 16–35. pmid:10261275 doi: 10.1086/268764
3. Grilli R, Ramsay C, Minozzi S (2002) Mass media interventions: effects on health services utilisation (Review). Cochrane Database Syst Rev;(1):CD000389. pmid:11869574 doi: 10.1002/14651858.cd000389
4. Phillips DP, Kanter EJ, Bednarczyk B, Tastad PL (1991) Importance of the lay press in the transmission of medical knowledge to the scientific community. N Engl J Med 325 doi: 10.1056/nejm199110173251620
5. Baum MA, Potter PB (2008). The relationships between mass media, public opinion, and foreign policy: Toward a theoretical synthesis. Annu Rev Polit Sci. 11: 39–65. doi: 10.1146/annurev.polisci.11.060406.214132
6. Kingdon J (1984) Agendas, Alternatives and Public Policies. Boston: Little Brown & Co.
7. Buse K, Mays N, Walt G (2005) Making Health Policy. Open University Press, Maidenhead, England.
8. Dorfman L (2003) Studying the news on Public Health: How content analysis supports media advocacy. American Journal of Health Behavior 27: 217–226. doi: 10.5993/ajhb.27.1.s3.5

9. Soroka S, Lawlor A, Farnsworth S, Young L (2012) Mass Media and Policymaking. Routledge Handbook of the Policy Process, Eduardo Araral, Scott Fritzen, Michael Howlett, M. Ramesh and Xun Wu, eds.
10. Wolfe M (2012). Putting on the brakes or pressing on the gas? Media attention and the speed of policymaking. Policy Studies Journal 40: 109–126. doi: 10.1111/j.1541-0072.2011.00436.x
11. Oxman AD, Lewin S, Lavis JN, Fretheim A (2009). SUPPORT Tools for evidence-informed health policymaking (STP) 15: Engaging the public in evidence-informed policymaking. Health Policy Research and Systems 7 (Suppl 1):S1. doi: 10.1186/1478-4505-7-s1-s15
12. Lavis JN, Lomas J, Hamid M, Sewankambo NK (2006) Assessing country-level efforts to link research to action. Bulletin of the World Health Organization 84: 620–628. pmid:16917649 doi: 10.2471/blt.06.030312
13. Jones N, Datta A, Jones H (2009) Knowledge, policy and power: Six dimensions of the knowledge–development policy interface. Overseas Development Institute, London.
14. Abeslon J, Collins P (2009) Media Hyping and the "herceptin access story": An analysis of Canadian and UK newspaper coverage. Healthcare Policy 4. doi: 10.12927/hcpol.2009.20474
15. Bubela TM, Caulfield TA (2004) "Do the print media 'hype' genetic research? A comparison of newspaper stories and peer-reviewed research papers." Canadian Medical Association Journal 170: 1399–407. pmid:15111473 doi: 10.1503/cmaj.1030762
16. Woloshin S, Shwartz LM (2002) Press releases: Translation research into news. JAMA 287: 2856–8. pmid:12038933 doi: 10.1001/jama.287.21.2856
17. Ashorkhani M, Gholami J, Maleki K, Nedjat S, Mortazavi J, Majdzadeh R. (2012) Quality of health news disseminated in the print media in developing countries: a case study in Iran. BMC Public Health 12. doi: 10.1186/1471-2458-12-627
18. Wilson A, Bonevski B, Jones A, Henry D (2009) Media reporting of health interventions: Signs of improvement, but major problems persist. PLOS One 4: 4831. doi: 10.1371/journal.pone.0004831
19. Larsson A, Oxman AD, Cheryl C, Herrin J (2003) Medical messages in the media—barriers and solutions to improve medical journalism. Health expectations 6:323–331. pmid:15040794 doi: 10.1046/j.1369-7625.2003.00228.x

20. Voss M (2002) Checking the pulse: Midwestern reporters' opinions on their ability to report health care news. Journal of Public Healt, 92:1158–1160. doi: 10.2105/ajph.92.7.1158
21. Besley JC, Nisbet M (2011) How scientists view the public, the media and the political process. Public Understanding of Science doi: 10.1177/0963662511418743.
22. Peters HP, Brossard D, De Cheveigne S, Dunwoody S, Kallfass M, Miller S, et al. (2008) Science communication: Interactions with the mass media. Science 321: 204–205. doi: 10.1126/science.1157780. pmid:18625578
23. Gascoigne T, Metcalfe J (1997) Incentives and impediments to scientists communicating through the media. Science Communication 18: 265–282. doi: 10.1177/1075547097018003005
24. Cheung A, Lavis JN, Hamandi A, El-Jardali F, Sachs J, Sewankambo N, et al. (2011) Knowledge-translation platform evaluation team: Climate for evidence-informed health systems: A print media analysis in 44 low- and middle-income countries that host knowledge-translation platforms. Health Research Policy Systems, 9(7). doi: 10.1186/1478-4505-9-7
25. El-Jardali F, Lavis JN, Ataya N, Jamal D (2012) Use of health systems and policy research evidence in the health policymaking in eastern Mediterranean countries: Views and practices of researchers. Implementation Science 7:2. doi: 10.1186/1748-5908-7-2. pmid:22236561
26. El-Jardali F, Lavis J, Ataya N, Jamal D, Ammar W, Raouf S. (2012) Use of health systems evidence by policymakers in eastern Mediterranean countries: Views, practices, and contextual influences. BMC Health Services Research 12:200. pmid:22799440 doi: 10.1186/1472-6963-12-200
27. El-Khazen F. (2003). Political Parties in Postwar Lebanon: Parties in Search of Partisans. Middle East Journal, 57(4), 605–624.
28. Reporters Without Borders (2014) Syrian crisis impacts freedom of information in region. World Press Freedom Index 2014. Available: http://rsf.org/index2014/en-middle-east.php
29. Ammar W. (2009). Health beyond politics. World Health Organization. Eastern Mediterranean Regional Office. Beirut, Lebanon.
30. Robinson A, Coutinho A, Bryden A, McKee M (2013) Analysis of health stories in daily newspapers in the UK. Public Health 127:39–45. doi: 10.1016/j.puhe.2012.10.001. pmid:23219265
31. Teixeira RA, Carlini M, Sousa ACJ, Fernandes PT, Camargo VRT, Vogt C, Li LM (2012). Reporting on health-related research in two prestigious

Brazilian newspapers. Clinics;67(3):261–264 pmid:22473408 doi: 10.6061/clinics/2012(03)10

32. Crewe E, Young J (2002) Bridging research and policy: context, evidence and links. London: Overseas Development Institute.
33. Fenech AM, Kiger A (2005) The use of triangulation for completeness purposes. Nurse Researcher 12: 19–29. pmid:16045044 doi: 10.7748/nr2005.04.12.4.19.c5956
34. Bartlett C, Sterne J, Egger M (2002) What is newsworthy? Longitudinal study of the reporting of medical research in two British newspapers. BMJ, 325: 81–84. pmid:12114239 doi: 10.1136/bmj.325.7355.81
35. Albæk E (2011). The interaction between experts and journalists in news journalism. Journalism 12: 335–348. doi: 10.1177/1464884910392851
36. Korownyk C, Kolber MR, McCormack J, Lam V, Overbo K, Cotton C, Finley C, Turgeon RD, Garrison S, Lindblad AJ, Banh HL, Campbell-Scherer D, Vandermeer B, Allan GM (2014). Televised medical talk shows—what they recommend and the evidence to support their recommendations: a prospective observational study. BMJ, 349:g7346 doi: 10.1136/bmj.g7346. pmid:25520234
37. Wilson A, Robertson J, McElduff P, Jones A, Henry D (2010). Does it matter who writes medical news stories? PLOS medicine, 7. doi: 10.1371/journal.pmed.1000323
38. Cassels A, Lexchin J (2008). How well do Canadian media outlets convey medical treatment information? Initial findings from a year and a half of media monitoring by media doctor Canada. Open Medicine 2.
39. El-Jardali F, Ataya N, Jamal D, Jaafar M (2012) A multi-faceted approach to promote knowledge translation platforms in eastern mediterranean countries: climate for evidence-informed policy. Health Research Policy Systems, 10:15. pmid:22559007 doi: 10.1186/1478-4505-10-15
40. Schwitzer G, Mudur G, Henry D, Wilson A, Goozner M, Simbra M, et al. (2005). What are the roles and responsibilities of the media in disseminating health information? PLOS Med, 2. doi: 10.1371/journal.pmed.0020215
41. Waddell C, Lomas J, Lavis JN, Abelson J, Shepherd CA, Bird-Gayson T. (2005) Joining the conversation: Newspaper journalists' views on working with researchers. Healthcare Policy, 1: 123–39. pmid:19308107 doi: 10.12927/hcpol..17571
42. Innvær S, Vist G, Trommald M, Oxman A (2002). Health policy-makers' perceptions of their use of evidence: a systematic review.

Journal of Health Services Research & Policy 7: 239–244. doi: 10.1258/135581902320432778

43. Mitton C, Adair CE, McKenzie E, Patten SB, Perry BW (2007) Knowledge transfer and exchange: review and synthesis of the literature. Milbank Quarterly, 85: 729–768. pmid:18070335 doi: 10.1111/j.1468-0009.2007.00506.x
44. Leask J, Hooker C, King C (2010) Media coverage of health issues and how to work more effectively with journalists: a qualitative study. BMC Public Health 10:535. doi: 10.1186/1471-2458-10-535. pmid:20822552

Chapter 5

CRIMINAL RISK, MEDIA REPRESENTATION AND ROLE OF THE CRIMINAL LAW CULTURE

Mario Caterini

University of Calabria, Rende, Italy

ABSTRACT

First of all, the essay is about the media's redundant emphasis on risks and the elitist specious creation of collective worries, in particular with relation to the criminal phenomenon, presenting the results of criminological researches that validate the empirical demonstration of the media representation's artificiality of criminal risk. The second part of the essay is dedicated to the influence of the media representation on the legislative choices of criminal politics, in particular in the actual contexts of the so-called "liquid democracy" developed around the new media, focusing the attention on the risks that it might involve with reference to the violation of some fundamental principles in the democratic modern systems. The conclusion is dedicated to the criminal law culture in a possible process of criminal-political paideia adapted to democratic and mass media postmodern needs, trying to track the ontological content of the minimum levels of knowledge of the citizens, such as the internalization of those fundamental values that constitute the ethos of the contemporary civil society.

INTRODUCTION

In today's society—it has been affirmed authoritatively—security is only a social pretense and, as a consequence, the overcoming of risks is merely symbolic[1]. And as a matter of fact, the role of the mass media follows this direction in an increasingly crucial way, especially through the Internet today, which is able to progressively influence the perception of such phenomenon[2]. These considerations are also valid for the risks related to the criminal happenings and the associated pretension of security[3]. To this end, the risk has a socio-cultural derivation, whether in its objective construction or in its subjective perception[4]. In these cases, the criminal risk frequently appears as socially produced through the creation of fake "enemies"[5].

THE MEDIA'S REDUNDANT EMPHASIS ON RISKS AND THE ELITIST SPECIOUS CREATION OF COLLECTIVE WORRIES

The perception of the risk doesn't follow a linear way (that is, starting from the happenings, passing through the mass media, to finish with the partners), but through a circular process of sources that reciprocally stoke one another[6]. Through the use of the collective experience and also the horse sense, in fact, the communications media perceive and intercept the supposed risks that attract the partners and, through the factitious typical of the media representation, they are able to influence and emphasize such a collective perception. This perception, then, is strengthened further by the same media that gain it one more time from that horse sense, according to an increasing amplification mechanism, comparable to such an autopoiesis reproduction that is a faulty, swirling spiral not always containable[7].

From this vicious circle, furthermore, often a "security question" arises, coming from the media and the so-called public opinion conditioned by the media, to which frequently corresponds the so-called "public response" that, with relation to the criminal phenomenon, has a political nature, which is the emanation of new rules [frequently symbolic to face the perceived risk; or it has a judicial nature, that is to say the initiatives of the magistracy that increasingly result in the so-called "lively jurisprudence", in which there is a "stretching" of the letter of the rules to satisfy the supposed needs of security coming from the public opinion[8]. The vicious circle can continue with the socio-political effects caused by the so-called "public response", effects that in turn attract other media reactions that in turn give rise to another social perception, which consequently often require a new "public response". Therefore, the perception of the risk is founded on a system of mutual urges and interferences that, when all is said and done, culminates in a clash to impose such an interpretation of the reality[9].

In this chasing and endless [short] circuit, the task to select the news represents the main power of the mass media, including on the web[10]. To ascertain that a precautionary evaluation of the news susceptible of diffusion must occur, the matter is based especially on criterion chosen for that[11]. The communication media makes a discrimination between what is considered information against what is not, in the sense that it does not cause interest for the audience[12]. Within the free economies, in fact, the popular logic is to divulge only the news that is more commercial, more desirable and that which, more so than others is able to stimulate the emotions, just like some criminal events[13]. This usually happens to the detriment of the information on phenomenon without any media appeal, which would be more relevant, for example, in a serious political-criminal discussion. The "commercial" selection of the news susceptible of diffusion and, therefore, the subjects of public debate, is also able to produce an unbalanced distribution of resources concerning the political, legislative and financial choices, which if conditioned by populist pushes, will not be very sensitive to the more real and serious risks, but those more manifest instead[14].

The media's redundant emphasis on the more "marketable" risks, can lead to instinctive social alarms; a sort of collective anxiety that frequently does not have a real defense; it is only the so-called paradox of fear in which the emotion intensifies the reality[15]. The theorization of the fear as an instrument of social control has remote and very authoritative origins[16]. Today, however, the mass media and particularly internet, in which the emotionality arrives to the parameter of choices, can supply extraordinary instruments of persuasion through the fear, more and more central in the politic world, to such an extent that phenomenon-producing social fear, emphasized, frequently conditions the legislative initiatives of [symbolic] contrast of the same phenomenon, intended to attract the approval of voters[17]. At this point is very clear that fear can be catalyzed, manipulated, exploited, to such an extent that it can be totally created and, when it happens, the supporters are the political, economic and media elites[18]. The role of mass communication—in which the internet is going to have a growing influence—becomes indispensable to create fear spreading through the perception of the risks[19].

THE EMPIRICAL DEMONSTRATION OF THE MEDIA REPRESENTATION'S ARTIFICIALITY OF CRIMINAL RISK

In order to confirm what has been outlined until now, in particular referring to the risks and the alarms connected to criminal events, it is useful to gain the empirical-criminal research to understand which events susceptible of criminal significance are popularized through the media, and how[20]. The inclination is to intensify the risk perceived by the community in relation to the criminal events, especially several criminal typologies, represented by mass media as a much more widespread phenomenon than it is in reality, expanding its consistence compared to that which can be officially found in the verified statistical data[21].

The majority of the news concerning criminal events is rejected in favor of execrable events presented with a strong charge of disvalue. The agenda setting related to the criminal typologies is tight and restrictive, with news concerning various traditional, violent crimes (e.g. murder, terrorism, etc.) almost exclusively reaching the audience, while other events do not grasp any media attention or rather it is very limited, with the exception of some types of events (e.g. sexual crimes or against childhood) that, even if they are ignored generally, usually appear in the limelight of news stories referring to specific events emphasized for seriousness. Furthermore, often the crimes that are statistically more frequent, such as those against property, if in some cases (especially in newspapers) they appear frequently in relation to the number of news, they also lack total media divulgation, whether in column space or time dedicated to them[22]. Mass media, moreover, tends to overestimate the seriousness of some crimes compared to the "official" non-value assigned to the system through the "edictal provisions"[23].

So mass communication tends to mainly publish the rarer criminal events, although considered serious and emotionally exciting, and unquestionably less in the case of the most common crimes, considered less relevant because they do not capture interest in the community. Mass communication, therefore, is apt to invert the order of the real statistics, neglecting crime as a wide social phenomenon and instead focusing on single events able to attract audience and profit[24]. The empirical data emerging from the criminological research validates the artificiality of the criminal risk perception as it appears in the media system, and also explains—according to the mechanisms that will be explained better later—many populist and "omnivorous" political-criminal choices, that in the last decades have contributed to the formation of the so-called emergency criminal legislation[25]. In fact, if irrational social instances of criminal repression are created in the media, politics tend to prepare criminal answers that are usually symbolic, aimed at social reassurance and also to gain approval, but ineffective, useless, unsuitable and oriented towards the affiliated nonetheless[26].

THE INFLUENCE OF THE MEDIA REPRESENTATION ON CRIMINAL POLITICS CHOICES

The artificiality of the media representation of the criminal risk, empirically demonstrated as such by crime investigations, is also useful to evaluate how legislative choices are made, increasingly conditioned by the actual methods carried out in politics, especially after the decline of the clearest ideological conflicts in history[27]. In fact, as the so-called "affiliation vote" is weakened, the political forces must distinguish themselves from others in order to attract a not entirely ideological consensus. So, the systems which intend to gain the favor of voters—on the model of the so-called “take-all party”—are based especially on the electoral “market” analysis, increasingly oriented toward techniques comparable to marketing[28]. The archetype is borrowed from a typically commercial rationality, in the sense that the political organizations are equalized to the companies, and exactly like them, they succeed more with reaching their objectives, putting the consumer needs at the beginning and not at the end of the production process, just as the political parties, in order to attract consensus, need to base the creation of their programs primarily on the needs of voters. For this reason, the political project of a party, according to this model, should not be an ideological standard product, but the result of research conducted on the electoral “market”.

Political marketing seems to have been inspired by a higher sense of democracy, simply because the legislator could not dictate his ideology, but was limited to gathering the preferences of the citizens[29]. The validity of this conclusion is subordinated to correctness, directness and democracy of the processes that give birth to and develop ideas, expectations and anxiety of the citizens. It can be affirmed that the democratic nature of such model for the most part is tied to the objectivity and democracy of the mass communication[30].

Indeed, the fact that the media system is able to influence the political agenda implies that the same political options will be subjected to the philosophy subtended to the functioning of the mass communication[31]. If these logics are guided mainly by economic interests, profit and also the models and the ideas instilled into the political programs and the criminal legislation, they will be shaped indirectly to less democratic and more economic reasons[32].

The methodology of marketing, in order to adapt to the mass communication, is also established on a maximum simplification of themes and debates. The complexity of the questions and the relative argumentations is removed to leave space for a slogan, brief and easy to understand assertions, able to obtain the approval of voters[33]. Furthermore, in this case it can be that the marketing strategies are more democratic because—following an inclusive philosophy—they mark a political communication in line with the common language of the citizens[34]. In this case, however, the value of this conclusion must be verified by analyzing the risks connected to a deleterious simplicity, inadequate to tackle complex questions, such as the criminal politics destined to infringe on the fundamental freedoms of humankind. In this perspective, therefore, the political marketing does not seem to be a more democratic strategy in itself, because—almost as if the problematic nature was incompatible with democracy—it pushes toward a banality of the questions, toward suffocating themes, simply because they are popular, easily understandable and subject to voter anxiety conditioned by the media[35]. A mature model of democracy, instead, cannot tolerate the media shutdown and the political oblivion of more serious and complex questions and argumentations[36].

The symbolism that has characterized the criminal politics of the last decades, therefore, seems to be a consequence of the bigger concept of "symbolic government" in which the objective of the power has become the management of the same power[37], that is, moreover, a consequence of the difficulty of mass circulation of the most imposing and serious ideas inspired by the fundamental values of a social state of law.

To summarize, if, on the one hand, the system's democracy is not safeguarded per se by the political marketing, on the other, the same marketing nonetheless is orienting the so-called "public response"—also the criminal legislation—more and more toward the "commercial" and simple trends coming from the media system[38]. The worries that generally derive from the effect of the marketing on politics[39], that is from the commercialization and trivialization of ideas, are even more serious, with particular reference to the criminal politics that affect the fundamental human rights, such as freedom and dignity[40]. "Marketing" the ideas of criminal politics, in conclusion, may be equivalent to simplifying, exploiting, commercializing and "selling" the most personal characteristics of human kind[41].

"LIQUID DEMOCRACY" THROUGH THE INTERNET: THE DANGERS FOR LEGITIMATE CRIMINAL POLITICS

The communication based on new technologies is facilitating the hopes of overcoming the so-called representative democracy in favor of the direct one[42]. "Liquid democracy" means a system in which, through free software, every citizen has the power to choose and exercise their political rights that consist of express proposals and vote them, or empower them, even if always in a revocable way, in order to render useless a unitary and periodic mechanism of election of spokespeople[43].

For this reason, the new media are supporting the conviction that the best ruler should be the public opinion. Through its dialogue structure, the Internet would permit a counter-revolution able to change the democratic mechanism, permitting the overcoming of the representative crisis of politics through the power bestowed upon every citizen to frequently demonstrate their preferences through a sort of permanent referendum method[44]. This topic is very current, especially after the assertions, as well as the criminal politics initiatives, of organizations that have founded on the Internet their philosophy intended to obtain a direct participation of the voters for the decisions, eliminating the mediation of the elected[45]. The idea would be to virtually create a new Ancient Agora of Athens through interactive technologies, able to keep citizens increasingly well-informed and able to guide public choices without any mediation of professional politicians.

Unlike the traditional media, the dialogue feature of the Internet—that is to say its bidirectional nature that permits the exchange of information—is considered the main requirement of its strong democratic vocation. This technological characteristic, in fact, is a great innovation compared with the press, radio or television which do not permit the users to "converse" directly. This fundamental quality of the Internet in itself, after all, does not seem to guarantee the democracy of a political system, and a contrary conclusion probably reveals itself as a myth. In fact, new technologies, on the one hand, can also be used for a distorted use, such as, for example, the legitimization of authoritative wills through the ratification of despotic decisions; on the other hand, the Internet alone cannot completely substitute the traditional democratic processes representative of the social-political conflict, but if anything, it can enrich them by establishing, with duly guarantees, valid help able to improve the level of democracy of a system[46].

On the one hand, the problems posed by the new media, are analogue to those of traditional mass communication, connected to the logic of the economic advantage and old or new lobbies that are able to condition the strategies[47]. On the other hand, they present additional problems coming from the enormity and the usual low quality of information published on the web, which also precisely due to the exorbitant quantity and the popular chaos stemming from it, with great difficulty, in fact, can instill in the citizen a better knowledge of the social-political questions[48].

The revolution presented by the interactive "liquid democracy", once again seems to be mainly symbolic. At least at the moment, in fact, the opinion as a slogan, according to which the problems of democracy could also be immediately solved through the Internet, cannot be shared. For many reasons: first of all, not everyone can use the new technologies and even those who do use them, often cannot use them effectively; those who are familiar with it are a minority. Furthermore, today the prevalence of web contents is managed by a small group of "transmitters", but using the same market logics, therefore with the famous antidemocratic implications. In the end, the information chaos deriving from the vastness of the content published, in essence corresponds to misinformation[49].

Recently, also among the promoters of internet as an indispensable instrument to improve the democracy of a system, new critics in the form of the so-called "liquid democracy" have emerged, due to the inappropriateness to give citizens the possibility to directly vote for law proposals, because it would require great knowledge that citizens do not have. Therefore, a different model of democracy has been proposed, known as "enunciating", nevertheless based on the usage of new technological media. This idea, even if it continues to consider the necessary parliamentary institutions, implies the abandonment of the classic representative democracy (that is the obligation of the mandate), but in favor of a system in which the elected representatives only have the task of expressing in the laws the will of the representatives. The elected, considered as a sort of simple nuncius, for this reason should be a perfect representative, able to express the will of the majority of his voters every time. This, after all, presupposes the possibility of the representative knowing perfectly this will, provision that could be carried out nowadays through new technologies, particularly through an IT platform able to guarantee the whole participation of the community in the political choices and, more specifically, a direct relation and control between the representative and the voter[50].

This model abandons the utopic idea of "liquid democracy" founded on the direct power of citizens to create laws, to move themselves toward an obligation that is the parliamentary mandate in which the voters should have the power, to practice through information technology, to impose on their representatives the "preliminary objectives" to follow, as well as to stimulate and control the realization of these objectives. Apart from the classic terms on the Rousseauian idea of the imperative mandate[51], the model of the "enunciating democracy", although constitutes an interesting democratic effort of internet, does not seem to overcome the questions mentioned before, relating to the preconditions of "how" the citizens will mold the ideas around the "preliminary objectives" to follow[52]. If this happens, even if in the way described before, through the mass media filters able to commercialize, trivialize and falsify the messages, therefore—remaining in the field of criminal politics—the unique shelter against the possible demagogic, repressive, emotive and irrational pushes, remains a "knowledgeable" "non-commercialized" legislator without any obligation of mandate.

Today, after all, it is not possible to ignore the pushes toward a democratic use of the Internet and a phobic attitude toward the new technologies would constitute the outmoded sign of reactionary short-sighted politics. Instead, we need to recognize the democratic potential of new media, not as the miracle cure for all the democratic deficiencies, but as a useful instrument, with the proper guarantees, to assign popular sovereignty to the citizens. However, it does not obstruct the awareness that the cornerstone of democracy exists not only and not so much in the moment of voting, but primarily in the participation in the discussion that requires correct information about socio-political questions.

Well then, starting from this prerequisite, the problems of democracy are the same for the traditional communication media and also for those that use new interactive technologies. In both cases, the difficulty to overcome is first and foremost always the same: the correct and balanced training and information of citizens, which after all, in relation to the Internet, sometimes seems delicate whether for the lack of rules of guarantee or for the informative chaos which derives from them.

The principle of criminal law and democratic legitimateness of the legislator should tend to guarantee representativeness, rationality and extreme prudence in the recourse of the punitive sanction[53]. If these features of the penal system have been threatened for decades by the so-called legislation of emergency, they should be threatened even more by the hasty usage of the Internet. In fact, a politic use of the dialogue capacity of the Internet (such as, for example, the instantaneous referendum, or the political marketing polls, or the "vote" of proposal to transfer into the Parliament), if not accompanied by a mass of guarantees of real democracy of the media tools, seems modestly compatible with a penal system truly shaped on a extrema ratio[54]. The economic interests buried in the web, the information technology chaos of the web, the scarceness of those who have adequate information technology knowledge, will probably direct the citizens toward emotive, little representative, irrational and repressive reactions. Reactions that, pursuant to the political marketing processes described, can concretely influence several criminal-political choices[55].

The interactivity, therefore, if not accompanied by some guarantees, might stoke plebiscitary swerves, according to a grotesque model of direct democracy, in which the reasoning and the public control are annulled, in favor of an illusionary decisional capacity founded on the oppression of an inexistent majority or exploited by the media[56]. The media system in its entirety, a fortiori considering the further dangers coming from the internet, seems to install the basis of the criminal constitutional law, under more than one profile: a single apparent democracy of the media choices that influence heavily and delegitimize criminal politics[57]; a consequent legislation that frequently, in fact, commercializes the person sacrificing it to the interests of the media system, according to "exclusion" logics of the "dangerous class" contrary to the fundamental guarantees of a social State of law[58]; a legislation, again, that communicates through the information media in the attempt to chase the public opinion, throwing together rules of a system increasingly irrational, disproportionate, chaotic and, therefore, in contrast with the need of extrema ratio of the crime law.

A PREFERRED POLITICAL-CRIMINAL BILDUNG AND THE ROLE OF THE CRIMINAL LAW CULTURE

Since, on the one hand, it is undeniable that in the democratic model the control of the institutions cannot be the prerogative of a knowledgeable elite apart from its people representativeness, but it should be extended in some way—even if indirectly—to all the citizens; on the other hand, it is similarly evident that the citizens, so that the institutions have greater opportunities to operate correctly, should have apolitical competence, understood like the awareness of the "public good" and the political lato sensu questions[59]. This awareness, as it is known, can be obtained through the educational agencies, in which a very important role is carried out by the communication media and by the Internet in particular nowadays[60].

It is hardly questionable, therefore, that the democratic processes operate more adequately only if there are the minimum levels of knowledge for the majority of voters. These standards—increasingly hard to reach when the difficulty level of the public questions increases little by little—are not quantitative, but more importantly qualitative. A superior knowledge of the citizens, therefore, is not connected per se to superior information. Actually, as for the new media, the access to information, de facto, impedes the formation of an adequate knowledge of the phenomenon. The cluster of many news pieces, aside from their possible manipulation, renders the citizens saturated with information, but deprived of knowledge, accustomed, distracted, and unable to exercise the true sense of critique[61].

The verification of the shortcomings and perversions of the criminal-media system does not mean exemption from promulgating the need of an effort towards the progression of this system and suggesting possible modalities. A sort of Bildung or paideia political-crime would be preferred, adequate to the postmodern democratic and mass media necessity, attempting, ambitiously, to track the ontological content of the minimum levels of knowledge of the citizens, as internalization of those fundamental values constituting the ethos of the civil society. This knowledge could be spread, into the limits of compatibility, also using the mass communication[62]. Naturally, not in the sense of "state pedagogy" through compulsory control instruments of mass media, but in the sense of Bildung as "contact with the culture", as "human education", objectification of freedom through a continuous process that obligates humankind to affirm its own nature, essentially in social and political realms. Therefore, a continuous education of humankind that increasingly approaches faces the culture, does not have a passive attitude, but instead the intention to face the problems, developing intelligence through doubt[63].

The necessity of this sort of political-criminal Bildung is especially perceived and proved that, currently, the majority of the associated does not come into contact with the criminal law and criminological culture, however, through the mass media, it comes into contact exclusively with the simplistic and "commercialized" described versions of the criminal phenomenon. The model which takes inspiration from this political-criminal paideia should be pursuant to the principles of legitimate criminal politics of a social State of law, directed toward an "inclusive" logic that endorses guarantees and rights, and not "exclusive", which instead currently seem to quantify the media representation of the criminal phenomenon[64]. A model, in other words, of an "open society" in which "freedom of people, non-violence, protection of minorities, defeat of the weak are important values"[65].

As it is not possible to imagine omniscient citizens, this Bildung clearly could not push itself toward more complicated and refined concepts, but at the most it should maintain itself, through simplistic communication methods, on the importance level of legitimate criminal politics principles that constitute the main structure of the occidental modern criminal law systems. The purpose, therefore, should be to give the citizens the minimum cultural instruments to permit a conscious reading of the criminal phenomenon, to know the essential requirements of legitimacy of the legislative choices of penalization, and to permit a basic critical analysis of the judicial tendencies. This process would need a long time, so that these principles and virtues are progressed, "digested", internalized by the citizens until the reduction of the most emotive, irrational and repressive pushes that currently characterize the crime-media system.

This idea might appear naïvely utopic, unattainable if compared to the concreteness of reality. However, this conclusion perhaps darkens the capacity, the collective intelligence if put in "contact with the culture", something that currently does not happen. After all, until the legitimate democratic politics principles are not internalized in the ethos of society, de facto the democratic mechanisms will not function properly and the conflicts will remain more or less latent in the public opinion, mass media, politics, magistracy and science.

The acquisition of this political-criminal ethos, after all, is proof that it encounters difficult obstacles to overcome. In primis within the media system, inasmuch as it is evident that a Bildung rebelling against principles and values does not have the seductive capacity of that information that stimulates more directly the emotions of the audience. This implies that the mass media should abandon, at least in part, the agenda setting concentrated exclusively on the commercialization of information, in order to spread itself, through information operators equipped with adequate cultural instruments, to read the criminal phenomenon more critically and less sensationally.

The obstacles of the political system, instead, are connected to the "commercialization" of choices. Politics, instead, should express itself in an effective and high-cultured debate adopting some decisions, sometimes unpopular at first blush, but inspired by basic ideological/value options able to carry out a pedagogic role. In this, the political world should open mainly to the criminal culture, accepting at least those results reinforced by decades of unequivocal research[66].

Among the tasks of the jurist, in fact, alongside the most traditional ones such as the interpretation of rules, the dogmatic abstraction and the systematization, there are also those ones related to the criminal politics and the legislative reform[67]. For this reason, coherently with the freedom of research and opinion, the assignment of the "juridical science is to listen to its own voice, formerly in the planning phase of rules, in order to guide the choices of the legislator, in accordance with the principles of legitimate criminal politics and proper actions of standardization [...] Science may demand attention only through its authority, connected to a strong capacity of communication"[68].

It is indispensable, therefore, a rational communication between science and the legislator, but even if this objective is achieved, in light of the "commercialized" mechanisms described before that condition the criminalization politics of today, it is plausible that the advantageous authority of the doctrine nevertheless proves to be powerless against the legislative options that are exhausted in what seems like a desire to condition the electorate by the media, apart from the principles of legitimate criminal politics, currently nearly unknown to the "general public"[69]. The science, then, apart from the essential channel of communication with the legislator, might also open a less indirect communication with the citizens, with that stratum of society that form the so-called public opinion; communication, at a time almost indispensable, and now, instead, could be facilitated exactly through new technologies such as the Internet.

CONCLUSION

The criminal-legal science, starting from the earliest one, should involve more criminal politics, displaying itself as more open to the needs and hopes of the citizens. The doctrine should dismount the "ivory tower". It should abandon the most "aristocratic" attitude that keeps in part, detached, barely interested in the most "popular" implications of criminal politics, undertaking instead an active role of this sort of crime-political Bildung through the media[70]. After all, the possibility to firmly carry out this leading role in the collective process of "contact with the criminal law culture", is tied to a more unitary force of the doctrine, at least about the cardinal questions, that is, the principles of a legitimate criminal law. In the absence of a harmonious scientific message, on one hand, there would be the creation of the pretext of politics to divert the reforms; on the other hand, the conflicting message would be deceptive and unable to stabilize that common ethos which is proposed.

The imaginable unattainability of the presumed criminal-political Bildung might be proved only after having seriously certified its practical failure. Before then, before having adopted concrete and long-lasting actions in that sense, even if with all the difficulties involved, it seems to be an instrument on which it is craved the desire to attempt to reduce the symbolic and emergency nature that the criminal system currently presents. The efforts aimed at the social internalization of the principles to establish a legitimate criminal politics, probably do not solve the entire critical scope of the crime system, but most likely do not aggravate it. Every "contact with the culture", also by the media, not commercialized, not simplistic, might only benefit the community; otherwise the necessity would be to completely distrust the discernment capacities of the citizens, which is to say to deny the very bases of every democratic model.

NOTES

[1]See Moccia, 2013: p. 410 , according to which "Security, therefore, is not anymore the consequence of a social order that tends to justice, but it is the result of vague political choices, oriented in the best of cases to the "damage reduction"; in any case, as the experience of these years demonstrates, they are condemned to collapse, also because the person, his individuality, more or less anguishing, do not let substitute himself for mathematical sets or statistical clusters. In these terms, security is only a social fiction: so the overcoming of risk is destined to be only symbolic. The actuarial average of private emotions, casually confused with the public opinion, is often supported by a very inattentive, misinformed and, maybe, bad faith legislator".

[2]In general about the influence of the communication media in the social perception of reality, seeEco (2012) ; in particular about the influence by means of new media see Meyrowitz (2002) .

[3]The right to security has been object of many authoritative researches in the field of criminal law studies; within them, recently, see Pulitanò,2009: p. 547; Donini, 2008: p. 3558; Hassemer, 2008: p. 15; Baratta, 2000: p. 19; at last, Cavaliere, 2009: p. 111 .

4About the perception of risks see Savadori & Ruminati, 2005: p. 44; Slovic (2000) , passim. About the so-called "risk society" and the deep alteration of the structure of the criminal justice system in contradiction with its fundamental principles, see Stella (2001) , passim, spec. p. 387, p. 415. For a risk analysis by the criminal law point of view, endo and esosystemic, more recently see Perini (2010) , passim, spec. p. 4, p. 168.

[5]About the media's emphasis on risks see, within others, Vianello & Padovan, 1999: p. 247 . About the influence of the communication media in the social perception of the "enemy", see Dino, 2006: p. 824 . In general, about the social construction of the risk see Beck, 2000: p. 35 ss., spec. p. 337; Amendola, 1995: p. 20 .

[6] Priulla, 2005: p. 63 .

[7]With reference to the criminal phenomenon and the capacity of media to supply deformed interpretation models, see Erickson (1991) , p. 219 ss., according to which the information media are not able to create opinions o convictions, but stimulate and develop the inclinations of citizens, according to a relational model in which the media offer an interpretation of reality that coincide with the citizens point of view.

8It is very plausible, in fact, that the media system might also influence the magistrates into the phase of taking some decision, orienting not only the inspection of the event but also the interpretation of the norms, toward a result instead of another, according to the expectations of the so-called public opinion. Romano, 1985: p. 413 , as well as a social consensus that can be referred to the creation of the norms, it is also about a social consensus "with reference to the dialog-communicative structure of the process [...] which last result—the decision to condemn or acquit—conditions the social comprehension of the judicial activity and it is probably conditioned in turn". Many researches, especially into the common law systems have verified empirically the mass media influence on the decision process of the professional judges and also jury members especially about the proof of fact; see Costantini & King, 1981: p. 36; Studebaker & Penrod, 1997: p. 428; Tyler, 2006: p. 1050 ; in Italy, for the psycological profiles, see the report of the meeting "Magistrates and Mass Media", organized by CSM, Rome, 2004, in particular Arcuri, 2004; Rumiati, 2004 .

[9] Ericson, Baranek, & Chan, 1989 .

[10]About the topic see Marini, 2011 ; also see Bentivegna (2002) , in particular the first part with the writings of McCombs & Shaw (2002), Benton & Frazier (2002) and Iyengar & Kinder (2002) .

[11]It has been asserted that the strongest influence of the mass media on politics and voters does not happen through a sort of imposition and ideological contents, but for the selective processes of the information inspired to internal logics of the media system; cfr. Caniglia, 2000: p. 180 .

[12]Just as the law is conformed to the licit/illicit, the communication media are

conformed to the different code: information/not information; cfr. Luhmann, 1990: p. 62; Luhmann, 1995: p. 17 .

[13] Garland, 2004: p. 174 .

[14] Priulla, 2005: p. 67 . For the debate about the so-called penal populism, recently see Fiandaca, 2013: p. 95; Pulitanò, 2013: p. 123 .

[15]The literature about the fear of crime is very vast; see Simon (2008) , passim; Cornelli (2008) , passim; Merzagora Betsos & Travaini, 2003: p. 51; Travaini (2002), passim, spec. p. 19 ; for a recent attempt to overcome fear through security policies oriented toward the democracy, seeCeretti & Cornelli (2013) .

[16]For the political usage of fear in the thinking of Hobbes, Montesquieu and Tocqueville, see Robin (2005), p. 41, p. 81, p. 91 .

[17]In this sense the words of Zaffaroni, 1989: p. 139 are particularly important, according to what he says "The mass media—and especially the television—are indispensable elements to exercise the power of the whole penal system. If they didn't exist [...] it would be impossible to provoke fear [...] the communication media are the creators of the illusion related to the penal systems [...] they deal with the early introjection of the penal model as a pretended solution model of the conflicts [...] which are in charge of creating the illusion of the system efficiency".

[18] Chomsky & Herman (1998) , trad. it. S. Rini (2014) , passim, have proved the elitist mechanism through which the world of information activates the public opinion to sustain and defend the particular interests that control the society: "The main social goal of the media is to instill and defend the economic, social and political projects of the privileged groups that control the society and the State. The media are at the service of this goal in many ways: selecting themes, distributing them according to a level of priority and importance, contextualizing the questions, screening the information, choosing emphasis and tone, and maintaining the debate within the limits of the acceptable premises" (p. 363). Robin, 2005: p. 199 , affirmed that "The elites [...] as official protectors of the community security, decide which threats are more relevant [...], define the nature of the threat, from where it comes and how it must be fought, deploying the citizens against it". In the political-criminal perpective there is the campaign of law & order to recover or reinforce the consensus; cfr. Paliero, 2006: p. 523 ; in general about the role of the consensus of criminal law, Paliero, 1992: p. 849 .

[19]If then the political power is able to control the mass media—through new impositions or property concentrations—, the alteration of the democratic system is further as the political forces might be able to stimulate the public

opinion and the reforms they desire; see Palazzo, 2009: pp. 202-203; Giostra, 2007: p. 66 .

[20]In general see Forti & Bertolino (2005) , passim; more recently also see Bianchetti (2012) , passim, spec. p. 154 ss.; less recently Grandi, Pavarini, & Simondi (1985) , passim.

[21] Forti & Redaell (2005) , passim, spec. p. 12 ss., p. 18 ss., p. 179; Gebotys, Roberts, & DasGupta, 1988: p. 3 . For more numeric imbalances and significant super-representations (due to omission), in particular criminal reports relating to citizens and foreigners, see Calvanese 2011: p. 115 . About this topic see also Paliero, 2006: p. 493 . For the analysis of the considerable growth of criminal news into the English press, see Robert, Livingstone, & Allen, 2001: p. 174 . For some synthetic problematic observations about the difference between "effective" and "perceived" criminality, see Padovani, 2008: p. 690 , who highlights that the presumed misinformation operated by the media, should be compared with the possible statistics ignorance of the criminal phenomenon to test the effective consistency; with eventual different territorial relocations and gravity of criminal events, and with the "unclear number" of crimes not reported.

[22] Forti & Redaelli, 2005: p. 92 . About the selection of distorting crime news, see also Surette (2007) , passim. The tendency is present also in other experiences, for example the Irish one, seeO'Connell, 1999: p. 191 , who analyzed more than 2000 articles and the distortions operated by the media, connected to the inclination to popularize serious crime news even if they are frequent. For the Scottish experience, see Ditton & Duffy, 1983: p. 159 . For the Austrian one, Gunz, 1980: p. 3; for the German one, Kury, 2005: p. 319 .

[23]Cfr. Forti & Redaelli, 2005: pp. 140, 158.

24About the inversion of the real statistical order, see Forti & Redaelli, 2005: pp. 140, 182 , that, during the comparison of the media presence data of the crime typologies with the numbers expressed into the criminal law statistics have taken into account the Istat data related to year 2000. See, furthermore, Paliero, 2006: p. 494 . See also, Surette, 2007: p. 63; Schneider, 1995: p. 148 .

[25]In general, about the problems connected to the emergency legislation, see the fundamental and by now classical work of Moccia (1997) , passim. More recently, again, Moccia, 2013: p. 414 , it is about a "globalizing, 'omnivorous' criminal law" that shows the crisis that the criminal, formal and content legality experiences currently. "The penal laws by now are, too often, became simply 'written rules', with a casual content: but they are connected, or maybe probably, to a strict punishment, without the emersion of a legitimateness of the sanctionatory treatment by the content of the prohibition". About Donini,

2004: p. 55 , in the last decades, in Italy, the "criminal law of the enemy" has been called "criminal law of emergency".

[26]See Donini, 2006: p. 735 , that in the matter of the impossibility of controlling the distorting use of mass media, talks about press and/or political invention of "monsters" as exploitation of the person that creates the second significance of the term "enemy", that is to say the exploitable use of the criminal law as a function of "fight" against "evil" committed by a normal kind of author. More recently Schiaffo, 2012: p. 52 , in particular about the "announced disaster" of privatization in the management of public security of the Italian legislation during the years of the media sudden growth of criminality.

[27]About the influence of mass media on the political agenda, in particular, with reference to the media indication of the criminal phenomenon as a permanent question of the same agenda, seeFuentes Osorio, 2005: pp. 16, 23

[28]The theory of the "take-all" parties comes from Kirchheimer, 1966: p. 177 , ora in G. Sivini (1971), p. 177, in particular p. 192.

[29] Harrop, 1990: p. 277; Scammell, 1995: p. 298; Cattaneo & Zanetto, 2001: p. 13 .

[30]For some critics to the political marketing inspired to the democratic models, see Franklin (2004); Jamieson (1991) .

[31]According to Qualter, 1985: p. 138 , marketing reduces politics to marketable images.

[32]In the Italian literature, for the relation between democracy and political marketing, see Mori, 2011: p. 563; Mori, 2012: p. 711. Palazzo, 2009: p. 203 , in the matter of law of markets that strongly regulate the representation of the criminal phenomenon, he speaks about "a methodologically anti-democratic drift".

[33]They are informative shortcuts "that function as 'second choice' of other kinds of data" cfr. Popkin & Dimock, 1996: p. 182 .

[34] Harrop, 1990; Scammell, 1995.

[35]About the strong uncertainties related to the excessive simplification of the political and information language, with obvious consequences on the honesty of the electoral choices, seeCaniglia, 2000: p. 191 .

[36] Smith & Saunders, 1990, p. 295 .

[37]Cfr. O'Shaughnessy, 2004: p. 232 .

[38]If the social science doesn't agree on the nature and the power of mass media, as it is not easy to distinguish their influence compared to the influence of the education, religion, etc., everyone agrees on the power they have on the

political agenda; cfr. Butler & Collins, 2004: p. 98 . For the intimate implications between political marketing and mass media, distinguished between free and paid media, see Scammel, 2004: p. 39; Wring, 2004: p. 121; O'Shaughnessy, 2004: p. 228 .

[39]Constriction of the public agenda, caution of the media messages rather than arguments, depletion of the political "bravery", etc. Cfr. Scammel, 2004: p. 57; Butler & Collins, 2004: p. 85 .

[40]For some consideration about the alteration of the democratic circuit coming from the distorted media representation, in particular the trial cases, see G. Giostra (2007), p. 66 . About the*spectacularization of the trial, see* Canestrari, 1995: p. 52 .

[41]See S. Moccia (2013), p. 411 , according to which "L'orientamento attuale ai flussi emotivi dei consociati o di lobbies, anche per demagogiche finalità elettorali, spinge il legislatore—o chi per esso—ad esaudire i desideri di criminalizzazione, al di là di parametri di effettiva meritevolezza di pena di talune condotte".

[42]About this topic, see De Rosa (2014) , passim; Putini, 2013: p. 42 .

[43]For a more complete definition of "liquid democracy" see Bernabè, Marcolini, & Rostello, 2013: p. 13 . The authors might permit the practice of the delegate voting in connection with free computer programs, for example currently the most famous: "Liquid Feedback", that is a platform used by the so-called Pirate party. About "liquid democracy" and the Pirate party, see De Rosa, 2014: p. 105.

[44] Shapiro (1999) , passim.

[45]The reference is related to the electoral affirmation obtained by the Movimento 5 Stelle in Italy. About it, recently, see Floridia & Vignati (2013) . According to the authors, in the ideas of the Movimento mix three different challenges to the representative democracy, causing more than a contradiction: reformatory (through instruments of direct democracy, such as referendums and petitions, in a context that preserve the centrality of the Parliament), utopic (overcoming of the representative democracy through computer instruments); and a plebiscitary challenge (through web and squares). See also Bernabè, Marcolini, & Rostello, 2013: p. 17 ss., according to which """Movimento 5 Stelle" is the continuation of the old but in new forms". Also see Fornaro, 2012: p. 253 . The members of the parliament belonging to the M5S presented numerous political-criminal bills: political exchange between politics and mafia, prevention and conflict of the corruption, auto-money laundering and possession of financial activity abroad, company, taxation and bankruptcy crimes, prohibition to carry out the electoral propaganda at the expense of

people belonging to mafia associations and exposed to prevention measure of special surveillance of public security. The so-called "democratic emergency", after all, and the rising protest that demands new forms of direct democracy, also concern the rest of Europe and Occident, as proved by the communicative success of movements such as the Indignados, Occupy and the so-called Pirate party.

[46]The topic about the relation between democracy and new communicative technologies is object of a vast literature. See: Rodotà, 1997; Lévy (2002); Lévy (2008); de Kerckhove & Tursi, 2006; Pittèri, 2007 . More recently Corchia, 2011 .

[47] Lombardini, 2001: p. 62; Longo, 2001: p. 70 , that is about a network strongly identified with the market, of which the anti-democratic dimension of money is exalted.

[48] Eco (2012) , in the chapter Veline e silenzio claims: "The Internet, naturally, represents, without any intention to censor, the maximum noise through which it is impossible to receive any information. In other words: first, if an information is received, it is hard to know if it is reliable; second, try to search an information on the Internet: only we, scholars, spending ten minutes on it, start to screen and find the information we need. All the other users are fixated on a blog, on a specific porn, e.g., but at the end they don't surf the web so much, because surfing doesn't permit to collect a reliable information". Also see Lombardini, 2001: p. 64 .

[49] Davis (1999) , passim; Mazzoleni, 2001: p. 80 .

[50]The model is proposed by Bernabè, Marcolini, & Rostello (2013) , passim.

[51]The topics in favor of the idea that gives to the representative a consistent space of autonomy, in fact, traditionally are founded on reasons of principle and technical nature. About the first ones, the freedom of mandate is considered connected to the idea of "common good" whereby all those instruments able to favor particular interests into the public field must be rejected. On the technical point of view, instead, the obligation of mandate would find an obstacle into the institution of Parliament, as it would be a mechanism able to limit or block the operation. About the topic in general, see Girelli (2007) , passim; Scarciglia (2005) , passim. About the theoretical reasons of the imperative mandate ban, less recently, see the important, even if short work written by Burke, 1983: p. 66 ; and also Zanon, 1991 , passim., spec. p. 87.

[52]About the civil liberties as a precondition of the practice of participation rights, see Pace, 2003: p. 21 .

[53]For all, Fiandaca, 2007: p. 1251; De Vero, 2012: p. 243 .

[54]According to Ceri, 2001: p. 98 , more than a transfer of power to the citizens, it is a concealment of the same, as—also excluding the use of tested distortion, psychological and statistics technics—, the transfer is deceptive because the participation is subject to manipulation and no responsibilities, and in general the answers are reactions to emotional events when they are not mere effects of "dragging".

[55] Artusi & Maurizzi, 2010: p. 75 , is about internet as an instrument of public participation to a movement or political idea through marketing techniques.

[56] Rangeri, 2001: p. 116; Pittèri, 2007; Ceri, 2001: p. 98 .

[57]About the implications of democratic nature of the media system over that one of the criminal system, see the fundamental observations by Palazzo, 2009: p. 200 .

[58] Paliero, 2006: pp. 536-537 .

[59]About these topics see Dahl, 1992: p. 45 , now in Dahl, 2001: p. 134 , who defines also the concept of public good, according to a classic (general good) and a more actual and coherent vision through the modern individualism (aggregation of the individual interests).

[60]Education consists mainly in the transmission through communication", cfr. Dewey, 2000: p. 12 .

[61] Giostra, 2007: p. 64 .

[62]About the educational dimension of media, recently see Aroldi, 2012: p. 101 .

[63]For a complete analysis of the Bildung concept and its re-elaborated versions, see Cambi, 1994: p. 63 .

[64] Paliero, 2006: pp. 536-537 .

[65] Popper, 1989: p. 176 .

[66]About the relation between crime and political science, the literature is vast. Within many, see, K. Roxin (1970), trad. it. S. Moccia (1998); Vassalli, 1978: p. 999; Moccia, 1984; Bricola, 1988: p. 3; Palazzo, 1997: p. 693; Donini, 2001: p. 27 ; more recently, Donini, 2010: p. 1067; Palazzo, 2011: p. 4064 .

[67]See Moccia, 2013: p. 415 , that, within other things, has highlighted a solid interaction between crime and dogmatic politics, in such a manner that the function of the crime science is legitimately directed to criminal politics and legislation, too. The mere technical dogmatism, according to the Author, in the end supports the illiberal choices when unblocks theoretical defenses intended to exclude the criminal political problems of the crime system theory. For the necessity of a crime system construction that assumes as principles of reference the criminal politics virtues with a liberal-solidaristic derivation,

frequently with norms at the base in Constitutions oriented to principles of the social State of law, see the fundamental work written by Roxin, 1970: p. 37 .

[68]Cfr. again Moccia, 2013: pp. 417, 419 .

[69]The words of the recent Discorso del Santo Padre Francesco alla delegazione dell'Associazione internazionale di diritto penale, in Bollettino Sala stampa della Santa Sede n. B0787, held at Sala dei Papi on October 23rd, 2014 are emblematic: "There is the risk to preserve not even the proportionality of the punishments, which historically reflects the values scale protected by the State. The conception of the penal law as last ratio became weak, as last recourse to the punishment, limited to the serious facts against individual and collective interests more worthy of protection. The debate about the substitution of the prison for other alternative penal sanctions also became weak. In this context, the mission of the jurists is to limit and contain some politicians without any hesitations and the impulse to revenge present in the society, under the pressure of the mass communication media" (Francesco I, 2014) .

[70]About this topic see Donini (2006) , that is about a permanent task of crime science to control critically the irrational excesses of "penal democracy", that should be carried out also in the mass media, because in other levels the subject remains specialized, without any influence on the public opinion. Recently, about the general debate over the role of the doctrine in the education and legitimation of crime law, see González Cussac, 2013: p. 363; Manna, 2013: p. 389; Moccia, 2013: p. 409 .

REFERENCES

1. Amendola, G. (1995). Qualità della vita, bene comune, rischio accettabile: I topoi retorici e/o le strettoie concettuali della valutazione d'impatto ambientale. In F. Beato (Ed.), La valutazione dell'impatto ambientale. Un approccio integrato. Milan.
2. Arcuri, L. (2004). Ruolo dei mezzi di comunicazione di massa nell'organizzazione delle rappresentazioni sociali e del giudi- zio delle persone (analisi dei processi attraverso cui i prodotti mediatici possono influenzare la decisione). The Report of the Meeting "Magistrates and Mass Media", Rome: CSM.
3. Aroldi, P. (2012). La responsabilità difficile. Media e discernimento. Soveria Mannelli.
4. Artusi, M., & Maurizzi A. (2010). Le nuove frontiere del marketing politico. Internet come strumento di costruzione e ges- tione del consenso. Mercati e Competitività, 75.
5. Baratta, A. (2000). Diritto alla sicurezza o sicurezza dei diritti. Democrazia

e Diritto, 19.

6. Beck, U. (2000). La società del rischio. Verso una seconda modernità. Rome.
7. Bentivegna, S. (2002). Mediare la realtà. Mass media, sistema politico e opinione pubblica. Milan.
8. Benton, M., & Frazier, P.J. (2002). La funzione di agenda-setting dei mass media ai tre livelli di "complessità" dell'infor- mazione. In S. Bentivegna (Ed.), Mediare la realtà. Mass media, sistema politico e opinione pubblica. Milan.
9. Bernabè, M., Marcolini, S., & Rostello, A. (2013). Democrazia nunciativa. Un sistema solido per società liquide, Rome.
10. Bianchetti, R. (2012). Mass media, insicurezza sociale e recenti orientamenti di politica penale, Milan.
11. Bricola, F. (1988). Rapporti tra dogmatica e politica criminale. Rivista italiana di Diritto e Procedura Penale, 3.
12. Burke, E. (1983). No al mandato imperativo. In D. Fisichella (Ed.), La rappresentanza politica. Milan.
13. Butler, P., & Collins, N. (2004). Il marketing politico tra prodotto e processo. In A. Mellone, & B. I. Newman (Eds.), L'Apparenza e l'Appartenenza. Teorie del marketing politico (p. 98).
14. Calvanese, E. (2011). Media e immigrazione tra stereotipi e pregiudizi. La rappresentazione dello straniero nel racconto giornalistico. Milan.
15. Cambi, F. (1994). I grandi modelli della formazione. In: F. Cambi, & E. Frauenfelder (Eds.), La formazione. Studi di peda- gogia critica. Milan.
16. Canestrari, R. (1995). Reazioni psicologiche differenziali e spettacolarizzazione del processo. In F. Galgano (Ed.), Quaderni dell'avvocatura. Padova.
17. Caniglia, E. (2000). Berlusoni, Perot e Collor come political outsider. Media, marketing e sondaggi nella costruzione del consenso politico. Soveria Mannelli.
18. Cattaneo, A., & Zanetto P. (2001). (E)lezioni di successo. Milan.
19. Cavaliere, A. (2009). Può la "sicurezza" costituire un bene giuridico o una funzione del diritto penale? In W. Hassemer, E. Kempf, & S. Moccia (Eds.), In dubio pro libertate. Festschrift für Klaus Volk zum 65. Geburtstag (p. 111). München.
20. Ceretti, A., & Cornelli, R. (2013). Oltre la paura. Cinque riflessioni su criminalità, società e politica. Milan.

21. Ceri, P. (2001). Promesse e realtà della teledemocrazia. In P. Fantozzi (Ed.), Politica, istituzioni e sviluppo (p. 98). Soveria Mannelli.
22. Chomsky, N., & Herman, E. S. (2014). La fabbrica del consenso. La politica e i mass media. (1998). Trad. it. Rini, S., Milan.
23. Corchia, L. (2011). La democrazia nell'era d internet. Per una politica dell'intelligenza collettiva. Florence.
24. Cornelli, R. (2008) Paura e ordine nella modernità. Milan.
25. Costantini, E., & Kin, J. (1981). The Partial Juror: Correlates and Causes of Prejudgment. Law & Society Review, 15, 9-40.
26. Dahl, R. A. (1992). The Problem of Civic Competence. Journal of Democracy, 3, 45-59.
27. Dahl, R. A. (2001). Politica e virtù. La teoria democratica nel nuovo secolo. Revision by Fabbrini, S., Rome and Bari.
28. Davis, R. (1999). The Web of Politics: The Internets Impact on the American Political System.
29. De Rosa, R. (2014). Cittadini digitali. L'agire politico al tempo dei social media. Santarcangelo di Romagna.
30. De Vero, G. (2012). Corso di diritto penale. Turin.
31. Dewey, J. (2000). Democrazia e educazione (1916). Florence.
32. Dino, A. (2006). I media e i "nemici" della democrazia. Questione Giustizia, 824.
33. Ditton, J., & Duffy, J. (1983). Bias in the Newspaper Reporting of Crime News. The British Journal of Criminology, 23, 159-165.
34. Donini , M. (2001). Metodo democratico e metodo scientifico nel rapporto fra diritto penale e politica. Rivista italiana di diritto e procedura penale, 27.
35. Donini, M. (2004). Il volto attuale dell'illecito penale. Milan.
36. Donini, M. (2006). Il diritto penale di fronte al "nemico". Cassazione Penale, 735.
37. Donini, M. (2008). Sicurezza e diritto penale. Cassazione Penale, 3558.
38. Donini, M. (2010). Democrazia e scienza penale nell'Italia di oggi: Un rapporto possibile? Rivista italiana di diritto e pro- cedura penale, 1067.
39. Eco, U. (2012). Costruire il nemico e altri scritti occasionali. Milan.
40. Erickson, R. V. (1991). Mass Media, Crime, Law, and Justice. An Institutional Approach. The British Journal of Criminology, 31, 219-249.
41. Ericson, R., Baranek, P., & Chan, J. (1989). Negotiating Control. A Study

of News Sources. Toronto.

42. Fiandaca, G. (2007). Legalità penale e democrazia. Quaderni Fiorentini, 1251.
43. Fiandaca, G. (2013). Populismo politico e populismo giudiziario. Criminalia, 95.
44. Floridia, A., & Vignati, R. (2013) Deliberativa, diretta o partecipativa: Quale democrazia per il Movimento 5 stelle? The Annual Convention of the Italian Society of Political Science.
45. Fornaro, F. (2012). Un non-partito: Il Movimento 5 stelle. Il Mulino, 253.
46. Forti, G., & Bertolino, M. (2005) La televisione del crimine. Milan.
47. Forti, G., & Redaelli, R. (2005). La rappresentazione televisiva del crimine: La ricerca criminologica. In G. Forti, & M. Bertolino (Eds.), La televisione del crimine. Milan.
48. Francesco I (2014) Discorso del Santo Padre Francesco alla delegazione dell'Associazione internazionale di diritto penale. Bollettino Sala stampa della Santa Sede no. B0787.
49. Franklin, B. (2004). Packaging Politics. Political Communications. Britain's Media Democrac.
50. Fuentes Osorio, J. L. (2005). Los medios de comunicación y el derecho penal. In Revista electrónica de ciencia Penal y criminología (p. 16).
51. Garland, D. (2004). La cultura del controllo. Crimine e ordine sociale nel mondo contemporaneo. Milan.
52. Gebotys, R. J., Roberts, J. V., & DasGupta, B. (1988). News Media Use and Public Perceptions of Crime Seriousness. Canadian Journal of Criminology and Criminal Justice, 30, 3.
53. Giostra, G. (2007). Processo penale e mass media. Criminalia, 66.
54. Girelli, F. (2007). Insindacabilità parlamentare e divieto di mandato imperativo. Turin.
55. González Cussac, J. L. (2013). Gli orizzonti, vecchi e nuovi, della dogmatica. Criminalia, 363.
56. Grandi, R., Pavarini, M., & Simondi, M. (1985) I segni di Caino: L'immagine della devianza nella comunicazione di massa. Naples.
57. Gunz, J. (1980). Kriminalberichterstattung in unseren Tageszeitungen Vergeltung oder Vorbeugung: Eine inhaltsanalytische Dokumentation. Linz.
58. Harrop, M. (1990). Political Marketing. Parliamentary Affairs, 277.
59. Hassemer, W. (2008). Sicurezza mediante il diritto penale. Critica del

diritto, 15.

60. Iyengar, S., & Kinder, D. (2002). L'effetto di agenda-setting. In S. Bentivegna (Ed.), Mediare la realtà. Mass media, sistema politico e opinione pubblica. Milan.

61. Jamieson, K. H. (1991). Dirty Politics: Deception, Distraction, and Democracy. New York, Oxford.

62. Kirchheimer, O. (1996). The Transformation of the Western European Party System. In J. La Palombara, & M. Weiner (Eds.), Political Parties and Political Development (p. 177). Princeton. Ora in Sivini G. (1971). Sociologia dei partiti politici, Bologna.

63. Kury, H. (2005). Mass media e criminalità: L'esperienza tedesca. In G. Forti, & M. Bertolino (Eds.), La televisione del crimine (p. 319). Milan.

64. Lévy, P. (2002). L'intelligenza collettiva. Per un'antropologia del cyberspazio. Trad. it. di Feroldi, D., & Colò, M., Milan.

65. Lévy, P. (2008). Cyberdemocrazia. Saggio di filosofia politica. Edited by Bianco, G., Milan.

66. Lombardini, S. (2001). Accelerare non è fare. In J. Acobelli (Ed.), Politica e Internet (p. 62). Soveria Mannelli.

67. Longo, G. O. (2001). Un rapporto problematico. In J. Acobelli (Ed.), Politica e Internet (p. 70). Soveria Mannelli.

68. Luhmann, N. (1990). La differenziazione del diritto. Contributi alla sociologia e alla teoria del diritto. Trad. it. di De Giorgi, R., & Silbernagl, M., Bologna.

69. Luhmann, N. (1995). Die Realität der Massenmedien. Opladen.http://dx.doi.org/10.1007/978-3-663-16287-2

70. Manna , A. (2013). La dottrina tra legislazione e giurisprudenza nel sistema penale. Criminalia, 389.

71. Marini, R. (2011). Mass media e discussione pubblica. Le teorie dell'agenda setting. Rome and Bari.

72. Mazzoleni, G. (2001). Una rivoluzione "simbolica". In J. Acobelli (Ed.), Politica e internet (p. 80). Soveria Mannelli.

73. Mc Combs, M., & Shaw, D. (2002). La funzione di agenda-setting dei mass media. In S. Bentivegna (Ed.), Mediare la realtà. Mass media, sistema politico e opinione pubblica. Milan.

74. Merzagora Betsos, I., & Travaini, G. V. (2003). Criminalità e paura: Una relazione complessa. Difesa Sociale, 51.

75. Meyrowitz, J. (2002). Oltre il senso del luogo. Come i media elettronici

influenzano il comportamento sociale. Trad. it. Gabi, N., Bologna.

76. Moccia, S. (1984). Politica criminale e riforma del sistema penale: L'Alternativ-Entwurf e l'esempio della Repubblica federale tedesca. Naples.
77. Moccia, S. (1997). La perenne emergenza: Tendenze autoritarie nel sistema penale. Naples.
78. Moccia, S. (2013). L'odierna funzione di "controllo" e "orientamento" della dottrina. Criminalia, 410.
79. Mori, L. (2011). Il marketing politico e il consenso in democrazia. Iride, 563.
80. Mori, L. (2012). Procedure democratiche, legittimazione e consenso nell'età del marketing politico: Considerazioni filoso- fico-politiche. Diritto e questioni pubbliche, 711.
81. O'Connell, M. (1999). Is Irish Public Opinion towards Crime Distorted by Media Bias? European Journal of Communication, 19, 191-212.
82. O'Shaughnessy, N. (2004). Il marketing del marketing politico: Un ossimoro? In A. Mellone, & B. I. Newman (Eds.), L'ap- parenza e l'appartenenza. Teorie del marketing politico (p. 232). Soveria Mannelli.
83. Pace, A. (2003). Problematica delle libertà costituzionali. Parte generale: Introduzione allo studio dei diritti costituzionali. Padua.
84. Padovani, T. (2008). Informazione e giustizia penale: Dolenti note. Diritto penale e processo, 690.
85. Palazzo, F. (1997). Scienza penale e produzione legislativa: Paradossi e contraddizioni di un rapporto problematico. Rivista italiana di diritto e procedura penale, 693.
86. Palazzo, F. (2009). Mezzi di comunicazione e giustizia penale. Politica del diritto, 202.
87. Palazzo, F. (2011). "Requiem" per il codice penale? (Scienza penale e politica dinanzi alla ricodificazione). Cassazione penale, 4064.
88. Paliero, C. A. (1992). Consenso sociale e diritto penale. Rivista italiana di diritto e procedura penale, 849.
89. Paliero, C. A. (2006). La maschera e il volto. Percezione sociale del crimine ed "effetti penali" dei media. Rivista italiana di diritto e procedura penale, 493.
90. Perini, C. (2010). Il concetto di rischio nel diritto penale moderno. Milan.
91. Pittèri, D. (2007). Democrazia elettronica. Rome.
92. Popkin, S., & Dimock M. (1996) La conoscenza dei cittadini, le

scorciatoie informative ed il ragionamento politico. In S. Bentivegna (Ed.), Comunicare politica nel sistema dei media (p. 182). Genoa.

93. Popper, K. (1989). Il futuro è aperto. Milan.
94. Priulla, G. (2005). Raccontar guai. Che cosa ci minaccia. Che cosa ci preoccupa. Soveria Mannelli.
95. Pulitanò, D. (2009). Sicurezza e diritto penale. Rivista italiana di diritto e procedura penale, 547.
96. Pulitanò, D. (2013). Populismi e penale. Sulla attuale situazione spirituale della giustizia penale. Criminalia, 123.
97. Putini, A. (2013). Al di là di Internet: Fra recupero e dissoluzione della democrazia. Sociologia, 42.
98. Qualter, T. H. (1985). Opinion Control in the Democracies. London. 138 p.
99. Rangeri, N. (2001). Il rischio della democrazia diretta. In J. Acobelli (Ed.), Politica e internet (p. 116). Soveria Mannelli.
100. Robert, R., Livingstone, S., & Allen, J. (2001). Casino Culture: Media and Crime in a Winner-Loser Society. In K. Stenson, & R. Sullivan (Eds.), Crime, Risk and Justice: The Politics of Crime Control in Liberal Democracies (p. 174). Cullomp- ton.
101. Robin, C. (2005). Paura: La politica del dominio. Milan.
102. Rodotà, S. (1997). Tecnopolitica: La democrazia e le nuove tecnologie della comunicazione. Rome and Bari.
103. Romano, M. (1985). Legislazione penale e consenso sociale. Jus, 413.
104. Roxin, C. (1970). Kriminalpolitik und Strafrechtssystem. Berlin. Trad. it. Moccia, S. (1998). Politica criminale e sistema del diritto penale. Naples.
105. Rumiati, R. (2004). L'influenza mediatica sulla decisione. The Report of the Meeting "Magistrates and Mass Media". Rome: Organized by CSM.
106. Savadori , L., & Ruminati, R. (2005). Nuovi rischi, vecchie paure. Bologna.44 p.
107. Scammel, M. (2004). Cosa insegna il marketing alla scienza politica. In A. Mellone, & B. I. Newman (Eds.), L'Apparenza e l'Appartenenza. Teorie del marketing politico (p. 39).
108. Scammell, M. (1995). Designer Politics: How Elections Are Won. London.
109. Scarciglia, R. (2005). Il divieto di mandato imperativo. Contributo a uno studio di diritto comparato. Padua.
110. Schiaffo, F. (2012). La creazione della insicurezza in Italia e negli USA:

Gli esiti istituzionali tra effetti simbolici e disastri reali. Critica del diritto, 52.

111. Schneider, H. J. (1995). La criminalité et sa représentation par les mass media. Revue internationale de criminologie et de police technique, 48, 148.
112. Shapiro, A. L. (1999). The Control Revolution: How the Internet Is Putting Individuals. In Charge and Changing the World We Know. New York.
113. Simon, J. (2008). Il governo della paura. Guerra alla criminalità e democrazia in America. Milan.
114. Slovic, P. (2000). Thc Pcrccption of Risk. London.
115. Smith, G., & Saunders, J. (1990). The Application of Marketing to British Politics. Journal of Marketing Management, 5, 295-306.
116. Stella, F. (2001). Giustizia e modernità. La protezione dell'innocente e la tutela delle vittime. Milan. 387 p.
117. Studebaker, C. A., & Penrod, S. D. (1997). Pretrial Publicity: The Media, the Law, and Common Sense. Psychology, Public Policy, and Law, 3, 428-460.
118. Surette, R. (2007). Media, Crime, and Criminal Justice: Images, Realities, and Policies. Belmont.
119. Travaini, G. V. (2002). Paura e criminalità. Dalla conoscenza all'intervento. Milan.
120. Tursi, A., & de Kerckhove, D. (2006) Dopo la democrazia? Il potere e la sfera pubblica nell'epoca delle reti. Milan.
121. Tyler, T. R. (2006). Viewing CSI and the Threshold of Guilt: Managing Truth and Justice in Reality and Fiction. The Yale Law Journal, 115, 1050-1085.
122. Vassalli, G. (1978). Politica criminale e sistema penale, ne Il Tommaso Natale. Scritti in memoria di Girolamo Bellavista, 2, 999.
123. Vianello, F., & Padovan, D. (1999). Criminalità e paura: La costruzione sociale dell'insicurezza. Dei delitti e delle pene, 247.
124. Wring, D. (2004). Le teorie del marketing politico. In A. Mellone, & B. I. Newman (Eds.), L'Apparenza e l'Appartenenza. Teorie del marketing politico (p. 121).
125. Zaffaroni, E. R. (1989). En busca de las penas perdidas. Delegitimacion y dogmatica juridico-penal. Bueons Aires. Trad. it. di Seminara, G., Revision by Cavaliere, A. (1994). Alla ricerca delle pene perdute. Delegittimazione e dommatica giuri- dico-penale. Naples. 139 p.

126. Zanon, N. (1991). Il libero mandato parlamentare. Saggio critico sull'articolo 67 della Costituzione. Milan.

Chapter 6

MODELING THE ADOPTION OF INNOVATIONS IN THE PRESENCE OF GEOGRAPHIC AND MEDIA INFLUENCES

Jameson L. Toole[1], Meeyoung Cha[2], Marta C. Gonza´lez[3]

[1] Engineering Systems Division, Massachusetts Institute of Technology, Cambridge, Massachusetts, United States of America

[2] Graduate School of Culture Technology, Korea Advanced Institute of Science and Technology, Daejeon, Korea

[3]Department of Civil and Environmental Engineering, Massachusetts Institute of Technology, Cambridge, Massachusetts, United States of America

ABSTRACT

While there is a large body of work examining the effects of social network structure on innovation adoption, models to date have lacked considerations of real geography or mass media. In this article, we show these features are crucial to making more accurate predictions of a social contagion and technology adoption at a city-to-city scale. Using data from the adoption of the popular micro-blogging platform, Twitter, we present a model of adoption on a network that places friendships in real geographic space and exposes individuals to mass media influence. We show that homophily both among individuals with similar propensities to adopt a technology and geographic location is critical to reproducing features of real spatiotemporal adoption. Furthermore, we estimate that mass media was responsible for increasing Twitter's user base two to four fold. To reflect this strength, we extend traditional contagion models to include an endogenous mass media agent that responds to those adopting an innovation as well as influencing agents to adopt themselves.

INTRODUCTION

In an increasingly digital and connected world, the processes by which information is shared and consumed are changing rapidly. Services and content are now distributed through on-line social networks where the flattening effects of the Internet distort spatial diffusion. These factors are quickly shifting the balance between word-of-mouth and mass media advertisement and along with it, changing the prominent spatiotemporal scales on which spreading occurs. Aiding our ability to characterize and quantify this shift are unprecedented amounts of data elucidating how people communicate with each other and how that communication translates into choices or behaviors such as adopting an innovation or technology.

In this article, we update and unify traditional models of information spread and technology adoption to more accurately reflect the novel economic and social environments in which spreading now occurs. We expand on metapopulation models by embedding social networks in real geography to reflect the spatial distribution of social ties and better understand how local demographics and topology affect contagion. Furthermore, we introduce an endogenous media agent to our network simulation, capturing the role of hyper-influential social forces. Our model is informed by a case study examining the *viral* (as it is colloquially referred) adoption of a social micro-blogging platform, Twitter, where we focus on the accumulation of users in cities across the US over a three year period.

Traditional models of contagion have generally focused on the spread of disease [1] or the diffusion of innovation [2]–[4]. Simple approaches such as the susceptible - infected (SI) model have proven extremely informative, but suffer from overly simple assumptions such as homogeneous mixing of populations. The diffusion of innovations literature has had made use of similar frameworks, such as the Bass model [5], to characterize the adoption of technologies that feature considerable cost and risk. We show, however, that these models perform poorly when applied to goods and services that are nearly cost- or risk-free and demonstrate massive positive externalities like social web applications.

These spreading processes have been placed on networks, revealing how the topology of our social connections aids or hinders outbreaks. The importance of this work continues to grow as the world that becomes increasingly connected by the Internet or cheap and fast travel by cars, trains, and planes [6]–[10]. Few, however, have placed such networks in real geography while preserving individual interactions, thinking carefully about properties such as homophily[11], [12].

More recently, massive popular interest in social networks has lead scholars to recognize the potential of using these platforms as natural experiments on how word-of-mouth information spreading occurs. For example, it has been shown that different types of information, be it political or sports related, follow different patterns as they are shared and consumed by millions of individuals [13], [14]. Some information even takes on a life of its own, evolving into self-sustaining 'memes' [15]. In many cases, however, predicting the outcomes of such processes has proven extremely difficult [16].

Social scientists have used similar frameworks to study collective action in the form of binary decisions in order to understand a wide variety of phenomena. Neighborhood segregation [17], riots, technology adoption [18], and standards setting are just a few examples of behavioral contagion studied [19]–[23]. Current events have proven this work increasingly relevant as revolutions and protests are coordinated through these online social networks.

Studies have also explored the many forces influencing the speed and success of information spreading from blogs to traditional news outlets [14], [24], [25]. Research revealed a number of patterns whereby mass media drives conversation on social networks or vice versa. In some instances, it has been found that when advertising effects are controlled for, word-of-mouth diffusion is a negligible force driving adoption [26]. Finally, marketers and retailers have long been examining the various roles of celebrity endorsements as well as spatial diffusion of information about products and services in an attempt to optimize business outcomes [5],[27]–[32].

In this article, we address significant gaps in the above literature. Namely, we show that the geographic distribution of individuals› with differing propensities to adopt (such as early versus late adopters), combined with a preference for friendship with others who share similar tastes and geographic locations, are crucial features to accurately describe micro (at the city level) and macro (at the national level) adoption trends. Furthermore, we propose a model that includes an endogenous mass media that responds to adoption patterns of users while at the same time influencing individuals to adopt an innovation. Based on adoption data from the popular social blogging platform, Twitter, we present a model of contagion to capture salient features. The remainder of this article is organized into three parts: (*i*) we present analysis of the spatiotemporal adoption of Twitter as a case study, examining the roles of word-of-mouth spreading as well as mass media, (*ii*) we use insights from the case study to construct a network model and simulate adoption, (*iii*) and finally we present and discuss results and important parameters of our model.

MATERIALS AND METHODS

A case study of Twitter

As with most complex systems, there are many different scales at which to analyze dynamics. We start at the national level, counting the number of new users that signed up for Twitter within the US each week. Fig. 1 shows time series for both week-to-week user gains as well as the cumulative sum over the first 3.5 years of Twitter's existence. In addition, we have gathered data from Google's Trends and Insights web application measuring weekly search volume news reference volume for the query "Twitter" on Google News. Information on how search and news values are scaled can be found athttp:// www.google.com/intl/en/trends/about.html.

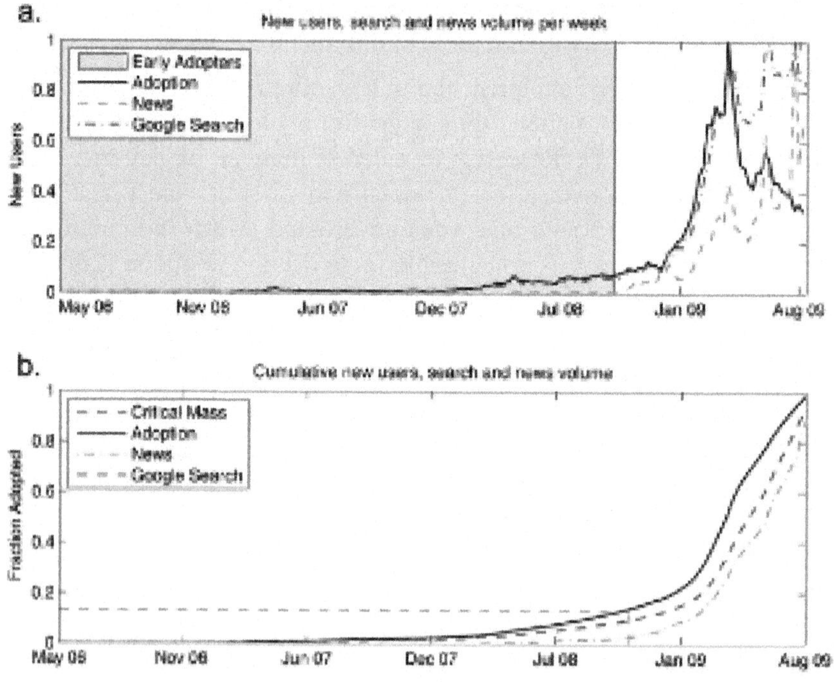

Figure 1: Plots of weekly national adoption. (a.) The number of new U.S. Twitter users is plotted for each week, normalized by the maximum weekly increase during the entire period of data collection. (b.) The cumulative total number of U.S. Twitter users is plotted for for the same time period. Google search and news volumes are normalized such that the maximum value is 1.

Following diffusion of innovations literature we label users according to when they adopted relative to all other adopters. For the purposes of this analogy, we make the simplifying assumption that adoption stopped in late 2009. Though this assumption is inaccurate given the subsequent growth of the platform, we do not have data passed this point. Furthermore, our time series suggest that Twitter's growth was slowing down significantly compared to a brief period of extremely fast growth. Those who adopt earlier than 1σ (standard deviation) before the average adoption time are labeled as early adopters. Those adopting between 1σ before and the mean adoption time are the early majority, with the late majority and laggards adopting in further deviations past the mean time. For more on the motivations behind this, see Rogers, 1995 [2].

At the lowest level of spatial resolution available in our data set, we examine the adoption patterns for individual cities. Though we find users in nearly 16,000 cities across the country, many of these locations have only a few users signed up. To ensure enough statistical power, we select only cities with over 1000 users, leaving 408 locations for the remainder of our analysis. Despite this threshold, we still retain data for roughly 70% of all users. Fig. 2 shows three different locations representing a young, early adopting demographic (Ann Arbor, MI), a large metropolitan region consisting mostly of late majority adopters (Denver, CO), and a mixed area (Arlington, VA). While these cities still show the classic S-shaped adoption curves, there are some significant differences such as the large spike in adopters during April, 2009 seen in Denver, CO, but not in Ann Arbor, MI. Later, we argue that these differences are the result of demographics that have different propensities to adopt and respond differently to media influences.

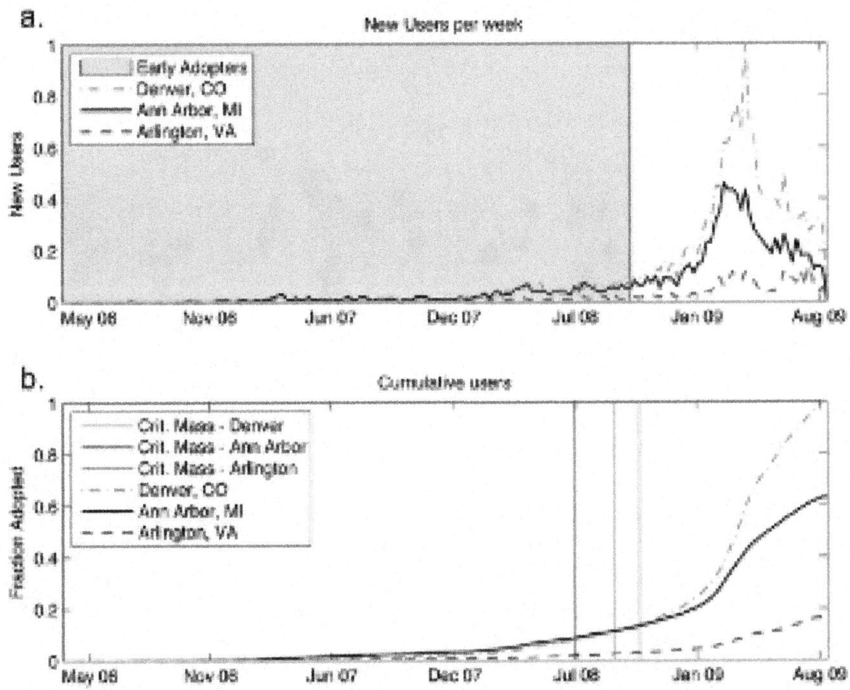

Figure 2: Plots of weekly adoption for select cities. (a.) Time series display the number of new U.S. Twitter users for three separate locations (Ann Arbor, MI, Denver, CO,

and Arlington, VA) from mid-March 2006 through late-August 2009, normalized by the largest weekly increase in Denver users. (b.) Shows a plot of the cumulative fraction of each city's user base normalized by the total number of users in Denver, CO.

Having labeled adopters relative to the national population, we then measure the composition of each city in terms of the percentage of users who are early adopters, early majority, late majority, or laggards. This step also serves to normalize locations with respect to population. We find, unsurprisingly, that cities with the most early adopters tend to have large universities or are technology centers that tend to attract large numbers of young, tech-savvy persons who are likely to adopt social web applications. Importantly, these locations are not necessarily co-located near each other. College towns all across the country saw early growth of Twitter users despite being very far from major metropolitan areas usually known for driving innovation. Later, we show that the empirical composition of cities and the demographics they represent is critical to reproducing spatiotemporal diffusion patterns.

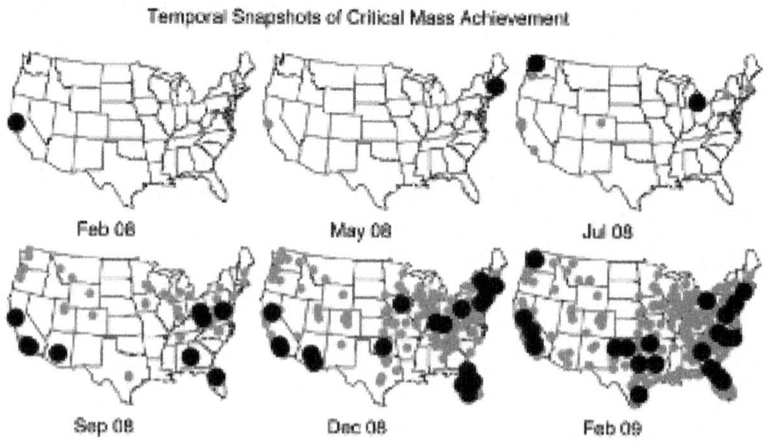

Figure 3: Temporal snapshots of critical mass achievement at locations across the US. For snapshot, the smaller, gray markers indicate locations that have already reached critical mass. The larger, black markers denote locations that achieved critical mass during that week. We note that locations achieving critical mass at very early times are clustered around Twitter's birthplace, San Francisco, CA, suggesting local word-of-mouth diffusion. There are, however, a few locations on the other side of the country, namely the suburbs of Boston, MA that are equally early in adoption, contrasting local diffusion with the flattening effects of the Internet.

We next focus on a key moment for any contagion process, critical mass achievement. Again following conventions from the diffusion of innovations literature, we mark a city as reaching critical mass when 13.5% of all eventual users have signed up [3]. Fig. 3 shows a series of snapshots in time indicating when various US cities reach critical mass. These snapshots reveal the diffusion path of Twitter from its birthplace in Silicon Valley, to college towns such as Cambridge, MA, Ann Arbor, MI, or Austin, TX, to metropolitan areas such as Los Angeles, CA, or Denver, CO, then finally to more suburban and rural areas. As noted above, this pattern is non-local in space. Whereas disease can only be transmitted via physical contact, or at least being in the same place at nearly the same time, online innovations are not necessarily constrained by geography and can travel coast-to-coast almost instantaneously. Despite reaching critical mass very early in the San Francisco Bay Area, Twitter did not diffuse spatially up and down the California coast. Instead, it hopped thousands of miles to Cambridge, MA, another highly tech-savvy population. As we shall see later, however, diffusion is not entirely non-local.

Just as individuals users were labeled as early adopters or laggards, cities were also placed into groups according to when they reached critical mass relative to the entire population. For example, many of the early adopting cities are home to large, public universities whose students are young internet users. Smaller rural towns make up the majority of the lagging cities, with large metropolitan areas falling somewhere in between.

As with any product or service, we expect at least some influence from marketing and advertising, done either explicitly by the creators in the form of advertising and marketing or done implicitly by the users through word-of-mouth. As explained above, we use Google news and search volumes as a proxy for these media influences. Importantly, we note that media coverage (Fig. 1) of Twitter was nearly non-existent during the first two years. The company itself did almost no official advertising. During this time, Google search volume was highly correlated with user growth. After a critical mass of users was reached, media coverage began to increase super-linearly. Many of the spikes in adoption rates were the result of celebrity endorsements such as Oprah's decision to officially sign up on-air during her show on April 17th, 2009 and political events like the Iranian protests in July and August 2009 that sparked debate over the use of social media to coordinate revolution.

Qualitatively, we recognize the media as having an enormous role in driving adoption. We also find that news coverage did not pick up until after the nation had achieved a critical mass of users, suggesting strong endogeneity where media responds to the very adoption it produces. This is much different than the traditional modeling of media [4], [5]. We seek to capture these stylized facts by including a powerful media agent whose coverage both grows with adoption and produces powerful and random shocks, simulating hyper-influentials and major media events.

Model Introduction

To capture both geographic effects as well as media influence, we introduce our model as follows:

(i) We begin by initializing the agent population and social network. Contagion spreading is simulated by a mechanism resembling the susceptible - infected (SI) model, which is also a special case of the Bass model, widely used in the diffusion of innovations literature. We create a population of N agents and place each agent into one of L cities, creating city level meta-populations. Each agent can be one of two types, *early adopter* or *regular adopter*. The geographic placement and and agent types are chosen to reflect empirical distributions of real Twitter users as well the composition of cities. Thus, if a city was measured to have 4% of all US Twitter users, 4% of our agents are placed there. Furthermore, of the agents placed in that city, if the composition was measure empirically to be 30% early adopters, 30% of agents will have an early adopter type, with the remainder marked as regular.

Agents are then connected by links to form a social network. The empirical characteristics of links and distances can be set to reflect those measured in on-line social networks. Liben-Nowell et al. [33] show that P_r, the probability of being connected to someone located a distance r from your city, follows a truncated power-law, $p_r = r^{-\gamma} + \nu$, where $\gamma = 1.2$ and the probability of connection becomes roughly constant for distances greater than $\nu = 1000$ km. We are also able to set the degree distribution and density of the social network to reflect different topologies.

(ii) Next, we add dynamics to the simulation. At any given time, each agent can be in one of two states, susceptible (S) or infected (I). Initial adoption is seeded to a small fraction of agents who are initialized as infected. Spreading is modeled over a series of T time periods, where the number of agents in each state is tracked (subject to $S(t)+I(t)=N$). Each time period, all infected agents attempt to infect their neighbors. With probabilities and β_e, a regular or early adopter, respectively, will heed a recommendation and adopt the technology. We use the ratio, $R = \frac{\beta_e}{\beta_r}$ to control differences in propensity to adopt for early versus regular adopters.

These features mimic social dynamics that suggest the pressure to adopt increases as more friends adopt and that more connected people receive greater benefits from adopting social technologies [3]. Some models assume that an individual will adopt an innovation once a specific number [18], [34], [35] or proportion [19] of their contacts have also adopted. Others have found evidence that occupying similar positions in social networks is more predictive of adoption [36]. While we do not attempt to test these hypotheses, Kleinberg has suggested that the dynamics of these adoption schemes are quantitatively similar [37].

(*iii*) In addition to word-of-mouth spreading, we also incorporate a media agent. This agent can be thought of as an influence in addition to word-of-mouth spreading, similar to the Bass model. Each time period, the media broadcasts its message to adopt a technology, and each agent flips a coin determining if adoption occurs. The media transmission probability is given by, $\Pr(\textit{media infection}) = \alpha M$, where $\alpha \in [0,1]$ is a model parameter, and M is the endogenous media volume. Media volume itself is determined as a function of the number of previously infected agents, $I(t-1)$, and a random term ε such that $M(t) = I(t-1)^{\gamma} + \varepsilon$. For convenience, we normalize the media so that, $M(t) \in [0,1]$. The parameter, γ, reflects the super-linear growth displayed in Google news media volume. Finally, we set the size of random shocks ε to be on the order of $M(t)$, reflecting stylized features seen in Google News volume data.

In essence, the amount of media exposure an innovation is given depends explicitly on the number of people who have adopted it as well as a random error term. Just because the media is reporting on a new product, however, does not mean a consumer will adopt it. To model this, we have included the parameter α, which adjusts how receptive agents are to the media. The probability that any given agent will adopt due to the medias influence, αM, is then given by the product of how much the media is reporting and how closely an individual is listening.

RESULTS

Replicating Standard SI Model

We first present results for parameter settings that reduce our simulation to the traditional SI model. We set $\beta_r = \beta_e$ (leaving only one type of agent), $\alpha = 0$ (removing the media), and populate each of $L = 408$ cities uniformly with 1000 agents for a total population of $N = 408,000$. We initialize the network to have a completely random spatial distribution of links so as to remove any geographic bias in friendship and simulate homogeneous mixing in the population. We choose a Poisson degree distribution because the qualitative structure of the adoption network is more selective than a scale free structure found in measurements of all connections in online social networks [25], [38], [39]. For example, Leskovec et al. [25]found that individuals who recommended a product to tens or even hundreds of contacts influenced no more purchases on average than those who sent recommendations to just a few friends.

Thus, we expect the number of people who can influence a person to adopt a technology is smaller than the number of acquaintances they have and the distribution is not likely to be long tailed. Scaling these numbers to fit our simulation size we choose a reasonable average degree of $\langle k \rangle = 7$.

Fig. 4 displays the simulated number of adopters per week for a variety of values for β. The simulation was run 500 times for each parameter configuration. The bands surrounding the average represent ranges between which 75% and 95% of simulations fell. In this simple form of the model, it is not possible to reproduce the empirical shape of the cumulative adoption curve seen in the Twitter case study suggesting more complicated dynamics are required to accurately predict the adoption of these technologies.

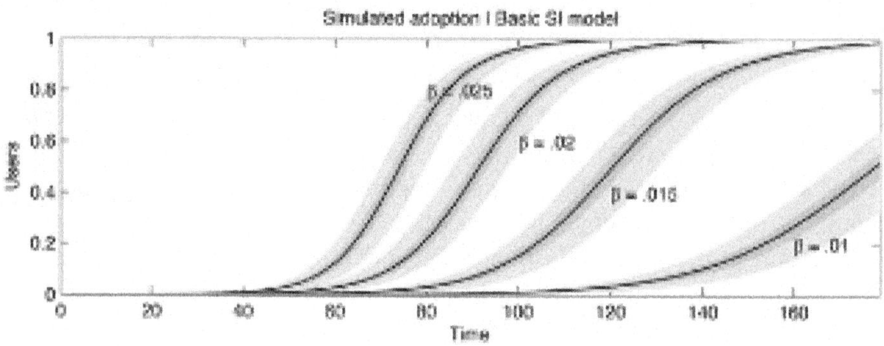

Figure 4: Verification of the basic SI model. Four different transmission rates β are displayed, each run 500 times and averaged. The bands surrounding the average value are bounds containing 75%, and 95% of simulation runs.

Next, we add more diverse geography to the model in the form of city populations, geographically distributed friendships, and early adopters that are three times as likely to adopt when than regular adopters ($R = \frac{\beta_e}{\beta_r} = 3$). To understand how these additions affect adoption at the local level, we first examine the importance of network structure in the presence of two agent types.

Our analysis shows that homophily based solely on agent type (i.e. early versus late adopter) is not enough to reproduce the observed trends in the spatiotemporal diffusion of information. A very specific type and strength of homophily must be present to ensure that the early adopters are connected to each other, forming a giant component in the early adopter sub-network, and not leaving members of their type isolated by regular adopters. To introduce these different types of homophily into the network, we simulate two types of networks, homogenous mixing and spatially embedded networks, and also vary the fraction of similarly typed neighbors each agent prefers. In order to form giant component of early adopters, we find that not only must agents prefer friendships with other agents of similar type (homophily by type), but they must also prefer friendships with those closer to them geographically, forming a *spatial social network.* Spatially embedded friendships are selected as a function of distance with probability,P_r, of selecting a friend who is a geographic distance r away is described in the previous sections [33].

Fig. 5 plots the size of the giant component of early adopters produced at a given level of homophily measured among early adopters for networks either spatially embedded or not. Here we define homophily as the average fraction of an early adopter›s friends who are also early adopters. These estimates were obtained by creating and consolidating results over 100networks, each with $N = 10{,}000$ nodes and a given level of homophily, then measuring the size of the giant component. For the remainder of this paper, all configurations labeled *spatial network* can be assumed to have a giant component containing over 95% of all early adopters.

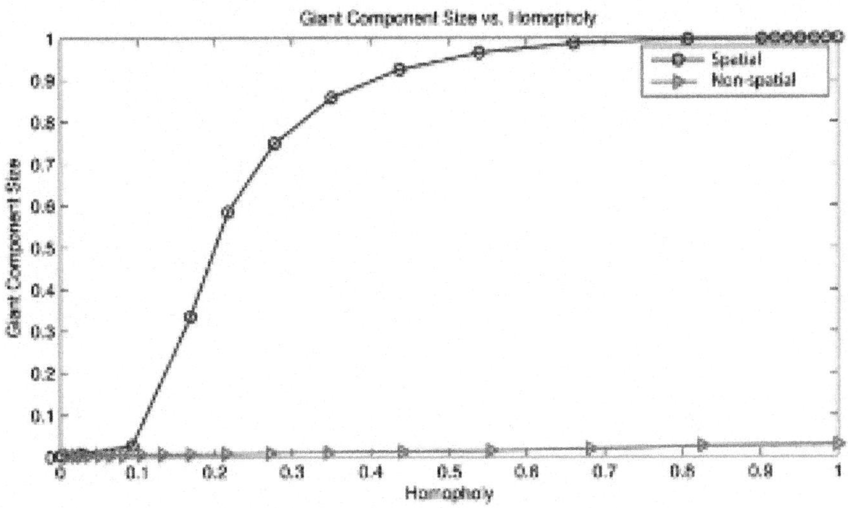

Figure 5: The size of the giant component plotted against homophily. Two configurations are shown, one in which the social network is explicitly spatial, the other ignoring geography of nodes. The figure illustrates that preference for friendship with similar agents is not enough to connect early adopters in a giant component and that spatial friendships are produce this structure.

To see how this giant component of early adopters affects adoption, Fig. 6 compares the predicted and actual times of critical mass achievement both with and without spatial friendships. In the absence of a giant component, nearly all cities peak at the same time. When spatially embedded friendships are introduced such that a giant component of early adopters is formed, we are able to simulate city level Twitter adoption, while preserving national trends. Though global cumulative adoption can be reproduced without the spatial social network, adoption cannot is not geographically resolved to the city level. Embedding the social network in real space, however, makes it possible to accurately simulate the critical mass achievement times in most cities. Fig. 7 shows these simulated times when compared to times empirically measured in data. We have divided specific cities into four groups based on when they reached critical mass relative to all locations. For selected cities, simulation quartiles are plotted along with actual peak times. In the on-line supporting information we provide data files containing the composition and adoption times of different cities, with the goal of facilitating future studies of other hypothesis and types of adoption.

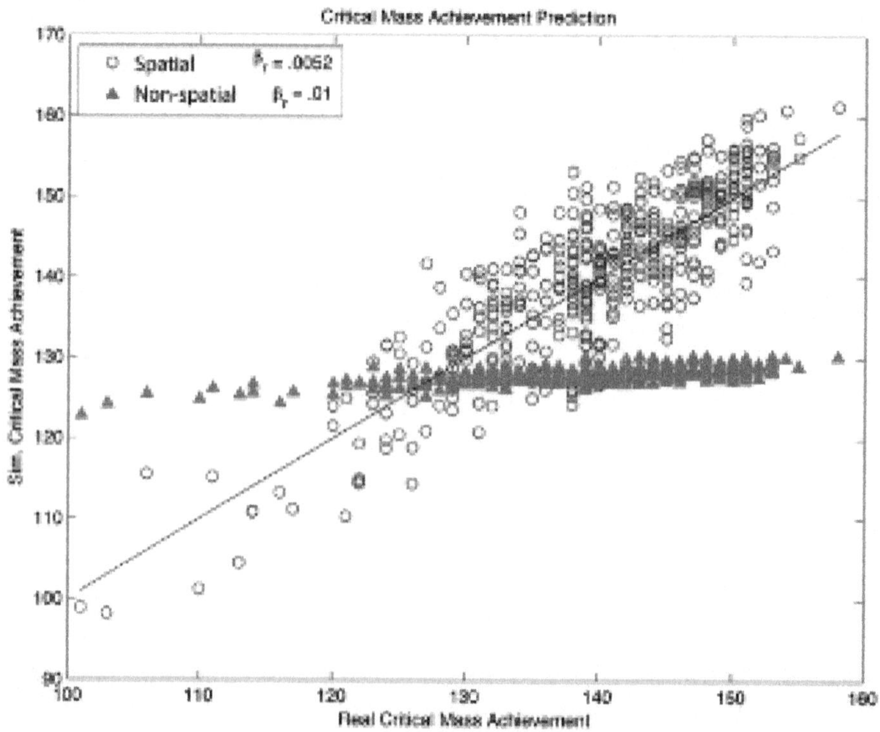

Figure 6: Simulated critical mass achievement times are compared to times measured from Twitter data. We find spatially embedded friendships are necessary to reproduce the inter-city spread of Twitter.

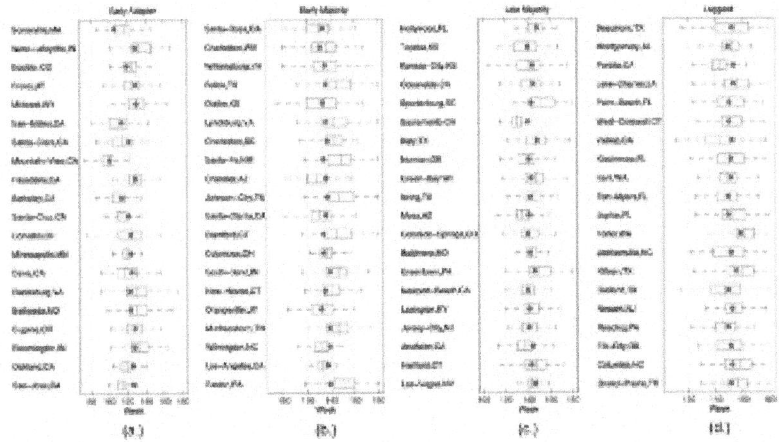

Figure 7: Simulation results are compared to actual critical mass achievement times for different subsets of locations. Borrowing from the diffusion of innovations literature, we use four groups (a.) Early adopting, (b.) Early Majority, (c.) Late Majority, (d.) Laggards. We are able to reliably predict adoption times for cities in each category.

Media Influence

Fig. 8 compares predictions of national adoption with the above model conditions. Examining news volume as collected by Google, we note that purely word-of-mouth simulations start diverging from reality around week 120 after launch. This is just around the time when mass media begins to report on the web application. Because of this sharp transition, we can measure the relative strength of word of mouth spreading versus mass media influence.

Predicting when the individual media events like celebrity endorsements will occur is beyond the scope of this work. We can, however, simulate adoptions in the presence of empirical news volume from Google's database. In order to achieve the national adoption pattern similar to that seen in real data, we find that agents must be highly susceptible to media influence, with the parameter $\alpha = 0.15$. Contrasting aggregate adoption predictions both with and without media influence suggests that the mass media was responsible for at least half of the newly joined Twitter's users, most of whom adopted in later stages. Coupled with our early results showing the importance of homophily and geography during the early stages of spread, our model paints a much more complete picture of adoption, capable of reproducing both aggregate and local trends in space and time.

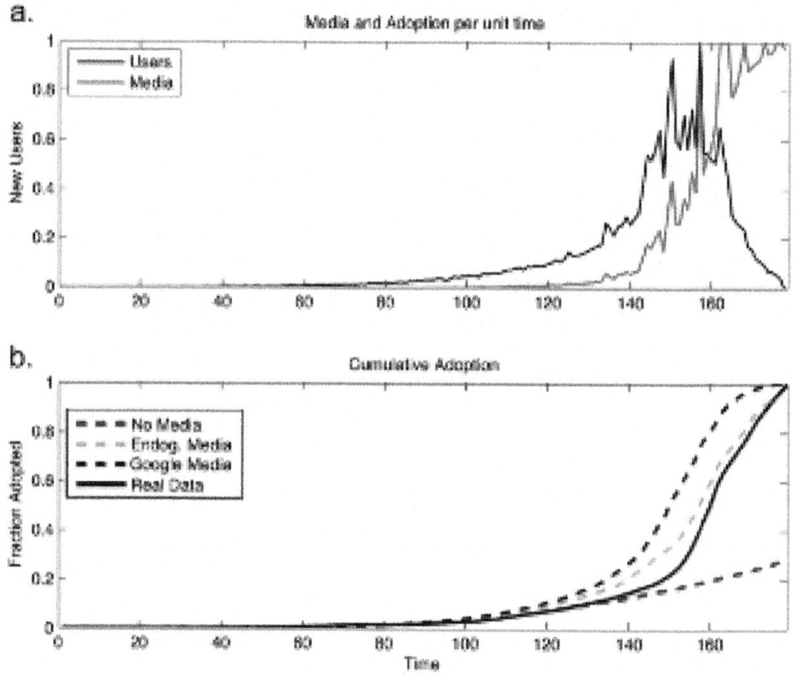

Figure 8: Simulated adoption treating the media as endogenous and increasing with the number of adopters. (a.) Shows simulated new users per week (normalized to the maximum over the period) as well as normalized media volume each week. (b.) A comparison of all model scenarios is shown. Traditional models, models which do not include media influence are capable of predicting adoption in early periods, but dramatically underestimate total adoption. Including endogenous media effects allows us to make adoption predictions that more closely resemble real data.

Next, we expand our model to treat news volume as endogenous such that adoption may be simulated without requiring external empirical data on media influence. We introduce an endogenous mass media, implemented as described above in step *iii.* of our model introduction. Reflecting trends seen in the real data, the growth of media volume is super-linear with respect to adopters and random spikes in media coverage are introduced to reflect discrete and unpredictable media events. For these simulations, we found an exponent of media growth with respect to adopters, $\gamma = 3$, produced reasonable fits to real data. Fig. 8displays simulation results for various model settings described in this paper. While spatial friendship networks are able to reproduce early adoption trends, real data quickly diverges in later times. Introducing an endogenous mass media agent which grows super-linearly in the number of current adopters produces, along with random media spikes, produces much more accurate adoption trends and reflects features seen real media coverage.

DISCUSSION

In light of a globalized world with near universal access to the Internet, previous models of adoption fail to characterize the interplay of media and word of mouth. In this article, we have presented descriptive statistics of the spatiotemporal adoption of a web application and proposed a model of technology adoption or, more generally, social contagion, to replicate features seen in data from city to national scales. For early stages, when spreading occurs primarily through word-of-mouth, we find that adoption is strongly correlated with traditional demographic covariates. Early adopting cities tend to be those with large, young, and tech-savvy populations. Media influences during later stages, however, were found to be very strong, accounting for a two to four fold increase in the number of people who adopted. This finding is consistent with earlier work that suggests advertising campaigns are enough to confound any word-of-mouth spreading [26].

Our model extends previous work in two important ways. First, we demonstrate that spatial social networks are crucial to reproducing the dynamics of adoption at a city scale. Secondly, the media features of the model reflect empirical observations that the news volume reacts to the number of adopters with a super-linear trend after a product has reached a critical mass and with random shocks emanating from super-influential people like celebrities or major media events like massive demonstrations.

These results suggest that our model is capable of replicating both micro (at the city level) and macro (at the national level) adoption phenomena and may provide substantial improvement over existing frameworks such as the SI or Bass models. We do, however, urge some caution in the interpretation of our results. Because our simulation relies upon the fraction of a city denoted as early adopters and this fraction was measured empirically from data, the model may be sensitive to errors in this measurement. While our empirical results are intuitive, for example finding that Silicon Valley and college towns have the most early adopters of a viral web application, they may not hold for other products such as durable goods. Our model is best applied to goods and services that are very low cost, very easy to tell someone about, and display large positive externalities.

We hope it inspires future work in the area. Specifically, it would be interesting to compare and contrast the spatial diffusion of web apps such as Twitter, with more tangible products such as gadgets, medicine, or cars. For example, it may be possible to use the composition of the cities as characterized by the adoption of Twitter to predict or even try to accelerate the adoption of other related kinds of technological innovations. To facilitate further research in this area, we have provided a readme and data file, containing city level compositions as well as time series data in the online supporting information as well as our web page, http://humnet.scripts.mit.edu/wordpress/2011/06/13/project-modeling-the-diffusion-of-social-contagion/. This work also represents advances in models of spreading in networks where the roll of demographics, i.e. node attributes, as well as geography is critical for future predictions. These insights may be particularly useful in modeling opinion spreading such as in elections and collective action.

ACKNOWLEDGMENTS

The authors would like to thank Krishna Gummadi, Fabricio Benevenuto, and Alan Mislove for help in gathering data.

AUTHOR CONTRIBUTIONS

Conceived and designed the experiments: JLT MC MCG. Performed the experiments: JLT MC MCG. Analyzed the data: JLT MCG. Contributed reagents/materials/analysis tools: MC. Wrote the paper: JLT.

REFERENCES

1. Dietz K (1967) Epidemics and Rumours: A Survey. Journal of the Royal Statistical Society Series A (General) 130:
2. Rogers EM, Rogers E (2003) Diffusion of Innovations, 5th Edition. Free Press, 5th edition.
3. Valente TW (1995) Network Models of the Diffusion of Innovations (Quantitative Methods in Communication Subseries). Hampton Press (NJ).
4. Katz E (1957) The Two-Step Flow of Communication: An Up-To-Date Report on an Hypothesis. The Public Opinion Quarterly 21: 61–78.
5. Bass FM (1969) A New Product Growth for Model Consumer Durables. Management Science 15: 215–227.
6. Dodds PS, Watts DJ (2005) A generalized model of social and biological contagion. Journal of Theoretical Biology 232: 587–604.
7. Newman MEJ, Jensen I, Ziff RM (2002) Percolation and epidemics in a two-dimensional small world. Physical Review E 65: 021904+.
8. Karrer B, Newman MEJ (2010) Message passing approach for general epidemic models. Physical Review E 82: 016101+.
9. Rahmandad H, Sterman J (2008) Heterogeneity and Network Structure in the Dynamics of Diffusion: Comparing Agent-Based and Differential Equation Models. Management Science 54: 998–1014.

10. Castellano C, Fortunato S, Loreto V (2009) Statistical physics of social dynamics. Reviews of Modern Physics 81: 591–646.
11. Watts DJ, Muhamad R, Medina DC, Dodds PS (2005) Multiscale, resurgent epidemics in a hier-archical metapopulation model. Proceedings of the National Academy of Sciences of the United States of America 102: 11157–11162.
12. Jones BF, Wuchty S, Uzzi B (2008) Multi-University Research Teams: Shifting Impact, Geography, and Stratification in Science. Science 322: 1259–1262.
13. Liben-Nowell D, Kleinberg J (2008) Tracing information ow on a global scale using Internet chain-letter data. Proceedings of the National Academy of Sciences 105: 4633–4638.
14. Romero DM, Meeder B, Kleinberg J (2011) Differences in the Mechanics of Information DiffusionAcross Topics: Idioms, Political Hashtags, and ComplexContagion on Twitter.
15. Leskovec J, Backstrom L, Kleinberg J (2009) Meme-tracking and the dynamics of the news cycle. Proceedings of the 15th ACM SIGKDD international conference on Knowledge discovery and data mining. New York, NY, USA: ACM, KDD '09. pp. 497–506. doi:10.1145/1557019.1557077.
16. Salganik MJ, Dodds PS, Watts DJ (2006) Experimental Study of Inequality and Unpredictability in an Artificial Cultural Market. Science 311: 854–856.
17. Schelling TC (1973) Hockey Helmets, ConcealedWeapons, and Daylight Saving: A Study of Binary Choices with Externalities. The Journal of Conict Resolution 17: 381–428.
18. Granovetter MS (1973) The Strength of Weak Ties. American Journal of Sociology 78: 1360–1380.
19. Centola D, Eguiluz V, MacY M (2007) Cascade dynamics of complex propagation. Physica A: Statistical Mechanics and its Applications 374: 449–456.
20. Centola D, Macy M (2007) Complex Contagions and the Weakness of Long Ties. American Journal of Sociology 113: 702–734.
21. Centola D (2010) The Spread of Behavior in an Online Social Network Experiment. Science 329: 1194–1197.
22. Watts DJ, Dodds PS (2007) Inuentials, Networks, and Public Opinion Formation.
23. López-Pintado D, Watts DJ (2008) Social Inuence, Binary Decisions and

Collective Dynamics. Rationality and Society 20: 399–443.

24. Yang J, Leskovec J (2011) Patterns of temporal variation in online media. Proceedings of the fourth ACM international conference on Web search and data mining. New York, NY, USA: ACM, WSDM '11. pp. 177–186. doi:10.1145/1935826.1935863.

25. Leskovec J, Adamic LA, Huberman BA (2007) The dynamics of viral marketing. ACM Trans Web 1:

26. Van den Bulte C, Lilien GL (2001) Medical Innovation Revisited: Social Contagion versus Marketing Effort. American Journal of Sociology 106: 1409–1435.

27. Pease A, Brewer PR (2008) The Oprah Factor: The Effects of a Celebrity Endorsement in a Presidential Primary Campaign. The International Journal of Press/Politics 13: 386–400.

28. Baum MA, Jamison AS (2006) The Oprah Effect: How Soft News Helps Inattentive Citizens Vote Consistently. The Journal of Politics 68: 946–959.

29. Fowler JH (2008) The Colbert Bump in Campaign Donations: More Truthful than Truthy. PS: Political Science & Politics 41: 533–539.

30. Garber T, Goldenberg J, Libai B, Muller E (2004) From Density to Destiny: Using Spatial Dimension of Sales Data for Early Prediction of New Product Success. MARKETING SCIENCE 23: 419–428.

31. Allaway A (2003) Spatial diffusion of a new loyalty program through a retail market. Journal of Retailing 79: 137–151.

32. Onnela JP, Reed-Tsochas F (2010) Spontaneous emergence of social inuence in online systems. Proceedings of the National Academy of Sciences 107: 18375–18380.

33. Liben-Nowell D, Novak J, Kumar R, Raghavan P, Tomkins A (2005) Geographic routing in social networks. Proceedings of the National Academy of Sciences of the United States of America 102: 11623–11628.

34. Granovetter M (1978) Threshold Models of Collective Behavior. American Journal of Sociology 83: 1420–1443.

35. Watts DJ (2002) A simple model of global cascades on random networks. Proceedings of the National Academy of Sciences 99: 5766–5771.

36. Burt RS (1987) Social Contagion and Innovation: Cohesion Versus Structural Equivalence. American Journal of Sociology 92: 1287–1335.

37. Kleinberg J (2007) Cascading behavior in networks: Algorithmic and economic issues.

38. Wu F, Huberman B, Adamic L, Tyler J (2004) Information ow in social

groups. Physica A: Statistical and Theoretical Physics 337: 327–335.

39. Gonalves B, Perra N, Vespignani A (2011) Modeling users' activity on twitter networks: Validation of dunbar's number. PLoS ONE 6: e22656.

Chapter 7

ACT CLXXXV OF 2010 ON MEDIA SERVICES AND MASS COMMUNICATION

INTRODUCTION

The Parliament, with a view to promote community and individual interests and social integrity, to ensure proper operation of the democratic order and to strengthen national and cultural identity, with due respect to the Fundamental Law, the constitutional principles, and the norms of international law and of the European Union, by taking into consideration the circumstances created by the developments in technology, by preserving the freedom of expression, speech and the press, and considering the key importance of media services in cultural, social and economic terms, and the importance of ensuring competition on the media market, hereby adopts this Act on Media Services and Mass Media, as follows:

SCOPE OF THE ACT

Article 1 (1) The Act shall apply to media services and press products provided and published by media content providers established in Hungary.

(2) For the purposes of this Act, a media content provider shall be deemed as established in Hungary if it meets the following criteria:

a) the analogue distribution of the media service provided by it is performed through the use of a frequency owned by Hungary, or the press product is primarily accessible through the electronic communications identifier designated for the users of Hungary;

b) the seat of its central administration is located on the territory of Hungary and the editorial decisions related to the media service or the press product are made on the territory of Hungary;

c) if either the seat of its central administration or the place where editorial decisions are made is located on the territory of Hungary, however the significant part of the media content provider's staff being employed on the territory of Hungary;

d) a significant part of the media content provider's staff is employed both in and outside the territory of Hungary but the seat of its central administration is located on the territory of Hungary;

e) either the seat of its central administration or the place where editorial decisions are made is located on the territory of Hungary, however its activity was commenced on the territory of Hungary and it maintains actual and continuous contact with the players of the Hungarian economy; or

f) it distributes its media service by exercising its temporary digital broadcasting right as per Point b) of Article 43/A (1) of Act LXXIV of 2007 on the Rules of Broadcasting and Digital Switchover (hereinafter referred to as: Digital Switchover Act).

(3) The scope of the Act shall also cover media services provided by media content providers which do not qualify as a media content provider established on the territory of Hungary based on Paragraphs (1)-(2) and which do not qualify as a media content provider established in another Member State either, provided that such media content providers use a satellite uplink station located on the territory of Hungary or use such transmission capacity of the satellite that is owned by Hungary.

(4) If, on the basis of Paragraphs (1)-(3), it cannot be determined whether a particular media content provider falls under the jurisdiction of Hungary or some other Member State, the media content provider shall fall under the jurisdiction of the state where it is established, according to the provisions of Articles 49-55 of the Treaty on the Functioning of the European Union.

(5) This Act shall also apply to media services and press products which, although outside the scope of Paragraphs (1)-(4), are targeted at or distributed or published on the territory of Hungary, subject to the conditions set forth in Articles 176-180.

(6) The Act shall also apply to the media services and press products targeted at or distributed or published on the territory of Hungary by such media content providers that are not deemed as established in any Member State, provided that their media services or press products are not subject to the jurisdiction of any one of the Member States either.

(7) The Act shall apply to media content providers rendering media services or publishing press products that fall under the scope of the Act pursuant to Paragraphs (1)-(6).

Article 2 (1) In certain instances stipulated herein, the scope of the Act shall also cover ancillary media services, and their providers, that are provided within the territory of Hungary or that are related to media service distribution provided within the territory of Hungary. (2) In certain instances stipulated herein, the scope of the Act shall cover a) media service distribution, carried out wholly or partially with electronic communications equipment installed within the territory of Hungary or transmitting to the territory of Hungary; b) the technical activities of the media service provider in connection with the media service distribution stipulated in Point (a); c) the activity of the ancillary media service provider in connection with the media service distribution stipulated in Point (a); d) publications. (3) In certain instances stipulated herein, the scope of the Act shall cover natural or legal persons or other organizations without legal personality and the executive officers of such persons or entities carrying out the activities or providing the services stipulated under Paragraph (2) or carrying out any activity or providing any service related thereto. (4) In certain instances stipulated herein, the scope of the Act shall also cover the intermediary service provider transmitting the media service or the press product and the services of such provider. (5) In certain instances stipulated herein, the scope of this Act shall also cover the viewers, the listeners or the readers of the media services, ancillary media services and press products and the user, consumer and subscriber of the media service distribution falling within the scope of the Act.

FUNDAMENTAL PRINCIPLES

Article 3 Media services may be provided and press products may be published freely, information and opinions may be transmitted freely through the mass media, and Hungarian and foreign media services intended for public reception may be accessed freely in Hungary. The content of the media service and the press product may be determined freely, nevertheless the media service provider and the publisher of press product shall be liable for compliance with the provisions of this Act.

Article 4 The diversity of media services is a particularly important value. The protection of diversity shall also include the avoidance of the formation of ownership monopolies and any unjustified restriction of competition on the market. The provisions of this Act shall be interpreted in consideration of the protection of diversity.

Article 5 The right to information and the right to be informed of those living within the territory of Hungary and of the members of the Hungarian nation and, in connection with this, the development and strengthening of publicity in the democratic society are fundamental constitutional interests. The provisions of this Act shall be interpreted with a view to the interests of democratic public opinion.

Article 6 Existence of public media services represents an essential condition of the appropriate functioning of a democratic social order. The interests of public media service shall be considered with particular emphasis in the course of the application of this Act.

Article 7 (1) In the course of carrying out the tasks falling within the scope of this Act, the media service providers, publishers of press products, ancillary media service providers and media service distributors shall act as required by good faith and fairness, and in accordance with the provisions of this Act shall be obliged to mutually cooperate with one another and the viewers, the listeners, the readers, the users and the subscribers. (2) The media service distributors, media service providers, and ancillary media service providers shall be obliged to operate and provide the electronic communications networks, electronic communications services, digital programme flows and ancillary media services between each other in accordance with a set of coordinated technical criteria, so that these form a unified system required to establish the necessary connection and to provide the service either directly or with the incorporation of proper interfaces, network parts, elements, devices or services.

Article 8 The professional self-regulatory bodies comprising the media service providers, publishers of press products, intermediary service providers and media service distributors, as well as the various self- and co-regulatory procedures applied play an important role in the field of media regulation and in the application of and compliance with the provisions of this Act. Such bodies and procedures shall be respected in the application of this Act.

REQUIREMENTS REGARDING THE CONTENT OF MEDIA SERVICES

Article 9 (1) A media service provider providing linear media services shall assign a rating to each and every programme it intends to broadcast in accordance with the categories under Paragraphs (2)-(7) prior to broadcasting, with the exception of news programmes, political programmes, sports programmes, previews and advertisements, political advertisements, teleshopping, public service advertisements and public service announcements.

(2) Category I shall include programmes which may be viewed or listened to by persons of any age.

(3) Category II shall include programmes which may trigger fear in persons under the age of six or may not be comprehended or may be misunderstood by such viewer or listener owing to his/her age. These programmes shall be classified as “Not recommended for audiences under the age of six”.

(4) Category III shall include programmes which may trigger fear in persons under the age of twelve or may not be comprehended or may be misunderstood

by such viewer or listener owing to his/her age. These programmes shall be classified as "Not recommended for audiences under the age of twelve".

(5) Category IV shall include programmes which may impair the physical, mental or moral development of persons under the age of sixteen, particularly because they refer to violence or sexuality, or are dominated by conflicts resolved by violence. These programmes shall be classified as "Not recommended for audiences under the age of sixteen".

(6) Category V shall include programmes which may impair the physical, mental or moral development of minors, particularly because they are dominated by graphic scenes of violence or sexual content. These programmes shall be classified as "Not recommended for audiences under the age of eighteen".

(7) Category VI shall include programmes which may seriously impair the physical, mental or moral development of minors, particularly because they involve pornography or scenes of extreme and/or unjustified violence.

(8) The Media Council of the National Media and Infocommunications Authority (hereinafter as: the Media Council) shall issue recommendations on the most important conceptual aspects of the enforcement practice applied by it concerning the detailed criteria governing the ratings as per Paragraphs (2)-(7), the signs to be used prior to and in the course of broadcasting the various programmes and the method of communicating the rating, if justified by public interest related to the protection of minors or by the uniform approach to the protection of minors.

(9) Upon request of the media service provider the Media Council shall adopt a regulatory decision on the rating of the programme within fifteen days from having received the programme in question, for an administrative service fee. (10) It shall not qualify as the violation of Paragraphs (1)-(7) if the media service provider rates a programme into a higher category than it would be required pursuant to Paragraphs (2)-(6).

Article 10 (1) In linear media services (

a) programmes classified into Category II cannot be aired between programmes intended for persons under the age of six, but may, at any time, be aired using the proper rating; (b) programmes classified into Category III cannot be aired between programmes intended for persons under the age of twelve, but may, at any time, be aired using the proper rating; (c) programmes classified into Category IV may be aired between 9.00 p.m. and 5.00 a.m. using the proper rating; (d) programmes classified into Category V may be aired between 10.00 p.m. and 5.00 a.m. using the proper rating; (e) programmes classified into Category VI may not be aired;

(f) a preview may not be aired at a time when the programme it introduces or presents is not allowed to be aired or at a time when upon the proper rating of such preview it is not allowed to be aired;

(g) the preview of a programme classified into Category III may not be aired during the interval of or immediately prior or subsequent to a programme intended for persons under the age of twelve; (h) sports programmes, commercial communications and public service advertisements may not be aired at such times when it is foreseeable that these would not be allowed to be aired, if they were provided with a proper rating based on their content. (2) In linear media services

(a) a programme may only be aired in compliance with its rating, subject to the exceptions provided by this Act; (b) the rating of the programme shall be communicated at the time the airing of the programme begins. (3) In the case of linear radio media services, the rating does not have to be communicated if (a) the programme falling within Categories II or III is aired between 9.00 p.m. and 5.00 a.m.; (b) the programme falling within Categories IV or V is aired between 11.00 p.m. and 5.00 a.m. (4) In linear audiovisual media services, at the time the specific programme is aired, a sign corresponding to the rating of the programme shall also be displayed in the form of a pictogram in one of the corners of the screen so that it is clearly visible throughout the entire course of the programme. The pictogram shall indicate with numbers the age group affected by the given category. In case of programmes falling into Category I it is not necessary to display the sign. In case of a linear radio media service it is not necessary to use permanent signs. (5) In case of linear audiovisual media services the continuous display in accordance with Paragraph (4) of the sign corresponding to the rating of the programme may be disregarded, provided that

a) the programme classified as Category II or III is aired between 9.00 p.m. and 5.00 a.m.; (b) the programme classified as Category IV is aired between 10.00 p.m. and 5.00 a.m.; or (c) the programme classified as Category V is aired between 11.00 p.m. and 5.00 a.m. In this case the sign corresponding to the rating of the programme shall be displayed when the programme begins, and at the time the programme is continued following the commercial break. (6) The stipulations in Points (c)-(f) and (h) of Paragraph (1) and under Paragraphs (2) and (4) shall not be applied if the media service contains the programme in an encrypted form and decryption may only be executed by using a code, which the media service provider or the media service distributor only made accessible to subscribers over the age of eighteen, or which uses another effective technical solution to prevent viewers or listeners under the age of eighteen from accessing the programme. The Media Council shall issue recommendations in respect of effective technical solutions subsequent to holding a public hearing, if necessary. (7) The rating of each and every programme in accordance with Article 9 shall be displayed in a conspicuous manner in the press product specifying the programme flow of the media service provider, on the website, noninteractive teletext and teletext of the media service provider, provided it has any of these.

Article 11 (1) The provisions under Article 9 (6)-(7) shall be applied to on-demand media services. (2) Pursuant to Article 19 (2) of Act CIV of 2010 on the Freedom of the Press and the Fundamental Rules of Media Content (hereinafter referred to as: Press Freedom Act), the media service provider or the media service distributor (distributing the given service) of an on-demand media service shall use an effective technical solution to prevent minors from accessing its programmes classified as Category V or VI programmes. (3) The Media Council shall issue recommendations in respect of effective technical solutions mentioned in Paragraph (2) subsequent to holding a public hearing, if necessary.

Information Activities

Article 12 (1) The information activities of media services shall comply with the obligation set forth under

Article 13 of the Press Freedom Act. (2) Subject to the nature of the programmes, the balanced nature of the information provision shall be ensured either within the given programme or within the series of programmes appearing regularly. (3) Save for the explanation of the news, employees of the media service provider appearing regularly in the programmes providing news service and political information as presenters, newsreaders or correspondents may not add any opinion or evaluative explanation to the political news appearing in the programme aired by any media service provider. (4) Any opinion or evaluative explanation added to the news provided in a programme shall be made in a form distinguishing it from the news themselves, indicating its nature as such and identifying its author. Article 13 [not in effect]

Warning about Offensive Content

Article 14 The viewers or listeners shall be given a forewarning prior to the broadcasting of any image or sound effects in media services that may hurt a person's religious, faith-related or other ideological convictions or which are violent or otherwise disturbing.

Managing Crisis Situations through the Media Services

Article 15 During a state of distress, state of emergency or state of extreme danger, or in the event of the unforeseen invasion of the territory of Hungary by foreign armed groups, or in connection with operations for the protection of the state's territory by air defence and air forces of the Hungarian Army, the Parliament, the Defence Council, the President of the Republic and the Government, as well as the persons and organizations defined by law may order the media service provider, to the extent necessitated by the existing state of affairs or situation, to publish, free of charge, any public service announcements in connection with the existing state of affairs or situation, in the prescribed form and time, or may prohibit the publication of certain announcements or programmes. The Media Service Support and Asset Management Fund (hereinafter as: Fund) shall be responsible for providing the conditions necessary for publishing. At the time of publication, the person or institution ordering the publication must be clearly identified.

Exclusive Broadcasting Rights

Article 16 (1) The audiovisual media service provider may not exercise the exclusive broadcasting right so as to deprive a substantial part – more than twenty percent – of the Hungarian audience having access to the audiovisual media services of the possibility to follow the events, live or in a subsequent broadcast, regarded to be events of major importance to society, through an audiovisual media service accessible without the payment of a subscription fee. (2) In connection with the audiovisual media service providers determined under Paragraph (1), the list of events of major importance to society shall be prepared by the Media Council, subsequent to a public hearing. As for the events included in the list, the Media Council shall also determine whether the given event should be aired by full or partial live coverage or, where necessary for objective reasons in the public interest, full or partial deferred coverage. (3) When preparing the list as per Paragraph (2) it must be taken into account that the events classified as events of major importance must meet the following criteria a) the event, besides the usual audience of the given sport or activity, also raises the interest of a broad section of society or it has a generally recognised, distinct cultural importance for the population, in particular as a catalyst of cultural identity, and b) the Hungarian team or athlete participate in the given event organised as part of a championship or cup having international significance, or the event has traditionally been broadcast on free television (without payment of a subscription fee) and has commanded large television audiences. (4) The Media Council shall send the draft list defined under Paragraph (2) to the European Commission, with detailed explanation attached, to obtain approval thereto. The list as per Paragraph (2) shall become effective as of the day it is published in the Official Journal of the European

Union. The preparation and acceptance of the list as per Paragraph (2) shall not qualify as a regulatory procedure or official matter, as defined under the Act on the General Rules of Administrative Proceedings and Services (hereinafter as: Act on Administrative Proceedings). (5) The Media Council may amend the list as per Paragraph (2), taking into account the criteria defined under Paragraph (3). The provisions of Paragraph (4) shall be applied respectively regarding the amended list. (6) Paragraph (1) and Article 18 (1) shall not be applied regarding the exclusive rights lawfully acquired prior to the entry into force of the first list prepared according to Paragraph (2) or the entry into force of its subsequent amendment. (7)

Article 17 (1) The exclusive broadcasting right shall not be exercised so as to deprive a substantial part of the audience in a Member State from following those events of major importance for them via an audiovisual media service, which are indicated on the list compiled and published in advance by

the Member State concerned. (2) Exclusive audiovisual broadcasting rights obtained subsequent to the effective date of the Act promulgating the Protocol on the amendment of the European Convention on Transfrontier Television signed in Strasbourg on 5 May 1989 (hereinafter, for the purposes of this Paragraph and Article 18: "Protocol"), promulgated by Act XLIX of 1998, shall be exercised in conformity with the provisions on the broadcasting of events of major importance for society in the States which are party to the Protocol.

Article 18 (1) If exercising of the exclusive broadcasting right would deprive at least twenty percent of the Hungarian audience from following the events as per Article 16 (2) via an audiovisual media service, the audiovisual media service provider shall be obliged to make a contract proposal – subject to reasonable terms and conditions and in exchange for consideration appropriate under the prevailing market conditions – to the linear audiovisual media service provider (hereinafter as: contracting authority), who provides services accessible for at least eighty percent of the citizens of Hungary without the payment of a subscription fee, when approached by such service provider, for the broadcasting of the said event live or subsequently. Under such circumstances, the media service provider having obtained exclusive rights may not refer to not being entitled to transfer the exclusive right. (2) Any media service provider, that acquired exclusive rights for the broadcasting of an event through audiovisual media service which has been designated by any State being a party to the Protocol as being of major importance to society, shall be required to make a contract proposal – subject to reasonable terms and conditions and in exchange for consideration appropriate under the prevailing market conditions – to the foreign linear audiovisual media service provider –

who falls within the jurisdiction of that State, complies with the requirements defined by that State, and is accessible without a subscription fee by at least eighty percent of the citizens of that State by taking any and all media service distribution techniques into consideration – when approached by such a service provider concerning the broadcast of the said event. (3) Any media service provider, that acquired exclusive rights for the broadcasting of an event that has been designated by a Member State as being of major importance to society, shall be required to make a contract proposal – subject to reasonable terms and conditions and in exchange for consideration appropriate under the prevailing market conditions – to the foreign audiovisual media service provider – who falls within the jurisdiction of that Member State and complies with the requirements defined by that Member State – when approached by such a service provider concerning the broadcast of the said event. (4) The parties concerned shall agree on the detailed terms and conditions of the contracts defined under Paragraphs (1)-(3). (5) In the cases specified under Paragraphs (1)-(3) the parties shall be subject to an obligation to contract. In the event the parties fail to conclude an agreement or fail to agree on the fees within fifteen days subsequent to the offer having been made, the contracting authority or the media service provider with exclusive broadcasting rights may initiate the legal dispute procedure stipulated in Articles 172-174. Within the framework of such legal dispute procedure, the Media Council shall adopt its decision within fifteen days. The administrative deadline may be extended by fifteen days, if justified. (6) For the purposes of Articles 16 and 18, the records of the Media Council shall prevail as far as the accessibility of the media services are concerned.

Short News Reports Article 19 (1)

Any linear audiovisual media service provider established within the territory of the European Union may have, for the purpose of a short news report, access in a fair, reasonable and non-discriminatory manner to the broadcast on the event of major importance, which appears on the list defined under Article 16 (2) or designated as such in any Member State and broadcasted under an exclusive broadcasting right by the audiovisual media service provider established in Hungary. The access may take place by obtaining the signal of the media service, by making a record at the location of the event or by receiving the footage recorded on the event. (2)

If an audiovisual media service provider, who is established in the same Member State where the audiovisual media service provider requesting the access is established, obtained exclusive rights in connection with the event of major importance, access may only be requested from this audiovisual media service provider. (3)

In the case specified under Paragraph (1) the parties concerned shall be subject to an obligation to contract. The contract shall be entered into upon reasonable terms and conditions; the consideration for the right of access may not exceed the costs arising directly as a result of providing access. In the event the parties fail to conclude an agreement within fifteen days subsequent to the offer having been made, any of the parties may initiate the legal dispute procedure stipulated in Articles 172-174. Within the framework of such legal dispute procedure, the Media Council shall adopt its decision within fifteen days. The administrative deadline may be extended by fifteen days, if justified. (4)

The audiovisual media service provider, which obtained a right of access, may freely select the parts of the programme it intends to broadcast in the short news report. (5) The total length of the parts to be broadcasted may not exceed ten percent of the total length of the programme concerned, but fifty seconds at most. The contract may permit the broadcasting of parts with a longer total length. (6) The audiovisual media service provider having obtained a right of access shall identify the holder of the exclusive broadcasting right with which it entered into an agreement on broadcasting. (7)

The parts of the programme, which may be used on the basis of the agreement, cannot be broadcasted individually but only as part of general news and information programmes. If the linear audiovisual media service provider intends to broadcast the short news report in an on-demand audiovisual media service as well, it may only do so if the programmes containing the short news report are identical in both the linear and in the on-demand audiovisual media services.

Programme Quotas

*Article 20 (1)*The media service provider a) shall allocate over half of its annual total transmission time of linear audiovisual media services to broadcasting European works and over one-third of its transmission time to broadcasting Hungarian works; b) shall allocate at least ten percent of its annual total transmission time of linear audiovisual media services to broadcasting such European works, and at least eight percent of its transmission time to broadcasting such Hungarian works that were ordered by it from an independent production company, or were purchased from an independent production company within five years of production. (2) Over one-quarter of the total length of the programmes made available in a given calendar year in the form of on-demand audiovisual media services shall be European works, and at least ten percent shall be Hungarian works. (3)

The public media service provider shall be obliged to allocate its total annual transmission time of linear audiovisual media services in the following way: (a) over sixty percent of its annual transmission time to broadcasting European works; (b) over half of its annual transmission time to broadcasting Hungarian works; (c) over fifteen percent of its annual transmission time to European works which were ordered by it from an independent production company or which were purchased from an independent production company within five years of production.

(4) The obligation stipulated under Paragraphs (1)-(2) in terms of the broadcasting of Hungarian works shall be applied exclusively for the media services targeted at the territory of Hungary. Article 21 (1) In linear radio media services at least thirty-five percent of the total annual transmission time dedicated to broadcasting musical works shall be allocated to broadcasting Hungarian musical works. (2) In average, annually at least twenty-five percent of the Hungarian musical programmes to be broadcasted in linear radio media services shall consist of musical works released within five years or from sound recordings produced within five years. (3) Those musical recordings recorded prior to 1990 the sound quality of which was improved by digital means less than five years before their publication, shall be considered for purposes of Paragraph (2) as sound recordings made less than five years ago. Article 22 (1) The provisions laid down in Articles 20-21 shall not apply to (a) media services dedicated exclusively for advertising purposes and the broadcasting of teleshopping; (b) media services advertising exclusively the media service provider or another media service of the media service provider; (c) the media service which broadcasts its service exclusively in a language other than the languages of the Member States of the European Union; where programmes are broadcasted in this language or languages in the significant part of the transmission time, the provisions shall not apply to the respective part of transmission time; (d) the local media service with the exception of community media service; (e) the media service which is exclusively broadcasted in countries outside of the European Union. (2) The media service provider may, upon its request addressed to the Media Council, also attain the proportions defined in Articles 20-21 gradually, in a manner stipulated in a public contract concluded with the Media Council. Such an exemption in a public contract may only be granted for a maximum period of three calendar years upon the condition that the media service provider – until it reaches the prescribed proportions – shall gradually increase the proportion of broadcasted Hungarian and European works and works produced by an independent producer in its media service. (3) A public contract entered into with a media service provider offering radio media services and on-demand media services

may, in justified cases, permit a long-term or permanent deviation from the proportions defined in Articles 20-21. A public contract entered into with a media service provider offering linear audiovisual thematic media services may, in justified cases, permit the media service provider to fulfil its obligation under Article 20 (1) (b) and Article 20 (3) (c) by broadcasting works produced over five years earlier. (4) Save for the case stipulated under Paragraph (3), no general exemption may be granted from compliance with the provisions concerning programme quotas. (5)

The proportion of European works set forth in Article 20 (1) (a) and the proportions set forth in Article 20 (3) (a) and 21 (1), as well as the proportions specified in the public contract concluded according to Paragraphs (2)-(3) of this Article – in relation to Point a) of Article 20 (1), Point a) of Article 20 (3), and *Article 21 (1)* – must also be ensured during the transmission time of the different media services between 5.00 a.m. and 12.00 p.m. (6) Media service providers providing more than one media service shall attain the proportions defined in Articles 20-21 as an average of the total transmission time of all of their media services, with the provision that the proportion of Hungarian musical works shall be at least twenty percent of the transmission time for each media service in relation to the performance of the obligation set forth in *Article 21 (1)*. This provision can be applied only for those individual programme quota obligations concerning which the media service provider was not granted an exemption as per Paragraphs (2)-(3) of Article 22, specified under the public contract.(7)

For the purposes of Articles 20-21, transmission time devoted to news programmes, sports programmes, games, advertisements, teleshopping, political advertisements, public service announcements, sponsorship announcements, public service advertisements and the noninteractive teletext shall not be considered in the course of determining the total transmission time. (8) The media service provider shall provide data monthly to the Media Council for the verification of compliance with the provisions concerning programme quotas. The application for exemption, with justifications attached, regarding the forthcoming calendar year in accordance with Paragraphs (2)-(3) shall be filed to the Media Council by 30 September each year at the latest. In the case of a new media service, the application may be lodged at the same time when the registration procedure is initiated.

Commercial Communications Article 23

The provisions laid down in Article 20 (1)-(7) of the Press Freedom Act shall also be applied to commercial communications broadcasted in media services. Article 24 (1) The commercial communication broadcasted in the media service (a) shall not violate human dignity; (b) shall not contain and shall not support discrimination on grounds of gender, racial or ethnic origin, nationality, religion or ideological conviction, physical or mental disability, age or sexual orientation; (c) shall not directly call upon minors to purchase or rent products or to use services; (d) shall not directly call upon minors to persuade their parents or others to purchase the advertised products or to use the advertised services; (e) shall not exploit the special trust of minors placed in their parents, teachers or other persons or the inexperience and credulity of minors; (f) shall not show minors in dangerous situations, if this is not justified; (g) shall not express religious, conscientious or ideological convictions except for commercial communications broadcasted in thematic media services with religious topics; (h) shall not violate the dignity of a national symbol or offend religious conviction. (2)

Commercial communications broadcasted in media services pertaining to alcoholic beverages (a) shall not be aimed specifically at minors; (b) shall not show minors consuming alcohol; (c) shall not encourage immoderate consumption of such beverages; (d) shall not depict immoderate alcohol consumption in a positive light and refraining from alcohol consumption in a negative light; (e) shall not show exceptional physical performance or the driving of vehicles as a result of the consumption of alcoholic beverages; (f) shall not create the impression that the consumption of alcoholic beverages contributes to social or sexual success; (g) shall not claim that the consumption of alcoholic beverages has stimulating, sedative or any other positive health effects or that alcoholic beverages are a means of resolving personal problems; (h) shall not create the impression that immoderate alcohol consumption may be avoided by consuming beverages with low alcohol content or that high alcohol content is a positive attribute of the beverage. Article 25 The person who orders the publication of the commercial communication and the person who has an interest in such publication may not exert editorial influence over the media service, except for the time of publication.

Sponsoring Media Services and Programmes

Article 26 (1) Provisions of Article 20 (8)-(10) of the Press Freedom Act shall be applicable to the sponsorship of media services and programmes. (2) In the case of a sponsored media service or programme the identification of the sponsor – pursuant to Article 20 (8) of the Press Freedom Act – may take place by reference to the name or the trademark of the sponsor or another undertaking designated by it, or by the publication or use of a symbol of the sponsor or another undertaking designated by it, or by reference to its product, activity or service or the publication or use of the distinguishing sign or logo of the aforesaid. (3) The publication under Paragraph (2) may take place simultaneously with the programme, prior to the programme or subsequent to the end of the programme in a manner not damaging the nature and content of the sponsored programme.

Article 27 (1) The following entities may not sponsor media services or programmes: a) political parties, political movements; b) undertakings manufacturing tobacco products; c) undertakings organising gambling games without the permission of the state tax authority. (2) In addition to the provisions of Point (b) of Paragraph (1), undertakings, which – as their core business – manufacture products that may not be advertised pursuant to the provisions of this Act or under any other piece of legislation or which provide services related to such products, may not sponsor media services or programmes by the display or promotion of such products or services. (3) The prohibition laid down in Article 20 (7) of the Press Freedom Act shall not apply to the sponsorship tied to the publication of the name and trademark of an undertaking in connection with a medicine or a therapeutic procedure, or sponsorship tied to the promotion of medicines, medicinal products or therapeutic procedures, which may be used without a medical prescription. Programmes sponsored by an undertaking engaged in the manufacture or distribution of medicines, medicinal products or the supply of therapeutic procedures may not promote medicines, medicinal products or therapeutic procedures accessible only upon medical prescriptions. (4)

The name, slogan or emblem of a political party or a political movement may not appear in the name or the displayed name of the sponsor. (5) It shall not qualify as the sponsorship of an audiovisual media service or programme or as a surreptitious commercial communication, if a public event, or the name or logo of the sponsor of the participants of the event, or the name of the product or the service of the sponsor is displayed on the screen in the course of the broadcast from the event – including the interviews made in connection with the event before or after the event or during the interval of the event –, provided that the media service provider has no material interest in such appearance and the manner of appearance does not provide the sponsor with an unjustified emphasis. (6) If a person or an undertaking sponsoring another person or undertaking, which appears in a programme of the audiovisual media service provider or the name, the symbol or the logo of such sponsoring person or undertaking appears in the programme – with the exception of the case referred to under Paragraph (5) –, the rules concerning the sponsorship of media services and programmes shall be applicable, not including the obligation to identify the sponsor. Article 28 (1) The following may not be sponsored in audiovisual media services: (a) news programmes and political programmes; (b) programmes reporting about the official events of national holidays. (2)

Programmes reporting about the official events of national holidays may not be sponsored in a radio media service. (3) The restriction defined in Point (a) of Paragraph (1) does not affect the sponsorship of thematic media services broadcasting news and political programmes. Article 29 [not in effect]

Product Placement in Programmes

Article 30 (1) With the exceptions provided under Paragraph (2), product placement in media services shall be prohibited. (2) Product placement in programmes shall be permitted (a) in cinematographic works intended for showing in movie theatres; cinematographic works or film series intended for showing in media services; sports programmes and entertainment programmes; (b) in programmes other than those stipulated in Point (a), provided that the manufacturer or distributor of the product concerned, or the provider or intermediary of the service concerned does not provide the media service provider or the producer of the given programme with any financial reward, neither directly nor indirectly, beyond making available the product or service free of charge for product placement purposes. (3) No product placement shall be used (a) in news programmes and political programmes; (b) in programmes intended specifically for minors under the age of fourteen, with the exception of the case specified in Point (b) of Paragraph (2); (c) in programmes reporting about the official events of national holidays; (d) in programmes with religious or ecclesiastic content. (4) Programmes shall not contain product placements of the following products: (a) tobacco products, cigarettes or other products originating from undertakings, the primary activity of which is the manufacture or sale of cigarettes or other tobacco products; (b) products that may not be advertised pursuant to this Act or other pieces of legislation; (c) medicines, medicinal products, or therapeutic procedures, which may only be used upon medical prescription; (d) gambling services provided without the permission of the state tax authority. Article 31 (1) Programmes containing product placements shall comply with the following requirements: (a) their content – and in the case of linear media services, the programme schedule – may not be influenced so as to affect the responsibility and editorial independence of the media service provider; (b) they shall not call upon the purchase or rent of a product or the use of a service in a direct manner; (c) they shall not give unjustified emphasis to the product so displayed, which does not otherwise stem from the content of the programme flow. (2) Viewers and listeners shall be unequivocally informed on the fact of product placement. At the beginning and at the end of the programme containing the product placement, and when the programme resumes after advertisements, attention shall be drawn to the fact of product placement in an optical or acoustic form. (3) The obligation stipulated under Paragraph (2) shall not apply to programmes which were not produced or ordered by the media service provider or another media service provider or production company operating under the qualifying holding of its owner. (4) The Media Council – subsequent to holding a public hearing, if necessary – may publish recommendations concerning the compliance of the product placement and the related warning with the provisions stipulated in this Act.

Political Advertisements, Public Service Announcements, Public Service Advertisements

Article 32 (1) The person or entity ordering the publication of political advertisements, public service announcements, public service advertisements, and the person or entity with an interest in the publication thereof shall not exert editorial influence over the media service, except for the time of publication. (2) The political advertisement, public service announcement and public service advertisement shall be immediately recognizable in nature and distinguishable from other media contents. The method of distinguishing from other media contents in linear media services (a) shall take place in the form of optical and acoustic notice in the case of audiovisual media services; (b) shall take place in the form of acoustic notice in the case of radio media service. (3)

During election campaign periods, political advertisements may only be published in accordance with the provisions of the Act on Electoral Procedures. Outside of election campaign periods, political advertisements may only be published in connection with referendums already ordered. The media service provider shall not be responsible for the content of the political advertisement. If the request for the publication of the political advertisement is in compliance with the provisions of the Act on Electoral Procedures, and in such case the media service provider shall be obliged to publish the advertisement without further consideration. (4) Upon the publication of political advertisements, public service announcements and public service advertisements, the person or entity ordering the publication shall be identified unequivocally. (5) The media service provider may not request any remuneration for the publication of public service announcements. (6)

The public or community media service provider or the media service provider with significant market power shall be obliged to publish the public service announcements of the professional disaster management agency if it provides information on the potential occurrence of danger to safety of life or property, on the mitigation of the consequences of an event that has already occurred or on the tasks to be carried out. Such publication shall take place in the media service of the media service provider which has the highest audience share per year on average and in the manner defined by the media service provider, with the exception of the instance stipulated under Article 36 (6). The obligation of publishing shall also apply to the media service provider of the local media service operating in the reception area where the given events take place. (7) The duration of the public service announcement may not exceed one minute. This restriction shall not apply to public service announcements specified in Article 15 and in Paragraph (6). (8) Upon request of the media service provider, the Media Council shall decide – within fifteen days of receipt of the request and against an administrative service fee – by a regulatory decision whether the announcement in respect of which the request is lodged qualifies as a public service announcement, a public service advertisement or a political advertisement. (9) Information concerning the corporate social responsibility of an undertaking shall not qualify as a surreptitious commercial communication, but such reports may only contain the name, logo and trademark of the undertaking and its product or service, if it is closely connected to its social responsibility. The slogan of the undertaking or any parts of its commercial communication may not appear in the report and the information may not expressly encourage the purchase of the product or the use of the service offered by the undertaking.

Advertisements and Teleshopping in Linear Media Services

Article 33 (1) The method of distinguishing advertisements and teleshopping from other media content in linear media services (a) shall take place in the form of an optical or acoustic notice in case of advertisements and teleshopping broadcasted in an audiovisual media service; (b) shall take place in the form of an optical and an acoustic notice in the case of teleshopping windows broadcasted in an audiovisual media service; (c) shall take place in the form of an acoustic notice in the case of a radio media service. (2) In linear media service the advertisement or teleshopping broadcasted by interrupting the programme – taking natural breaks, the duration and nature of the programme into consideration – may not interfere with the coherence of the programme to an unjustified extent or violate the rights or legitimate interests of the holder of the copyrights or the related rights to the programme. (3) The programme broadcasted in a linear media service, which (a) broadcasts political news or contains political information and its duration does not exceed thirty minutes; (b) is intended for minors under the age of fourteen and its duration does not exceed thirty minutes; (c) reports about the official events of national holidays; (d) has religious or ecclesiastic content, save for cinematographic works, may not be interrupted with advertisements or teleshopping. (4) The average volume, or the volume perceived by the viewer or the listener, of advertisements, teleshopping and previews broadcasted in a linear media service, and that of the acoustic notice indicating the broadcasting of advertisements or teleshopping or previews may not be higher than the volume of adjacent programmes. (5) Virtual advertisements may only be broadcasted in a linear audiovisual media service if the media service provider draws attention to such broadcasting by an optical or acoustic notice immediately prior to the given programme and also immediately after the given programme. This obligation shall not apply to programmes which were not produced or ordered by the media service provider or another media service provider or production company under the qualifying holding of its owner. (6) Virtual or split screen advertisements may not be published in a programme broadcasted in a linear audiovisual media service, which programme (a) contains political news or political information and its duration does not exceed thirty minutes; (b) is intended for minors under the age of fourteen and its duration does not exceed thirty minutes; (c) reports about the official events of national holidays; (d) has religious or ecclesiastic content; or (e) is a documentary and its duration does not exceed thirty minutes. (7)

Split screen advertisements may only be broadcasted in a linear audiovisual media service if these are separated from the programme in terms of visual appearance in a clearly recognizable manner, on half of the screen at most, indicating the nature of the advertisement on the screen in a clearly visible manner. Article 34 (1) In sports programmes and other programmes featuring natural breaks, broadcasted in linear media services, advertisements may only be broadcasted between the parts and during such breaks, with the exception of split screen advertisements and virtual advertisements. (2)

A cinematographic work, news or political programmes, the duration of which exceeds thirty minutes – with the exception of television series or documentaries – broadcasted in a linear audiovisual media service may only be interrupted with advertisements or teleshopping once every thirty minutes, including the duration of advertisements and previews as well. Article 35 (1) The duration of advertisements broadcasted in linear media services may not exceed twelve minutes within any 60-minute period, i.e. hour to hour (from the top of the hour), including split screen advertisements, virtual advertisements and the promotion of the programmes of other media services, with the exception provided for in Point (e) of Paragraph (2). (2) The time restriction defined under Paragraph (1) shall not apply to (a) teleshopping windows; (b) political advertisements;

(c) public service announcements; (d) public service advertisements; (e) previews on the own programmes of the media service or the programmes of another media service operating under the qualifying holding of the given media service provider or its owner; (f) sponsorship announcements as defined under Article 26 (2); (g) product placements; (h) noninteractive teletext, if it is broadcasted in a local media service; (i) virtual advertisements appearing in programmes which were not produced or ordered by the media service provider or another media service provider or production company operating under the qualifying holding of the given media service provider or its owner; (j) media service providers solely broadcasting advertisements and teleshopping; (k) linear audiovisual media services advertising exclusively the media service provider or its other media services; (l) announcements intended solely for the purpose of advertising the media service itself or the products complementing the programmes broadcasted in the media service. (3) The transmission time used for broadcasting teleshopping windows may not exceed three hours per calendar day, not including the transmission time of the thematic media service broadcasting primarily teleshopping or teleshopping windows.

Advertisements and Public Service Announcements in Public and Community Media Services

Article 36 (1) The duration of the advertisements and teleshopping broadcasted in the linear media service of the public media service provider may not exceed eight minutes within any 60-minute period, i.e. hour to hour (from the top of the hour). The duration of the advertisements and teleshopping broadcasted in the community media service may not exceed six minutes within any 60-minute period, i.e. hour to hour (from the top of the hour). (2)

The broadcasting of noninteractive teletext containing advertisements shall also be counted into the duration of advertisements defined under Paragraph (1) in the case of public media service. (3) Advertisements in public and community media services may only be broadcasted in between the individual programmes – in the case of complex programmes composed of several parts, between the individual parts of the programme –, or before or after the programmes. In sports and other broadcasts with natural breaks, advertisements may also be broadcasted in between the parts and during the breaks. (4) Presenters, reporters or newsreaders appearing regularly in the news and political programmes broadcasted in public and community media services cannot appear or play a role in advertisements or political advertisements broadcasted in any media service, except for the self promotion of public media services. (5) In public and community media services, split screen advertisements and virtual advertisements may only be broadcasted in conjunction with the broadcast of sports programmes. (6) [not in effect]

Disclosure Obligation

*Article 37 (1)*The media service provider shall ensure that the following data are continuously available to the public (a) its name or company name; (b) its address or registered office or mailing address; (c) its electronic mailing address (d) its telephone number; (e) the name and contact details of the regulatory or supervisory authorities that are competent to proceed against it upon violation of rules concerning media administration; (f) the name and contact details of the professional self-regulatory bodies authorised by them to proceed against the media service provider. (2) The media service provider shall publish the data specified under Paragraph (1) on all of its websites and teletext pages connected to its media services, provided that it has any such websites or teletext pages. In the case of on-demand media services, such data shall also be published at the access point of the media service. Moreover, the media service provider shall also ensure that the interested parties may also receive information about the data defined in Points (a)-(c) and (e)-(f) on the telephone

Public Service Obligations of Media Service Providers with Significant Market Power

Article 38 (1) Linear audiovisual media service providers with significant market power shall be obliged to broadcast a news programme or general information programme of at least fifteen minutes in duration on each working day between 7:00 a.m. and 8:30 a.m., and a separate news programme of at least twenty minutes in duration on each working day between 6:00 p.m. and 9:00 p.m. without interruption. Linear radio media service providers with significant market power shall broadcast a separate news programme of at least fifteen minutes in duration on each working day between 6:30 a.m. and 8:30 a.m. without interruption. News content or reports of a criminal nature taken over from other media service providers, or the news content or reports of a criminal nature which do not qualify as information serving the democratic public opinion, shall not be longer in duration on an annual average than twenty percent of the duration of the news programme. (2) The linear media service provider with significant market power shall meet its obligation stipulated under Paragraph (1) above and in Article 32 (6) in its media service which has the highest annual average audience share. (3) Linear media service providers with significant market power shall ensure in the course of all of their media services transmitted by digital media service distribution, that at least one quarter of the cinematographic works and film series originally produced in a language other than Hungarian, broadcasted between 7:00 p.m. and 11:00

p.m., shall be available in their original language, with Hungarian subtitles, including programmes starting before 11:00 p.m. but ending later

Programmes Accessible to People with Impaired Hearing

Article 39 (1) Media service providers of audiovisual media services shall make efforts to gradually make their programmes accessible to people with impaired hearing as well. (2) Public and – in respect of their media services with the highest annual average audience share – linear media service providers with significant market power shall be obliged to ensure that all public service announcements, political advertisements, news programmes (including traffic news, sports news and weather forecasts), political programmes, programmes about people with disabilities and programmes about equal opportunities, cinematographic works, games and programmes serving public service objectives defined under Article 83 are also accessible with Hungarian subtitles – for example through teletext – or with sign language. (3) The obligation specified in Paragraph (2) shall not apply to the programmes made available in their original language, excluding the programmes published pursuant to Article 99 (2). (4) The obligation specified in Paragraph (1) shall oblige the obligors for at least six hours of programmes per day in 2012, at least eight hours of programmes per day in 2013 and at least ten hours of programmes per day in 2014. (5) Media service providers shall provide subtitles or sign language throughout the entire duration of a programme that was begun with subtitles or with sign language, without interfering with the coherence of the programme, as well as in the case of programme series which are organically and closely connected to each other. (6) It shall be indicated in media services prior to subtitled programmes that the respective programme is also available in that form through the teletext service connected to the media service. The subtitled version of the text of each programme shall be accurate and synchronised to the events displayed on the screen and can contain the brief summary of the words spoken in the programme only if the subtitles (due to their length) would not allow that the words spoken be followed. (7) In case of programmes not prerecorded, the subtitles must be accurate and synchronised to the events displayed on the screen to a reasonably expected extent. (8) Media service distributors shall be obliged to transmit the teletext signal or other subtitles provided by the audiovisual media service provider, synchronously with the image and sound signals, on all transmission systems, networks or media service distribution transmission platforms.

Rules Concerning Ancillary Media Services

Article 40 Articles 14-18, Article 19 (2) and Article 20 of the Press Freedom Act shall apply to ancillary media services mutatis mutandis.

THE RIGHT TO PROVIDE MEDIA SERVICES AND PUBLISH PRESS PRODUCTS

General Provisions

Article 41 (1) The provision of linear media services subject to this Act provided by media service providers established in Hungary may commence subsequent to the notification of and registration by the Office of the National Media and Infocommunications Authority (hereinafter as: the Office), with the exception of analogue linear media services using state-owned limited resources, which may be provided subject to winning a tender announced and completed by the Media Council and entering into an agreement thereto, or entering into a provisional public contract as per Article 65 of this Act. (2) On-demand media services and ancillary media services provided by media service providers established in Hungary, as well as press products published by a publisher established in Hungary, falling under the scope of this Act, shall be notified to the Office for registration, within sixty days from commencement of the service or activity. The registration shall not be a precondition for starting such a service or activity. (3) Under the framework of this Act, the notifier initiating such registration may be any natural person or person. (4) The Office shall keep a register of a) linear audiovisual media services; b) linear radio media services; c) audiovisual media services, the providers of which obtained the media service provision rights via tendering; d) radio media services, the providers of which obtained the media service provision rights via tendering; e) on-demand audiovisual media services; f) on-demand radio media services; g) ancillary media services; h) printed press products; i) online press products and news portals. (5)

In the event a media service provider provides both linear and on-demand services, or if a press product publisher publishes both printed and online press products, it shall notify each of its media services or press products separately. (5a) In the event the publisher makes available on the Internet a printed press product in the form of a digital copy (having fully identical contents) of such printed press product, then such Internet content shall be considered as a copy of the printed press product and shall not be required to be notified as a separate online press product. (6) The data recorded in the registers mentioned in Paragraph (4) concerning the names, contact information of media service providers, press product founders and publishers, as well as the names and titles of the media services and press products shall be publicly available and accessible on the website of the National Media and Infocommunications Authority (hereinafter as: the Authority). For the purposes of monitoring media services and press product publishing, the Authority shall handle the identification data of natural person media service providers and of natural persons founding and publishing press products until such data are deleted from the register. (7) Linear media service provision rights shall not be transferable.

Article 41/A (1) The following are not allowed to be included in the name or title of press products and media services: a) the name of a person who had a leading role in the foundation, creation or maintenance of any of the authoritarian political regimes of the 20th century, or b) an expression or the name of an organisation that can be directly associated with an authoritarian political regime of the 20th century. (2) In the course of the registration process, the Office shall examine fulfilment of the conditions specified under Paragraph (1). If there is any doubt or uncertainty, the position of the Hungarian Academy of Sciences must be obtained by the Office in the course of the registration process, or by the court in the course of the court procedure connected to the registration process.

Linear Media Service Provision Rights Based on Notification

Article 42 (1) The registration of linear media services may be initiated by the future media service provider thereof. Notifiers intending to provide linear media services without using state-owned limited analogue resources shall notify the Office of the followings at least forty-five days prior to taking up the media service provision activity: a) particulars of the notifier: aa) name, ab) address (registered office), designation of place(s) of business directly affected by the media service provision, ac) contact information (telephone number and electronic mailing address), ad) name and contact information (telephone number, postal and electronic mailing address) of its executive officer, representative, and of the person appointed to liaise with the Authority, ae) company registration number, or registration number, b) the notifier's effective Deed of Foundation and the specimen of signature of its representative authenticated by a notary public [except for the case stipulated under Paragraph (2a)], if the notifier is not a natural person; c) basic particulars of the planned media service: ca) kind (radio or audiovisual), cb) type (general or thematic), cc) character (commercial, community),cd) permanent name, ce) name, address (registered office), contact information (telephone number and electronic mailing address) of the electronic communications service provider likely to perform broadcasting, cf) planned number of subscribers, cg) type of the electronic communications network planned for broadcasting, ch) name of the settlements affected by broadcasting, ci) media service transmission time, transmission time schedule and planned programme flow structure, cj) daily, weekly, monthly minimum transmission time intended for broadcasting public service programmes, programmes dealing with local public affairs, or programmes supporting local everyday life, ck) minimum transmission time intended for daily regular news programmes, cl) planned daily minimum transmission time serving nationalities, cm) planned ancillary media services, cn) the media service signal, and – in case of audiovisual media services – the emblem of the media service, co) the fact of expansion of the reception area, or connecting to the network, if applicable. d) in case of satellite media services, a statement of intent from the provider of the satellite capacity the notifier plans to use, with respect to the lease of the channel, also indicating its frequency, technical specifications and fee, e) data on the size of direct or indirect ownership stake held by the notifier or by any other person with a qualifying holding in the notifier undertaking, in any undertaking providing media services, or applying for media service provision rights, within the territory of Hungary, f) planned date of launching the media service. (2)

The notifier shall make a statement that no grounds for exclusion under the Act would arise against it in case of its registration. (2a) If the notifier is a company registered in the company register and if it has submitted to the court of registration the specimen of signature of its representative authenticated by a notary public or countersigned by an attorney-at-law and this fact is indicated in the company register, the Office shall obtain the given deed by downloading it electronically directly from the company register. (3) Linear media service provision may only be commenced after the completion of registration. The Office shall adopt a regulatory decision on the registration of the linear media service within forty-five days, wherein it shall set forth the media service provision fee payable after each linear media service by the media service provider. (4) In the event that the Office fails to adopt the decision on the registration within forty-five days after the notification, the notification shall be deemed as registered, with the provision that the rights holder shall be informed about the fact of registration and the amount of the media service provision fee by virtue of a decision within fifteen days. (5) In the course of the registration procedure, the Office shall examine whether the jurisdiction of Hungary can be established in relation to the notified media service pursuant to this Act. (6) The Office shall refuse the registration of the linear media service, if a) a conflict of interests set forth in

Article 43 exists vis-à-vis the notifier, b) the notifier, or any of its owners, has overdue fees from earlier media service activities, c) it would be in violation of the provisions set forth in Article 68 on the prevention of media market concentration, d) the notification does not contain the data provision required under Paragraph (1), even after notice to remedy the deficiencies, e) the name of the notified media service is identical with – or is confusingly similar to – the name of a linear media service already registered, having valid records at the time of notification, or

f) the notifier failed to pay the administrative service fee. (7) The Office shall delete the linear media service from the register, if a) refusal of registration would be applicable, b) the media service provider requested its deletion from the register, c) the media service provider failed to pay its overdue fees within thirty days from the Office's written notice thereto, d) the rights holder fails to commence the media service within six months from the date of registration, or interrupts the ongoing service for more than six months, except if the media service provider provides adequate justification thereto, e) a final decision by a court has ordered the cessation of trade mark infringement perpetrated through the use of the media service's name and barred the infringer from further violation of the law, or f) based on repeated and serious violation of the media service provider, the Media Council ordered the application of this legal sanction with regard to the provisions of Articles 185-187. (8) The provisions of Paragraphs (1)-(7) shall also apply to linear media service provision via satellite involving the use of satellites not subject to Government control. (9)

The media service provider of a linear media service shall notify the Office about any changes concerning its registered data within fifteen days after the change. (10) The Office shall have the right to impose a fine as per Points (ba) or (bb) of Paragraph (3) of Article 187 on the media service provider in case of late performance or non-performance of the notification on such data changes. (11) The permission of the Media Council granted in the form of a regulatory decision in line with the provisions set forth in Article 64 of this Act shall be required for every media service provider to connect to the network or to expand their reception area.

Conflict of Interest Rules of Linear Media Service Providers

Article 43 (1) For persons authorized to provide linear media services, the provisions set forth in Article 118 (1) (a)-(c) concerning the Authority's President, Vice-President, Director General and Deputy Director General shall be applicable. (2) Furthermore, the following persons shall not be entitled to provide linear media services: a) judges and public prosecutors; b) executive officers of public administration bodies, the National Bank of Hungary, the Hungarian Competition Authority, and the Hungarian State Holding Company (Magyar Nemzeti Vagyonkezelő Zrt.), the President, Vice-President, secretary general, executive officer, or auditor of the State Audit Office of Hungary, and Members of the Hungarian Competition Council; c) the Authority's President, Vice-President, Director General, Deputy Director General, and any person in work-related legal relationship with the Authority; d) a close relative of persons falling within the scope of Article 118 (1) (a)-(b) and of those specified under Points (b)-(c) above. (3) The following organisations shall not be entitled to provide linear media services: a) political parties or undertakings established by political parties; b) state and public administration bodies, unless provided otherwise by legislation applicable in the event of an extraordinary situation or state of emergency; c) undertakings in which the Hungarian state has a qualifying holding; d) undertakings in which any of those listed under Paragraphs (1)-(2) hold a direct or indirect ownership stake, or have acquired the right to influence its decisions pursuant to a separate agreement or by other means; or a person or organisation otherwise subject to acquisition restrictions. (4)

An undertaking shall not be entitled to provide local linear media service in a reception area of which at least twenty percent falls within the limits of local government jurisdiction, if any local government representative or employee, the Mayor, Deputy Mayor, the Mayor of Budapest, the Deputy Mayor of Budapest, or any of their close relatives hold an office in the Board of Directors, management or the Supervisory Board of such an entity, or in the Board of Trustees of a Foundation or a Public Foundation. (5) For the purposes of Paragraph (3) (d), an undertaking in which the Mayor of Budapest, the Deputy Mayor of Budapest, the Mayor, or Deputy Mayor, the chairperson or deputy chairperson of the county-level general assembly, or a close relative of a member of the local or county level government holds a direct or indirect qualifying holding, or is entitled to influence the decisions thereof under a separate agreement or otherwise, may not be entitled to provide linear media services if the reception area of the respective media service covers at least twenty percent of the territory of the affected local government.

Media Service Provision Fee

Article 44 (1) Persons or entities entitled to provide linear media services by virtue of registration shall pay a media service provision fee specified by the Office. (2) The media service provider shall pay a quarterly media service provision fee in advance, as a consideration. In the event of connecting to a network, the networked media service provider shall pay the media service provision fee payable by the media service provider joining the network in proportion to its networked transmission time. (3) In the event of late payment of the fee, the Media Council may terminate the agreement with a fifteen day notice period. (4) Default in fee payment shall be deemed a serious breach of law. (5) With respect to media services subject to public contract or broadcasting agreement, the media service provision fee shall be the sum total of the media service provision basic fee applicable to the given media service provision rights and the fee instalment undertaken by the tenderer winning the tender procedure. The Media Council shall determine the media service provision basic fee in the invitation to tender. (6)

The media service provision basic fee shall be proportionate to the area of the given media service's reception area. At the same time, it shall give due consideration to the purchasing power indicator of the given area's population, as well as to the market share attained by media service provider groups grouped according to their reception area, media service type, mode of distribution, or other significant criteria. (7) The media service provision fee payable on linear media services subject to registration shall be proportionate to the reception area of the given media service. At the same time, it shall give due consideration to the purchasing power indicator of the given area's population, as well as to the market share attained by media service provider groups grouped according to their reception area, media service type, mode of distribution, or other significant criteria. (8) When setting the media service provision fee payable with respect to linear media services provided via terrestrial digital broadcasting systems or satellite systems accessible without payment of a subscription fee, due consideration shall be given to data about the reception area of the given media service, as well as to the availability (prevalence) of equipment suitable for reception of such media service. (9) No media service provision fee shall be payable for community media services. (10) In the event of expansion of the reception area, the media service provision fees established for each individual reception area shall be added up.

Notification of On-Demand Media Services

Article 45 (1) The registration of on-demand media services may be initiated by the media service provider thereof. The notification to the Office of the on-demand media service shall include: a) particulars of the notifier: aa) name, ab) address (registered office or place of business), designation of place(s) of business that are directly affected by the media service provision, ac) contact information (telephone number and electronic mailing address), ad) name and contact information (telephone number, postal and electronic mailing address) of the executive officer, representative of the media service provider, and of the person appointed to liaise with the Authority, ae) company registration number, or registration number, b) basic particulars of the planned media service: ba) kind (radio or audiovisual) bb) name bc) type (general or thematic)

c) the planned date of launching the media service. (2) The following shall not be entitled to provide on-demand media services: the National Media and Infocommunications Authority's President, Vice-President, Director General, Deputy Director General, or the Chairperson or member of the Board of Trustees of the Public Service Foundation or the Chairperson or member of the Board of Public Services, the CEO of the Fund, the President, Deputy President or member of the National Council for Communications and Information Technology, the CEO of the public media service provider, the Chairperson or member of the Supervisory Board thereof, members of the Media Council, and persons in work-related legal relationship with any of the aforesaid organizations. The notifier shall make a statement that no conflict of interest under the Act exists or would arise vis-à-vis him/her/it as a result of registration of the media service. (3)

The Office shall register the on-demand media service within thirty days. (4) The Office shall withdraw the registration if a) a conflict of interests exists vis-à-vis the notifier, or b) the name of the notified media service is identical with – or is confusingly similar to – the name of an on-demand media service already registered, having valid records at the time of notification. (5) The on-demand media service shall be deleted from the register, if a) the registration is to be withdrawn pursuant to Paragraph (4), b) the media service provider requested its deletion from the register, c) the media service is not commenced for more than a year, or the ongoing media service is interrupted for more than a year, or d) a final decision by a court has ordered the cessation of trade mark infringement perpetrated through the use of the media service's name and barred the infringer from further violation of the law. (6)

The media service provider of an on-demand media service shall notify the Office about any changes concerning its registered data within fifteen days. (7) In the event of a change in the media service provider's person, the media service provider making the original notification shall initiate a modification of the data on record. Paragraphs (1)-(4) shall be applied mutatis mutandis to such procedure. (8) In the event the media service provider fails to comply with its obligations related to registration, the Office may impose a fine up to one million forints, taking into consideration the principles set forth in Article 185 (2).

Notification of Press Products

Article 46 (1) Registration of a press product may be initiated by its publisher or founder. In the event that the founder and publisher of a press product are different persons or undertakings, they shall enter into an agreement wherein they shall define their relationship, and their responsibilities and rights regarding the press product. (2) Notifications for the registration of press products shall contain the following information: a) particulars of the notifier: aa) name, ab) address (registered office or place of business), ac) contact information (telephone number and electronic mailing address), ad) name and contact information (telephone number, postal and electronic mailing address) of its representative, and of the person appointed to liaise with the Authority, ae) company registration number, or registration number, b) the title of the notified press product, c) the web address (URL) of the online press product, news portal, and the digital copy of the printed press product made available on the Internet, d) in the event the founder and the publisher are different persons or undertakings, the particulars of both of them, as defined in Point (a). (2a) Unless otherwise regulated by other pieces of legislation, the copy of the deed verifying the right of representation shall be attached to the notification for the registration of the press product (if the notifier is not a natural person), hence in particular the copy of the specimen of signature or authorisation. (3)

The following persons may not be founders or publishers of press products: the National Media and Infocommunications Authority's President, Vice-President, Director General, Deputy Director General, or the Chairperson or member of the Board of Trustees of the Public Service Foundation or the Chairperson or member of the Board of Public Services, the CEO of the Fund, the President, Deputy President or member of the National Council for Communications and Information Technology, members of the Media Council, not including the founding or publishing of press products aimed to publish scientific results or to disseminate popular science. The notifier shall make a statement that no conflict of interest under the Act exists or would arise vis-à-vis him/her/it as a result of registration. (4)

The Office shall register the press product within fifteen days. (5) The Office shall withdraw the registration if a) a conflict of interests exists vis-à-vis the notifier, or b) the title of the notified press product is identical with – or is confusingly similar to – the title of a press product already registered, having valid records at the time of notification, or if the name of the press product does not meet the requirements specified under *Article 41/A* (1). (5a) Point b) of Paragraph (5) shall not be applied for those press products that are required to provide data in accordance with Article 208 (2). (6) The press product shall be deleted from the register, if a) the registration is to be withdrawn pursuant to Paragraph (5), b) the founder or – if the founder and the publisher are different undertakings, with the approval of the founder – the publisher requested deletion from the register, c) publication of the press product is not commenced within two years from the date of registration, or ongoing publication is interrupted for over five years, d) a final decision by a court has ordered the cessation of trade mark infringement perpetrated through the use of the title of the press product and barred the infringer from further violation of the law, or e) the founder of the legal entity or organisation without legal personality has been dissolved or terminated without legal successor at least fifteen days ago. (7) The publisher and founder of the press product shall notify the Office about any changes concerning the registered data within fifteen days. The title of the press product registered in the official register cannot be changed. (8) In the event of a change in the publisher's person, the publisher on record shall initiate modification of the data on record. In case of failure of this, the founder may also initiate the modification. Paragraphs (1)-(5) shall be applied mutatis mutandis to such procedure. (8a) In the event the publisher or the founder fail to comply with their obligations related to registration, the Office may impose a fine up to one million forints, taking into consideration the principles set forth in Article 185 (2). (9)

Press products and – unless legislation provides otherwise – other publications must display the key editorial and publication data (imprint). The imprint shall display the following information: a) publisher's name, registered office, and the name of the person responsible for publishing, b)-c) [not in effect] d) the name of the person responsible for editing. (10) An international identifier of printed press products (ISSN), other international markings, and the price of the publication shall be determined and displayed pursuant to separate legislation. (11) Legislation may also prescribe the use of a short imprint, the obligation of displaying special data, or other specific rules. (12)

For academic and administrative purposes, a free legal deposit copy of printed press products and other publications shall be provided to the bodies designated by separate legislation. The legal deposit copy shall remain in the ownership of the body entitled thereto. Detailed rules for making available legal deposit copies shall be regulated by a government decree. (13) Free legal deposit copies of printed press products and other publications shall be delivered to the bodies designated by separate legislation in order to preserve cultural assets, to ensure national bibliographical accounting and public library services. The legal deposit copy shall remain in the ownership of the body entitled thereto. (14) A legal deposit copy for preservation purposes may only be removed from the public collection records, if it was destroyed or has become irreparably damaged.

Notification of Ancillary Media Services

Article 47 The registration of ancillary media services shall be subject to the regulations applicable to the registration of on-demand media services.

OBTAINING THE RIGHT TO PROVIDE LINEAR MEDIA SERVICES VIA TENDER

General rules

Article 48 (1) Analogue linear media services using state-owned limited resources may be provided – unless provided otherwise by this Act – subject to winning a tender announced and conducted by the Media Council and entering into a public contract. (2) The procedures applied for tenders announced concerning the rights to provide linear media services using state-owned limited resources (hereinafter as: tender procedure) shall be governed by the provisions of the Act on Administrative Proceedings, subject to the deviations set forth in this Act. (3) The Media Council shall – subject to the deviations set forth in this Act – be in charge of managing the tasks related to the tender procedure.(5)

The right to provide analogue linear media services using state-owned limited resources shall, in the case of radio, be valid for a maximum period of seven years or, in the case of audiovisual media service provision, for a maximum period of ten years, and it may be – upon expiry – renewed one time for a maximum of five years without a tender procedure upon the media service provider's request, with the provision that the audiovisual media service provision agreements shall expire on the date set forth under *Article 38* (1) of the Digital Switchover Act. The request for renewal must be notified to the Media Council fourteen months prior to the expiry. Renewal shall be refused in case of failure to meet this deadline. The Media Council shall adopt its decision about renewal of the right no sooner than four months prior to expiry of the right and no later than two months prior to expiry of the right. (6) [not in effect] (7)

The right may not be renewed, if a) the Media Council established, in its final and binding decision, that the media service provider repeatedly or seriously violated the provisions set forth in the agreement or in this Act, b) the media service provider had been subject previously to the sanction specified in Article 112 (1) (b) of Act I of 1996 on Radio and Television Broadcasting due to any breach of the agreement, or c) the media service provider is in arrears with the media service provision fee at the time of submission or evaluation of the request. (8) The Media Council, with due regard to the appropriate application of the provisions of Chapter III and the unique characteristics deriving from the nature of these media service facilities, shall determine and publish on its website the principles of the tender procedure regarding the small community media service facilities. Small community media service facilities may not be subject to tendering and may not be operated commercially. (9) Upon the Media Council's request, the Office shall compile the register of media service facilities.

Preparation of Tender Procedures for Media Service Provision

Article 49 (1) The Media Council shall, for purpose of preparing tender procedures regarding media services, request the Office to draw up frequency plans. (2) In the request as per Paragraph (1), the Media Council shall establish the conceptual criteria required for drawing up a broadcast frequency plan, in particular: a) the objective of frequency use, b) the preferences to be applied in frequency planning, c) the frequency planning schedule. (3) The frequency plan prepared shall contain: a) the broadcasting stations' nominal places of business, and other technical requirements of installation, b) the expected reception area of the stations, c) the frequency band according to the International Radio Regulation markings. (4)

The Media Council may return the frequency plan for modification. (5) The Office shall publish the frequency plan for at least fifteen days, prior to approval by the Media Council. The Office shall issue a public notice on the website of the Media Council concerning the publication of the plan and its location, at least one week prior to the starting date of publication of the plan. During the period when the frequency plans are published and for five days after closing the frequency plans, any person may submit written comments – addressed to the Media Council – with respect to the frequency plans. (6) The Media Council shall make a decision with respect to the approval of the frequency plan and the preparations for a draft invitation to tender within forty-five days from the last day of publication.

(7) The frequency plans and the conceptual criteria of planning shall be public and available for inspection at the Office. (8) For the purpose of planning the media service facility, the Authority may, in exchange for a fee and upon the request of clients, provide data, provided that the Media Council approved the planning of media service facility in advance with respect to the reception area specified in the request and with due consideration of media market and media policy considerations. Media service facilities thus planned shall henceforth be subject to the provisions of this Act applicable to tender procedures.

Draft Invitation to Tender

Article 50 (1) The Media Council shall, with a view to preparing the invitation to tender, compile a draft invitation to tender about the tender conditions. The

Media Council shall publish the draft invitation to tender, with justification, via public notice and on its website. (2) Between the twentieth – the earliest – and the thirtieth – the latest – day from publishing the draft invitation to tender, the Office shall hold a public hearing (hereinafter as: hearing). (3)

The Office shall publish, via public notice and on the Media Council's website, an announcement about the time and venue of the hearing, at least ten days prior to the hearing. (4) Anyone may comment on the draft invitation to tender verbally or in writing, at the hearing and anyone may lodge a question or submit a comment to the Office in writing within five days from the hearing. (5) Minutes of the hearing shall be prepared within eight days and shall be available for inspection at the Office. (6) The Media Council shall decide about the finalisation of the draft invitation to tender within forty-five days from the hearing, and, as far as possible, it shall take into account the comments received and the recommendations made at the public hearing.

The Tender Procedure

Article 51 (1) The tender procedure shall – with the exceptions specified in this Act – commence ex officio with the publication of the invitation to tender. (2) The administrative deadline for the tender procedure shall be eighty-five days. This deadline shall not include – beyond those set forth in the Act on Administrative Proceedings – the time period from the day the invitation to tender is published to the submission of the tender. In justified cases, the deadline may be extended on one occasion, with the maximum of twenty days.

The Invitation to Tender

Article 52 (1) The Media Council shall publish invitations to tender for the utilisation of media service facilities. (2) The invitation to tender shall include: a) the data of the media service facility as per Article 49 (3), b) the objective of the invitation to tender, c) the fundamental rules governing the rules of procedure, d) the tender fee and the payment method thereof, e) the minimum amount of the media service provision fee (media service provision basic fee), below which media service provision rights cannot be awarded, with the exception of the provision of community media services, f) the form of and deadline for the submission of tenders, g) the required contents of tenders,h) the principles of evaluation and the criteria to be taken into consideration during evaluation, the categories for evaluating tenders, the quantified evaluation framework allocated to specific evaluation categories, as well as the rules of evaluation based on which the Media Council adopts its decision about the winning tenderer, i) the starting date of the provision of the media service, j) the term of the media service provision right, k) the formal requirements of tenders, l) the validity criteria of tenders concerning their form and contents, m) other criteria according to the Media Council's decision.

(3) In addition to the criteria defined under Paragraph (2), the invitation to tender may also include the following criteria, in particular: a) commitment concerning the offer validity of the submitted tenders, the term thereof, b) the specific proportion of programmes serving public service objectives set forth in Article 83, c) the ratio of programmes on subjects related to local public affairs or facilitating local everyday life, d) predefined extent of service to nationalities and other minority needs, e) the obligation to provide news services, f) tender criteria for connecting to a network and expanding the reception area, g) criteria for the provision of ancillary and value-added media services.

(4) The Media Council shall publish the invitation to tender through a public notice and on its website. (5) The invitation to tender shall be announced so that, from the day of its publication a) at least sixty days are available for the submission of tenders for the provision of national media services, b) at least forty days are available for the submission of tenders for the provision of regional media services, c) at least thirty days are available for the submission of tenders for the provision of local media services.

Amending and Withdrawing the Invitation to Tender

Article 53 (1) The Media Council shall be entitled to amend the invitation to tender along the principles of an objective, transparent and non-discriminative procedure. (2) The invitation to tender may be amended until no later than the fifteenth day prior to the submission of the tenders. (3) Any amendment to the invitation to tender shall be published in accordance with the rules governing the publication of the invitation to tender. (4) In the event the invitation to tender is amended, the Media Council shall be obliged to extend the deadline for the submission of tenders, ensuring that the period available for the submission of tenders as defined under Article 52 (5) remain available from the date of the publication of the invitation to tender. (5) The Media Council may withdraw the invitation to tender until no later than fifteen days prior to the deadline for submission of the tenders, by taking into consideration media market and media policy aspects. The Media Council shall publish this decision in the same manner as the invitation to tender, and give reasons for its decision.

The Tender Fee

Article 54 Tenderers submitting a tender shall pay a tender fee. The tender fee shall be five percent of the published media service provision basic fee. Eighty percent of the tender fee shall be offset against (deducted from) the media service provision fee.

The Tenderer

Article 55 (1) Only those undertakings may participate in the tender procedure that a) have no customs or social security contributions overdue for longer than sixty days or overdue taxes registered by the central tax authority, or any overdue payment obligations to separate state funds, except if the creditor has agreed to the payment of the debt at a subsequent date in writing, b) are not under bankruptcy, liquidation, members' voluntary liquidation, or other winding up proceedings, and c) in regard to which no final public administration ruling has established a serious breach of obligations stemming from a broadcasting agreement or a public contract undertaken on the basis of a previous tender procedure – closed not more than five years ago – and the broadcasting agreement or public contract of which has not been terminated, d) does not have overdue debts to the Media Council. (2)

Any undertaking with a qualifying holding in the tenderer or in which the tenderer has qualifying holding must also meet the criteria laid down under Paragraph (1) (a)-(d). (3) Only those entities shall be eligible to participate in the tender procedure that comply with the provisions on conflict of interests defined under the Act. A conflict of interest shall hold, regarding the tenderer in the tender procedure announced in terms of the national analogue media service provision right, if the given tenderer or an undertaking having a qualifying holding in the tenderer is declared by the Media Council as the winner of another ongoing tender procedure. A conflict of interest shall hold, regarding the tenderer in the tender procedure announced in terms of the regional or local analogue media service provision right, if the given tenderer or the undertaking having a qualifying holding in the tenderer is declared by the Media Council as the winner of another ongoing tender procedure announced in terms of the reception area of the local or regional media service, except if the extent of overlapping between the reception areas of the two media service provision rights does not exceed twenty percent. (4)

If the tenderer, or the undertaking having a qualifying holding in the tenderer, or the undertaking in which the tenderer holds a qualifying holding, has a media service provision right falling under the scope of this Act which excludes acquisition of the right announced in the invitation to tender, it may only submit a tender if it declares in a legally binding declaration, forming part of its tender, that if it is declared as the winner of the tender, it shall either relinquish the affected media service provision right or any claim to such right as of the date of the conclusion of the agreement, or undertake to terminate the situation violating the restrictive provisions in another manner, as of this same date. (5) Undertakings holding a qualifying holding in one another, or an undertaking in which the other undertaking holds a qualifying holding, or in which the same third party holds a qualifying holding shall not be permitted to participate in the tender procedure simultaneously.

The Tender

Article 56 The tender shall contain: a) the particulars of the tenderer: aa) name, ab) address or registered office, ac) company registration number or registration number, ad) contact details (telephone number and electronic mailing address),ae) name and contact information (telephone number, postal and electronic mailing address) of its executive officer, representative as well as the specimen of signature certified by a notary public or countersigned by an attorney-at-law, b) the tenderer's effective Deed of Foundation, c) the tenderer's declaration on the ownership share, either direct or indirect, held by the tenderer or by another undertaking holding an ownership share in the tenderer, in the undertaking providing media services in the territory of Hungary or applying for media service provision rights in Hungary, d) basic particulars of the planned media service: da) type (general or thematic), db) reception area, dc) the broadcasting transmission facility wished to be used, de) kind (commercial, community), df) the transmission time and transmission time schedule of the service, dg) the planned ancillary media services, dh) permanent name and signal of the media service, di) the fact of expansion of the reception area, or connecting to the network, if applicable, dj) the planned programme flow structure, dk) daily, weekly, monthly minimum transmission time intended for broadcasting programmes serving the public service objectives set forth in Article 83, programmes dealing with local public affairs, or programmes supporting local everyday life, dl) daily, weekly, monthly minimum transmission time intended for broadcasting news programmes, dm) planned daily minimum transmission time serving the needs of nationalities or other minorities, e) with the exception of community media service, the offer for the media service provision fee, f) the media service provider's business and financial plan, g) a bank certificate confirming that the amount required to cover the operating costs of the planned media service for at least the first three months of operation, excluding advertising revenue, is available for the tenderer on a separate current account, h) the tenderer's declaration stating that no grounds for exclusion, as defined in this Act, exist vis-á-vis it, and that the possible acceptance of another pending tender of the tenderer will not create such grounds for exclusion either, i) any other data, documents and declarations defined in the invitation to tender.

Evaluation and Formal Validity of Tenders

Article 57 (1) The Media Council shall examine whether the tenderer complies with the applicable formal and content requirements. (2) Tenders shall be deemed formally invalid if a) the tenderer does not meet the personal or participation criteria set forth in Article 55, or the conflict of interest requirements under this Act, b) the tender was not submitted by the deadline, at the place, in the number of copies or in the manner defined in the invitation to tender, c) the tender fee was not paid in time, d) the tender does not comply with the formal requirements defined in the invitation to tender, e) the data and information listed in Article 56 are not included in the tender or are included inadequately. (3) No remedy of deficiencies is permitted with regard to the formal requirements specified under Points a)-d) of Article 57 (2). Only those deficiencies revealed in terms of the requirement of form specified in Article 57 (2) e) shall be allowed to be remedied which relate to the information and data as per Article 56 b), c), dc), df)-dm), and f)-i). (4) Deficiencies may be remedied by the tenderer within fifteen days of delivery. If the tenderer duly remedies the deficiencies within the deadline set forth in the invitation to tender, the tender shall be deemed as if it was correct and complete right from the start. The deadline defined for remedying deficiencies represents the expiry of the limitation period; no petition for excuse may be submitted after its expiry. No remedy of deficiencies is permitted with regard to those elements of the tender that are subject to evaluation pursuant to the invitation to tender. (5) Fifty percent of the tender fee shall be reimbursed in the case of formally invalid tenders.

Tender Register and Formally Invalid Tenders

Article 58 (1) The Media Council shall record the tenderers having submitted a formally valid tender in an official register (hereinafter referred to as: tender register) within forty-five days of expiry of the submission deadline. The Office shall notify the tenderers – i.e. participants from then on – of their entry into the tender register, and publish the list of tenderers recorded in the tender register on the Media Council's website. (2) In the case of tenders that are formally invalid pursuant to Article 57 (2), the Media Council shall reject the registration of the tenderer in the tender register by way of an order. The order rejecting the registration shall terminate the tenderer's client status under the procedure. The tenderer may request the Budapest Administrative and Labour Court to review the order rejecting the registration in the tender register on grounds of a breach of law, within eight days of the communication of the order. The court will pass its decision, based on the hearing of the parties, if necessary, in out-of-court proceedings within fifteen days. No appeal can be lodged against the decision of the Budapest Administrative and Labour Court. If a request is submitted for an out-of-court proceeding, the Media Council shall suspend the tender procedure until the final decision of the court is made. No independent legal remedy against the Media Council's order to suspend the tender procedure can be obtained. (3) If the Media Council discovers causes of formal invalidity only after registration in the tender register, in the course of the tender's evaluation on the merits, it shall not establish the formal invalidity of the tender in a separate order; rather, it shall stipulate such invalidity in the decision closing the tender procedure.

Substantive Validity of Tenders

Article 59 (1) When examining the substantive validity of the tenders, the Media Council shall evaluate and check the tender submitted by the tenderer entered into the tender register both as a whole and also in respect of each tender component separately. (2) If the tender is deficient in terms of content, the Media Council shall call on the tenderer to remedy the deficiencies. Article 57 (4) shall apply to the remedy of deficiencies. If the tender is not adequately clear, the Media Council may, without prejudice to the principle of equal opportunities, request clarification from the tenderer. The tenderer shall have fifteen days for clarification from the date of delivery of the respective request. Clarification may not result in modification of any financial or other commitments pertaining to value or other material statements; it may only serve the interpretation thereof. (3) A tender shall be deemed substantively invalid if a) it contains – among the commitments forming part of the evaluation criteria of the invitation to tender – incomprehensible, contradicting or clearly unfeasible commitments or conditions that impede the evaluation of the tender on the merits, b) in the opinion of the Media Council, the tender contains commitments that are unfeasible, excessive or insufficient or highly disproportionate, or contains such clearly irrational or unfounded commitments or conditions that contradict the facts and data available to the Media Council, and thus render evaluation in accordance with the set of criteria defined in the invitation to tender impossible, c) the tender is unsuitable for achieving or implementing the objectives defined in this Act and in the invitation to tender since the tender itself is unfounded, or d) it does not comply with the substantive requirements defined in the invitation to tender. (4) The Media Council shall not establish the substantive invalidity of the tender in a separate order; rather, it shall stipulate such invalidity in the decision closing the tender procedure. (5) Fifty percent of the tender fee shall be reimbursed in the case of substantive invalidity.

Evaluation of Tenders

Article 60 (1) Tenders shall be evaluated on the basis of the principles and criteria defined in the invitation to tender. Evaluation criteria shall be based on quantitative or other assessable factors, and be in line with the subject of the tender or the material conditions of the public contract. (2) The Media Council may, in connection with a tender component related to the evaluation criteria, determine, in the invitation to tender, a requirement compared to which no less favourable offer can be made. (3) The evaluation principles shall be transparent, free from discrimination and proportionate. (4) Tenders must be evaluated in the way defined in the invitation to tender: no deviation shall be allowed in this respect.

Termination of the Tender Procedure

Article 61 (1) The Media Council may terminate the tender procedure through an order if a) no tenders are submitted for the invitation to tender, b) the tender procedure loses its original purpose due to circumstances or conditions arising in the course of the tender procedure, thus in particular if the national or international economic environment changes substantially following the invitation to tender, or if the economic, legal, spectrum management or media service market circumstances or conditions prevailing at the time of the publication of the invitation to tender change materially, c) in the opinion of the Media Council, the media policy aspects or the fundamental principles or objectives defined under this Act or in the invitation to tender cannot be guaranteed by executing the tender procedure, or d) based on the tenders submitted or the information available, the Media Council establishes that none of the tenders submitted by the tenderers satisfy the objectives or basic principles laid down in this Act, or that declaring any one of the tenderers as the winner would jeopardise the responsible, proper and effective management of frequencies constituting state property. (2) The Media Council shall publish its decision as per Paragraph (1) in the same place and in the same manner as the invitation to tender.

Result of the Tender

Procedure, Announcement of the Result and Public Availability of Tenders Article 62 (1) The Media Council shall establish through a regulatory decision a) the success or the failure of the tender procedure, and b) the winner of the tender procedure in the case of a successful procedure. (2) The tender procedure shall be unsuccessful if all submitted tenders are invalid in terms of form or content. (3) Only such a tenderer may be declared winner that have consistently complied with the participation requirements laid down in this Act and in the invitation to tender from the date of the submission of the tender. In case of tenders on local media services, if only one tenderer meets the statutory requirements or the requirements of the tender, the Media Council determines the winner of the tender in line with Point b) of Paragraph (1). (4) The Media Council shall publish its decision as per Paragraph

(1) in the same place and in the same manner as the invitation to tender. (5) A review of the Media Council's decision as per Paragraph (1) may be requested from the Budapest Administrative and Labour Court by the client and by any other participant in the proceeding as regards the provisions expressly applicable to him/her, within fifteen days of the decision's announcement, on the grounds of breach of law. (6) The Media Council shall forward the statement of claim, together with the documents and representations of the case, to the Budapest Administrative and Labour Court within fifteen days of receipt thereof. The court shall assess the statement of claim for a judicial review within sixty days from the submission of the statement of claim by the Media Council to the court and shall put down its decision in writing until the day of its announcement. No appeal may be lodged against the decision of the court and no retrial can be requested.

The petition for review of the decision can be lodged within fifteen days from announcement of the decision, with the provision that the petition for review must be actually received by the Budapest Administrative and Labour Court within the time limit set for filing. If this deadline (limitation period) is missed, no petition for excuse will be accepted. The Curia shall assess the petition for review within sixty days and shall put down its decision in writing within this deadline. The Budapest Administrative and Labour Court and the Curia shall hold an accelerated procedure. (7) The tender shall qualify as a secret protected by law as defined under Paragraph (2) of Article 153, right until the completion of the tender procedure. The tender shall be handled by the Media Council within the document folder separately, as restricted data. The Media Council shall not disclose any information concerning the data contained in the tenders to third parties until the contract is concluded. (8) Eighty percent of the tender fee shall be reimbursed in the case of tenders which are valid in terms of form and content, but which have not been declared winner.

Public Contract

Article 63 (1) Simultaneously with notifying the winning tenderer about the decision as per Article 62 (1) (b), the Media Council shall, ex officio, launch a regulatory procedure for the purpose of concluding a public contract with the winner of the tender procedure. The administrative deadline of such regulatory procedure shall be forty-five days. (2) If the winning tenderer does not participate in the regulatory procedure specified under Paragraph (1), or if the winning tenderer hinders the conclusion of the public contract, the public contract may not be concluded beyond the administrative deadline defined under Paragraph (1). In such cases, the Media Council shall terminate the procedure on the forty-fifth day from the starting date of the procedure. No petition for excuse may be lodged in the procedure. (3) [not in effect] (4) If the procedure of the Budapest Administrative and Labour Court has been requested according to Article 62 (5), the public contract may not be concluded until the final and binding decision of the Budapest Administrative and Labour Court. The duration of the review procedure of the Budapest Administrative and Labour Court shall not be included in the administrative deadline of the regulatory procedure.

(5) The Media Council may, pursuant to Article 187, impose fines if the winning tenderer withdraws its tender or does not conclude the public contract. (6) The Media Council may, in addition to imposing a fine, also oblige the winning tenderer to bear and pay all the costs arising from the withdrawal of the tender or from hindering the conclusion of the public contract. (7)

The conditions pertaining to the production, safekeeping, availability and disclosure of the information required for verifying the fulfilment of the media service provider's obligations must be determined in the public contract. (8) If the media service is not provided by the deadline specified in the public contract – due to reasons within the tenderer's reasonable control – the Media Council may, in addition to enforcing the legal sanctions determined in the public contract, terminate the public contract with immediate effect. (9) The media service provider shall pay the media service provision fee defined in the public contract in advance on a quarterly basis. Upon obtaining the media service provision right, the media service provision fee shall be paid in advance for the following half year. (10) If the media service provider is in default with the payment of or fails to pay any portion of the media service provision fee, the Media Council may, in addition to enforcing the legal sanctions determined in the public contract, terminate the public contract with a fifteen-day notice period. (11) The consequences of breach of contract must be defined in the public contract. (12) The media service provider shall be entitled and obliged to broadcast the programme flow meeting the requirements specified under the public contract, via its own network maintained by it, using its own equipment and instruments or using an electronic communications service provider (broadcasting service). No telecommunications license is required for the media service provider's broadcasting or distribution activity using own equipment. This, however, does not affect the obligations of the media service provider to acquire other permits and licenses required by legislation. (13)

The original applicant as per Article 49 (8) may claim from the winner of the tender the reimbursement of the justified expenses incurred in relation to data disclosure and planning. (14) The media service provider shall report to the Media Council within five days any changes taking place to its ownership structure or its data indicated in the public contract.

Connecting to a Network, Expansion of the Reception

Area, Amendment of the Agreement Article 64 (1) The Media Council shall decide on connecting to a network based on the joint request of those connecting to the network, within the framework of a regulatory procedure. If the permission is granted, the Media Council shall amend the public contract of the media service providers. (2) Community media service providers may only connect to a network with other community media service providers.

National media service providers shall not be allowed to connect to a network. (3) Connecting to a network shall not be allowed if a) the length of the regional or local media service provider's own media service does not reach the daily threshold of four hours, b) any of the media service providers owe overdue media service provision fees to the Media Council, c) as a result of connecting to the network, any of the media service providers would not meet the conditions laid down in Article 71, d) the reception area of the networked media service provider and the media service provider connecting to the network overlaps in excess of twenty percent, e) as a result of connecting to the network, the media service provider would depart from its original commitments made in its tender. (4)

The Media Council shall adopt its decision about expansion of the reception area, within the framework of a regulatory procedure, initiated at request. If the permission is granted, the Media Council shall amend the public contract of the media service provider. (5) The condition for permitting the expansion of the reception area shall be that the reception areas of the media service provider's rights of similar nature are situated at a distance of at most forty kilometres from each other. (6)

Expansion of the reception area shall not be permitted a) if the media service provider owes overdue media service provision fees to the Media Council, b) if, as a result of expansion of the reception area, the media service provider would not meet the conditions laid down in Article 71. (7) No new rights shall be created through the expansion of the reception area. The validity period of the expanded reception area right shall remain unchanged, with the full right remaining in force until the expiry of the extended basic right. The media service provider shall broadcast the same programme flow over the entire reception area throughout the entire transmission time. (8)

If the media service provider's reception area increases from local to regional or from regional to national as a result of an increase in the population reached with the media service distribution system, or as a result of connecting to a network, or as a result of the reception area expansion, the Media Council shall amend the public contract on condition that the media service provider satisfies the requirements applicable to the media service with the increased reception area, as defined under this Act. (9) At the media service provider's request, the Media Council may – based on media market and media policy considerations, and with due regard to essential public interests – offer, in place of the existing media service provision right, another media service provision right registered in the register of media service facilities under similar terms and conditions, with regard to the frequency band and the frequency, without inviting tenders. Such amendment shall not affect the term of the media service provision right.

Temporary Media Services

Article 65 (1) Upon request, the Media Council may – taking into consideration media market and media policy considerations – conclude provisional public contracts for a period of at most thirty days for the utilization of such local media service facilities a) the frequency plan of which has been published by the Office as per Article 49 (5), but for which no public contract has been concluded yet, b) [not in effect] c) regarding which the Authority certifies that the media service may be pursued without disturbing others and without violating international requirements. (2) The applications shall include: a) the name, address, registered office, telephone number of the applicant, b) the effective Deed of Foundation of the applicant undertaking, c) the purpose of the proposed temporary media service, d) the planned transmission time broken down by day, week or month, e) the programme flow plan, f) the starting and ending date of the proposed temporary media service, g) [not in effect] h) the description of the media service facility or in case of Paragraph (1) (c) the place of business of the proposed temporary media service.

(3) Applications shall be evaluated within twenty days of their submission. If the application does not meet the conditions set forth under Paragraph (2), the Media Council shall call on the applicant to remedy the deficiencies. Applicants shall have five days from the date of delivery to remedy the deficiencies. The deadline set for remedying deficiencies represents a limitation period; if it is not met, the Media Council shall reject the application. The Media Council

shall reject the application without examining it on the merits if at least thirty days have not passed between the date of submission of the application and the start date of the proposed temporary media service. (4)

If several applications are submitted regarding a media service facility, the Media Council shall evaluate the applications in the order they were received. If the Media Council concludes a public contract based on an application received earlier, the provisions of Paragraph (5) shall be applied regarding the evaluation of applications received later, and applicants shall be called upon to amend the dates under Paragraph (2) (f), if necessary. (5) A provisional public contract may be concluded a) once a year with the same undertaking, b) three times a year in the same public administration area. A period of at least fifteen days shall elapse between the terms of two provisional public contracts. (6) The media service provider authorised to provide temporary media services may not initiate connection to a network with another media service provider, nor the expansion of its reception area. (7) The community media service provider shall not be required to pay a media service provision fee based on the provisional public contract. (8) The requirements defined under Article 71 shall not be taken into account when applying Paragraphs (1)-(7). (9) The temporary media service provision period specified under Paragraph (1) may not be extended. (10) If the audiovisual media service provision right expires between 1 January 2010 and the target date set in Article 38 (1) of the Digital Switchover Act in a way that it cannot be renewed pursuant to Article 48 (5), the Media Council may conclude a provisional public contract at the media service provider's request concerning the media service provision right, until the deadline defined in legislation as the target date of digital switchover of media service distribution provided by audiovisual media service providers. (11) If the linear radio media service provision right expires after having been renewed on one occasion by the Media Council, and the tender procedure for the given media service facility has already been started, the Media Council shall have the right to conclude a provisional public contract with the media service provider formerly holding the right, even on several occasions, at the request of such media service provider, for a term of sixty days at most. The provisional public contract based on this Paragraph can only be concluded until the completion of the tender procedure or until the judicial review procedure is terminated in a final and binding manner, if a judicial review procedure was started against the decision adopted on the merits of the tender procedure or against the order terminating the tender procedure. The provisional public contract shall be terminated as of the day when the public contract is concluded with the winner of the tender procedure. (12) When applying Paragraphs (10)-(11), Paragraphs (1)-(5) and Paragraph (9) shall not be applied. (13) For the purposes of Paragraphs (10)-(11), the Media Council may conclude a provisional public contract, if the media service provider has no overdue debts toward the Media Council and certifies, on the day of conclusion of the contract at the latest, the payment of the media service provision fee payable for the entire period – in case of audiovisual media services, for six months – of the provisional right.

COMMUNITY MEDIA SERVICES

Article 66 (1) Linear community media services a) are intended to serve or satisfy the special needs for information of and to provide access to cultural programmes for a certain social, national, cultural or religious community or group, or b) are intended to serve or satisfy the special needs for information of and to provide access to cultural programmes for residents of a given settlement, region or reception area, or c) in the majority of their transmission time such programmes are broadcasted which are aimed at achieving the objectives of public media services as defined in Article 83. (2) The media service provider providing linear community media services shall define in its media service policy a) the objective of its activity, b) the cultural areas and topics which it has undertaken to present, c) the objectives of public media services which it has undertaken to serve, d) the community or communities (social groups or residents of a specific geographic area) that it intends to serve, e) if it serves the needs of a specific community as per Paragraph (1) (a)-(b), then such community and the minimum percentage ratio of the programmes targeted at such community as compared to the total transmission time shall be defined. (3)

The media service provider shall report annually to the Media Council on compliance with the applicable legislative provisions governing community media services and with the media service policy. (4) Linear community media service shall a) provide information about social or local community news regularly, and perform other news services, b) broadcast cultural programmes, c) strive to take into consideration the needs of persons with impaired hearing, in the case of audiovisual media services, d) operate, in the case of audiovisual media services, in line with the requirements of Article 20 pertaining to Hungarian and European programme quotas, without applying the exemption opportunity specified under Paragraph (2) of Article 22, excluding any possible exemptions regarding programme quotas, as per Paragraph (2) of Article 22, applicable to independent production companies, e) have at least four hours of daily transmission time allocated to it, f) broadcast weekly at least four hours of programmes aired for the first time (not reruns) prepared and edited by it during the given calendar year, g) broadcast programmes serving public service objectives set forth in Article 83 in over two-thirds of its weekly transmission time, including the news programme, political programme and cultural programme aimed at the community served by it, as well as other similar programmes not primarily aimed at the community in question, h) allocate, in the case of radio media services, at least fifty percent of its weekly transmission time committed to programmes presenting musical works to the presentation of Hungarian musical works. (5) The recognition of local or regional media services as community media services shall be established through the Media Council's decision, adopted within the framework of the tender procedure started by the Media Council pursuant to this Act regarding the usage of the media service provision rights, on the winner of the media service tender or under the Media Council's procedure initiated specifically for this purpose, based on the Media Council's decision. This procedure may be initiated by the media service provider following the registration of the media service in the register in accordance with the provisions of Article 42. In the course of its procedure, the Media Council shall examine whether the existing or proposed media service and the provisions of its respective media service policy satisfy the criteria laid down under Paragraphs (1)-(4), and issue a regulatory decision within sixty days. National media services may not be recognised as community media services. (6) Following recognition as per Paragraph (5), the Media Council shall, ex officio, examine the operation of the media service provider in depth, over a period of at least seven days of service, at least every two years – and also following the first year in the case of new services –, and for that purpose the media service provider shall disclose detailed data regarding the programmes broadcasted by it and the contents of the media service. If, in the opinion of the Media Council, the media service examined does not meet the criteria of linear community media services, the Media Council shall, through a decision passed by it, withdraw recognition as community media service. (7) In case a decision on the refusal or withdrawal of the recognition as a community media service is adopted, the media service provider may not initiate the proceeding under Paragraph (5) within six months of communication of the decision on the refusal or withdrawal.

General Rules on the Prevention of Media Market Concentration

Article 67 The market concentration of media service providers providing linear media services may be limited within the framework of this Act in order to maintain the diversity of the media market and to prevent the formation of information monopolies. Article 68 (1) Linear audiovisual media service providers with an average annual audience share of at least thirty-five percent, linear radio media service providers, and media service providers having a joint average annual audience share of at least forty percent on the linear audiovisual and linear radio markets, any owners of the media service provider and any person or undertaking having a qualifying holding in the media service provider's owner a) may not launch new media services, may not acquire shares in undertakings providing media services, and b) shall take measures in order to increase the diversity of the media market by modifying the programme flow structure of its media services, by increasing the proportion of Hungarian works and programmes prepared by independent production companies, or in any other way. (2)

In the case presented under Paragraph (1) (a), if the media service provider affected by the rule restricting media market concentration wishes to acquire a share in an undertaking providing media services, the Media Council shall be obliged to reject the special authority approval under its procedure as per Article 171. (3) In the case presented under Paragraph (1) (b), in order to determine the measures aimed at increasing diversity, the Media Council may conclude a public contract – for a term of at least one year – with the media service provider, at the media service provider's request, and under such procedure the Media Council shall be entitled to assess whether it accepts the obligations the media service provider wishes to undertake or not. Such applications may be submitted within thirty days from the communication of the Media Council's regulatory decision as per Article 70 (7). If the public contract – due to failure to reach an understanding – is not concluded within three months from the communication of the regulatory decision specified in Article 70 (7), the Media Council shall terminate the procedure by a decision. (4) In the absence of the conclusion of a public contract specified under Paragraph (3), the media service provider shall submit its application for the approval of its measures aimed at increasing media market diversity, within six months of the communication of the Media Council's regulatory decision specified in Article 70 (7).

In its procedure conducted regarding the approval of the application, the Media Council shall assess whether the proposed measures are suitable for decreasing the former information monopoly and for increasing media market diversity and information pluralism. In the event of the late fulfilment of such obligation, the Media Council shall impose a procedural fine. (5) If the application complies with the conditions specified under Paragraph (4), the Media Council shall approve it by its decision. (6) In case of any doubt, it is the media service provider's responsibility to prove that the proposed measures comply with the conditions specified under Paragraph (4). (7)

If the Media Council does not approve the proposed measures, it shall adopt a decision wherein it shall identify the causes of non-compliance, as far as the principles specified under Paragraph (4) are concerned. (8) In the case presented under Paragraph (7), the media service provider shall submit a new plan for proposed measures by the deadline set by the Media Council, but, within thirty days at most, taking into account the considerations specified in the Media Council's decision as per Paragraph (7). In the event of the late fulfilment of such obligation, the Media Council shall impose a procedural fine. If the measures specified in the new application also fail to satisfy the criteria defined under Paragraph (4), the Media Council may enforce the respective legal sanctions in accordance with Articles 185-187. (9) The Media Council shall supervise the implementation of the measures approved through its decision within the framework of general regulatory supervision. (10) The average annual audience share jointly reached on the linear audiovisual and linear radio market shall, for the purposes of Paragraph (1), be determined by adding the individual average annual audience shares, expressed as a percentage, attained separately on the linear audiovisual and linear radio markets.

Identifying Media Service Providers with Significant Market Power Article 69 (1) Linear audiovisual media service providers and linear radio media service providers with an average annual audience share of at least fifteen percent shall qualify as media service providers with significant market power, provided that the average annual audience share of at least one their media service reaches three percent. (2) The Media Council shall regularly monitor the fulfilment of the obligations prescribed for media service providers with significant market power under Article 32 and Articles 38-39. (3) The Authority may conclude an agreement with an external contractor for measuring the average annual audience share defined in Article 68 and Paragraph (1). The contracting party shall be selected in an open tender procedure. When preparing the agreement and determining the tender result, the Authority shall cooperate with the media service providers. The agreement shall define the method for measuring audience share, the professional criteria thereof, and the procedure for auditing the results. (4) The Authority shall publish on its website the methodology used for measuring audience share and the average annual audience share of media services for the previous calendar year.

Rules of Procedures

Aimed at Preventing Media Market Concentration and Identifying Media Service Providers with Significant Market Power Article 70 (1) For the purposes of the procedures aimed at the prevention of media market concentration and at identifying media service providers with significant market power, the Media Council shall examine market facts and circumstances important (hereinafter as: relevant) for the assessment of the level of concentration, in particular the media service provider's average annual audience share for the previous calendar year, under the regulatory inspection as per the Act on the General Rules of Administrative Proceedings and Services, with the deviations defined under Paragraphs (2)-(6). (2) In order to clarify the relevant facts and circumstances, the Media Council may require the media service providers to provide data in the course of its regulatory inspection, by way of an order. No independent legal remedy shall be available against the order; the order may be challenged in a legal remedy procedure brought against the decision on the merits made in a procedure that may follow the regulatory inspection and is aimed at the prevention of media market concentration and at identifying media service providers with significant market power. (3)

In the event of failure to provide data or upon inadequate provision of data, the Media Council may, pursuant to Article 175 (8), impose a procedural fine. Over and above the fine, if the data are not provided or if data are provided inadequately, the Media Council shall be entitled to, and in case of a repeated breach of law, shall be obliged to impose a fine ranging from fifty thousand forints to three million forints on the officer or registered representative, as per Article 45 (1) (ad), of the media service provider found in breach of the law. (4)

The following shall be taken into account when determining audience share, or added to the audience share a) the audience share of all linear media services distributed by the media service provider on the territory of Hungary, b) the audience share of the linear media services distributed on the territory of Hungary by media service providers in whom the affected media service provider has a qualifying holding, and c) the audience share of linear media services distributed on the territory of Hungary by a media service provider in whom any owner of the affected media service provider, or the owner of the owner thereof has a qualifying holding. (5)

If, based on the regulatory inspection, the Media Council established that there is a circumstance providing grounds for conducting a procedure aimed at the prevention of media market concentration and at identifying media service providers with significant market power, then, notwithstanding the relevant provisions of the Act on the General Rules of Administrative Proceedings and Services, it shall only decide to launch the procedure in an order. (6) No procedure shall be launched by the Media Council if it establishes on the basis of the regulatory inspection that neither the media service provider affected by the rules restricting media market concentration identified in the decision made earlier as per Paragraph (7), nor the group of media service providers with significant market power identified in the decision as per Paragraph (7) or in the public contract as per Paragraph (10) have changed. (7)

In the procedure aimed at the prevention of media market concentration and at identifying media service providers with significant market power, the Media Council shall identify the media service provider affected by the rules restricting media market concentration as per Article 68 or the media service provider with significant market power as per Article 69 in a regulatory decision, and shall decide on the termination of such status determined in its earlier decision. (8) In its decision made within the framework of a procedure aimed at identifying media service providers with significant market power, the Media Council shall also define the exact contents of the obligations imposed on the media service provider with significant market power pursuant to Article 32 and Articles 38-39, taking into account the assessment criteria defined therein. (9) A review of the Media Council's decision made within the framework of the procedure aimed at the prevention of media market concentration and at identifying media service providers with significant market power may be requested from the Budapest Administrative and Labour Court by the client and by any other participant in the proceeding as regards the provisions expressly applicable to him/her, within fifteen days of the decision's announcement, on the grounds of breach of law.(9a)

The Media Council shall forward the statement of claim, together with the documents and representations of the case, to the Budapest Administrative and Labour Court within fifteen days of receipt thereof. The court shall assess the statement of claim for a judicial review within sixty days from the submission of the statement of claim by the Media Council to the court and shall put down its decision in writing until the day of its announcement. No appeal may be lodged against the decision of the court and no retrial can be requested. The petition for review of the decision can be lodged within fifteen days from announcement of the decision, with the provision that the petition for review must be actually received by the Budapest Administrative and Labour Court within the time limit set for filing. If this deadline (limitation period) is missed, no petition for excuse will be accepted.

The Curia shall assess the petition for review within sixty days and shall put down its decision in writing within this deadline. The Budapest Administrative and Labour Court and the Curia shall hold an accelerated procedure. The court shall have the right to change the decision of the Media Council. (10) In the procedure aimed at identifying media service providers with significant market power, the Media Council, rather than issuing a decision, may also conclude a public contract with the media service provider in order to identify whether the media service provider has significant market power and to define the exact contents of the obligations imposed on the media service provider with significant market power pursuant to Article 32 and Articles 38-39. In such case, the parties may depart from the assessment criteria for determining the obligations specified in Article 32 and Articles 38-39 with the provision that the media service provider with significant market power may not be exempted, not even in the public contract, from its obligations defined therein. (11) The Media Council shall conduct its procedure aimed at the prevention of media market concentration and at identifying media service providers with significant market power, with the deviations determined under Paragraph (6), by 30 September each year. When identifying media service providers with significant market power, their average audience share during the previous calendar year shall be taken into account. Media service providers with significant market power shall fulfil their obligations from 1 January of the year following the Media Council's decision. The Media Council's decision made within the framework of the procedure aimed at the prevention of media market concentration and at identifying media service providers with significant market power and also the public contract concluded shall remain in force until the entry into force of the subsequent decision made, or public contract concluded on the same subject as a result of a procedure conducted in the following year. (12) For the purposes of Paragraphs (1)-(11), sales revenue shall mean the net sales revenue achieved by the participant of the procedure through sales relating to media service activities in the course of the previous business year.

Rules Governing Media Service Providers of Analogue Linear Radio Media Services Acquiring Media Service Provision Rights by Virtue of a Public Contract or Broadcasting Agreement

Article 71 (1) Those authorised to provide analogue linear radio media services based on a public contract or broadcasting agreement shall have the right to simultaneously provide a) maximum one national analogue linear radio media service, b) maximum two regional and four local analogue linear radio media services, or c) maximum twelve local analogue linear radio media services. (2) With the exception of thematic analogue linear radio media services, providers authorised to provide national analogue linear radio media services and those having a qualifying holding therein may not acquire a qualifying holding in undertakings providing or distributing other media services. (3) The same undertaking may only acquire a qualifying holding in organisations authorised to provide analogue linear radio media services within the limits defined under Paragraph (1). (4)

The media service provider's own rights and the rights of the undertakings in which it has a qualifying holding shall be taken into account jointly for the purposes of Paragraphs (1) and (3). (5) A regional or local linear radio media service provider or its owner may not, with the exceptions defined under Paragraph (6), acquire a qualifying holding in other undertakings providing regional or local linear radio media services falling within the reception area of their media services, and the regional or local linear radio media service provider or its owner may not provide another regional or local linear radio media service falling within the reception area of their media services. (6) The restriction defined under Paragraph (5) shall not be applied if a) the reception areas of the two media service providers overlap up to twenty percent at most, or b) unused transmission time remains following the evaluation of the tender and, parallel to an invitation being issued to a new tender, an agreement is concluded with the media service provider defined under Paragraph (5) in respect of the unused transmission time, provided that the transmission time thereby acquired by it differs from its existing transmission time by eighty percent, and neither transmission time exceeds four hours. (7) Concentration of companies as per the Act on the Prohibition of Unfair and Restrictive Market Practices shall not be permitted if such were prejudicial to this Act.

Diversity in Media Service Distribution Article 72 (1)

The number of media services in the media service providers of which the same undertaking has a qualifying holding shall not exceed one quarter of the audiovisual media services or half the radio media services distributed on the given transmission system. (2) The number of media services the providers of which also perform media service distribution activities or in the providers of which the same media service distributor undertaking has an ownership stake shall not exceed one quarter of the audiovisual media services or half the radio media services broadcasted on the given transmission system. (3) The ratios defined under Paragraphs (1)-(2) shall also apply to the programme package, offered by the media service distributor undertaking to viewers or listeners, which had the highest number of subscribers at the end of the previous calendar year in the given transmission system. (4) The obligations defined under Paragraphs (1)-(3) shall not apply to media service distribution activities carried out by the public media service provider.

"Must carry" Obligation regarding Media Services

Article 73 (1) In order to preserve, protect and further develop Hungarian and European culture and the culture of nationalities, support and sustain the languages of nationalities, satisfy the information needs of citizens and facilitate their participation in democratic public affairs and preserve diversity of opinions, the media service distributor defined under Paragraphs (2)-(3) shall be subject to the obligations defined in Articles 74-75 (hereinafter as: "must carry" obligation). (2) Media service distributors distributing media services on a transmission system or network used for broadcasting radio and audiovisual media services to the public shall be subject to a "must carry" obligation. (3) Transmission systems or networks used for broadcasting radio and audiovisual media services to the public include, in particular, cable television networks, satellite and terrestrial media service distribution networks (with the exception of analogue audiovisual broadcasting networks), as well as transmission systems allowing for transmission of media services by use of Internet Protocol, if the nature and conditions of the service are identical to those of media service distribution, or if this substitutes the media service distribution carried out by any other means. (4) The "must carry" obligation shall also extend to service providers and operators distributing media services on other transmission systems or networks, if this transmission system or network is the one which is widely used by subscribers and users as the main instrument for receiving radio and audiovisual media services.

The Media Council shall monitor such transmission systems or networks regularly, but at least every three years, as far as compliance with the "must carry" obligation is concerned, and shall perform their analysis within the framework of such monitoring. If, in the course of the regulatory procedure launched, if necessary, as a result of such monitoring, the Media Council establishes that it is reasonable to impose a "must carry" obligation in respect of the given transmission system or network, then it shall, in its decision, establish such "must carry" obligation in respect of all service providers and operators distributing media services on the given transmission system or network. (5) [not in effect] (6) If the media service distributor simultaneously provides media service distribution on several transmission systems, media service distribution networks, or media service distribution transmission platforms, the "must carry" obligation as per Paragraphs (1)-(4) shall apply to the media service distributor for each transmission system, media service distribution network or media service distribution transmission platform separately, except if the media service distributor provides a unified, complex programme package, containing several media service distribution transmission platforms.

Where a unified, complex programme package containing several media service distribution transmission platforms is provided, the "must carry" obligation shall apply to the media service distributor separately for each programme package. (7) A media service distributor shall qualify as influential from a media market perspective (hereinafter as: influential media service distributor) if a) the number of subscribers to its media service distribution, irrespective of the media service distribution platform or network used, exceeds one hundred thousand, or b) in case of publicly accessible media service distribution available without payment of a subscription fee, the reception area of the media service distributor covers more than one-third of the population of Hungary, and the sales revenue of the media service distributor or any undertaking having a qualifying holding in it or in its owner, or of any other undertaking operating under the qualifying holding of the media service distributor or its owner, arising from media service distribution or related services, with the exception of analogue broadcasting transmission, performed in the territory of Hungary, exceeds one billion forints annually. (8)

In case of any doubt, the influential media service distributor shall be obliged to prove that the conditions defined under Paragraph (7) do not prevail. Article 74 (1) The media service distributor shall be obliged to transmit a total of four linear audiovisual media services and three linear radio media services of the public media service provider free of charge, with the exception of media service distribution performed by means of broadcasting transmission. The media service distributor may not claim an additional fee from subscribers in excess of the costs of access related to ensuring access to such media services. The public media service provider shall not claim consideration from the media service distributor for the distribution of its media services. (1a) The media service distributor defined in Article 73 (2), operating a digital transmission system, shall be obliged to transmit, in addition to the linear audiovisual media services specified in Paragraph (1), two further linear audiovisual media services of the public media service provider, under the terms specified in Paragraph (1)(1b)

The media service distributor defined in Article 73 (2) that also transmits audiovisual media services in HD quality on the given transmission system shall be obliged to transmit on that transmission system the public media service provider's audiovisual media services defined in Paragraphs (1) and (1a) in HD quality, under the terms specified in Paragraph (1). (1c) The media service distributor defined in Article 73 (2) shall be obliged to set the audiovisual media services defined in Article 74 (1)-(1c) on the first places of the channel order, as a default. (2) The media service distributor shall transmit the public media services defined in Paragraph (1) and falling under the scope of the "must carry" obligation as a basic service in such a manner that these services, with the exception of analogue media service distribution networks, may also be available to subscribers as a separated subscription service. The media service distributor may not claim an additional fee for the use of such subscription service packages from subscribers in excess of the costs of access related to ensuring access to such media services. In case of analogue media service distribution networks, all public media services falling under the scope of the "must carry" obligation shall be made available to subscribers in all programme packages. (3) The public media service provider shall make its media services as per Paragraph (1), distributed using broadcasting transmission, available to subscribers free of charge. (4) The Office shall monitor due performance of the provisions defined under Paragraphs (1)-(3) ex officio or upon request. (5) The media service distributor providing media service distribution through terrestrial broadcasting with a local or regional reception area shall not be subject to the "must carry" obligation as per Paragraphs (1)-(3) with regards to their above mentioned activity. Article 75 (1) The media service distributor shall, up to ten percent of its total capacity but in respect of three media services at most, be subject to an obligation to contract regarding the technically and economically founded contract offers made by the media service providers regarding the provision of their regional or local audiovisual community media services. (2) The media service distributor shall – in respect of no more than two further media services – be subject to an obligation to contract, regarding the technically and economically founded contract offers made by the media service provider with a local reception area, regarding the provision of its audiovisual media service, provided that, based on the data in the register of the Authority, the reception area of the given media service provider falls within the given media service distributor's reception area or within the separate service area as per Paragraph (4), and that it provides its media service specifically for the given area's population. Pursuant to Paragraphs (1)-(2), the media service distributors performing their services via satellite or terrestrial broadcasting networks shall not be subject to the "must carry" obligation in respect of the local media services subject to the "must carry" obligation. (3)

Over and above the media services falling under the "must carry" obligation defined under Article 74 (1) and Paragraphs (1)-(2), the Media Council may, ex officio or upon the media service provider's request, define in a regulatory decision no more than two additional linear public media services or one linear community media service, serving the media policy objectives of public interest laid down in this Act, in respect of which the media service distributor has an obligation to contract according to a technically and economically founded contract offer. When passing its decision, the Media Council shall assess the extent by which the decision contributes to the diversity of the media market and information, to the achievement of the public service objectives defined in this Act and to the preservation and improvement of culture. Media service distributors shall not have the legal status of a client in such regulatory procedures. (4) If the transmission system of the media service distributor, as per Paragraphs (1)-(3), consists of parts serving several areas that can be technically distinguished from each other, the media service distributor shall be subject to the obligations, as per Paragraphs (1)-(3) mutatis mutandis, in respect of each technically distinguishable area separately. As far as the "must carry" obligation is concerned, technically distinguishable area shall mean the geographical area served by those parts of the transmission system within which no other media service can be installed into or removed from the transmitted complex programme signal under economically or technically reasonable conditions, in other words within such an area all users choosing the same programme package shall have access to an identical programme structure. (5) For the purposes of Paragraphs (1)-(2) and (7), the media service provider shall be considered as being entitled to be the beneficiary of the "must carry" obligation in respect of that media service provided by it a) in respect of which it requests the media service distributor to distribute the media service, and b) in respect of which it proceeded in good faith and in line with the requirements of fairness in the course of the contract offer procedure and the negotiations held to prepare the conclusion of the contract, and it negotiated on the merits regarding the responses, statements and requests for information given to the media service distributor in connection with the contract offer of the media service provider, in order to bring about the conclusion of the contract. For the purposes of Paragraph (3), the Media Council may appoint only linear community media services provided by media service providers other than those providing linear community media services under Paragraphs (1)-(2). (6) For the purposes of Paragraphs (1)-(4), neither the media service distributor's information channel nor such media service shall be taken into account in the provider of which, or in the owner of the provider of which the media service distributor undertaking or its owner has a qualifying holding. (7) The influential media service distributor shall have an obligation to contract in respect of three further linear community audiovisual media services at most in addition to those defined under Paragraphs (1)-(3), according to the technically and economically founded contract offers made by the media service providers for distributing their audiovisual community media services. (8) The obligation to contract must be performed according to the order of the offers.

The order of the contract offers, as far as the performance of the obligation to contract is concerned, shall be determined on the basis of the day when the written contract offer regarding the distribution of the media service was received (in an evidenced manner) by the media service distributor, or on the basis of the day when the media service distributor obtained knowledge (in an evidenced manner) of the verbally communicated contract offer. The fact of receipt of the offer by the media service distributor or of obtaining knowledge of the offer by the media service distributor shall be evidenced, verified in case of any doubt, by the media service distributor. If, in the course of joint fulfilment of the "must carry" obligation specified under Paragraphs (1) and (2) or on the basis of the "must carry" obligation specified under Paragraph (7), the media service distributor is only obliged to transmit one authorised media service provider but several authorised media service providers simultaneously also require transmission, the media service distributor shall be obliged to assess the authorised media service providers' contract offers, impartially and based on objective criteria, under a public and transparent procedure. (9)

Offers may be rejected on objective technical grounds if the service requirement indicated in the offer jeopardises the safety of operation or the unity of the network. (10) Offers may be rejected on objective economic grounds if the service claim indicated in the offer jeopardises the operation of the media service distributor and thereby the agreement is impossible. (11) In case of any doubt, the media service distributor shall be responsible to prove that transmission of the programme flow is either economically or technically unfounded. (12) The Media Council shall notify the affected media service providers about the launch of the regulatory procedure as per Paragraph (3) in an order. Such notification shall only contain the subject-matter of the case and a brief description thereof.

The Media Council shall publish such notifications through public notices. In the course of such a regulatory procedure only clients participating in the procedure shall be entitled to exercise the respective client rights. The Media Council shall announce its regulatory decision issued in the course of this procedure through public notices. (13) Taking into account the assessment criteria defined under Paragraph (3), the Media Council may amend its regulatory decision as per Paragraph (3) if this is justified by a substantial change in circumstances. The provisions of Paragraph (12) shall apply to the communication of the amended decision. (14) The submission of a statement of claim within the framework of the judicial review of the regulatory decision specified under Paragraphs (3) and (13) shall not have a suspensive effect on the enforcement of the decision, and the court shall not suspend the enforcement of the regulatory decision challenged by the statement of claim. The decision shall be enforceable immediately, irrespective of the filing of the statement of claim. (15) The Media Council may, ex officio or on the basis of a complaint specified in Article 145, may monitor the due application and performance by the media service distributor of the provisions laid down in Paragraphs (1)-(11) within the framework of general regulatory supervision. (16) If the Media Council concludes, as the result of the regulatory inspection, that the media service distributor had violated the provisions laid down in Paragraphs (1)-(11) and the violation may be rectified by termination of the violating behaviour or by restoring the lawful situation – without completing another regulatory procedure, the Media Council shall notify the media service distributor about the violation of law and shall, in the form of an order, oblige the media service distributor to terminate such violation by setting a deadline of at least twenty days for compliance and including a warning on the consequences of failure to comply. (17) If the deadline set in the notification mentioned in Paragraph (16) expires without result or if the provisions contained in Paragraph (16) cannot be applied, the Media Council shall ex officio launch the proceeding falling within its own competence. (18) The contents and framework of the "must carry" obligation of the public media service designated according to Paragraph (3) by the regulatory decision of Media Council, as well as the respective rights and obligations shall remain unaffected even if the number of "must carry" public media services specified in Article 74 (1) are reduced subsequent to the decision on the designation as per Paragraph (3) became final. Article 76 (1) The media service provider shall be entitled to initiate the legal dispute procedure as per Articles 172-174 if a) none of the agreements, as per Paragraphs (1)-(3) and (7) of Article 75, is concluded within thirty days of the offer being made, despite the media service provider's attempts to reconcile with the opposing positions on the merits, or b) the media service distributor violates the authorised media service provider's media service distribution right or legitimate interest set forth by law or an agreement. (2)

If the media service provider requests the Media Council to bring the contract into existence or determine its content, under a legal dispute procedure, in the absence of an agreement regarding the content of the contract, in line with the provisions of Article 172 (3), the Media Council, in the course of exercising its powers, shall have the right to determine the content of the contract, provided that the application is substantiated, only in the following manner: a) the media service is also distributed in the subscription service or programme package of the media service distributor providing the largest access, b) the media service distributor shall not have the right to receive any consideration (including the fee for the installation of the reception of the programme distribution) for the transmission of the media services as per Paragraphs (1)-(3) and (7) of Article 75, and the media service provider shall not have the right to receive a programme fee, c) the term of the contract concluded in terms of the distribution of the media service shall be one year, with the proviso that if neither party notifies the other contracting party, in writing, of its intention to discontinue the contract at least 90 days in advance of the expiry of the term of the contract, the term of the contract shall be automatically extended by one year, on one occasion, under unchanged contractual conditions. Article 77 (1)

The media service distributor shall send to the Office all agreements concluded with media service providers within the framework of its "must carry" obligation defined in this Chapter, as well as the amendments thereto, within thirty days from their conclusion or amendment, and shall notify the Office of the termination of such agreements within thirty days following the date of termination. (2) The media service distributors and media service providers shall provide data upon the Authority's request in connection with the "must carry" obligation regulated in this Chapter.

Obligation to Offer Media Services

Article 78 (1) Media service providers with significant market power and media service providers in which or in the owner of which an influential media service distributor or the owner thereof has a qualifying holding (for the purposes of Articles 78-81 hereinafter jointly referred to as obliged media service provider) shall be subject to the obligations defined under Paragraph (2) in respect of all their linear media services. (2) The obliged media service provider shall have an obligation to contract in respect of all its linear media services according to the fair and reasonable contract offers of the media service distributor. The obliged media service provider shall be subject to an obligation to contract in respect of each linear media service separately. (3) The conclusion of an agreement subjecting any of the other media services of the obliged media service provider, which are not essential for the distribution of the given media service, or the purchase or use of other services or products may not be set by the obliged media service provider as a precondition of the conclusion of an agreement pertaining to any of its media services or of the determination of the material contents of such agreement (prohibition on tying). (4)

The obliged media service provider and media service distributor shall determine the agreement and the contractual terms and conditions thereof – in particular, but not exclusively, the fee – in line with the principle of equal treatment, by setting an affordable price level and by taking into account the principles of technological neutrality and economies of scale. In the course of this, the obliged media service provider shall not differentiate between the contract offers of the media service distributors, unless it is justified. Parties shall be entitled to amend the agreement in terms of the fee once a year, reckoned from the date the agreement was concluded. (5) For the purposes of this Act it shall be regarded as a behaviour violating the principle of equal treatment, in particular, if the obliged media service provider a) unreasonably subjects distribution of the programme flow to technical conditions which a decisive proportion of media service distributors are unable to meet, or b) determines such pricing terms and tariffs – including volume discount – in the course of determining the fee payable by the media service distributors, so that upon application of these terms and tariffs, the most advantageous terms would become available only to a few media service distributors. (6) The offer may be rejected if performance of the commitments contained in the offer is impossible due to objective technical or economic reasons, and the parties cannot come to an agreement regarding these terms within the framework of the procedure aimed at conclusion of the agreement. (7) In case of any doubt, the obliged media service provider shall be responsible to prove that refusal of the offer was well-founded.

Article 79 (1) In order to ensure the proper and transparent satisfaction of the obligation to contract defined in Article 78 (2), the obliged media service provider shall determine the general contractual framework conditions related to the distribution of its media service, and shall publish such conditions on its website. (2) The obliged media service provider shall determine its general contractual framework conditions as per Paragraph (1) in line with the requirements of rationality in such a way as to ensure that they are justified, transparent and verifiable. Conditions contrary to these shall not be applied. (3) The provisions of Paragraphs (1)-(2) shall apply to the following contractual terms and conditions: a) the contractual framework conditions regarding the programme fee payable to the obliged media service provider, in particular the principles, method, period of application of the pricing policy of the obliged media service provider and the method and date of payment, b) the procedure applicable for the conclusion of the agreement, the method and terms for using the service and its technical, economic or other restrictions, if any, c) cases and conditions of amendment or termination of the agreement, d) cases of interruption of the service, e) breach of the agreement and the legal sanctions thereof. (4)

In the event of modification of the contractual terms and conditions, the obliged media service provider shall make the new contractual terms and conditions available at least thirty days prior to the entry into force of the new contractual terms and conditions. (5) The Office shall monitor the fulfilment of the obligations set forth under Paragraphs (1)-(4). Article 80 (1) The media service distributor shall be entitled to initiate the legal dispute procedure as per Articles 172-174 if a) the agreement as per Article 78 (2) is not concluded within thirty days of making the offer, or b) the obliged media service provider has violated the authorised media service distributor's right or legitimate interest laid down by law or in an agreement, affecting distribution of the media services. (2) If the amount of the fee payable by the media service distributor is contested, the obliged media service provider shall be responsible to prove the legitimacy of the pricing and that the proceedings have been conducted in line with the requirement of equal treatment. Article 81 (1) The obliged media service provider shall send to the Office all agreements, and the amendments thereof, concluded with media service distributors within the framework of the obligation defined in Article 78 within thirty days of their conclusion or amendment, and shall notify the Office of the termination of such agreements within thirty days of termination. (2) The obliged media service providers and the media service distributors shall provide data upon the Authority's request in connection with the obligation defined in Articles 78-79.

BASIC PRINCIPLES AND OBJECTIVES OF PUBLIC MEDIA SERVICES

Article 82 Public media service is characterised by the following: a) it operates independently from both the State and from economic operators, furthermore the managers of the public media service provider and those involved in its activities have professional autonomy within the applicable legislative framework, b) its system ensures accountability and the existence of social control, c) its operations are financed primarily from the joint voluntary contributions of those living in Hungary, from public funding, d) its activities cannot be primarily focused on profit-making.

The Objectives of Public Media Services Article 83 (1) The objectives of public media service are as follows:

a) to provide media services which are comprehensive in both the social and the cultural sense, aiming to address as many social classes and culturally distinct groups and individuals as possible,

b) to support, sustain and enrich national, community and European identity, culture and the Hungarian language,

c) to promote and strengthen national cohesion and social integration, and to respect the institution of marriage and the value of family,

d) to provide information about and support constitutional rights, the fundamental values of law and order and the rules of democratic social order,

e) to satisfy the media related needs of nationalities, religious communities and other communities, present their culture, support and sustain the mother tongues of nationalities,

f) to satisfy the media service related special needs of underprivileged groups who are at a great disadvantage due to their age, physical, mental or psychological state or social circumstances, as well as of people with disabilities,

g) to serve the cultural needs of Hungarians living abroad, promote preservation of their national identity and mother tongue and enable them to have spiritual relations with their mother country,

h) to broadcast programmes serving the physical, mental and moral development and interest of minors and widening their knowledge, as well as educational and information programmes serving child protection purposes,

i) to accomplish educational and information tasks and present the latest scientific findings,

j) to disseminate information promoting healthy lifestyles, protection of the environment, nature and landscape conservation, public security and transport safety,

k) to present programmes about the social, economic and cultural life in Hungary and of various areas within the Carpathian Basin,

l) to present Hungary and Hungarian culture, as well as the culture of the nationalities living in Hungary to Europe and to the world,

m) to provide a balanced, accurate, thorough, objective and responsible news service and information,

n) to confront dissenting opinions with one another, conduct debates about community affairs, contribute to the freedom of opinion based on the provision of reliable information,

o) to broadcast a rich palette of diverse programme flows representing different values, present high quality entertainment, as well as programmes generating widespread interest,

p) to implement high quality programme-making across every segment of the programme flow, reasonable and justified involvement in media market competition. (2) Public media service strives to: a) ensure innovation in the media profession, the continuous improvement of professional standards and the use of high ethical standards in the media service, b) boldly use new technologies and methods serving media service distribution, play a pivotal role in discovering new digital and Internet media services and exploit these in the public's interest, c) promote acquisition and development of knowledge and skills needed for media literacy through its programmes and through other activities outside the scope of media services,

d) support Hungarian cinematographic art and present new Hungarian cinematographic works, e) serve public interest through activities outside the scope of media services, such as book publishing or active involvement in theatre events. (3) The public media service provider shall contribute to the long-term preservation, archiving and professional collection and care of cultural values and documents of historical significance that come into its possession in the course of performing its activities.

THE PUBLIC SERVICE FOUNDATION

Article 84 (1) The Parliament establishes the Public Service Foundation (hereinafter as: Public Foundation) to ensure the provision of public media service and public news service and to protect their independence. The Public Foundation is the owner of the Duna Media Service Provider Non-Profit Private Limited Company (hereinafter referred to as: the public media service provider). (2) The initial assets of the Public Foundation shall be determined by the Parliament in a parliamentary decision. (3) The Parliament shall adopt and may amend the Public Foundation's Statutes. Issues relating to the operation and organisational structure of the Public Foundation not regulated in this Act or the Statutes shall be specified in the Public Foundation's By-laws. (4) Unless otherwise specified by this Act, the general rules governing foundations shall apply to the Public Foundation.

Board of Trustees of the Public Service Foundation

Article 85 (1) The managing body of the Public Foundation is the Board of Trustees. (2) The responsibilities and the framework of the activities of the Board of Trustees shall be determined in the Public Foundation's Statutes, in line with this Act. (3) The Board of Trustees shall, within the framework of this Act and the Public Foundation's Statutes, define and adopt its own procedural rules, as well as the Public Foundation's By-laws. These procedural rules shall include the rules governing the substitution of the Chairperson of the Board of Trustees. (4) The activities of the Board of Trustees shall be supported by the Board of Trustees' Office (hereinafter as: Board of Trustees' Office). The administrative, management and procedural duties of the Board of Trustees shall be fulfilled by the Board of Trustees' Office. The Board of Trustees and the members of the Board of Trustees shall be entitled to avail themselves of expert assistance via the Board of Trustees' Office. The terms and conditions of employing experts as well as the operating conditions of the Board of Trustees' Office shall be set out in the Public Foundation's By-laws.

Composition of the Board of Trustees

Article 86 (1) The Parliament shall elect six members to the Board of Trustees by voting for each member individually. (2) Half of the members who may be elected by the Parliament to the Board of Trustees shall be nominated by the governing factions, while the other half shall be nominated by the opposition factions. Both the governing factions and the opposition factions shall agree among themselves upon the candidates who may be nominated by the respective side. (3) Nominations for candidates shall be made within eight days following the commencement of the election procedure. The election shall be held within eight days of the nomination of candidates. (4) Should any faction fail to participate in the nomination, the other factions of the given side may exercise the given side's right to nominate. (5) A new candidate shall be nominated in place of a non-elected candidate within eight days, and the new election shall be held within the subsequent eight days. A person who did not receive at least one-third of the votes of all the Members of Parliament in the course of the previous election may not be renominated. (6)

The Chairperson of the Board of Trustees and one other member shall be delegated by the Media Council for a term of nine years. (7) The Board of Trustees shall be deemed to have come to existence when its members have been elected, and its Chairperson, and one other member, have been delegated by the Media Council. The member of the Board of Trustees elected by the Parliament shall take an oath according to the provisions of the Act on the Oath and Pledge of Certain Public Law Officials, whereas the Chairperson and the delegated member shall take the oath upon taking up their offices, in front of the President of the Parliament, with text determined under the Act on the Oath and Pledge of Certain Public Law Officials. (8)

The formation of the Board of Trustees shall not be prevented by failure of either the governing or the opposition side to make a nomination, or by not all nominees obtaining the necessary majority or, upon the application of Paragraph (5), by the new nominee not obtaining the necessary majority. In this case the Board of Trustees shall come into existence with the election of at least three members. (9) When formed with less than the full headcount, the Board of Trustees may be completed up to the full headcount in accordance with the provisions of Article 87. (10)

Members of the Board of Trustees shall be elected by the Parliament for a term of nine years. The mandate of the elected and delegated members shall expire at the same time, i.e. after nine years from the date of election of the elected members by the Parliament. Article 87 (1) If the mandate of an elected member terminates before the expiry of the period defined in Article 86 (10), the nomination and election of the new member shall take place in accordance with Paragraphs (2)-(7). (2)

If the nomination of a new member takes place within the same Parliamentary cycle as the one in which other members of the Board of Trustee are elected, or if no change has occurred in respect of the factions of the governing side and the opposition side following Parliamentary elections held after this Parliamentary cycle, then the provisions of Article 86 (2)-(4) shall apply to the nomination, with the provision that the right of nomination shall be vested in that (governing or opposition) side that originally nominated the member (who was elected) and who is to be replaced through the new nomination process, after his/her mandate expired. (3) If the nomination of a new member takes place after the Parliamentary cycle during which the members of the Board of Trustee were elected, then, provided that there is a change regarding the factions of the governing and the opposition side following the Parliamentary elections held after the Parliamentary cycle during which the Board of Trustees was elected, a nominating committee consisting of one member of each Parliamentary faction shall propose a candidate by unanimous vote within fifteen days following the establishment of the nominating committee. (4)

Should the nominating committee fail to nominate a member within the deadline defined under Paragraph (3), the nominating committee may then propose a candidate within another period of eight days with at least two-thirds of the votes. In the course of this, the number of votes held by the individual members of the nominating committee shall be proportionate to the size, at the time of voting, of the Parliamentary faction nominating the given member. (5)

In the course of candidate nomination under Paragraphs (3)-(4), the nominating committee shall take into consideration any changes taking place regarding the governing and the opposition side, such as when a Parliamentary faction changes the side to which it belongs, or in case of establishment of a new faction or the termination of an existing faction. (6)

Should the nominating committee fail to nominate a sufficient number of candidates even under the scenario defined in Paragraph (4), a new nominating committee shall be established. (7)

After a successful nomination, the Parliament shall elect the new member for the remaining term of the mandate of the members of the already operational, elected Board of Trustees. The new member of the Board of Trustees shall take an oath according to the provisions of the Act on the Oath and Pledge of Certain Public Law Officials. (8) In case of early termination of the mandate of the Chairperson of the Board of Trustees or a Board of Trustees member delegated by the Media Council, the Media Council shall, within fifteen days, delegate a new Chairperson/member for the period lasting until the mandate of the members of the Board of Trustees expires. Article 88 (1)

Conflict of interest rules stated in Article 118 (1)-(2) pertaining to the Chairperson and members of the Board of Trustees, the President, Vice President, Director General and Deputy Director General of the Authority, as well as the rules stated in Article 118 (3) shall apply as appropriate. (2) Neither the Chairperson of the Board of Trustees nor its members may be engaged in an employment relationship with the Public Foundation, and may not accept remuneration under any legal title from the public media service provider. (3) The Chairperson and members of the Board of Trustees may not establish any work-related legal relationship with the public media service provider within one year following the termination of their mandate. (4) If the Chairperson of the Board of Trustees or any of its members fail to meet their verification obligation despite being asked to do so as defined in Article 89 (4) due to their own fault, or if any conflict of interest arises in respect of a member of the Board of Trustees or its Chairperson, and the conflict of interest is not eliminated within thirty days of the emergence of the cause of the conflict of interest or of the date of the meeting establishing the conflict of interest, the plenary meeting of the Board of Trustees shall adopt a decision terminating the Board membership of the Chairperson or the member of Board of Trustees. The Chairperson or member of the Board of Trustees may not exercise his/her powers arising from his/her office as of the date of the adoption of the decision establishing a conflict of interest. (5)

The mandate shall be terminated by way of dismissal if the Chairperson or any member of the Board of Trustees is placed under guardianship affecting his/her legal capacity. (6)

The mandate shall be terminated by exclusion, if a) the Chairperson or member of the Board of Trustees is unable to fulfil his/her responsibilities arising from his/her mandate for more than six consecutive months for reasons within his/her control, or b) if as a result of criminal proceedings instituted against any member or the Chairperson of the Board of Trustees, the Chairperson or member is declared guilty by the court's final judgement delivering a term of imprisonment, or banning him/her from exercising his/her profession corresponding to the activities of the Board of Trustees or prohibition from participation in public affairs. (7) The mandate of the Chairperson or a member of the Board of Trustees shall terminate upon his/her death. Article 89 (1) Termination of the mandate of the Chairperson or a member of the Board of Trustees due to conflict of interest, dismissal or exclusion shall be established and announced by the plenary meeting of the Board of Trustees. (2) In the plenary meeting of the Board of Trustees adopts a decision about a conflict of interest, dismissal or exclusion, the Chairperson or member affected by such decision may not take part in the voting process, and the unanimous decision of those entitled to vote is required to resolve such matters. If an unanimous decision is not reached in case of a repeated voting concerning the issues mentioned above, the Chairperson of the Board of Trustees shall initiate the decision making of the Parliament on the subject matter. In this case, the Parliament shall adopt a decision on the conflict of interest, dismissal or exclusion. (3)

If any suspicion of a conflict of interest arises in relation to the Chairperson of the Board of Trustees, then the member designated in the procedural rules of the Board of Trustees shall exercise the powers of the Chairperson in the proceedings defined under Paragraphs (5)-(6). (4) If any information comes to light suggesting that any of the legal sanctions defined in Article 88 (6) (b) are applicable to any member of the Board of Trustees, then the Chairperson of the Board of Trustees shall call upon the concerned member of the Board of Trustees in writing, by designating a deadline and by specifying the legal sanctions of failure to comply, to verify having a clean criminal record and not being banned from exercising a profession corresponding to its activities with the Board of Trustees or prohibited from participating in public affairs. (5) The Chairperson of the Board of Trustees shall be in charge of handling the personal data of the members of the Board of Trustees that have come to his/her knowledge pursuant to Paragraph (4) until termination of the mandate of the member of the Board of Trustees. (6)

The provisions of Paragraphs (4)-(5) shall apply to the Chairperson of the Board of Trustees, with the difference that the Chairperson of the Board of Trustees shall fulfil his/her verification obligation defined under Paragraph (4) to the Board of Trustees, whereas the right defined under Paragraph (5) shall be exercised by the Board of Trustees. The Chairperson of the Board of Trustees shall not be involved in exercising the powers of the Board of Trustees defined in this Paragraph.

Powers and Responsibilities of the Board of Trustees

Article 90 (1) The Board of Trustees: a) monitors whether the objectives of the public media service are fulfilled through the activities of the public media service provider, b) if, according to the opinion of the Board of Trustees, the behaviour of the public media service provider seriously violates or threatens the attainment of public media service objectives, then it may initiate the Media Council's proceedings, c) safeguards the independence of the public media service provider, d) establishes and amends the Statutes of public media service provider, and publishes these in the Hungarian Gazette, e) elects the CEO of the public media service provider, and determines the terms and conditions of his employment contract and remuneration, f) may terminate the employment relationship of the CEO of the public media service provider, g) elects the Chairperson and members of the joint Supervisory Board of the public media service provider, and may also remove these, h) appoints the auditor of the public media service provider, and may terminate the mandate of such auditor. The responsibilities, powers and competence of the auditor are regulated by the Board of Trustees in the Statutes of the public media service provider, in accordance with the provisions of the Civil Code applicable to business associations and the Accounting Act, i) approves the annual financial management plan of the Public Foundation and adopts its balance sheet, j) exercises the rights of the General Meeting in relation to public media service provider pursuant to the provisions of the Civil Code applicable to business associations, subject to the deviations set forth in this Act, k) manages the Public Foundation's assets in its capacity as trustee of the Public Foundation

l) may increase or decrease the equity capital of the public media service provider, as regulated by the Public Foundation's Statutes,

m) approves the principles and key accounts of the public media service provider's annual financial management and financial plans,

n) approves the public media service provider's balance sheet and profit and loss statement,

o) monitors the funding and financial management of the public media service provider in terms of compliance with applicable requirements of the European Union, p) may grant prior authorisation for negotiating such contracts having a value of more than three hundred million forints which the public media service provider wishes to conclude, q) may grant the prior approval necessary for the public media service provider to take out a loan or to conclude contracts having a value of more than one hundred million forints, or to amend or terminate any of the contracts concluded according to the above mentioned provisions, r) carries out other duties defined in this Act. (2) For the purposes of Paragraph (1) (p)-(q), the value of the services to be provided by the public media service provider under various contracts concluded with the same contracting party during the same calendar year, regardless of their content, shall be aggregated. Article 91 (1) The Public Foundation shall exercise the founders' and shareholders' rights in respect of the public media service provider, as defined by the provisions of the Civil Code applicable to business associations. However, it is not entitled:

a) to change the basic scope of activities of the public media service provider,

b) to terminate or transform the public media service provider or to transform it into another organisational form,

c) to withdraw assets from the public media service provider,

d) to define the programme flow structure of the public media service provider, as well as the content of its programme flow, other services or programmes,

e) to give instructions to the CEO of the public media service provider in respect of the employer's rights exercised by such CEO,

f) to decide in matters falling within the competence of the CEO of another organisation or of the public media service provider pursuant to this Act. (2) The Public Foundation's Board of Trustees cannot extend its powers defined in Article 90, not even with the founder's rights defined by the provisions of the Civil Code applicable to business associations, but not included in Article 90.

Operation of the Board of Trustees

Article 92 (1) The Board of Trustees shall meet with the frequency required for fulfilling its responsibilities, but at least once every month. The CEO of the public media service provider shall be invited to attend the discussions of any items on the agenda relating to General Meeting issues. The Chairperson of the Board of Trustees shall convene an extraordinary meeting of the Board of Trustees within eight days if the majority of the members of the Board of Trustee so requests by determining the agenda of such meeting. In case of failure to do so, the initiators are collectively entitled to convene the extraordinary meeting. (2) Members of the Board of Trustees, including the Chairperson of the Board of Trustees, shall have equal voting rights. In the event of a tie vote, the vote of the Chairperson shall be decisive. (3) The Board of Trustees has quorum when more than half of its members are present. (4) The Board of Trustees shall adopt its decisions by a simple majority of the votes of its members and the Chairperson, unless otherwise stipulated by the Act. (5) The Chairperson of the Board of Trustees shall draw up the agenda for the meeting and preside over the meeting. Any member may make a proposal concerning the agenda in advance and in

Remuneration of the Chairperson and Members of the Board of Trustees

Article 93 The Chairperson of the Board of Trustees shall be entitled to a honorarium equalling sixty-five percent of the remuneration of state secretaries, whereas members of the Board of Trustees shall be entitled to forty percent of the remuneration of state secretaries, and they may require reimbursement of expenses up to fifty percent of the amount of their honorarium at most. Further rules pertaining to the rate of reimbursement of expenses shall be set forth in the Public Foundation's By-laws

Financial Management of the Public Foundation

Article 94 (1) The revenues of the Public Foundation shall comprise the following: a) financial support received from the Fund to finance operations, b) the proceeds from the assets of the Public Foundation, c) the proceeds from the utilization of assets managed by the Public Foundation, d) other revenues serving foundation purposes (subsidies, targeted subsidies from the state budget, payments made to the foundation). (2) The expenditures of the Public Foundation comprise the following: a) contributions to the operating and development expenses of the public media service provider, b) the Public Foundation's own expenses, expenditures. (3) The Public Foundation may not carry out for-profit economic activities, may not found other business associations and may not acquire shares in other operating business associations, and is not entitled to establish foundations.

THE PUBLIC SERVICE CODE AND THE BOARD OF PUBLIC SERVICES

Article 95 (1) The Public Service Code (hereinafter as: the Code) contains, in accordance with this Act, the basic principles governing public media services and fine-tunes the public service objectives defined in this Act. The Code may have a general content and also a content relating to individual public media services separately. Fundamentally, the Code is meant to provide guidance to the public media service provider regarding the appropriate operating principles of the public media services within the framework of the Act. (2) The Code will first be adopted by the Media Council with the consent of the Board of Trustees and with a view to the opinion of the CEO of the public media service provider. (3) The Code may be amended by the Board of Public Services, following its first approval in accordance with Paragraph (2), with the Board of Trustees' consent. Apart from the Board of Public Services, an amendment may also be initiated by the Board of Trustees and the CEO of the public media service provider. (4) The Institute for Media Studies operating under the aegis of the Media Council shall provide professional support to the drafting and amendment of the Code. (5)

Enforcement of the rules defined by the Code shall be supervised by the Board of Public Services. Article 96 The Code can, among other things, regulate the following: a) the means and method of attaining the statutory objectives of public media service, b) the basic principles of independence from political parties and political organisations, c) the principles regarding the presentation of the diversity, objectivity and balanced nature of news and timely political programmes, presentation of disputed matters and the diversity of opinions and views, d) the criteria for supporting and sustaining the mother tongue culture, e) the principles of the rules of presenting the culture and life of the nationalities living in Hungary, f) the principles of presenting cultural, scientific, ideological and religious diversity, g) the principles of performing tasks with regard to the protection of minors, h) the principles relating to ethical norms governing the broadcasting of commercial communications, advertising activities and the sponsorship of programmes, i) the principles of communicating public service announcements, j) the principles relating to the extent and guarantees of the autonomy and responsibility of production companies employed by the public media service provider, and to the guarantees of their participation in the definition of the principles of the production and editing of programmes,

k) the principles of keeping members of the Hungarian nation living abroad adequately informed, and also of providing adequate information about them, l) the principles of formulating basic ethical rules, other than those in this Act, applying to staff members, with special regard to those employed in relation to news and political programmes.

The Board of Public Services

Article 97 (1) The Board of Public Services is composed of fourteen members, its Chairperson is elected by its own members from among themselves, it adopts its decisions with a simple majority of votes, unless this Act stipulates otherwise. In the event of a tie vote, the vote of the Chairperson shall be decisive. (2) Members of the Board of Public Services are delegated by the nominating organisations defined in Annex 1 of this Act for a term of three years, in the manner as defined in the Annex. Members may be delegated several times. Failure by any of these organisations to exercise their delegation right shall not impede the operation of the Board of Public Services. (3) Members of the Board of Public Services shall be delegated at least thirty days prior to the expiry date of the previous members' mandate. (4) The secretarial duties of the Board of Public Services shall be provided for by the Public Foundation's Office and its costs – including the honorarium of the Chairperson and the members – shall be borne by the Public Foundation. (5) The Chairperson of the Board of Public Services shall be entitled to a honorarium equalling forty percent of the remuneration of state secretaries, whereas its members are entitled to twenty-five percent of the remuneration of state secretaries. In addition to this, the Chairperson and members may require reimbursement of their travel expenses as necessary for performing their tasks relating to the Board. The conflict of interest rules defined in Article 118 shall be applied regarding the Chairperson and the members – with the exception of those stipulated in Point e) of Article 118 (1) – as appropriate. (6) The Board of Public Services guarantees social control over the public media service provider. (7) The Board of Public Services constantly monitors how public service orientation is manifested, and exercises control in accordance with Paragraphs (8)-(13) over the public media service provider in relation to the enforcement of the provisions of this Act. (8) Once every year, by 28 February of the year following the current calendar year, the CEO of the public media service provider prepares a report on whether the media service provider, according to his own assessment, has fulfilled the requirements outlined in this Act regarding the objectives and basic principles of public media service. (9)

The Board of Public Services shall discuss the report and decide on the acceptance thereof by a simple majority. (10) If the Board of Public Services, after having personally interviewed the CEO, decides to reject the report, the Board of Public Services may consider submitting a proposal to the Board of Trustees for the termination of the CEO's employment relationship. Adopting such a proposal requires the two-thirds majority of the members of the Board of Public Services. (11) The Board of Trustees shall put on its agenda and debate the proposal for the termination of the CEO's employment relationship within eight days. The CEO and the Chairperson of the Board of Public Services shall be invited to the meeting of the Board of Trustees. (12) The Board of Trustees shall decide on the proposal to terminate the employment relationship by a simple majority of the members present. The decision needs to be accompanied with a justification. (13) If the Board of Trustees does not terminate the CEO's employment relationship despite the proposal, then in three months time the Board of Public Services shall put a new hearing of the CEO on its agenda. (14) If the CEO's employment relationship was terminated due to his/her failure to ensure implementation of public service objectives and principles, then he/she may not be re-nominated for the CEO's position of the public media service provider for a period of ten years.

THE PUBLIC MEDIA SERVICE PROVIDER

Article 98 (1) The public media service provider is responsible for implementing the objectives of public media service as defined in Article 83. The media service provider shall fulfil this task by coordinating the activities of the public media services. (2) The rules pertaining to companies limited by shares, as defined by the provisions of the Civil Code applicable to business associations shall apply, as appropriate, to the public media service provider, including the common rules applicable to business associations as well, unless otherwise provided for by this Act. (3) The public media service provider shall hold one non-marketable share. (4) The public media service provider shall not pay any media service provision fee. (5) The public media service provider shall provide at least one radio and at least one audiovisual linear public media service to the overwhelming majority of the population of Hungary. Services provided to the overwhelming majority of the population shall mean, for radio media services, terrestrial media services that may be received by eighty percent of the population in the 87.5 to 108.0 MHz frequency band, or, for audiovisual media services, media services available to ninety percent of the population. (6) In addition to its national media services, the public media service provider may also provide local or regional media services. (7)

The Media Council shall decide on the media service facilities used by the individual public media service provider – including media services targeted at foreign countries as well – on the basis of technical, economic, and media policy considerations and after consultation with the CEO of the Fund. (8) In relation to public audiovisual and radio media services, the Media Council – after consultation with the CEO of the Fund and taking into consideration economic and budgetary planning related considerations for the next year, and with regard to the fulfilment of the public service objectives set forth in Article 83 of this Act – may supervise the system of public media services annually and may decide whether to maintain the existing media services of the public media service provider or to change the system thereof. (9) For the purpose of facilitating the implementation of the objectives of public media service, to the required degree, the pieces of legislation governing the restriction (in terms of gross vehicle weight, axle load and size) of usage of vehicles in road traffic on the area of Hungary and the related tariff payment obligations and time limits shall not be applied for the motor-vehicles operated and used by the public media service provider and/or the Fund in the course of programme production.

Appearance of Nationalities in Public Media Service

Article 99 (1) All nationalities recognised by Hungary are entitled to support and sustain their culture and mother tongue, and to be regularly informed in their mother tongue by way of separate programmes aired through public media service. (2) The responsibility defined under Paragraph (1) shall be fulfilled by the public media service provider via national or, having regard to the geographic location of the nationality, via local media services by airing programmes satisfying the needs of the nationality in question, or via audiovisual media services using subtitles or broadcasting in multiple languages, as required. (3) The national local governments of nationalities, or (in the absence of such local governments) their national organisations, shall independently decide on the principles of allocation of the transmission time made available to them by the public media service provider. The public media service provider shall abide by these principles, but these may not affect the contents and editing of the programme.

Public Service Media Assets and the Archive of the Public Media Service Provider

Article 100 (1) All ownership rights and obligations associated with public service media assets that are owned by the State shall be exercised by the Fund, with the exceptions set forth under Paragraphs (2), (5) and (6). (2) The Fund may not alienate, transfer or encumber public service media assets in any way, neither in full nor in part. This prohibition does not exclude the utilisation of copyright, related rights and usage rights existing with respect to certain items of the public service media assets. (3) The Fund shall be responsible for the storage, safekeeping and use of public service media assets and also those physical data carriers containing works and other subject matter subject to Act LXXVI of 1999 on Copyrights (hereinafter referred to as: the Copyright Act), acquired by the public media service provider and the Fund, which do not fall within the scope of public service media assets (hereinafter jointly referred to as: the Archive). The Archive shall qualify as a public collection with a nationwide collection area. (4) The detailed archiving rules as well as detailed rules of preserving, maintaining and utilisation of the Archive shall be defined by the Fund's CEO in a regulation, with the agreement of the Media Council. (5) The Fund may transfer to the public media service provider any copyrighted works belonging to the public service media assets, as well as other intellectual property which fall outside the scope of public service media assets but in respect of which the Fund has a usage right, for purpose of utilisation required for performance of the public media service provider's public service tasks (among others, in particular, for the purpose of transmission to the general public), without the need for any separate permission or payment. The public media service provider is granted a free of charge right to use those items of the public service media assets which are used by it. (6) Copyrighted works and other intellectual property located in the Archive, constituting part of the public service media assets, as well as those that fall outside the scope of public service media assets may be used by the Fund and the public media service provider within the framework of the Copyright Act and the terms and conditions of agreements concluded with copyright owners and holders of related rights. (7) Unless otherwise agreed, the provisions contained in Article 30 (3) of the Copyright Act shall not be applied in terms of the acquisition of the right of use by the public media service provider over the items of the public service media assets which are used by it.

Strategic Plan of the Public Service Media and Measurement of Public Service Value

Article 100/A (1) The public media service provider shall be obliged to prepare a general strategic plan for each year, until 31 May of the year preceding the target year, wherein it shall identify and evaluate the possible directions and ways of improvement of the quality of public media services, taking into account, in particular, among others, the following criteria: a) international and Hungarian media market trends, b) technological developments and innovations, c) the experience learned from the procedures targeting the reviewing and monitoring of public service value as per Article 100/B, d) the contents of the Public Service Code, e) opinion of the Board of Public

Services, f) results of the examination of public service value, g) viewing and listenership figures and other media consumption data. (2) In addition to the general strategic plan, on an ad hoc basis, the public media service provider shall also be obliged to prepare strategic plans in terms of certain sub-issues of the media service, adjusted to the needs of the public media service. (3) The strategic plans specified under Paragraphs (1)-(2) must also be in line with the provisions of this Act, the requirements laid down in the Code, and the respective recommendations and rules of the European Union and the Council of Europe. (4) The strategic plans specified under Paragraphs (1)-(2) shall serve as the basis of the operation of the public media service, and the cooperation between the public media service provider and the Fund. Article 100/B (1) The public media service provider shall be obliged to examine and check the public service nature and value of its services as well as their impact on the diversity of the media market. (2) The detailed rules of examination of the public service value shall be regulated under the respective set of regulations, to be adopted jointly by all of the organisations or bodies affected by the procedure, at the initiative and under the coordination of the public media service provider. (3) In the course of creation and possible amendments of the regulations specified under Paragraph (2), the provisions of this Act, the requirements laid down in the Code, and the respective recommendations and rules of the European Union and the Council of Europe must be taken into account.

The News Agency Tasks of the Public Media Service Provider

Article 101 (1) The public media service provider shall perform the following news agency tasks in addition to implementing the objectives defined under Article 83: a) provides news items, news reports, photographs, data carriers, background materials, graphic images and documentary information about events of general public interest, taking place either in Hungary or abroad, b) provides access to all such news items and news reports, which the general public needs to know in order to adequately enforce community and individual rights and interests, c) plays a role in transmitting public service announcements made by public authorities, other organizations or natural persons to the printed and electronic media, d) provides regular and factual information about the actions of parliamentary parties, other political parties, significant non-governmental organizations, the Government, public administration entities, local governments, courts and prosecutor's offices, and shall make the official communications related to the above public, e) provides regular and factual information to foreign countries about the most important events taking place in Hungary and the main processes in the country's life, f) provides information regularly and factually about the lives of Hungarians living outside the borders of Hungary, and provides news services to them, g) provides regular and factual information about the life of nationalities living in Hungary, h) ensures provision of information, as outlined in a separate Act, during election periods, i) in a state of national crisis or state of emergency performs the duties outlined in a separate Act, j) ensures long-term preservation and protection of cultural values and original documents of historical importance that come into its possession in the course of performing its activities, k) participates in the work of international news agency organisations. (2) The public media service provider, in order to fulfil its news agency tasks, shall operate a) a network of correspondents covering all counties of Hungary as well as the Hungarian capital, b) a network of correspondents covering all areas within the Carpathian Basin which have a Hungarian population, c) a network of foreign correspondents as the country's international relations and interests may require. (3) In case of a national crisis, state of emergency or state of danger, or if the territory of Hungary is subject to unexpected attack by foreign armed groups, furthermore, in the event of having to defend the territorial integrity of the country by the anti-aircraft and stand-by air forces of the Hungarian Defence Forces, the Parliament, the National Defence Council, the President of the Republic and the Government, and/or persons and entities defined by law may, to the extent necessitated by the given situation, order the public media service provider (within the scope of its news agency activities), in accordance with Article 32 (6), to provide information.

Electing the CEO of the Public Media Service Provider

Article 102 (1) The public media service provider shall be managed by the CEO, as there is no Board of Directors. The CEO shall, within the framework of this Act, exercise all the powers referred to the Board of Directors of a company limited by shares by the respective provisions of the Civil Code applicable to business associations. An employment contract shall be executed with the CEO, and his/her remuneration shall be defined as a monthly sum payable by the public media service provider. (2) The Board of Trustees shall exercise the employer's rights in respect of the CEO of the public media service provider, which includes the appointment of the CEO and the termination of his employment relationship. The CEO shall be nominated and appointed in the following step-by-step order:

a) the President of the Media Council proposes two CEO candidates to the Media Council; b) if the Media Council approves of these candidates, then it shall submit the nominations to the Board of Trustees, in order to have one of the candidates selected; c) if the Media Council does not approve of one of the candidates proposed by the President of the Media Council, then the President of the Media Council shall propose a new candidate; the Media Council may make a proposal to the Board of Trustees only if it had approved two candidates; d) the Media Council may also make a proposal regarding the contents of the CEO's employment contract; e) during the first round of voting, the Board of Trustees shall come to a decision concerning the appointment of the CEO by a two-thirds majority of all of its members, including its Chairperson; f) if the Board of Trustees cannot make a selection from the two candidates by a two-thirds majority within thirty days from the date on which they were nominated by the Media Council, then a new nomination procedure shall be conducted; g) in the course of the new nomination, two new candidates shall be proposed again; h) during the vote, taking place after the new nomination, the Board of Trustees shall come to a decision concerning the appointment of the CEO by a simple majority of all of its members, including its Chairperson. (3)

The Board of Trustees shall come to a decision by vote concerning the appointment of the CEO and the terms and conditions of his/her employment contract, drawn up with a view to the Media Council's proposal. The CEO's employment contract shall be concluded for an indefinite period. Should the elected CEO refuse to accept the terms and conditions of the draft employment contract determined by the Board of Trustees, then the Board of Trustees shall take a repeated vote on the employment contract containing the amended terms and conditions. If no agreement can be reached on the terms and conditions of the employment contract, then a new CEO shall be elected. (4) The CEO's employment relationship shall terminate in the following cases: a) upon his/her dismissal; b) by termination with notice as per his/her employment contract; c) upon his/her death; d) in the event regulated by Article 97 (10)-(12), provided that the Board of Trustees decides in favour of termination based on the proposal made by the Board of Public Services. (5) The CEO's employment relationship shall be terminated by dismissal, if a) he/she is placed under guardianship affecting his/her legal capacity; b) if, as a result of criminal proceedings instituted against him/her, he/she is pronounced guilty by the court's final judgement delivering a term of imprisonment; c) he/she is unable to fulfil his/her responsibilities for three consecutive months for reasons beyond his/her control; d) he/she is in breach of conflict of interest rules, and fails to eliminate such conflict of interest within thirty days of the date on which such conflict of interest has arisen; e) he/she has been banned by the court from exercising his/her profession or has been prohibited from participating in public affairs. (6) In case of dismissal, the termination of employment shall be established by the Board of Trustees. (7)

The CEO has the right to appoint one or more Deputy CEOs. The terms and conditions of the employment contracts of the Deputy CEOs shall be approved by the Board of Trustees. Article 103 (1) Persons eligible for the position of the CEO of the public media service provider include those Hungarian citizens with a clean criminal record and a diploma of higher education, who have at least five years of relevant work experience. (2) Relevant work experience shall include previous experience in programme-making, broadcasting, information, as well as related technical, legal, managerial, administrative, economic, cultural, scientific and opinion polling activities. (3) Those, who at any time during the two years prior to the date of election, held the post of President of the Republic, Prime Minister, member of the Government, State Secretary, State Secretary for Public Administration, Deputy State Secretary, Member of Parliament, parliamentary spokesperson for ethnic minorities, Mayor of Budapest, Deputy Mayor of Budapest, Mayor, Deputy Mayor, or officer of a national or local organisation of a political party, may not be appointed as the CEO of the public media service provider. (4) The process to be applied for the verification of the clean criminal record of the CEO of the public media service provider and applicable legal sanctions shall be governed by the Labour Code.

Conflict of Interest Rules Applicable to the Executives of the Public Media Service Provider

Article 104 (1) The conflict of interest rules under Article 118 (1) (a)-(c) and (f) pertaining to the Authority's President, Vice-President, Director General, Deputy Director General, as well as the grounds for exclusion under Article 118 (3) shall apply to the CEO and executive employees of the public media service provider throughout the term of their employment relationship, as appropriate. (2) Apart from the conflict of interest rules under Paragraph (1), the CEO and executive employees of the public media service provider or their close relatives cannot be shareholding members or executive officers or Supervisory Board members in a business association which has a business relationship with the public media service provider headed by the CEO or employing the executive employee. If this rule is violated by a close relative of the public media service provider's CEO or executive employees, then it shall be considered as conflict of interest arisen in respect of the CEO or the executive employee, and the appropriate legal sanctions shall be applied. (3) Throughout the term of their employment relationship, the CEO and executive employees of the public media service provider shall not be engaged in any revenue generating profession, with the exception of scientific, educational, literary, artistic and other activities under copyright protection, and shall not be entitled to receive any remuneration from the public media service provider, not even by virtue of these titles. (4) The CEO of the public media service provider shall make a written statement, prior to entering into its employment contract, that no grounds for a conflict of interest exist in respect of him/her. (5) The CEO or executive employee of the public media service provider cannot conclude, on behalf of the public media service provider, an agreement in which he/she, or a close relative of him/her, or such business association is the other contracting party, in which he/she or his/her close relative holds an indirect or direct ownership share, has some other pecuniary rights, or a personal interest. Contracts within the sphere of interest of those affected by this restriction cannot be concluded by any other employee of the public media service provider either. Article 105 (1) The CEO shall direct the public media service provider within the framework of this Act, other legal regulations, the Statutes of the Public Foundation and the public media service provider and the decisions of the Board of Trustees. More particularly, he/she shall: a) decide on the programme schedule; b) establish the By-laws; c) ensure that the Public Service Code is enforced; d) draw up and submit to the Board of Trustees for approval the annual financial management plan, and ensure that it is implemented; e) draw up the balance sheet and profit and loss statement, and submit both to the Board of Trustees for approval; f) submit proposals for the authorisation of contracts or those needing prior approval, in line with

Article 90 (1) (p)-(q); g) exercise the employer's rights in respect of the employees of the public media service provider, including the employment of the Deputy CEOs; h) provide for the preparation of all further submissions as may be required by this Act and the Statutes of the Public Foundation or a decision of the Board of Trustees; i) ensure, in collaboration with the Fund, that those engaged in or contributing to the public media service provider's activities receive regular in-service training in media; j) have a seat in the Public Service Fiscal Council; k) exercise all the rights, subject to the provisions of this Act, which are referred to the Board of Directors of a company limited by shares by the provisions of the Civil Code applicable to business associations. (2) The CEO of the public media service provider shall receive no remuneration from the Public Service Foundation under any legal title, other than the allowances outlined in his/her employment contract.

The Supervisory Board of the Public Media Service Provider

Article 106 (1) The Supervisory Board monitors the management of the public media service provider (hereinafter as: Board). The Board is entitled to request reports or information from the CEO, the employees of the public media service provider, and may inspect the books, bank accounts, documents and petty-cash of the public media service provider at any time, or hire an expert to carry out such inspection at the cost of the public media service provider. (2) The Board consists of a Chairperson and four members. (3) The Chairperson of the Board and its members are elected by the Board of Trustees for a term and under the terms and conditions as defined in the Public Foundation's Statutes, with the exception of the Board member elected by the employees. (4) The Board of Trustees determines the remuneration of the Board's Chairperson and the members thereof. (5) The Board defines its own operating rules, and the Board of Trustees approves its rules of procedure. (6) The Board shall be responsible for inspecting all such reports to be submitted to the Board of Trustees that relate to matters of fiscal nature of the public media service provider, falling within the scope of competence of the General Meeting of the Board of Trustees. (7) The internal audit organisations of the public media service provider are under the control of the Board. (8) Otherwise, the organisational structure and operations of the Board is governed by the provisions of the Civil Code applicable to business associations, and the Public Foundation's Statutes and By-laws.

The Auditor of the Public Media Service Provider Article 107 (1)

The auditor of the public media service provider is elected by the Board of Trustees for a term of two years. It is also the Board of Trustees' competence to terminate the auditor's mandate. (2) The powers and responsibilities of the auditor shall be defined in the Statutes of the public media service provider, within the framework of the provisions of the Civil Code applicable to business associations.

Funding and Financial Management of the Public Media Service

Article 108 (1) The Fund shall support the fulfilment of the responsibilities of the public media service provider from its resources defined in Article 136 (3), and, if a specific order is placed, it shall perform the production, procurement and purchasing of the media contents of the public media service provider, as well as its other activities required for the public media service. (2) Based on the resources specified under Article 136 (3), the Fund shall propose an amount to be spent on production and purchasing of media contents, with a breakdown as per the service types of public media service determined under point 31 of Article 203. The Public Service Fiscal Council (hereinafter referred to as: the Council) shall provide its opinion on this proposal. (3) The Council is composed of three members, its members are the following: a) the CEO of the public media service provider; b) the CEO of the Fund, c) the member delegated, on an ad hoc basis, by the President of the State Audit Office for whom the conflict of interests rules laid down in Articles 104 and 118 shall be applied as appropriate. The remuneration of this member shall be determined by the CEO of the Fund. (4)

The Fund shall make its proposal as per Paragraph (2) until 30 June each year, in terms of the forthcoming target year. The Council shall provide its opinion as per Paragraph (2) on the proposal until 31 July each year. Its opinion shall be formulated with a view to the public service objectives and plans outlined in this Act, the Code, and the strategic plans prepared pursuant to Article 100/A, and to the special tasks of the public media service provider. The Council shall accept its opinion by simple majority, shall attach a reasoning to it, and shall publish it on the Fund's website. (5) In the event the Council's opinion rejects the Fund's proposal as per Paragraph (2), the Fund shall be obliged to submit a new proposal to the Council until 15 August each year. In such new proposal, it shall either accept the stipulations contained in the Council's opinion or shall reject them, with a reasoning attached. (6) The Council shall be convened by the Fund's CEO, who is also the Council's Chairperson, no later than by 30 June each year. The Council shall establish its own operating rules and rules of procedure within the framework of this Act. (7) The Fund, acting on behalf and in the interest of the public media service provider, shall conclude the agreements concerning the distribution of the linear media services of the public media service provider from its own budget. The provisions laid down in Paragraph (9) shall be applied to media service distribution agreements under which the public media service provider realizes any revenues in return for the distribution licence. (8) The CEO shall report to the Board of Trustees concerning the activities of the public media service provider, and approval of the balance sheet and the profit and loss statement shall take place within the framework thereof. The CEO's report shall be submitted to the Board of Trustees together with the opinion of the Supervisory Board of the public media service provider. (9)

The public media service provider may engage in business activities if those serve to promote its public service objectives. Any profits generated may be used exclusively for provision or development of public media service. The right to pursue business activities – with regard to the activities performed by the Fund without remuneration in order to support public media services – may be assigned to the Fund. Any revenues generated from this by the Fund may be used only to realize the objectives of the public media service. (10) The public media service provider cannot have a share in other media service providers and cannot set up foundations. (11) The public media service provider shall keep a separate register for its contracts. This register shall include the current data allowing for the company identification of the contracting parties, as well as the services to be performed by each of the contracting parties and the consideration thereof. (12) The public media service provider enjoys individually granted exemption from the payment of duties and is not subject to corporate tax. For the purposes of Article 8 of Act CXXVII of 2007 on Value

Added Tax (hereinafter referred to as: the VAT Act), the Fund and the public media service provider shall be considered as affiliated companies, which affiliated relationship may be joined by a new person by separate statutory provision only. (13) Procurements taking place within the legal relations between the Fund and the public media service provider are not covered by the application scope of the Public Procurement Act. (14) Having due regard to the provisions of this Act, the Media Council is responsible for determining the detailed rules, not regulated under law, governing the utilisation of the State owned assets, the ownership rights of which are exercised by the Fund, and the management of such assets, including the terms and conditions under which the public media service provider may use the specific asset elements and assets for the purpose of discharging its public service responsibilities.

The Special Labour Law Rules Applicable for the Employees Working in the System of Public Media Services

Article 108/A (1) The rules laid down in Act I of 2012 on the Labour Code (hereinafter referred to as: the Labour Code) shall be applied in terms of the employees employed by the public media service provider and the Fund, subject to the deviations specified under Paragraphs (2)-(5) and Article 108/B. (2) The activities of the public media service provider and the Fund related to media content services and news agency services shall be considered as activities performed on Sundays and non-working days as well, by their nature (based on their purpose). (3) As far as the employees are concerned, having regard to the unique characteristics of the different posts of employment, the actual working time (duration of the work phases) spent with the given activity shall be taken into account for purpose of calculation of the working time ordered by the employer and determination of the standby-type nature of the given post of employment. (4) Article 101 (3) of the Labour Code shall not be applied in terms of the employees. (5) The maximum of four hundred hours of extraordinary work per calendar year can be ordered for the employees employed full time, based on the provisions of the collective bargaining agreement. Article 108/B (1) Separate legislation shall define those posts of employment that are aimed to participate in the public media services and in the news agency activities of the public media service provider. (2)

The person employed in the post of employment affected by the legislation determined under Paragraph (1) shall be employed in a free work schedule. The nature of the work schedule shall not be affected by the compulsory availability arising from the unique nature of the post of employment or the work performed at the time or period determined by the employer. (3) Under the employment contract, the parties may deviate from applying the free work schedule specified under Paragraph (2), based on their ex nunc agreement. (4) As far as the employees employed under posts of employment affected by the piece of legislation specified in Paragraph (1) are concerned, the employer shall be obliged to determine the average number of hours per working day that can be recognised during the calendar year as working time required for preparation outside the workplace, in case of employees employed full time. As far as the employees employed part time are concerned, the working time required for preparation outside the workplace shall be recognised and taken into account in proportion to the ratio between the full time and the part time work stipulated under the employment contract. The preparation outside the workplace can be replaced by the employer with a proper possibility guaranteed at the workplace and during the working time. (5) As far as the employees employed in posts of employment affected by the piece of legislation defined under Paragraph (1) are concerned, in deviation from the stipulations contained in Article 122

(2) of the Labour Code, the employer, when granting the ordinary leave of the employee, is not obliged to take into account the employee's request with respect to one quarter of their base leave, exceptionally, if justified, as long as this would materially jeopardise the employer's normal operations.

The employer shall be obliged to notify the employee about this, without delay, and shall also specify when the employee can take their leave.

THE NATIONAL MEDIA AND INFOCOMMUNICATIONS AUTHORITY

an independent regulatory body solely subject to the law. (2) The Authority participates in the implementation of the Government's policy – as defined by law – in the areas of spectrum management and communications. Any function may be assigned to the Authority only by law or other legislation issued pursuant to law. (3) The Authority comprises the following entities with independent powers: President of the National Media and Infocommunications Authority (hereinafter as: President), the Media Council of the National Media and Infocommunications Authority and the Office of the National Media and Infocommunications Authority. (4)

The President of the Authority reports to the Parliament on the activities of the Authority once every year. (5) In relation to the communications sector, the Authority is responsible for ensuring – particularly in line with the objectives and basic principles of the Electronic Communications Act – the smooth and effective functioning and development of the communications market, safeguarding the interests of the users and of those pursuing communications activities, fostering the development and maintenance of fair and efficient competition within the electronic communications sector, and for the supervision of legal compliance of the conduct of organizations and persons pursuing communications activities. (6)

The Authority performs its tasks and exercises its powers independently, in compliance with applicable legislation. (7) The communications regulatory powers of the Authority cannot be withdrawn in any way. (8) The Government's public administration function pertaining to non-civilian spectrum management shall be provided for by the Office. (9) [not in effect] Article 110 In relation to the communications sector and subject to separate legislation, the Authority shall: a) comment on legislative and amendment requests and proposals concerning its competence; b) assess and continuously analyse the functioning of the communications market and of related information technology markets; c) continuously evaluate the state of the communications market and prepare comparative analyses; d) conduct market analysis; e) proceed in connection with the fulfilment and breach of certain obligations imposed on the obliged service providers; f) take action in connection with any breach of communications related provisions, as well as in proceedings launched in relation to legal disputes arising from the conclusion of contracts;g) perform regulatory tasks provided for under other pieces of legislation in respect of electronic communications and postal services; h) as part of its management functions, the Authority shall exercise – in accordance with this Act and other pieces of legislation – the state ownership rights pertaining to radio frequencies and identifiers, and shall manage the radio frequencies and identifiers; i) perform other regulatory and non-regulatory tasks defined by other pieces of legislation. Article 110/A (1)

The Authority shall establish the principles related to its personnel policy independently, in order to retain the specialist personnel with the special expertise and competences required for the performance of its duties as detailed under Articles 109-110. (2) The Director General and Deputy Director General of the Authority, as well as the employees of the Authority, shall perform their activities within the framework of a public service legal relationship, and their legal relationship shall be governed by the provisions of the Act on Civil Servants applicable to civil servants, subject to the differences specified under this Act. (3) The president of the Authority shall determine the system of the different posts of employment required for performance of the tasks of the Authority, the amount of the resources required for the performance of the tasks, and define, under the By-laws of the Authority, those employment positions not falling under Paragraph (2), where the employees perform their tasks under an employment relationship. (4) The president of the Authority, within his/her own powers which cannot be transferred, shall decide upon the principles of the remuneration policy of the Authority, the fringe benefits, the basic salary, and any deviations thereof. (5)

The president of the Authority can determine a special personal remuneration to civil servants who are in an employment position requiring a special, unique expertise or to civil servants in more than one executive position. Personal remuneration can be granted up to the maximum of twenty percent of the active employee headcount of the Authority and can be withdrawn without the need for any explanations. The president of the Authority shall determine the possible rules restricting the employment of the persons in the above-mentioned posts of employment, applied upon termination of the legal relationship of these persons, and these rules shall be specified in detail in the employment document. (6) The President of the Authority shall, on his/her own initiative, determine in the Public Service Policy of the Authority the detailed rules related to the performance assessment system and the related remuneration, recruitment and selection policies, as well as the planning and execution of the in-service training, courses, and individual development. (7) The Authority, being an independent regulatory body, shall not be subject to the data provision obligation related to public administration personnel activities.

The President and Vice-President of the National Media and Infocommunications Authority

Article 111 (1) The President shall a) perform the management of the National Media and Infocommunications Authority; b) from the powers defined in Article 110, exercise the powers conferred upon the President by separate legislation; c) submit the annual draft budget and annual institutional budget report of the Authority in accordance with Article 134; d) propose amendments to legislation concerning communications and media services; e) make decisions about the classification of data handled by the Authority in the course of performing its activities, in line with the provisions of the Act on the Protection of Classified Information.

(2) Further responsibilities of the President are the followings: a) if elected as President of the Media Council, convene and chair the meetings of the Media Council; b) if elected as President of the Media Council, arrange for the meetings of the Media Council to be prepared; c) appoint the Vice-Presidents and exercise the employer's rights over them, including dismissal and removal; d) appoint the Director General of the Office and exercise the employer's rights including dismissal and removal; e) appoint, dismiss or remove the Deputy Directors General upon the Director General's proposal; f) appoint, dismiss or remove the Media and Communications Commissioner and exercise the employer's rights; g) adopt the Authority's By-laws; h) represent

the Authority, particularly when keeping contact and consulting with the European Commission and with regulatory authorities from Member States; i) publish, by 28 February of each year, the annual work schedule of the Authority and key figures of its draft budget, and, by 30 June, the annual assessment of the Authority's financial management for the previous year; j) outline, on a yearly basis, tasks to be carried out in connection with professional preparatory works; k) notify the Minister responsible for electronic communications of any circumstances that may jeopardise the safety of communications and make recommendations for the measures deemed as necessary; l) proceed before international organisations on behalf of the state as mandated; m) sign cooperation agreements annually on behalf of the Authority with the consumer protection authority and the competition authority; n) act as second-instance authority on the field of communications concerning the official matters of the Office defined by law; o) [not in effect] (3)-(5) (6) The President may not be instructed with respect to his/her actions and decisions associated with the performance of his/her duties and exercise of powers. The President may not instruct the Office to take ad hoc decisions in respect of the Office's official matters defined by law. Article 111/A (1) The President shall be appointed by the President of the Republic for a period of nine years, on the recommendation of the Prime Minister. (2)

A person meeting the following criteria may be appointed as President: a person who may be elected at the election of Members of Parliament, has no criminal record, is not banned from exercising an occupation corresponding to his/her activities, has a higher education degree and a) has at least five years of work experience in the regulatory supervision of media services or press products, or the regulatory supervision of infocommunications, or b) with respect to a subject-matter relating to media or infocommunications he/she has ba) an academic degree recognised in Hungary, or bb) at least ten years of experience as a lecturer in an institution of higher education. (2a) The following activities shall be considered, in particular, as a work experience as per Paragraph (2) a): a) regulatory activity in management or administrative position at the Office or at the National Communications Authority, in the field of infocommunications, b) participation as a judge, public prosecutor or legal representative in appeal procedures related to the decisions of the Office or the National Communications Authority,

c) activity related to the supervision of media services, in administrative or management position at the National Radio and Television Commission, at its bodies or at the Media Council, d) participation as a judge, public prosecutor or legal representative in appeal procedures related to the decisions of the National Radio and Television Commission or its bodies, e) membership in the

Board of Trustees of the Hungarian Radio Public Foundation, the Hungarian Television Public Foundation, or the 'Hungária' Television Public Foundation, in accordance with Act I of 1996 on Radio and Television Broadcasting, or in any of their controlling bodies, or in the Board of Trustees as per Article 85. (3) The President, once his/her mandate expired, cannot be elected again. (4) The Prime Minister, prior to making his/her recommendation as per Paragraph (1), at least sixty days prior to expiry of the mandate of the President in office, or within fifteen days from termination of the mandate in any other case when the President's mandate is terminated, shall request the Board of Public Services, the National Council for Communications and Information Technology, as well as the professional, interest representative and self-regulatory bodies of the communications service providers, media content providers, media service distributors and journalists (having a national operating area and at least five years of operation) to make nominations for the candidate for President. (5)

The requested organisations shall make their nominations in writing and shall describe the professional career of the proposed person, taking into account the professional criteria set forth under Paragraphs (2) and (2a) as well, and they shall also state the reasons for their nominations. The organisations invited to make nominations are allowed to disclose to the public the name of their presidential candidate, subject to the candidate's consent. The Prime Minister shall also hold direct consultations to learn more details about the proposals made by the invited organisations, either personally or through a state executive appointed by him/her. (6) The Prime Minister shall name his/her candidate after considering the nominations made in the course of the consultations. Article 112 (1) The President is entitled to appoint two Vice-Presidents for an indefinite term. The provisions of Paragraphs (2) and (2a) of Article 111/A shall be applicable to the appointment of Vice-Presidents, as appropriate. (2) The President may be substituted by the Vice-President if the conditions specified in the By-laws are met. The President may delegate his/her second-instance regulatory decision-making powers to the respective Vice-President by virtue of an appropriately detailed authorisation. When acting within this delegated competence, the Vice-President may not be instructed in relation to making second-instance regulatory decisions. Other tasks of the Vice-President shall be defined by the By-laws. (3) The President shall be entitled to the remuneration and allowances of Ministers, whereas the Vice-President shall be entitled to the remuneration and allowances of State Secretaries. Any issues not regulated by this Act shall be governed by the provisions of other laws pertaining to the legal status of Ministers as far as the President is concerned, and those pertaining to the legal status of State Secretaries as far as the Vice-President is concerned. (4)

Rules applicable to those engaged in public service relationship shall be applicable to the social security status of the President and the Vice-President. The term of their mandate shall be regarded as time spent in public service relationship and pensionable service time. (5) The President shall – immediately upon being appointed – present an official certificate in verification of his/her clean criminal record and not being banned from occupations aligned with the scope of his/her activities. Should the President fail to fulfil this certification obligation for reasons attributable to him/her, the legal sanctions of conflict of interest shall apply. (6) The Prime Minister shall be responsible for handling the President's personal data disclosed pursuant to Paragraph (5) until the end of the President's mandate, and may call upon the President at any time to verify the data outlined in Paragraph (5). (7) The provisions of Paragraph (5) shall be applied to the Vice-President, whereas the powers defined under Paragraph (6) shall be exercised by the President in relation to the Vice-President. Article 113 (1)

The President's mandate shall be terminated if a) his/her mandate expires; b) he/she resigns; c) he/she dies; d) he/she is dismissed by the President of the Republic in accordance with Paragraph (2); e) if he/she is not elected as President of the Media Council by the Parliament within 30 days from his/her appointment, or, if such appointment takes place outside the parliamentary session, within 15 days from the starting date of the forthcoming parliamentary session. (2) The President of the Republic shall dismiss the President, if a) he/she fails to eliminate the conflict of interest as outlined in Article 118 (1) within thirty days of the date of appointment or the emergence of the ground for the conflict of interest; b) if as a result of criminal proceedings instituted against the President, the President is pronounced guilty in a final judgement of the court sentencing the President to imprisonment, or barring him/her from exercising an occupation aligned with his/her activities as President; c) the President is placed under guardianship affecting his/her legal capacity; d) the President fails to fulfil the responsibilities arising from his/her mandate for more than six months for reasons attributable to him/her. (2a) The President of the Republic shall pass his/her decision as per Paragraph (2) based on the recommendation of the Prime Minister. (3) In case the President's mandate is terminated pursuant to Paragraph (1) (a) or (b), the President shall be eligible to severance pay equivalent to two months' remuneration at the time of termination. If the President has been in office for less than three years, then the prohibition outlined under Paragraph (8) shall be applicable for six months after the termination of the President's mandate, and in this case the President shall be entitled to severance pay equivalent to one month's remuneration. (4) The Vice-President's mandate shall be terminated, if a) he/she resigns; b) he/she dies; c) he/she is dismissed by the President pursuant to Paragraph

(5); d) he/she is removed by the President pursuant to Paragraph (6); e) based on the mutual agreement of the President and the Vice-President. (5) The President shall dismiss the Vice-President, if a) he/she fails to eliminate the conflict of interest as outlined in Article 118 (1) within thirty days of the date of appointment or the emergence of the ground for the conflict of interest; b) if as a result of criminal proceedings instituted against the Vice-President, the Vice-President is pronounced guilty in a final judgement of the court sentencing the Vice-President to imprisonment, or barring him/her from exercising an occupation aligned with his/her activities as Vice-President. (6)

The President may also terminate the Vice-President's mandate by removal. No justification for the removal shall be required. (7) In case the Vice-President's mandate is terminated pursuant to Paragraph (4) (a) or (d), the Vice-President shall be eligible to severance pay equivalent to two months' remuneration at the time of termination. If the Vice-President has been in office for less than three years, then the prohibition outlined under Paragraph (8) shall be applicable for six months after the termination of the Vice-President's mandate, and in this case the Vice-President shall be entitled to severance pay equivalent to one month's remuneration. (8) For one year after the termination of their mandate, the President and the Vice-President a) may not be engaged in any form of employment or other work-related relationship with a business association; b) may not establish regular business relationship in the capacity of executive officer or company owner with a business association; and c) may not acquire an ownership share in a business association; the rights or lawful interests of which were affected by his/her decisions while serving as President or Vice-President. (9) With regard to the employment related prohibition affecting the operational sector set forth in Paragraph (8), the President and the Vice-President, upon termination of their mandate, shall be entitled to a compensation, the rate of which shall be the sum of the previous 12 months' net – that is reduced by personal income tax – salary paid by the Authority. The compensation shall be paid from the budget of the Authority. The flat rate compensation determined this way shall be tax-free in the context of compensating for damage. The same provision shall be applicable in relation to the prohibition laid down in Article 129 (9) which is applicable upon the termination of the mandate of the President and members of the Media Council. (10) If the mandate of the Vice-President is terminated under Paragraph (4) (d), the provisions applicable upon the withdrawal of the executive mandate during the public service relationship shall be applied to the termination of the mandate.

Office of the National Media and Infocommunications Authority

Article 114 (1) The Office shall be headed by the Director General appointed by the President for an indefinite period. (2) From the powers defined in Article 110, the Office shall exercise powers that are conferred upon the Office by separate legislation, furthermore it shall fulfil its functions conferred upon it by laws or by the President under the framework of this Act and other legislation. (3) The Office shall provide the President, the Vice-Presidents, the Media Council, and members of the Media Council with professional assistance for the performance of their duties. (4)-(5) [not in effect]

The Director General and Deputy Director General of the National Media and Infocommunications Authority

Article 115 (1) The Director General shall be appointed by the President. (2) The provisions of Paragraphs (2) and (2a) of Article 111/A shall be applicable to the appointment of the Director General, as appropriate. (3) The Director General shall be entitled to the remuneration and allowances of State Secretaries. (4) The Director General may not be instructed with respect to his/her first-instance powers in regulatory decision-making. (5) The mandate of the Director General shall be terminated, if a) he/she resigns; b) he/she dies; c) he/she is dismissed by the President pursuant to Paragraph (6); d) he/she is removed by the President pursuant to Paragraph (7); e) based on the mutual agreement of the President and the Director General. (6) The President shall dismiss the Director General, if a) he/she fails to eliminate the conflict of interest as outlined in Article 118 (1) within thirty days of the date of appointment or the emergence of the ground for the conflict of interest; b) if as a result of criminal proceedings instituted against the Director General, the Director General is pronounced guilty in a final judgement of the court sentencing the Director General to imprisonment, or barring him/her from exercising an occupation aligned with his/her activities as Director General. (7) The President may also terminate the Director General's mandate by removal. No justification for the removal shall be required. (8)

For a period of one year following the termination of his/her mandate, the Director General a) may not be engaged in any form of employment or other work-related relationship with a business association; b) may not establish regular business relationship in the capacity of executive officer or company owner with a business association; and c) may not acquire an ownership share in a business association; the rights or lawful interests of which were affected by his/her decisions while serving as Director General. (9) In case the Director General's mandate is terminated pursuant to Paragraph (5) (a) or (d), the Director General shall be eligible to severance pay equivalent to two months' remuneration at the time of termination. If the Director General has been in office for less than three years, then the prohibition outlined under Paragraph

(8) shall be applicable for six months after the termination of the Director General's mandate, and in this case the Director General shall be entitled to severance pay equivalent to one month's remuneration. (10) The provisions of Article 112 (5) shall be applicable to the Director General, and the powers defined in Article 112 (6) shall be exercised in respect of the Director General by the President. Article 116 Responsibilities of the Director General shall include the following: a) perform the organisational and professional leadership of the Office, with the exception of the organisational units subordinated directly to the President, and act as the President's deputy in respect of the management of the Office; b) exercise the powers conferred upon the Director General by separate legislation from those defined in Article 110; c) ensure the efficient operation of the Authority's organisation; d) make recommendations to the President for the appointment, dismissal and removal of Deputy Directors General, exercise employer's rights in relation to his/her Deputies and the employees of the Office, with the exception of organisational units subordinated directly to the President; e) ensure the publication of information defined in this Act; f) attend meetings of the Media Council with consultative powers on the basis of the invitation from the President of the Media Council; g) ensure that the Office provides professional assistance to the extent and in the manner as defined by the President – in case of the Media Council and the members thereof, as the President of the Media Council – to the President, the Vice-Presidents, the Media Council and members of the Media Council as necessary for the performance of their duties; h) fulfil the duties and exercise the powers conferred upon him/her by law or by the President – as the President of the Authority and as the President of the Media Council – within the scope of this Act. Article 117 (1)

Upon the Director General's proposal the President shall be entitled to appoint Deputy Directors General. The number of Deputy Directors General and the scope of their responsibilities shall be defined in the By-laws of the Authority. (2) The person who can be elected at the election of Members of Parliament, has a clean criminal record, is not banned from exercising an occupation corresponding to his/her activities, possesses a higher education degree and at least three years of work experience in programme distribution, media services, regulatory supervision of the media services, electronic communications, or in economics, social science, law, technology or management (including membership of management bodies) or in administration with a focus on the regulatory supervision of communications, can be appointed as Deputy Director General. (3) The Deputy Director General is entitled to the remuneration and allowances of State Secretaries. (4) The provisions of Article 115 (5)-(10) pertaining to the Director General shall be also applicable to the Deputy Director General.Conflict of Interests Rules

Article 118 (1) The following persons shall not be eligible for the position of President, Vice-President, Director General and Deputy Director General: a) the President of the Republic, the Prime Minister, members of the Government, State Secretaries, the State Secretary for Public Administration, Deputy State Secretaries, the Mayor of Budapest, the Deputy Mayor of Budapest, Mayors, Deputy Mayors, chairpersons of county-level general assemblies and their deputies, Members of Parliament, parliamentary spokesperson for ethnic minorities, Members of the European Parliament; b) the Chairperson and members of the Board of Trustees of the Public Foundation for Public Service Media and of the Public Service Board, the CEO and Deputy CEO of the Fund, the Chairperson, Deputy Chairperson or members of the National Council for Communications and Information Technology, the CEO of the public media service provider and the Chairperson and members of the Supervisory Board thereof, members of the Media Council, the President of the Media Council with the exception of the President of the Authority, and persons engaged in any other work-related relationship with any of the foregoing organisations; c) local or county-level municipal representatives, government officials, officials of the national or local organisations of political parties, and persons engaged in any work-related relationship with political parties; d) executive officers, management board members, supervisory board members of communications or media service providers, media service distributors, advertising agencies, press publishing and newspaper distribution companies; e) persons engaged in any form of employment or other work-related relationship with a communications or media service provider, programme distributor, media service distributor, advertising agency, press publishing and newspaper distribution company; f) persons holding direct or indirect ownership share in an undertaking providing communications or media services, pursuing programme distribution, media service distribution, press publishing, advertising agency or newspaper distribution activities; g) direct and indirect owners of business associations – in case of public limited company, with an ownership share of more than five percent – and persons engaged in any work-related relationship with the such companies, which are involved with the organisations defined in Point (d) under an agency or service agreement; h) the close relatives of the persons under Points (a)-(b) and (d). (2) For the purposes of Paragraph (1) (e), other work-related relationships entailing scientific work, the publication of scientific results and the dissemination of scientific information shall not be regarded as grounds for conflict of interest. (3) The President, the Vice-President, the Director General and Deputy Director General may not be engaged in party politics or make representations on behalf of political parties.

Report of the President of the National Media and Infocommunications Authority

Article 119 (1) By 31 May of each year, the President of the Authority shall submit a report to the Parliament to give account of the activities of the Authority during the previous year. In this report the President shall: a) evaluate the functioning and development of the electronic communications market; b) evaluate the decisions adopted in protection of the interests of providers and users of electronic communications services, as well as measures taken in the electronic communications sector to promote the development and maintenance of fair and effective competition; c) provide information on the supervision of compliance by entities and individuals engaged in electronic communications with applicable legislation; and d) evaluate the consequences of its management of state-owned limited resources. (2) The report shall be published both in printed format and on the websites of the Authority and of the Ministry overseen by the Minister responsible for electronic communications.

The National Council for Communications and Information Technology

Article 120 (1) The National Council for Communications and Information Technology (hereinafter as: NHIT) is a counselling and advisory body to the Government on information technology and communications related matters. (2) The NHIT shall consist of five members. The Chairperson and Deputy Chairperson of NHIT shall be appointed and dismissed by the Prime Minister. (3) Members of the NHIT – including its Chairperson and Deputy Chairperson – shall be appointed from persons having at least five years of experience in the field of communications or information technology. (4) Of all NHIT members a) two members shall be delegated by the Media Council; and b) one member shall be delegated by the Hungarian Academy of Sciences. (5) The NHIT shall be solely subject laws and its members may not be instructed with respect to their activities. (6) The Chairperson and Deputy Chairperson as well as members of the NHIT shall be mandated for four years. (7) Vacant seats shall be filled by the authorized organisation or person within thirty days. (8) Government officials and civil servants too are eligible for the position of NHIT's Chairperson, Deputy Chairperson or member. (9) The remuneration of the Chairperson of NHIT shall be equal to sixty-five percent of the remuneration of State Secretaries, the remuneration of the Deputy Chairperson of NHIT shall be equal to sixty percent of the remuneration of State Secretaries, and the remuneration of the members of the NHIT shall be equal to fifty-five percent of the remuneration of State Secretaries during the period between their appointment and the termination of their mandate, and the Chairperson, Deputy Chairperson and members shall also be entitled to a reimbursement of expenses. Article 121 (1) On the field of information technology, communications and the media related matters, the NHIT shall provide its opinion to the Government on a) the program for building an information society and strategic decisions concerning the promotion of information culture and information society; b) setting directions for research and development; c) decisions targeting dissemination of social attitudes and culture; and d) developing the regulatory framework of the communications market, fostering equal opportunities for market players; e) ensuring the harmonisation of civil and non-civilian spectrum management; f) the Hungarian position to be represented at international conferences concerning radio communications; and g) strategic submissions for regulating the infrastructure of the information society, and decisions concerning the program for building an information society. (2)

The NHIT shall provide the Government its opinion on: a) the drafts of Government and Ministerial decrees; b) all submissions, ad hoc decisions and draft legislation on communications and information technology, upon request from the Government, the Prime Minister, the Minister responsible for electronic communications, or the Minister responsible for information technology; c) strategic submissions for regulating the infrastructure of the information society, and the program for building an information society; in relation to which any submission may be presented to the Government after obtaining the comments by the NHIT and with the opinion of the NHIT only. (3) The Chairperson of the NHIT shall participate with consultative powers in state executive meetings preceding Government meetings and, by invitation, on Government meetings discussing submissions mentioned in Paragraphs (1)-(2). (4) The Chairperson of the NHIT may invite with consultative power the representatives of organizations interested in the utilisation of examined frequency bands and services provided thereon. (5)

In line with the Government program on the field of information technology, communications, and media, the NHIT, in relation to the topics mentioned in Paragraphs (1)-(2), may make independent recommendations and initiatives toward the Government, and toward bodies, other organizations controlled or supervised by the Government or a Minister, in order to increase the efficiency of the performance of the public functions concerning such topics. The head of the body or organization shall notify the Chairperson of the NHIT about its comments on the independent recommendation or initiative within 30 days. (6) Upon invitation by the Government or the Prime Minister, the NHIT shall, on the basis of communication, IT scientific, practicality, and economic considerations, examine the EU and other tenders of bodies and other organization controlled by the Government or a Minister and the implementation of such tenders, and their other projects and procurements as well, in the field of communications and information technology. The opinion of NHIT prepared upon completion of the examination shall be sent to the Prime Minister. On the basis of the examination, the NHIT may also submit independent recommendations and initiatives under Paragraph (5). The bodies and other organizations controlled or supervised by the Government or a Minister shall cooperate with NHIT in the course of completing the examination. (7) NHIT shall have quorum when more than half of its members are present, and at least the Chairperson or Deputy Chairperson is also present. With the exception of decisions regarding conflicts of interest, the NHIT shall adopt its decisions by majority voting, and in case of parity of votes, the vote of the Chairperson shall decide. (8) NHIT shall establish its own operational rules. (9)

The resources needed for the operations of the NHIT shall be ensured from the budget of the Authority. These resources may not be reallocated for any other purpose. (10) The financial operation of the NHIT shall be audited by the State Audit Office. The NHIT shall report on the fulfilment of its duties to the relevant Committee of the Parliament on an annual basis. Article 122 (1) The NHIT's Office (hereinafter as: NHIT Office) shall be an organizational unit of the Authority, the head of which shall be entitled to use the title of head of office. (2) The NHIT Office shall perform tasks related to the operations of the NHIT, and shall perform the necessary administrative activities in relation thereto. (3) The Policy of Functions and Competences of the NHIT Office shall be approved by the President of the Authority, with the consent of Chairperson of the NHIT. (4) The administrative activities of the NHIT Office shall be overseen by the head of the NHIT Office, in accordance with decisions of the NHIT and with the instructions of the Chairperson of the NHIT. (5) Based on Article 121 (1)-(2), the NHIT Office shall prepare for the NHIT preparatory documents for negotiating and decision-making concerning the opinion to be provided by the NHIT to the Government or the Prime Minister. (6) The Chairperson of the NHIT shall directly control the professional activities of the Office to be carried out in relation to drafting preparatory documents for negotiating and decision-making associated with the tasks defined in Article 121 (1)-(2). (7) Of employer's rights pertaining to the head of the NHIT Office, the right of appointment and terminating the public service relationship shall be exercised by the President of the Authority based on the proposal of the Chairperson of the NH

THE MEDIA COUNCIL OF THE NATIONAL MEDIA AND INFOCOMMUNICATIONS AUTHORITY

Article 123 (1) The Media Council shall be a body of the Authority with independent powers under the supervision of the Parliament and having legal personality. The Media Council shall be the legal successor of the National Radio and Television Commission. (2) The Media Council and its members shall be solely subject to laws and may not be instructed with respect to their activities. (3) The registered office of the Media Council shall be in Budapest. (4) The Office shall be the administrative unit of the Media Council. (5) On the basis of a mandate given through the Office, the Media Council and its members may also employ external experts.

Electing the Media Council Article 124 (1) The President and the four members of the Media Council shall be elected by the Parliament for a period of nine years by simultaneous voting by list, except if the mandate of the President is terminated for any of the reasons specified under Points b)-e) of Paragraph (1) of Article 113, or if the mandate of the member is terminated for any of the reasons specified under Points b)-f) of Paragraph (1) of Article 129. In the latter case, the Parliament shall vote separately regarding the president or member candidate. (2) A person meeting the following criteria may be elected president or member of the Media Council: a person who may be elected at the election of Members of Parliament, has no criminal record, is not banned from exercising an occupation corresponding to his/her activities, has a higher education degree and a) has at least five years of work experience in the regulatory supervision of media services or press products, or the regulatory supervision of infocommunications, or b) with respect to a subject-matter relating to media or infocommunications he/she has ba) an academic degree recognised in Hungary, or bb) at least ten years of experience as a lecturer in an institution of higher education.

(2a) The following activities shall be considered, in particular, as a work experience as per Paragraph (2) a): a) regulatory activity in management or administrative position at the Office or at the National Communications Authority, in the field of infocommunications, b) participation as a judge, public prosecutor or legal representative in appeal procedures related to the decisions of the Office or the National Communications Authority, c) activity related to the supervision of media services, in administrative or management position at the National Radio and Television Commission, at its bodies or at the Media Council, d) participation as a judge, public prosecutor or legal representative in appeal procedures related to the decisions of the National Radio and Television Commission or its bodies, e) memberahip in the Board of Trustees of the Hungarian Radio Public Foundation, the Hungarian

Television Public Foundation, or the 'Hungária' Television Public Foundation, in accordance with Act I of 1996 on Radio and Television Broadcasting, or in any of their controlling bodies, or in the Board of Trustees as per Article 85. (3) Media Council members shall be nominated a) not earlier than sixty and not later than thirty days before the expiry of the mandate of members, b) with the exception of cases outlined in Point (a), within thirty days from gaining knowledge of the termination of a mandate, by the unanimous vote of an ad hoc committee consisting of one member of each parliamentary faction (hereinafter as: nominating committee). (4) In each voting round, members of the nominating committee shall have a number of votes corresponding to the headcount of the parliamentary faction they were appointed by. (5) The parliamentary decision instituting the nominating committee shall specify the time period available for the parliamentary factions to appoint members to the nominating committee. The nomination process may commence even if a faction fails to appoint a member to the nominating committee within the deadline set by the parliamentary decision. (6) If, in the case outlined under Paragraph (3) (a), the nominating committee fails to nominate four members within the stated deadline, the nominating committee may propose a candidate in the second round of nomination with at least a two-thirds majority of votes. (7) If, in the case outlined under Paragraph (3) (a), the nominating committee fails to nominate four members within eight days in the second nomination round, its mandate shall be terminated and a new nominating committee shall be set up. (8) If, in the case outlined under Paragraph (3) (b), the nominating committee fails to nominate a member within the deadline stated therein, the nominating committee may propose a candidate with at least a two-thirds majority of votes. (9) If, in the case outlined under Paragraph (3) (b), the nominating committee fails to nominate four members within eight days in the second nomination round, its mandate shall be terminated and a new nominating committee shall be set up. Article 125 (1) The President of the Authority appointed by the President of the Republic shall become a candidate for the President of the Media Council by virtue and from the moment of appointment. (2)

The President and members of the Media Council shall take office upon being elected or – if elected before the termination of the mandate of the predecessor – upon the termination of the mandate of the predecessor. (3) If the mandate of the President of the Authority is terminated pursuant to Points b)-d) of Paragraph (1) of Article 113, his/her mandate as President of the Media Council shall be terminated simultaneously as well. In the event that the mandate of the President of the Authority expires the provisions of Article 216 (8) shall be applied. The new President of the Authority appointed by the President of the Republic shall become a candidate for the President of the Media Council by the fact and from the moment of appointment. His/her election shall be decided upon with a vote by list or with a separate vote in line with Article 124 (1). (4) [not in effect] (5) The President and members of the Media Council may not be re-elected. (6) The mandate of a new member shall be for the period remaining from the mandate of previously elected members of the Media Council. (7)

The duration of the mandate of the President of the Media Council corresponds to the duration of the mandate of the President of the Authority, except for the case specified under Article 216 (8). Article 126 (1) Once elected, members of the Media Council shall promptly verify to the President of the Media Council, by presenting an official certificate, that they have a clean criminal record and are not barred from exercising an occupation aligned with their activities as members of the Media Council. (2) The President of the Media Council shall handle the personal data of Media Council members that were disclosed to him/her pursuant to Paragraph (1) until the termination of their respective mandates and may call upon members at any time to verify the data under Paragraph (1). (3) Provisions of Paragraphs (1)-(2) shall apply to the President of the Media Council, with the deviation that the verification obligation of the President of the Media Council defined under Paragraph (1) shall be performed toward the Media Council, whereas the right defined under Paragraph (2) shall be exercised by the Media Council. The President of the Media Council shall not be involved in exercising the power of the Media Council defined in this Paragraph.

Conflict of Interests Rules Article 127 (1) The conflict of interest rules defined in Article 118 (1) with respect to the President and members of the Media Council, the President and Vice-President of the Authority, and the Director General and Deputy Director General, as well as the grounds for exclusion defined in Article 118 (3) shall be applied as appropriate. (2) With respect to members of the Media Council, employment relationships and other work-related relationship entered into with publishers or founders of press products for the performance of scientific activities, the publication of scientific results and the dissemination of scientific information shall not constitute a conflict of interests.

The Duties of Members of the Media Council Article 128 (1) Members of the Media Council shall keep all and any classified data and business secrets disclosed to them in relation to the fulfilment of their duties. (2) The President and member of the Media Council shall take an oath according to the provisions of the Act on the Oath and Pledge of Certain Public Law Officials. (3) Members of the Media Council shall make an asset declaration in accordance with the rules applicable to Members of Parliament, in the first instance within thirty days upon being elected. Such asset declarations shall be handled, registered and controlled in accordance with rules pertaining to the handling, registration and control of the asset declarations of Members of Parliament

Termination of the Mandate of Members of the Media Council Article 129 (1)

The mandate of the Media Council member shall be terminated upon a) the expiry of the Media Council's term of mandate; b) his/her resignation; c) the establishment of a conflict of interest; d) his/her dismissal; e) his/her exclusion; f) the member's death. (2) The mandate of the President or a member of the Media Council shall be terminated on the ground for conflict of interests, if such a ground for conflict of interests arises in relation to the President or member, or if the President or member refuses or fails to fulfil his/her obligations of making an asset declaration, or if his/her asset declaration contains misrepresentations of important data or facts, or if he/she fails to meet the verification obligation under Article 126 (1) for reasons attributable to him/her. (3) If a ground for conflict of interests is established in relation to the President or a member of the Media Council, and if the ground for conflict of interests is not eliminated within thirty days of the conflict of interests taking effect or the date of the meeting establishing the conflict of interests, the plenary session of the Media Council shall establish, by way of a decision, the termination of the Media Council membership of the President or member. Once the decision establishing the conflict of interest is adopted, the President or member of the Media Council may no longer exercise his/her powers associated with his/her position. (4)

Termination of the mandate of a member of the Media Council shall be established and announced by the President of the Media Council in case of Paragraph (1) (b) and (f), and by the plenary session of the Media Council in case of Paragraph (1) (c), (d) and (e). Termination of the mandate of the President of the Media Council shall be established and announced by the plenary session of the Media Council. (5) The mandate shall be terminated by dismissal, if the President or member of the Media Council is placed under guardianship affecting his/her legal capacity. (6) The mandate shall be terminated by exclusion, if a) the President or a member of the Media Council fails to meet his/her responsibilities arising from the position for more than six months for reasons attributable to him/her, b) as a result of criminal proceedings instituted against the President or member of the Media Council, the President or member is pronounced guilty in a final judgement of the court sentencing the President or member to imprisonment, or barring him/her from exercising an occupation aligned with his/her activities. (7) If the session of the Media Council decides on a conflict of interests, dismissal or exclusion, the President or member affected may not take part in the voting process, and the unanimous decision of those entitled to vote is required in such matters. If unanimous decision is not reached on the subject matter even in a repeated voting procedure, the President of the Media Council shall recommend to the Parliament to decide on the matter. In such cases, the Parliament shall adopt a decision on the conflict of interests, dismissal or exclusion. (8) If the proceedings outlined under Paragraphs (3), (6) and (7) concern the President of the Media Council, the President's powers shall be exercised by a member designated in the procedural rules. (9) For one year after the termination of their mandate, the President or member of the Media Council a) may not be engaged in any form of employment or other work-related relationship with a business association; b) may not establish regular business relationship in the capacity of executive officer or company owner with a business association; and c) may not acquire an ownership share in a business association; the rights or lawful interests of which were affected by his/her decisions while serving as President or member of the Media Council.

(10) If the mandate is terminated pursuant to Paragraph (1) (a) or (b), the President or member of the Media Council shall be eligible to severance pay equivalent to two months' remuneration at the time of termination. If the President or member has been in office for less than three years, the prohibition outlined under Paragraph (9) shall be applicable for six months from the termination of the mandate, and in this case the President or member shall be entitled to severance pay totalling one month's remuneration.

Remuneration of the Members of the Media Council

Article 130 (1) The President of the Media Council shall be entitled to a remuneration equal to sixty percent of the remuneration of Ministers and to the reimbursement of expenses. (2) Members of the Media Council shall be entitled to a remuneration equal to seventy-five percent of the remuneration of State Secretaries and to the reimbursement of expenses.

Operation of the Media Council

Article 131 (1) The Media Council shall set its own rules of procedure, which shall be published in the Hungarian Gazette. (2) If the President of the Media Council is unable to attend a meeting of the Media Council due to being detained elsewhere or if the Media Council does not have an elected President, the powers and responsibilities of the President and representation of the Media Council shall be performed by the members of the Media Council in turn, in the way defined in the procedural rules. The member performing the tasks of the President may participate in voting.

Responsibilities of the Media Council

Article 132 In accordance with Articles 182-184 the Media Council shall: a) oversee and guarantee the freedom of the press under this Act and the Press Freedom Act; b) ensure the performance of tasks related to the tendering and contract awarding procedure for media service provision rights using state-owned limited resources made available for media services; c) perform the supervisory and control tasks prescribed by this Act – by recording programme flows or programmes or examining the programme flows recorded by the media service provider, or by making official requests; d) operate a programme flow monitoring and analysis service through the Office; e) express its opinion regarding draft legislation on media and communications; f) review regularly compliance with public contracts concluded with it; g) elaborate official positions and proposals with respect to the theoretical aspects of developing the Hungarian system of media services; h) initiate proceedings with respect to consumer protection and the prohibition of unfair market practices; i) prepare a report to the European Commission on the fulfilment of obligations with regard to programme quotas; j) be entitled to initiate amendments to this Act as may be necessary vis-à-vis the Minister responsible for audiovisual policy; k) undertake a pioneering role in developing media literacy and media awareness in Hungary and, in this context, coordinate the activities of other state actors in the area of media literacy, assist the Government in drafting its upcoming interim report to the European Union on the subject matter; l) perform other tasks defined by this Act and by other legislation issued under the authorization of

The Report of the Media Council

Article 133 (1) By 31 May of each year, the Media Council shall submit a report to the Parliament to give account of its activities for the previous year. In this report it shall evaluate: a) the state of the freedom of speech, expression and the press, as well as balanced information provision; b) changes in the ownership status of media service providers and media service distributors; c) the status of spectrum management serving to satisfy needs for media services; d) the economic situation and changes in the financial conditions of media services. (2) The report shall be published both in printed format and on the websites of the Authority and the Ministry overseen by the Minister responsible for audiovisual policy. Financial Management of the Authority and the Media Council Article 134 (1) The Authority shall manage its finances in accordance with the legislation applicable to the financial management of budgetary entities as appropriate, shall be entitled to manage state assets under statutory provisions applicable to central budgetary entities, it shall cover costs incurred in connection with the fulfilment of its duties from its own revenues and from central budget funding, and its accounts shall be managed by the Hungarian State Treasury. Every year, the Authority may set aside a reserve from its own revenues defined under Paragraph (4) – with the exception of fines – up to twenty-five percent of its effective revenue for the subject year. The reserve thus generated may be used in subsequent years to finance the Authority's operations and the fulfilment of its duties but may not be allocated for any other purpose. (2) The consolidated budget of the Authority shall be approved by the Parliament in the form of separate legislation in accordance with the provisions of this Act, relying on resources specified under Paragraph (4), and Article 136 (3), which legislation shall also regulate the utilisation of residual amounts, if any, that may have been generated in the Authority's budget for the previous year – with the exception of reserves referred to under Paragraph (1) and residual amounts upon which a commitment had been established by 31 December of the same fiscal year when they were generated. Residual amounts earmarked by way of a commitment by 31 December of the same fiscal year when they were generated may be used in accordance with the terms set out in the legal statement serving as the basis for the commitment. The President shall be entitled to make reallocations between target expenditures stated in the already approved consolidated budget, with the provision that the authorisation of the Media Council shall be obtained for reallocations affecting the budget of the Media Council. Within the consolidated budget of the Authority, the Media Council shall enjoy financial independence as described in Article 135. (3) The Parliament's budgetary committee shall submit to the Parliament the draft law comprising the Authority's consolidated budget by 31 October of the year preceding the subject year – based on the proposal sent by the President by 15 September, which includes the draft budget of the Media Council as approved by the Media Council. The Authority and the Media Council shall operate on the basis of their previously approved budget until the new budget is approved. (4) The Authority's own revenue shall comprise frequency charges, fees received for the booking and use of identifiers as well as for regulatory procedures; it shall also include supervisory fees, which shall be used to ensure the efficient and highly professional operation of the Authority. Statements indicating the inflow and utilisation of own revenue, and the utilisation of central budget funding shall be published by the Authority on its website every year. (5)

The amount of frequency charges and fees payable for the booking and use of identifiers shall be regulated by the President of the National Media and Infocommunications Authority in a decree. Portions of frequency charges, that were not used by the Authority for operating purposes – under the Act defined under Paragraph (2) – or were not used to generate reserves as outlined under Paragraph (1), shall be paid into the Fund as instructed by the President. The President shall designate in his/her instructions the public purpose for which, and the manner, in which the amount paid into the Fund in accordance with this Paragraph may be used. Any amount transferred pursuant to this Paragraph may be used by the Fund strictly as instructed and for the purpose designated by the President. The CEO of the Fund may, in the course of utilising such amounts, request the President to amend the ordained purpose of use or utilisation rules, if necessitated by public interests. The President may reject or approve either wholly or partially the request of the CEO of the Fund, or may specify a new purpose of public interest or new utilisation rules. If the amount transferred is used by the Fund in violation of the instructions of the President, the Fund, upon notice by the President, shall reimburse the corresponding amount to the Authority without delay. The Authority shall generate reserves from such refunds, which, based on the President's decision, may be used to subsidise the Fund by designating a new purpose in the public interest, or may be used – wholly or partially – directly for a public purpose linked to communications and related markets, or for improving the living standards of consumers. With the exception of subsidies financed from reserves, the Authority shall complete such payments by 31 March of the year following the subject year. Parts of frequency charges earmarked by the President by 31 December of the subject year for payment into the Fund, and the reserves generated in accordance with this Paragraph – also in view of the provisions of Paragraphs (2) and (12) – shall not be deemed as effective residual amounts. (6)

A supervisory fee shall be paid by electronic communications service providers to cover the costs incurred in connection with the communications regulatory activity of the Authority, and by postal service providers to cover the costs incurred in connection with the postal supervisory activities. This fee shall be maximum 0.35 percent of net sales revenue generated by the electronic communications services of the electronic communications service provider in the course of the previous business year, and maximum 0.2 percent of net sales revenues generated by the postal services of the postal service provider in the course of the previous business year, or – in the absence of sales revenue from the previous year – a prorated part of sales revenue for the subject year projected for the entire year. The amount of the supervisory fee shall be defined every year by the President of the National Media and Infocommunications Authority in a decree within the limitations permitted by law. (7) The supervisory fee shall be paid to the Authority on a quarterly basis, by the end of every quarter. (8) If the Authority's supervisory revenues as defined by this Act exceed the amount of costs incurred in a budgetary year in connection with the performance of its statutory responsibilities, any surplus amount shall be credited, once the Authority's annual report was adopted, in the form of supervisory fees payable during the year following the subject year, in proportion of supervisory fees paid during the subject year and up to their amount. (9) The Authority shall use the entire amount of fines collected during the previous year from actors of the communications and media market for developing the informed decision-making culture of consumers in the area of communications and the media, including particularly for supporting academic and training programmes concerning communications and media law, competition and consumer protection policy, for training professionals specialising in communications and media law and consumer protection policy, and disseminating information in order to increase awareness concerning communications and media policy and consumer decision-making. Any amount earmarked for this purpose but not used in the subject year may be rolled over to the following year, and may be spent on developing the informed decision-making culture of consumers. (10) The Parliament shall make its decision about implementing the separate legislation referred under Paragraph (2) by adopting the draft law of final accounts as proposed in accordance with the procedure outlined under Paragraph (2), including the annex referred to in Article 136 (15).

The deadline for the submission of this Final Accounts Act shall be 31 May of every year. (11) [not in effect] (12) For the purposes of Paragraph (2), any legal statement made in accordance with the internal policies of the Authority and of the Fund and giving rise to a payment obligation to be financed from the consolidated budget in accordance with separate legislation as specified under Paragraph (2) shall be considered a commitment. (13) The fees and administrative service fees payable to the Authority and imposed in any piece of legislation issued under the authorization granted in this Act or in a decision of the Authority, as well as the fines imposed under this Act shall qualify as public debts to be collected as taxes. Article 135 (1) The Media Council shall manage its finances in accordance with statutory regulations pertaining to the financial management of budgetary entities, and its accounts shall be managed by the Hungarian State Treasury. (2) The budget of the Media Council shall be approved by the Parliament – in the Act on the budget of the Authority – as part of the consolidated budget of the Authority as a separate item thereof, to be financed from the amount that may be used to cover the operating costs of the Media Council from the Fund's resources defined in Article 136 (3) of this Act. The Media Council may re-allocate sums between target expenditure headings within its already approved budget.

Media Service Support and Asset Management Fund

Article 136 (1) The Fund is a separated asset management and monetary fund responsible to promote the structural transformation of public media services, the Public Service Foundation, the community media services and the public media service provider, to produce and support the public service programmes, to support contemporary musical works and cinematographic works intended to open at cinemas, to carefully manage and increase the Fund's own assets and the State owned assets the ownership rights of which are exercised by the Fund, as well as to promote and implement other activities related to the foregoing. (2) The Fund's own assets and the State owned assets the ownership rights of which are exercised by the Fund (including the income collected as a result of utilisation and transfer of title of these assets as well) can only be used for the purposes defined by law. (3) The Fund's revenues shall consist, in particular, of the following: media service provision fees, tender fees, default penalty and compensation levied for the breach of broadcasting agreement, fines, public service contributions, surplus frequency fee amounts transferred by the Authority to the Fund pursuant to Article 134 (5), support paid by media service providers providing linear audiovisual media services based on Paragraph (8), target subsidies from the central budget, proceeds from the disposal of assets, sale of assets, business activities, interest received and voluntary payments received. (4) Every year the Hungarian State shall pay a public service contribution based on the number of households using equipment suitable for receiving linear audiovisual media services. The amount of this public service contribution shall be defined in Annex no. 4 of this Act. The public service contribution shall be paid by the State in twelve equal instalments, always in advance by the third day of every month, by transfer to the Fund's bank account. With the consent of the Media Council, the Fund shall be entitled to assign its revenues received from public service contributions. (5) Acting on behalf of the Hungarian State, the Minister responsible for audiovisual policy may enter into agreement with the Fund for a maximum period of seven years on the payment of the public service contribution. The separate authorisation from the Parliament prescribed by the Public Finances Act shall not be required for the conclusion of this agreement. (6)

The Fund shall be a legal person, a business entity, and shall be managed by the Media Council. The Fund shall be the legal successor of the Broadcasting Fund and of the Broadcasting Support and Asset Management Fund. (7) The Fund must have a payment account with the Hungarian State Treasury, however, in addition to its payment account, it shall have the right to have other payment accounts at any credit institutions. (8) Media service providers with significant market power, providing linear audiovisual media services shall use two and a half percent of their annual advertising revenues on supporting new Hungarian cinematographic works. This obligation may be performed either by paying the relevant amount to the Fund, or by providing financial support for new cinematographic works specified in an agreement concluded by and between the Fund and the media service provider. The media service provider may deduct this amount paid or used as support from its corporate tax base. (9) Voluntary payments made into the Fund shall qualify as public service commitment. If the voluntary payment into the Fund is based on a commitment undertaken in a public contract made with the Authority or the Media Council or an agreement made with the Media and Communications Commissioner, the voluntary payment shall used in accordance with the provisions of such agreements. (10) The Fund's support and subsidy policy, business plan and annual report shall be adopted by the Media Council. The Media Council's prior consent shall be obtained before the Fund's financial resources and the assets in the accounts can be used for any purpose not stated in the Fund's support and subsidy policy or business plan, and for undertaking commitments to be financed from the foregoing, or for making payments that exceed the threshold amount defined by the Media Council. (11) The CEO shall be entitled to represent the Fund. All employer's rights vis-à-vis the Fund's CEO – including his/her appointment, determining his/her salary and allowances, and termination of his/her employment by the employer – shall be exercised by the President of the Media Council. (12) The CEO shall make a proposal to the President of the Media Council for the appointment of the Fund's Deputy CEOs as well as for termination of their employment, who shall decide about the appointment, wage and allowances, and termination by the employer. In other respects the CEO shall exercise the employer's rights in relation to Deputy CEOs. (13)

The rules of conflicts of interests defined in Article 118 (1)-(2) pertaining to the President and Vice-President, as well as the Director General and Deputy Director General of the Authority, and the rules of exclusion defined in Article 118 (3) shall be applicable to the CEO and Deputy CEO of the Fund as appropriate. (14) The Chairperson and four members of the Fund's Supervisory Board shall be appointed and removed by the President of the Media Council. Their remuneration shall be established by the President of the Media Council. (15) The Fund's annual budget shall be approved by the Parliament as an annex to the separate legislation referred to in Article 134 (2). (16) The detailed rules of managing the Fund shall be defined by the Media Council. (17) [not in effect] (18) The Fund shall be personally exempted from the payment of duties and shall not be subject to corporate tax or local tax obligations. Article 137 (1) Support for public service programmes, community media service providers, cinematographic works intended to open at cinemas – with the exception of cinematographic works supported as defined in Article 136 (8) of this Act –, and contemporary musical works shall be provided for by way of open tendering. (2) The general conditions of tendering elaborated by the Fund shall be approved by the Media Council. (3) The Fund shall prepare and publish its invitation to tender based on the already approved general conditions of tendering. The method for evaluating tender bids shall be regulated among the general conditions of tendering. (3a) The obligation undertaken in consideration for the support awarded under a tender, disbursed by the Fund based on its responsibility specified under Article 136 (1), directly influencing the price of the service, shall not be considered as a service provision in terms of Article 13 of the VAT Act. (3b) The services used and products purchased in connection with thc production of the work of art produced from the support awarded and disbursed by the Fund under a tender based on Article 136 (1) shall be considered as products and service provision used for the purpose of a taxable sale of merchandise and/or service provision in terms of Articles 120, 123 and Annex no. 5 of the VAT Act. (4) In order to achieve the purposes of public media services as defined in Article 83, the Fund shall provide further training for persons engaged in producing public service media content in order to promote the creation of media content of appropriate quality. The Fund shall be entitled to make the necessary training arrangements within the scope of its commercial activity.

The Fund's Financial Management of State Assets

Article 137/A (1) The Fund shall act as the entity exercising the ownership rights, as defined under point 17 of Article 3 (1) of Act CXCVI of 2011 on the National Assets (hereinafter referred to as: the National Assets Act) over all those State owned assets (the assets entrusted to it) (including the copyrights and other related rights due to the State) a) for which the law appointed the Fund or previously any of its predecessors, to exercise the ownership rights and obligations, furthermore b) which were transferred to State ownership in connection with the public media service or an activity supporting such service. (2) The Fund, for purpose of performance of the public media service, has the right to establish a business association on behalf of the Hungarian State, or for that purpose, to acquire shares in business associations or to exercise ownership rights (membership, shareholding) therein. (3) The primary purpose of the assets entrusted to it shall be to promote the performance of the public media service and the news agency service, being public functions (duties). (4) The primary purpose of the asset management shall be to efficiently operate the assets, protect their condition, maintain or increase their value in order to ensure the fulfilment of the public function determined under Paragraph (3).

(5) The Fund's activity aiming to exercise its ownership rights over the State assets belonging to the assets entrusted to the Fund shall not be subject to Act CVI of 2007 on State Assets (hereinafter referred to as: the State Assets Act). (6)

The Fund shall qualify as a transparent organisation as per point 1 of Paragraph (1) of Article 3 of the National Assets Act. Article 137/B (1) The provisions of the National Assets Act shall be applied in terms of the Fund's exercising of the ownership rights over the State assets belonging to the assets entrusted to the Fund, subject to the deviations specified under Paragraphs (3)-(9). (2) The Fund itself may use and utilise the State assets belonging to the assets entrusted to the Fund, or (unless otherwise stipulated by law) may transfer the ownership title of these assets (sale). The agreement on utilisation or transfer of ownership title shall be made in writing. (3) Any assets above the value limit specified under Article 11 (16) of the National Assets Act, unless otherwise stipulated by law, can be utilised or transferred only with public tendering, or, in exceptionally justified cases, with restricted tendering, proportionately to the value of the service and consideration. For purpose of determining the value limit, the market value of the asset or asset part subjected by the utilisation or sale or, in case of a transaction affecting several asset elements, the aggregate market value of the asset elements shall be taken into account. In case of real estates and other asset elements with an individual gross book value above HUF 5 million, the market value shall be determined on the basis of an independent expert's opinion. (4)

The obligation to conduct a tendering procedure shall apply even in the event of extension of use agreements concluded for a fixed-term. The contracting authority shall be obliged to guarantee equal opportunities under the tendering procedure to all participants in terms of access to the information required for the submission of the tender and the applied conditions of competition. (5) The tendering can be omitted a) if the utilisation is performed for the benefit of an organisation or public body falling within the scope of public finances, b) if the utilisation is performed for the benefit of an organisation operating under the separate or joint majority ownership of the Hungarian State and/or the Fund, c) if the utilisation is performed for the benefit of an organisation performing certain tasks of the State or municipalities, as stipulated by law, d) if the utilisation is performed for the benefit of the public media service provider, e) if the utilisation is performed for the benefit of a foreign state or foreign municipality, furthermore f) if provisions of law or other circumstances of transfer of usage restrict the selection of the potential user in such a material way or to such a significant extent so that the advantages arising from the tendering procedure cannot be ensured, g) if the duration of the contract to be concluded for a fixed-term ga) does not exceed 180 days in case of real estates, gb) does not exceed 3 years in case of contracts or license agreements concluded in terms of archive materials, gc) does not exceed 90 days in other cases, or h) if the utilisation is targeting the usage of the Fund's production capacities or the related studios and equipment. (6) The tendering can be omitted a) if the ownership title is transferred to an organisation falling within points a)-e) of Paragraph (5), or b) if the ownership title is transferred by means of exchange, or c) if the ownership title is transferred for purpose of implementation of an international convention, furthermore d) if the asset is made available to a business association as a contribution in kind, e) if a valid purchase option for an asset is exercised, f) in case of execution of a piece of legislation on lot formation or an agreement on ownership change required for execution of lot formations. (7) A restricted tender can be held, in particular, if the reasonable, planned costs of public tendering of the given asset element would significantly reduce the revenue that can be generated from the utilisation on an annual level or from the sale thereof, or if the previous public tendering procedure was unsuccessful and only a restricted tendering procedure can guarantee the efficient management of the State assets entrusted to the Fund. (8)

If a restricted tender is held, at least three concerned parties, independent from each other, shall be invited to the tendering procedure in writing, simultaneously, directly and in the same way (by sending them the invitation to tender). (9) A purchase option on the assets entrusted to the Fund can only be established in compliance with the rules on sale, as stipulated by law. (10) Except for the case specified under Article 11 (13) of the National Assets Act, the Fund, in the course of its asset management activity, shall ensure a free of charge use of the assets entrusted to it to the public media service provider, furthermore, it shall provide the related services free of charge, including also the services guaranteeing the continuous operation of the public media service provider. (11) In the event of a free of charge transfer of a scrapped tangible asset (not qualifying as a real estate) belonging to the assets entrusted to the Fund, the provision on the reporting obligation specified under Article 13 (4) (b) of the National Assets Act shall not be applied. Article 137/C (1) No contract on the utilisation or transfer of ownership title of the entrusted assets can be concluded with an entity a) that is under bankruptcy or liquidation proceedings, voluntary liquidation, or the proceedings of local governments for consolidation of debts; b) that has suspended its activities or whose activities have been suspended; c) that has any outstanding public debts overdue for more than sixty days, as per point 20 of Article 178 of Act XCII of 2003 on the Rules of Taxation; d) that has a criminal record for the following criminal offences: da) crimes against public justice as stipulated under Title VII of Chapter XV, and economic crimes stipulated under Chapter XVII of

Act IV of 1978 on the Criminal Code, in force until 30 June 2013, db) the following criminal offences specified under the following Chapters of Act C of 2012 on the Criminal Code: crimes of corruption stipulated under Chapter XXVII, criminal offences relating to counterfeiting currencies and philatelic forgeries stipulated under Chapter XXXVIII, criminal offences against public finances stipulated under Chapter XXXIX, money laundering stipulated under Chapter XL, economic and business related offences stipulated under Chapter XLI, crime against consumer rights and any violation of competition laws stipulated under Chapter XLII, or illicit access to data and crimes against information systems stipulated under Chapter XLIII; e) that is banned from exercising an occupation excluding the holding of an executive position in a business entity or business association, or whose activities have been restricted by a final and binding court judgement pursuant to Article 5 (2) of Act CIV of 2001 on Criminal Measures Applicable to Legal Persons; f) that provided false data under any previous proceedings subjecting the utilisation or sale of State assets, closed within the last three years, and hence was excluded from such a proceeding. (2) Prior to execution of the contract, the contracting party must make a written statement (signed personally by him/her or in case of a legal entity, by the authorised signatory) verifying that the grounds for exclusion specified under Paragraph (1) do not apply regarding such contracting party. In the absence of this statement the contract cannot be concluded. A contract concluded on the basis of false statements shall be null and void. (3) In the event any grounds for exclusion as per Paragraph (1) arises subsequent to conclusion of the contract on the utilisation of the entrusted assets, the Fund shall have the right to terminate the contract with immediate effect. Article 137/D The Fund, subject to the prior approval of the Media Council, and the Hungarian National Asset Management Inc may enter into an agreement regarding the free of charge transfer of the exercising of the ownership rights over any of the asset elements, to be registered at book value. This agreement shall enter into force as of its approval by the Minister responsible for State assets. The initiative regarding this shall be submitted to the Minister responsible for State assets jointly by the Fund and the Hungarian National Asset Management Inc. As of entry into force of the agreement, the concerned asset shall qualify as an asset defined under Article 3 (1) of the State Assets Act. Article 137/E (1) The register of the Fund's own assets and the register of the State assets entrusted to the Fund shall have to be separated within the Fund's registers. The entrusted assets shall be registered in a way allowing identification thereof, in line with the characteristics of the given asset, in the way agreed with the Hungarian Central Statistical Office, indicating their quantitative data and value, and also the date of creation (capitalisation). (2) The registration obligation at the value as per Paragraph (1) shall not apply to the asset elements the value of which cannot be determined due to their nature or characteristic, hence in particular, the copyrights and related rights of materials stored in archives. (3) The Fund shall meet its obligations of accounting and annual reporting regarding the State assets entrusted to it in compliance with the decree on the accounting of public finances. (4) Having regard to the public function stipulated under Article 137/A (3), the register does not have to include separately the public function as per the primary purpose of the asset.

Institute for Media Studies of the Media Council

Article 138 (1) The Institute for Media Studies of the Media Council (hereinafter as: Institute) is an independent entity of the Authority, assisting the operation of the Media Council, and pursuing independent scientific activity. The head and members of the Institute are all civil servants of the Authority. (2) Work at the Institute is supervised by the Media Council. (3) The Institute's tasks shall be as follows: a) support the operation of the Media Council by way of performing research and analysis; b) conduct social science research connected to the media; c) publish professional materials; d) organise professional conferences; e) perform other tasks defined for the Institute by the Media Council. (4) The Institute may also engage the services of external experts.

THE MEDIA AND COMMUNICATIONS COMMISSION-EROPERATES AS PART OF THE AUTHORITY.

The Commissioner contributes to the promotion of the equitable interests of users, subscribers, viewers, listeners, consumers of electronic communications services or media services, as well as the readers of press products, regarding electronic communications, media services and press products. The Commissioner shall act in matters vested in him/her under this Act. (2) The Commissioner shall be appointed and removed by the President, who shall also exercise the employer's powers over him/her. The Commissioner is a civil servant in the position of a Head of Division. In performing its duties specified in this Chapter, the Commissioner may not be given instructions. (3) The provisions of Paragraphs (2) and (2a) of Article 111/A shall apply mutatis mutandis to the Commissioner. (4) The Commissioner is assisted in performing its duties by the Office of the Media and Communications Commissioner (hereinafter as: Commissioner's Office) headed by the Commissioner, the civil servants of the Commissioner's Office shall be appointed and removed by the President; the employer's other powers over these civil servants shall be vested with the Commissioner. (5) The operation, organisational structure, internal and external relations of the Commissioner's Office is defined in the By-laws of the Authority and the rules of procedure of the Commissioner's

Office. The rules of procedure of the Commissioner's Office are prepared by the Commissioner and are approved by the President. (6) The budget of the Commissioner's Office shall be determined separately within the budget of the Authority. Article 140 (1) On detecting a conduct related to the provision of a media service, press product or electronic communications service, which conduct does not constitute a breach of a regulation on media administration or electronic communications and falls outside the scope of competence of the Media Council, the President or the Office, but is, or may be suitable to cause harm to the equitable interests of the users, subscribers, consumers, viewers, readers and listeners of media services, press products or electronic communications services, a) the person affected by the harm to interests (for the purposes of this Chapter, hereinafter as: harm to interests) or exposed to the direct danger of such damage to interests; or b) an association representing the interests of consumers, subscribers, users, listeners, or readers may file a complaint with the Commissioner's Office. (2) Requests and notifications received by the President, the Office or the Media Council that meet the conditions laid down under Paragraph (1) in terms of content and contain all the data required under Article 141 (5) shall be transferred to the Commissioner by the President, the Office or the Media Council within eight days, and the Commissioner shall adjudge such requests and notifications as complaints received by him/her. This fact, as well as the fact of the transfer shall be communicated to the requesting party or the complainant concurrently with the transfer. (3) The Commissioner shall act pursuant to the provisions specified under Article 142 in the case of complaints concerning electronic communications services, and shall act pursuant to the provisions specified under Article 142/A in the case of complaints concerning media services or press products.

The common rules applicable to proceedings of the Commissioner

Article 141 (1) The proceedings of the Commissioner shall not be deemed as a regulatory procedure, and the Commissioner shall not have the right to exercise regulatory powers. The complaints defined in Article 140 (1) shall not be deemed as official matters. The Commissioner may apply regulatory instruments – as stipulated in Article 142 – only in case of complaints concerning electronic communications services. (2) The Commissioner may proceed upon having received a complaint only. The Commissioner shall examine the complaint and if it is obviously unfounded or if the harm to interests therein described is of minor importance, or if the case falls outside the Commissioner's scope of competence, he/she shall notify the complainant accordingly within fifteen days. In his/her notification, the Commissioner shall – to the necessary extent – inform the complainant of his/her rights and obligations under the legislation on electronic communications and/or media administration or under the subscription contract, as well as the course of action and means of legal remedy available for such complainant. (3) If the Commissioner detects in the course of the conciliation procedure conducted according to Article 142 (4) or 142/A (1) that the complaint is unfounded or the harm to interests therein described is of minor importance, or if the case falls outside the Commissioner's scope of competence, he/she shall terminate the proceeding, and shall notify the complainant and the parties to the conciliation procedure accordingly within fifteen days. In his/her notification, the Commissioner shall – to the necessary extent – inform the complainant of his/her rights and obligations under the legislation on electronic communications and/or media administration or under the subscription contract, as well as the course of action and means of legal remedy available for such complainant. (4) The complainant shall have the right to request the restricted handling of his/her personal identification data and address. In such cases, the Commissioner, with a view to ensuring the right of access to the documents, shall make an extract of the complaint in a manner which prevents the identity of the complainant from being established. Only this extract may be disclosed to third parties by the Commissioner. For the purposes of investigating the complaint, the Commissioner will handle the personal data of the complainant disclosed to the Commissioner in the course of the procedure and directly related to the complaint until the procedure on the complaint is completed. This fact shall be brought to the complainant's attention. (5) The complaint shall contain the name, address or mailing address of the complainant, the particulars of the harm to interests that call for action by the Commissioner, or the action or conduct that suggest the harm to interests, as well as the circumstances that suggest or substantiate that the other conditions laid down in Article 140 (1) are fulfilled. In case of complaints filed with insufficient information, the Commissioner shall invite the complainant in any phase of the proceeding to rectify the deficiencies within a specified deadline. If the complainant fails to rectify the deficiencies appropriately despite of being invited to do so, the application may not be deemed as a complaint, and therefore the Commissioner shall not proceed. If the proceeding has already been launched, the Commissioner shall terminate the proceeding and shall notify the complainant and the other parties to the conciliation procedure thereof within fifteen days. In his/her notification, the Commissioner shall – to the necessary extent – inform the complainant of his/her rights and obligations under the legislation on electronic communications and/or media administration or under the subscription contract, as well as the course of action and means of legal remedy available for such complainant.

Proceeding by the Commissioner in case of complaints concerning electronic communications services

Article 142 (1) In order to investigate the harm to interests as defined in Article 140 (1) which the Commissioner has become aware of from the complaint, the Commissioner shall have the right to request data related to the harm to interests from any electronic communications service provider, by applying in the appropriate manner the measures defined in the Act on the General Rules of Administrative Proceedings and Services regarding regulatory inspections and the other measures stipulated in this Act concerning the establishment of the facts of the case. The electronic communications service provider concerned shall furnish the Commissioner with the requested data, information, documents or records (for the purposes of this Subtitle, hereinafter collectively as: data) within fifteen days, even if the particular data qualifies as a business secret. The Commissioner shall keep the business secrets revealed to him/her confidential and handle them at the request of the data supplier as a document with restricted access. (2) The Commissioner shall complete its proceedings under this Article within the deadline laid down in Article 151. This deadline shall not include a) the period between the date of invitation to rectify deficiencies as per Article 141 (5) and the date of such rectification, b) the period between the date of requesting data according to Paragraph (1) and the date of the actual data provision, c) the period of time necessary for the procedure as defined in Paragraph (3), d) the period between the invitation to make a statement according to Paragraph (5) and the date of making such statement. (3) If the particular electronic communications service provider fails to furnish the Commissioner with the requested data within the specified deadline, the Commissioner shall resort to the Office. The Office shall initiate verbal or written conciliation with the electronic communications service provider concerned about the necessity of such data provision and the scope of data to be provided. After such conciliation, the Office shall oblige the particular electronic communications service provider to furnish the data related to the harm to interests as specified by the Commissioner in accordance with Paragraph (1) and with the results of the completed conciliation procedure. An appropriate deadline of at least fifteen days shall be set for the provision of the particular data. The provisions of Paragraphs (5)-(7) of Article 155 shall be applied mutatis mutandis.

The obliged electronic communications service provider may seek legal remedy with suspensive effect by requesting the judicial review of the order by the Budapest Administrative and Labour Court. The Budapest Administrative and Labour Court shall decide in an out-of-court proceeding within eight days, and no further legal remedies may be sought against its order. In the event the electronic communications service provider fails to furnish the Office with the requested data, or furnishes it improperly or falsely, the Office may apply the legal sanctions defined in Article 156. The Office shall provide the Commissioner with the received data. (4) the Commissioner, in the course of his/her proceedings, will conduct verbal or written conciliation with the electronic communications service provider on the harm to interests (for the purposes of this Article, hereinafter as: conciliation procedure). The Commissioner will involve the complainant in the conciliation procedure, if the Commissioner finds it expedient and if it is requested by the complainant, and, if the matter concerns a large number of consumers, the Commissioner may also involve the representative of the association engaged in the protection of consumer interests. (5)

In the conciliation procedure the Commissioner will furnish the electronic communications service provider with the description of the harm to interests with the request to provide a statement with their response within a specific deadline of at least fifteen days. (6) In justified cases, the Commissioner, on the basis of the written statement of the electronic communications service provider, will call the representative of the particular electronic communications service provider and/or, if needed, the complainant or the representative of the association engaged in the protection of consumer interests to attend a personal consultation. (7) If the Commissioner and the electronic communications service provider fail to reach an agreement to remedy the harm to interests, the Commissioner shall record the results of the conciliation procedure in a report and proceed as defined under Paragraph (9).

If the conciliation procedure results in an agreement, the Commissioner and the electronic communications service provider concerned shall incorporate the agreement in writing, which the Commissioner shall send to the complainant and shall post the agreement on his/her website. In the agreement the parties shall provide for the manner of remedying the harm to interests. (8) The agreement is a concordant and voluntary legal statement of the parties, concluded between the Commissioner and the electronic communications service provider concerned whereby the contractual rights shall entitle the users, subscribers, and consumers, resorting to the electronic communications service. The agreement may not result in any obligations imposed on the users, subscribers, or consumers. The provisions of the agreement shall constitute part of the legal relationship – by modifying such legal relationship – of the particular users, subscribers, and consumers with the particular electronic communications service provider, whereby the provisions of the agreement will be applicable in individual cases and the particular users, subscribers, or consumers may make a reference to these provisions in individual cases, and the Authority will have the right to verify compliance with the provisions of the agreement in the course of a regulatory inspection. The extent of cooperation demonstrated by the electronic communications service provider concluding the agreement as per this Paragraph with regard to the effective enforcement of consumer interests shall also be taken into account by the Authority in other official matters involving the given electronic communications service provider. (9)

The Commissioner shall make a report of the results of the successful conciliation procedure as necessary, and shall make a report of any and all conciliation procedures not resulting in an agreement. Such reports shall be sent to the complainant, to the electronic communications service provider concerned, and to any associations representing the interests of consumers in the proceeding. In addition to the particulars of the harm to interests, in its report the Commissioner shall describe the conduct of the electronic communications service provider in detail regarding the handling of the harm to interests, and, in particular its willingness to cooperate in remedying the harm to interests and enhancing consumer well-being. The Commissioner shall publish his/her report if it affects or may affect a large number of consumers, or can issue a recommendation or guideline for the consumers for the purpose of avoiding further harm to interests. If no agreement was concluded, the electronic communications service provider concerned shall notify the Commissioner about the measures taken within the deadline of at least fifteen days specified by the Commissioner.

Proceeding by the Commissioner in case of complaints concerning media services and press products

Article 142/A (1) The Commissioner, in the course of his/her proceedings, will conduct verbal or written consultations regarding the harm to interests as per Article 140 (1) (for the purposes of this Article, hereinafter as: conciliation procedure), with the professional, interest representing or self-regulatory bodies of media content providers (for the purposes of this Article, hereinafter collectively as: professional organisation). (2) The Commissioner shall not proceed in relation to the complaint, unless a) the complaint concerns such an activity causing harm to interests, which arises repeatedly in the course of activities by the media content provider, or which arises in the course of activities of more media content providers, and b) the harm to interests specified in the complaint affects a significant part of the viewers, listeners, or readers. (3) The Commissioner shall notify the media content provider about any and all complaints concerning its activities, and shall ensure for the media content provider the possibility to present its position in all stages of the conciliation procedure. (4) The Commissioner shall, in the course of the conciliation procedure, forward the description of the harm to interests affecting a significant part of viewers, listeners, or readers to the professional organisations for commenting thereto within a specified deadline. (5) The Commissioner shall, in the course of the conciliation procedure, prepare a proposal for remedying the complaint, and shall forward such proposal to the professional organisations. The Commissioner shall prepare its proposal in a way so to represent the interests of viewers, listeners, and readers, while taking into consideration the observations made by the professional organisations and the media content provider concerned. (6)

Based on the response given by the professional organisations and the media content provider concerned regarding the proposal, the Commissioner, in justified cases, shall invite the complainant, the professional organisations concerned, and the media content provider concerned to a personal conciliation. (7) The Commissioner shall prepare a report of the results of the conciliation procedure, and shall forward the report to the complainant, the media content provider concerned, and the professional organisations concerned. In addition to presenting the circumstances of the harm to interests, the Commissioner shall present in the report the prepared proposals, and the respective responses and observations made by the media content provider and the professional organisations. The Commissioner may not publish its report. (8) For the purposes of this Article, the deadline specified in Article 142 (2) shall be applied regarding the preparation of the proposal mentioned in Paragraph (5). This deadline shall not include a) the period for making observations as defined in Paragraph (4), b) the time used to prepare the expert opinion, provided that an expert is required to be involved in the conciliation procedure.

The Commissioner's Report

Article 143 The Commissioner shall prepare a quarterly report on his/her observations regarding

the proceedings carried out, the results of the proposals, as well as on his/her reports and proposals, for the President concerning the cases affecting the electronic communications service providers, and for the Media Council concerning the cases affecting the media content providers. The report prepared for the Media Council shall include only the general observations of the Commissioner, without disclosing any specific data concerning any individual media content provider.

PROVISIONS ON THE PROCEDURES BY THE MEDIA COUNCIL AND THE OFFICE OF THE NATIONAL MEDIA AND INFOCOMMUNICATIONS AUTHORITY

Article 144 (1) The Media Council and the Office (hereinafter for the purposes of this Chapter: Authority) shall act in accordance with the provisions of the Act on the General Rules of Administrative Proceedings and Services subject to the provisions of this Act. (2) The members and the President of the Media Council shall have votes of identical value, that is, each person shall have one vote. (3) The Media Council shall be deemed to have quorum when a simple majority of the members, including the President of the Media Council, are present. (4) The decisions of the Media Council shall be passed with the simple majority of the votes of all members of the Media Council, including the President, with the exception of the case defined in Article 129 (7).

The Complainant

Article 145 (1) Anyone not deemed to be a client for the purposes of the subject of the notification (hereinafter as: complainant) may lodge a complaint addressed to the Authority in matters falling within the scope of powers and responsibilities of the Authority defined in this Act, claiming infringement of the rules on media administration. (2) The complaint shall contain the data of the complainant, the circumstances providing the grounds for the Authority's proceedings, the action or conduct that suggests infringement of the rules on media administration, as well as the facts providing the grounds for the complaint. (3) Based on the complaint the Authority shall have the right to initiate proceedings ex officio at its sole discretion. If the Authority does not initiate proceedings on the basis of the complaint, it shall duly notify the complainant in an official letter, without having to specify the reasons for its decision. (4) The complainant shall not become a subject in the legal relations arising under the regulatory procedure initiated on the basis of the complaint, the complainant shall not have the right to seek legal remedy against the regulatory decision of the Authority passed in the administrative proceedings initiated ex officio on the basis of the complainant's complaint. (5) The complainant may request the restricted handling of his/her data as stipulated in Article 153 (2). (6) [not in effect]

Legal Succession

Article 146 (1) The client having acquired rights under a final decision may be replaced by its legal successor. (2) The client bound by an obligation under a final decision is replaced by its legal successor, provided that such replacement is not impossible. In case of an obligation established under a final decision the legal successor may voluntarily fulfil the obligation, within a deadline extended upon its request, in justified cases, on one occasion at the most. The Authority and the legal successor may agree on the above in a public contract as well. (3) In case of an obligation established under a final decision, the third party to whom the original (legal predecessor) client, bound by an obligation, assigns the terms of its operations under a contract, shall also be deemed as a legal successor to such client. (4) If the legal succession arises in the course of the regulatory procedure and is based on a statutory legislation, the Authority shall establish the fact of legal succession in its order. No separate appeal shall lie against such order. (5) In the event that the legal succession arises in thc coursc of thc regulatory procedure and is based on a contract, the Authority shall establish the fact of legal succession necessary for exercising its regulatory powers in its order. No separate appeal shall lie against such order.

Confidentiality

Article 147 (1) During the term of their employment and after the termination thereof, persons currently or formerly employed by the Authority as civil servants or in other work-related relationship shall keep confidential any personal data, classified data and business secrets they may have learnt in relation to the operation and actions of the Authority as well as any other data, fact or circumstance that the Authority is not obliged to make accessible for the public, excepting those that are to be disclosed to other entities under relevant legislation. (2) The persons listed under Paragraph (1) may not unlawfully disclose, utilize or make known to any third party, any data, fact or circumstance they may have learnt in the course of performing their tasks.

Communications via Electronic Means

Article 148 In its scope of competence and procedures defined under this Act the Authority may require that contact is maintained via electronic means.

Commencement of Proceedings

Article 149 (1) In matters falling within its competence the Authority may initiate proceedings ex officio, except if under this Act the proceeding may be initiated only upon application. (2) If the Authority becomes aware of a breach of law falling beyond the scope of the particular official matter yet closely or indirectly related to such matter, it may ex officio extend its proceedings to that particular matter, before passing its regulatory decision. In accordance with the relevant provisions of the Act on the General Rules of Administrative Proceedings and Services the clients shall be notified of the fact that the proceedings were ex officio extended to the particular matter. On the ex officio extension of the proceedings, the administrative deadline of the proceedings shall be extended by the period of time applicable to the particular proceedings. (3) The proceedings of the Authority defined in separate legislation shall be subject to an administrative procedural service fee. (4) Proceedings of the Authority in relation to violations concerning media contents may be initiated (by request, notification) within three months of publication of the media content or, in case of continuous publication, after the first publication. (5) If the applicant gained knowledge about the violation only subsequently or was otherwise prevented from filing the request or notification, the deadline set forth in Paragraph (4) shall start

from the date of gaining knowledge or from the date the obstacle was overcome. No regulatory procedures may be initiated in relation to violations concerning media contents after six months of publication of the media content or, in case of continuous publication, after the first publication. This deadline shall represent the expiry of the limitation period. (6) Upon violation of Articles 14 and 16-20 of the Press Freedom Act, as well as Articles 9-11, Article 12 (3)-(4), Article 14, and Articles 23-36 of the Media Act, the authority may launch the regulatory procedure ex officio within one year after the media content was published or – in case of continuous publication – after the media content was published at the first time.

Assessment of Competence and Jurisdiction

Article 150 If the Authority has no competence or jurisdiction concerning a certain issue, the Authority shall have the right to reject the respective application and/or terminate the proceedings without examination thereof on the merits, without determining the competent authority and without transferring the case to such authority.

Administrative Deadline

Article 151 (1) Unless otherwise provided for in this Act the administrative deadline of the proceedings conducted by the Authority shall be forty days. (2) The period may be extended in justified cases on one occasion, by thirty days at the most.

Application

Article 152 The client shall submit its application in the appropriate official form of the Authority, and in case contact via electronic means, in electronic form, in the notification procedures defined in Articles 42-47

Access to Documents for Inspection, Secrets Protected by Law

Article 153 (1) Persons participating in administering the case and employed by the Authority as civil servants or engaged in other work-related relationship with such Authority, shall have unlimited access to the secrets protected by law. (2) The client and other participants involved in the proceedings may designate the range of data they deem necessary to be treated as restricted data, by reference to the protection of the secrets protected under the law, in particular business secrets, to other equitable interests as well as to any significant media policy considerations, save for data made public for general public interests and data defined in relevant legislation that may not be rated as data restricted under the law. In this case the client and/or other participants involved in the proceedings shall also prepare a version of the document which does not contain the data defined above. (3) Data defined under Paragraph (2) shall be handled by the Authority within the document folder separately, as restricted data. The Authority shall ensure that restricted data are not accessible for unauthorised persons in the course of the procedural acts. (4) Only the officer, the keeper of Minutes, the executives of the Authority, the member of the Media Council, the competent public prosecutor and, in case of judicial review, the acting judge shall be entitled to access the restricted data. (5) To the extent so required to perform their duties connected to the subject of the official matter, other administrative authorities or government entities may also have access to restricted data, as deemed appropriate by the Authority, provided that such entities ensure at least the same level of

protection for the data thus transferred as at the disclosing authority. (6) With a view to ensuring the right of access to documents for inspection, the Authority shall prepare an extract of the document generated in the course of the proceedings, which document is otherwise in compliance with statutory requirement as to form and content, whereby no conclusions may be made as to the data defined under Paragraph (2). (7) If the proper enforcement of the law, the enforcement of rights and the exercising of client rights justify it, the Authority may request that the client and other participants involved in the proceedings lift the restriction placed on the data management as defined under Paragraph (2). (8) In case the client or other participant in the proceedings does not lift the restrictions defined under Paragraph (2), the Authority – if such action is indispensable for law enforcement or for the enforcement of rights vested with clients – may provide for in its order that the restricted data management be lifted. This order may be challenged by the client or the other participant in the proceedings by submitting an appeal to the Budapest Administrative and Labour Court with a suspensive effect; the court shall decide in the matter with priority in out-of-court proceedings within eight days. No further appeal shall be available against the order of the Budapest Administrative and Labour Court.

Exclusion

Article 154 (1) In addition to those specified in the relevant provisions of the Act on the General Rules of Administrative Proceedings and Services on exclusions, no person may participate in handling of the case on the merits, who had a legal relationship as defined in Point (a) with the client or with an enterprise with a qualifying holding in the client or with an enterprise operating under the client's qualifying holding within one year of the commencement of the proceedings, or whose relative a) is in employment relationship, other work-related relationship or membership relationship with the client, or is an executive officer thereof; b) holds an ownership share in the client; c) is in employment relationship, other work-related relationship or membership relationship with a natural person or legal person that is in regular business relations with the client, or is an executive officer thereof, or has a shareholding in the above; d) is in a work-related relationship with an organisation that is a supervisory or subordinate entity to the client and/or which has provided any support or exclusive licence for the client, excluding the work-related relationship with the Foundation or the Authority. (2) The acting officer of the Office shall forthwith report to the Director General any grounds for exclusion on his/her part. The acting officer of the Office shall be bear disciplinary and financial liability for his/her failure to or delay in, making a notification. The decision on the exclusion of a particular officer of the Office shall be made by the Director General and, if necessary, he/she shall designate the officer acting on behalf of the Office. (3) The Director General shall forthwith report to the President any grounds for exclusion on his/her part. The Director General shall bear disciplinary and financial liability for his/her failure to or delay in, making the notification. The decision on the exclusion of the Director General shall be made by the President. When there are grounds for the exclusion for the Director General, the President – in making its decision – shall consider whether the Director General may proceed in the particular case under the condition that he/she shall notify the President of his/her decision, or whether the President will select one of the Deputy Directors General to exercise the scope of competence. (4) If the report submitted by the client with the aim of exclusion is obviously unsubstantiated, in the order on rejecting the exclusion the client may be subjected to a procedural fine laid down in Article 156.

(5) The decision on the exclusion of a Media Council member shall be made by the Media Council. The member thus excluded may not participate in handling of the case on the merits. When, as a result of exclusion, the Media Council does not have a quorum, the Media Council will proceed with the involvement of the excluded members in accordance with the relevant provisions of the Act on the General Rules of Administrative Proceedings and Services, irrespective of their grounds for exclusion, with such members also having a right to vote. (6) When there are grounds for exclusion in the case of the President, the Vice-President designated by the President shall proceed in handling of the case on its merits

Establishing the Facts of the Case

Article 155 (1) In establishing the facts of the case, the Authority shall apply the provisions of the Act on the General Rules of Administrative Proceedings and Services on establishing the facts of the case and on regulatory inspections subject to the provisions specified under Paragraphs (2)-(10). (2) In order to establish the facts of the case, the Authority shall have the right to view, examine and make duplicates and extracts of any and all instruments, deeds and documents containing data related to the media service, the publication of the press product or the media service distribution, even if such instrument, deed or document contains business secrets. (3) In order to establish the facts of the case, the Authority shall have the right to oblige a) the client and b) other participants in the proceeding, the agents and employees of the client or of the other participants in the proceeding, and persons in other legal relationship with the client or the other participants in the proceeding, and – in exceptionally justified cases – other persons or organisations (for the purposes of this Article, hereinafter as: other participants) – while warning them about the legal sanctions specified in Article 156 that can be applied if this obligation is not met in the appropriate manner – to make a statement, to provide data, or to provide either verbally or in writing data in a comparable format as defined by the Authority, and to furnish other information (for the purposes of this Article, hereinafter as: data provision). (4) The order mentioned in Paragraph (3) may be challenged by the other participants obliged to provide data by submitting an appeal to the Budapest Administrative and Labour Court, and such appeal shall have a suspensive effect. The court shall decide in the matter with priority, within the framework of an out-of-court proceeding, within eight days. No further appeal shall be available against the order of the Budapest Administrative and Labour Court. (5)

For the purposes of Paragraphs (2) and (3), a) the deeds, instruments, and documents generated during or for the purposes of the communications between a client and his or her legal representative or recording the contents of such communication, provided, in all above cases, that this characteristic is apparent directly from the deed, instrument or document itself, may not be used as evidence, may not be examined, may not be seized, and their holder may not be obliged to produce it during an inspection; b) the Authority may not oblige the media content provider or a person in an employment relationship or in a work-related legal relationship with a media content provider to provide any data, or to hand over any deed, instrument or document that would reveal the identity of the person delivering information to him/her in connection with the media content provider's activities. (6) The exemption specified under Paragraph (5) shall remain valid even after the legal relationship justifying the exemption is terminated. The client may grant an exemption regarding the prohibition stipulated in Point a) of Paragraph (5). (7) Any client or other participant of the proceeding obliged to provide data or to hand over or present any deed, instrument, or document despite of having recourse to the exemption stipulated in Paragraph (5) may seek legal remedy with suspensive effect from the Budapest Administrative and Labour Court against the order of the Authority, and the court shall decide in the matter with priority, within the framework of an out-of-court proceeding, within eight days. No further appeal shall be available against the order of the Budapest Administrative and Labour Court. (8) A witness may be heard on the business secret of the client even if the client has not granted him/her an exemption regarding the obligation of confidentiality. (9)

In particularly justified cases, the Authority shall have the right to resort to the deeds, data, documents and other means of evidence generated in the course of a regulatory procedure also for the purposes of another procedure, when necessary for reducing the procedural burden on clients or for proper and effective law enforcement. (10) The media service provider shall keep the authentic documentation on its programme flow, including the full recording of output signals of the media service, for a period of sixty days from the date of broadcast or, in case of on-demand media services, from the last day the concerned content was made available. For the purposes of regulatory inspection, the Authority shall be entitled to oblige the media service provider – within the period of statutory retention – to deliver the authentic documentation on its programme flow without delay and free of charge. In case of a regulatory procedure instituted or a legal dispute arising in relation to a media service, the media service provider shall keep the documentation for a period of one year from the conclusion of the proceedings with a final force

Procedural

Fine Article 156 (1) In case of hindrance on the proceedings, the Authority shall have the right to impose procedural fine on the client, other actors in the proceedings or other persons obliged to cooperate with a view to establishing the facts of the case, when these parties act in a manner aimed at the prolongation of the proceedings or preventing the actual facts of the case from being established, or in a manner which may result in the above. (2) The maximum amount of the procedural fine is twenty-five million forints or, for private person clients, one million forints. (3) In addition to the provisions of Paragraphs (1)-(2), the Authority shall have the right, and in case of repeated offence, shall be obliged, to impose a procedural fine also on the executive officer of the breaching entity in case of hindering the proceedings or in case of failure or improper fulfilment of the obligation to furnish data, in the maximum amount of three million forints. (4) When setting the amount of the procedural fine, the Authority shall take into account especially the net sales revenue generated by the breaching entity in the previous year and the fact whether the offence was committed on one or more occasions.

Public Hearing

Article 157 (1) When so required under this Act or to the extent it deems necessary and justified to perform its duties, the Authority, with a view to familiarizing itself with legislation on media administration and the measures pertaining to its enforcement, and with the experts' positions and opinions on the preparation and implementation of law enforcement procedures, shall hold a public hearing, inviting media service providers, entities providing ancillary media services, publishers of press products, media service distributors, intermediary service providers, self-regulatory professional organisations, civil associations and others. (2) Unless otherwise provided for in this Act, the Authority shall publish the date, time, place and subject of the public hearing at least thirty days before the scheduled date thereof. (3) The Authority shall publish the preparatory documents related to the subject of the public hearing, excepting business secrets, at least ten days before the scheduled date of the hearing.

Article 158 (1) Eight days before the scheduled date of the public hearing the Authority shall post on its website the documents received by it in an electronic format in relation to the public hearing. (2) The Authority shall prepare a summary or a protocol on the public hearing containing comments and proposals given and voiced at the hearing, excepting data classified by the commenter or proposer as business secret. The Authority shall publish the summary within thirty days of the date of the hearing.

Consultations with Stakeholders in Significant Issues

Article 159 (1) To the extent it deems necessary, the Media Council may initiate consultations with stakeholders in matters falling within its regulatory powers (hereinafter as: consultations). In so doing, the Media Council – at least fifteen days before passing its regulatory decision – shall publish the draft decision and preparatory documents necessary for the consultations, with the exception of data subject to restricted data handling within the proceedings. (2) Within eight days of publication of the draft regulatory decision as defined under Paragraph (1), anyone may submit to the Media Council in writing his/her position, proposal and other comments he/she may have concerning the draft decision (hereinafter as: comment). The Media Council shall not be bound by the comments so received, which serve for information purposes only, with no obligation on the part of the Media Council to take them into account for the purposes of passing its regulatory decision. (3) In its regulatory decision the Media Council shall not be under obligation to justify the necessity to hold consultations or – when it initiates consultations – to justify the reasons why comments were taken or not taken into account. (4) By virtue of the fact of submitting comments, the stakeholders having submitted comments as defined under Paragraph (2) will not become a party to the procedural relationship involving the regulatory decision being the subject matter of the consultations. Stakeholders shall not be entitled to legal remedies within the scope of its comments, even in relation to the portions of the regulatory decision pertaining to the comments.

Public Contract

Article 160 (1) In cases defined herein, the Authority shall have the right to conclude a public contract with a client, based on the provisions of the Act on the General Rules of Administrative Proceedings and Services and subject to the provisions of this Act. (2) Under the public contract concluded with the Authority, the client may assume obligations that are beyond the Authority's regulatory powers, and compliance therewith on the part of the client could not be prescribed otherwise under a regulatory decision. In this case, under the public contract the client agrees that in case of non-compliance on the client's part with the provisions of the agreement the entire agreement shall be regarded as a final and enforceable regulatory decision. (3) Regarding those contractual terms and conditions which could be imposed on the contractual party by way of regulatory decision under the law, the approval of third parties whose rights and lawful interests are affected by the contract is not a condition to the public contract being validly concluded. (4) The administrative deadline for the completion of the official matter by a public contract as defined in

Article 151 shall apply subject to the provisions of this Act. Article 161 (1)

The Authority shall check compliance with the provisions of the public contract in the course of a regulatory inspection. When under the regulatory inspection the Authority establishes breach of the public contract by the client, it shall assess, with a view to the facts revealed in the inspection, the gravity of the breach, the effective enforcement of rights, the social, economic and legal relations affected by the contract, the relevant media administration principles and objectives, and the effective enforcement of public interest underlying the contract, whether to initiate in the case involving the breach of the decision the enforcement proceedings as defined in the Act on the General Rules of Administrative Proceedings and Services, or the regulatory procedures to apply the legal sanctions specified in this Act. (2)

When the Authority initiates enforcement proceedings, the client may seek review of the order on enforcement, by claiming infringement of law, at an administrative court within fifteen days of the order being announced. The court will pass its decision, based on the hearing of the parties, if necessary, in out-of-court proceedings within fifteen days. The submission of the application for out-of-court proceedings shall have a suspensive effect on the enforcement of the order. No appeal may be lodged against the order of the Budapest Administrative and Labour Court. (3) When the Authority, under Paragraph (1), initiates proceedings to apply legal sanctions specified in this Act, no independent legal remedy shall lie against the institution of the proceedings. (4) In the regulatory procedure initiated as a result of the regulatory inspection and on account of breach of contract by the client, the Authority may apply the legal sanctions defined in Article 187 and in the public contract. (5) In case of material or repeated breach of contract by the client, the Authority, unless otherwise provided for in the public contract, shall have the right to terminate the public contract with immediate effect. (6)

An action brought before the court for the amendment of the public contract, shall not affect the fulfilment and enforcement of the public contract and shall not have a suspensive effect on the fulfilment and enforcement of the public contract.

Disclosure

Article 162 (1) The Authority shall comply with the provisions of the Act on the General Rules of Administrative Proceedings and Services on disclosure to the general public by notification posted through its website. (2) The Authority shall publish its regulatory decisions and the relevant court decisions through its website, having regard to the protection of personal data and restricted data handled in the proceedings. (3) When the law allows notification through public notice, the notice shall be made public by posting the notice on the bulletin board of the Authority and by posting such notice on the website of the Authority.

Legal Remedies

Article 163 (1) No appeal may be lodged against the regulatory decision of the Media Council passed in its capacity as authority of the first instance. Review of the regulatory decision of the Media Council may be requested only by the client, and as regards the provisions expressly applicable to him/her, the witness, the official witness, the expert, the interpreter, the holder of the object under inspection, the representative of the client and the liaison officer, by claiming infringement of law, at the court proceeding in administrative cases, within thirty days upon announcement of the regulatory decision, by bringing an action against the Media Council. (2) The court proceedings instituted on the basis of the statement of claim for review of the Media Council's decision shall be subject to the provisions of the Act on the Code of Civil Procedure on public administration lawsuits, subject to the provisions of this Act. (3) The submission of the statement of claim shall not have a suspensive effect on the enforcement of the decision; the court may be requested to suspend the enforcement of the regulatory decision challenged by the statement of claim.

(4) The Media Council shall forward the statement of claim, together with the documents and representations of the case, to the court within fifteen days of receipt thereof. (5) The application for out-of-court proceedings against the orders of the Media Council which can be challenged by an independent legal remedy shall be submitted within fifteen days of the notification of the order. (6) No supervisory proceedings may be instituted concerning the regulatory decisions of the Media Council. Article 164 (1) In proceedings specified under Article 163, courts of both first and second instance shall pass judgement within thirty days. (2) The judicial review proceedings shall fall within the exclusive competence of the Budapest Administrative and Labour Court. (3)

The court shall have the powers to alter the decision of the Media Council. Article 165 (1) The client shall have the right to appeal against the regulatory decision of the Office passed according to this Act at the Media Council, with the exception of decisions against which no appeal may be lodged under the Act on the General Rules of Administrative Proceedings and Services or under this Act. (2) The decision of the Office may be challenged under an appeal only by a client who has participated in the proceedings of the first instance. (3) Review of the second instance decision of the Media Council may be requested only by the client, and as regards the provisions expressly applicable to him/her, the witness, the official witness, the expert, the interpreter, the holder of the object under inspection, the representative of the client and the liaison officer, by claiming infringement of law, at the court proceeding in administrative cases, within thirty days upon announcement of the regulatory decision, by lodging a statement of claim. (4) The submission of the statement of claim shall not have a suspensive effect on the execution of the decision, the court may be requested to suspend the execution of the regulatory decision challenged by the statement of claim. (5) The application for out-of-court proceedings against the orders of the Office which can be challenged by independent legal remedy shall be submitted within fifteen days of the notification of the order. (6) The judicial review proceedings shall fall within the exclusive competence of the Budapest Administrative and Labour Court.

Specific Proceedings of the Authority

Article 166 In conducting its proceedings defined in Articles 68-70 and 167-181, the Authority shall apply the provisions of the Act on the General Rules of Administrative Proceedings and Services and this Act subject to the deviations determined for the various types of proceedings.

General Regulatory Supervision

Article 167 (1) At request or ex officio, the Authority, within the context of its scope of powers and responsibilities, shall have the right to supervise within a regulatory inspection or regulatory procedure the enforcement and observance of the provisions laid down in this Act and the Press Freedom Act, as well as fulfilment of the terms and conditions set forth in its regulatory decisions, broadcasting agreements and in the public contracts concluded by the Authority. (2) Should the Authority establish infringement of the provisions laid down in its regulatory decision as revealed in the supervision of compliance with its regulatory decision, it shall assess, on the basis of all circumstances of the case, the facts revealed in the inspection, the gravity of the infringement and the effective enforcement of rights, whether to resort to the enforcement procedure as defined in the Act on the General Rules of Administrative Proceedings and Services, or institute a regulatory procedure to apply the legal sanctions specified in this Act, in the case involving violation of the decision. (3) The Authority shall have the right to apply the legal sanctions defined in Chapter V in cases of infringements revealed in the course of general regulatory supervision.

Market Surveillance

Article 168 (1) The Media Council, within its scope of competence, with a view to protecting the smooth, fruitful and diverse operation of the media market and protecting the interests of those engaged in media service distribution and media service provision, publishers of press products, viewers, listeners, readers, subscribers and users, as well as preserving the diversity of the national culture and opinions, promoting the maintenance of fair and effective market competition, familiarization with market trends and the comprehensive assessment, analysis and regulatory supervision of media policy considerations and other purposes defined in this Act, shall perform market surveillance activities. (2) The specific market surveillance procedure may include a number of regulatory powers and official matter types, as defined in the Press Freedom Act and this Act, as a comprehensive regulatory procedure. (3) The Media Council, in performing its duties defined under Paragraph (1), shall prepare an annual market surveillance plan by 1 December of the year preceding the subject year – taking into consideration the market surveillance experiences of the previous year – and shall publish the same on its website within fifteen days thereof. The Media Council shall ensure that its market surveillance plans are in accordance with one another. The plans may be reviewed on the basis of its findings made in the first six months at the end of that half, and – if necessary – the Media Council shall have the right to modify these plans accordingly. The Media Council shall post its modified market surveillance plan on its website within fifteen days of its modification. (4) The market surveillance procedure shall be instituted ex officio. (5) The administrative deadline of a market surveillance procedure shall be sixty days. The period may be extended in justified cases on one occasion, by forty-five days at the most. (6)

In its comprehensive and consolidated regulatory decision, the Media Council, as the purpose and as a result of the market surveillance procedure, shall a) assess compliance of services and activities subject to the procedure with applicable legislation. In so doing, the Media Council shall establish the occurrence of infringements, make an assessment of these instances both on an individual and aggregate basis and shall determine the legal sanctions by suitably applying the provisions of Chapter V. In its market surveillance decision, the Media Council may impose obligations and define the terms of their fulfilment, when no infringement has occurred, b) determine the directions, methods, criteria for development and reshaping (if any), and media policy conclusions of state intervention with a view to preventing infringement of legislation, promoting voluntary compliance with the law and smooth flow of market trends. (7) The Media Council shall prepare an annual report on the fulfilment of the objectives in its market surveillance plans, the results and findings of its market surveillance operations and its proposals on amendment of legislation arising on the basis of market surveillance decisions. The Media

Council shall post its report on its website within fifteen days of its approval. (8) The Media Council shall have the right to conduct market surveillance activities ex officio beyond the scope of the market surveillance plan.

Inspection of the Media Market

Article 169 (1) With a view to assessing compliance with the provisions of this Act and revealing whether regulatory powers specified in this Act should be applied, when the price changes or other market circumstances suggest that competition in the media service market is being distorted or is restricted, the Media Council, in order to gather information on market trends and asses such trends, shall institute a regulatory inspection by its order. (2) This procedure of the Media Council shall be without prejudice to the competence of the Hungarian Competition Authority to conduct an inspection under the Act on the Prohibition of Unfair and Restrictive Market Practices. (3) The Media Council shall inform through public notice the media service providers of the commencement of the regulatory inspection, which – in deviation from the relevant provisions of the Act on the General Rules of Administrative Proceedings and Services – must contain the subject of the case and a brief description thereof. The explanatory section of the order shall designate the market conditions that gave rise to the inspection. The order shall be announced through public notice by posting on the bulletin board of the Authority and on the website of the Authority. The order on the institution of the procedure shall be deemed duly served on the fifteenth day from the posting of the notice on bulletin board of the Authority. (4) The amount of the procedural fine that may be imposed in an inspection, taking into account the net sales revenue generated by the breaching entity in the previous year and the fact whether the offence was committed on one or more occasions, shall be equal to 0.5 % of the sales revenue of the breaching entity, or, in the absence of revenues or reporting on revenues, it shall be minimum fifty thousand forints and maximum fifty million forints. In addition, in case of non- or improper provision of data, the Media Council shall have the right, and in case of repeated infringement, shall be obliged, to impose a fine on the executive officer of the breaching media service provider in the amount between fifty thousand forints and three million forints. Article 170 (1) If the Media Council, on the basis of the findings of the regulatory inspection, establishes that the market trends under review may cause distortions or restrictions in competition in the market for media services, and in its opinion these circumstances may not be remedied by exercising the powers available according to this Act, it shall initiate that the commencement of the Hungarian Competition Authority's competition authority proceeding in the matter. (2) The Hungarian Competition Authority will not commence the competition authority proceeding initiated by the Media Council as defined under Paragraph (1) if there is an inspection in progress in the same subject and for the same period or, if the Hungarian Competition Authority had already completed an inspection in the same subject for the same period beforehand. The Hungarian Competition Authority shall notify the Media Council of this fact. (3) When there are no grounds for, or due to absence of competence it is impossible to initiate competition authority proceeding, or when the market distortion may not be remedied within the scope of competence of the Media Council or the Office, it shall duly notify the body entitled for legislation

Proceedings of the Media Council as Special Authority

Article 171 (1) The Hungarian Competition Authority shall obtain the position statement of the Media Council for the approval of concentration of enterprises under Article 24 of the Act LVII of 1996 (hereinafter as: the Competition Act) on the Prohibition of Unfair and Restrictive Market Practices, which enterprises, or the affiliates of at least two groups of companies as defined in Article 15 of the Competition Act bear editorial responsibility and the primary objective of which is to distribute media content to the general public via an electronic communications network or a printed press product.

(2) If the level of independent opinion sources following the merger would still ensure the right for diversity of information within the particular market segment of media content service, then the Media Council, with the exception of the case defined in Article 68 (2), cannot reject granting an approval as special authority. (3) With regard to applying the provision or condition imposed by the Media Council as special authority in a decision on the merits of a case, Article 30 (3) of the Competition Act shall appropriately apply. (4) The position of the Media Council as special authority shall bind the Hungarian Competition Authority, however, this fact does not prevent the Hungarian Competition Authority from a) prohibiting a merger that has already been approved officially by the Media Council as special authority, irrespective of any condition the Media Council may have set; or b) imposing a condition or an obligation as defined in Article 30 (3) of the Competition Act that the Media Council has failed to set. (5) The statutory period for the proceedings of the Media Council as a special authority shall be twenty days, which may be extended on one occasion by another twenty days. The statutory period of the competition authority proceeding shall not include the period of proceedings of the Media Council as special authority. Failure by the Media Council to issue its position within the prescribed statutory period shall be deemed as an approval on its part. (6) The amount of the administrative service fee payable to the Media Council for its procedure as special authority shall equal two

million forints, which is payable to the Hungarian Competition Authority together with the procedural fee as defined in Article 62 (1) of the Competition Act, except when the applicant had submitted a request for a prior approval of the special authority as defined under Paragraph (7). (7)

On payment of the administrative service fee defined under Paragraph (6), at the request of the applicant defined in Article 68 of the Competition Act, the Media Council shall issue prior approval as a special authority. The applicant shall have the opportunity to request prior approval until the date of submitting a request for approval of merger but not later than the end of the period defined in Article 28 (2) of the Competition Act, and this approval can be used within six months from the date of issue, provided that facts, the market and the regulatory circumstances decisive for the purposes of the approval have – remained unchanged since the date of the position issued by the special authority. The prior approval issued by the Media Council as special authority or the request for approval shall be attached to the form set forth in Article 68 (2) of the Competition Act. When a specific requirement or condition laid down in the prior approval issued by the Media Council as special authority contradicts an obligation or condition deemed necessary by the Hungarian Competition Authority in part or in full, the government entities involved shall proceed as described in Article 45 (2) of the Act on the General Rules of Administrative Proceedings and Services.

Proceeding in Case of Legal Disputes Article 172 (1) In case of infringement of the rights or lawful interests concerning media administration – defined in an agreement concluded under a rule on media administration or in a rule on media administration – of a media service provider, an entity engaged in providing ancillary media services, a publisher of press products or a media service distributor, by another media service provider or media service distributor, and in cases defined in this Act, the affected party may resort to the Media Council to conduct a legal dispute procedure (hereinafter as: legal dispute procedure). The legal dispute procedure may be initiated within six months after the occurrence of the infringement. If the applicant gained knowledge about the infringement only subsequently or was otherwise prevented from filing the request, the period of six months shall start from the date of gaining knowledge or from the date the obstacle was overcome.

The legal dispute procedure may not be initiated after one year of occurrence of the infringement serving as ground for such procedure. This deadline shall represent the expiry of the limitation period. (2) The application for conducting a legal dispute procedure shall clearly describe, in addition to the requisites defined in the provisions of the Act on the General Rules of Administrative Proceedings and Services on applications, the facts and circumstances serving as grounds for claims under Paragraph (1), the legislative and contractual provisions that provide the grounds for the application and verification of its rights and lawful interests. (3) When the applicant requests the Media Council to bring the contract into existence or to determine its contents, he/she shall expressly and clearly define the particulars of the contractual provisions he/she wishes to be brought into existence or established, in a clear-cut text. (4) The application may also include a motion for evidence. (5)

When the application for the legal dispute procedure does not contain or contains improperly the requisites laid down under Paragraph (2), the Media Council shall request the applicant to remedy deficiencies within eight days at the latest. Should the applicant fail to, or improperly remedy the deficiencies within the specific deadline, the Media Council shall reject the application within fifteen days without assessment of the case in its merits. (6) When the application for the legal dispute procedure does not contain or contains improperly the requisites laid down under Paragraph (3), the Media Council shall request the applicant to remedy deficiencies with a deadline of five days. Should the applicant fail to, or improperly remedy the deficiencies within the specific deadline, the Media Council shall not adopt a decision in the context of bringing the contract into existence or determining its contents, and as regards the subject of the case and the infringement it shall adopt its decision in reliance on the data at its disposal, or it shall terminate the proceedings altogether. (7) The Media Council shall send the application, provided that it does not reject the same without assessing the case in its merits, to the adverse client and shall request such client to submit its position and the evidence at its disposal within a period of ten days at the most and to concurrently send the same to the adverse client. (8) If the Media Council holds a hearing in the course of the proceedings, it shall attempt to mediate a settlement between the parties in the course of the hearing. Article 173 (1) The parties and other stakeholders may attend the hearings as per Paragraph (8) of Article 172 in person or through their representatives, may make statements, put forward their comments and submit their pieces of evidence by the end of the hearing. The hearing shall not be public. (2)

Absence of persons duly summoned to and notified of the hearing shall not prevent the hearing from being held and the case from being concluded. In justified cases, persons summoned to and notified of the hearing may seek prior exemption from attending the hearing; in which case the Media Council shall have the right to postpone the hearing. (3) Absence from the hearing may not be subsequently excused. However, if the Media Council deems necessary to hear one of the persons who failed to appear, then, with regard to the above and by setting a new date, the Media Council may postpone the hearing. (4) Unless otherwise provided in this Act, the applicant shall provide credible evidence to verify the factual and legal grounding of the contents of the application. (5) The Media Council shall have the right to call upon or oblige the adverse client to provide data and/or put forth statements on his/her part. (6) The Media Council shall have the right to issue an interim injunction in the ongoing case at request or ex officio, if it can be established that in lack of such interim injunction the breach of the present Act – and in particular its core principles – will result in a grave and otherwise unavoidable infringement of rights or interests, or in the danger thereof, and provided that the disadvantages arising from issuing the injunction cannot exceed the advantages that may be achieved under the injunction. (7)

As an interim injunction, the Media Council may order that the activity at issue be discontinued, may set the conditions for the activity and may also set obligations. (8) The interim injunction shall be in place until the conclusion of the proceedings with a final force. During the proceedings the Media Council shall have the right to modify or cancel the interim injunction at request or ex officio. (9) If the Media Council resorts to an interim injunction, the client may lodge an application for remedy against the interim injunction to the Budapest Administrative and Labour Court. The court will pass its ruling in the case in out-of-court proceedings within fifteen days. No appeal may be lodged against the order of the Budapest Administrative and Labour Court. The submission of the application shall not have suspending effect on the execution of the order. (10) The Media Council will not issue a separate order on rejecting an application for an interim injunction; the grounds for rejection shall be set forth in the decision concluding the legal dispute procedure on its merits. Article 174 (1) In a legal dispute procedure, the Media Council shall have the right to bring into existence, modify and determine the contents of the agreement, if there is an obligation to contract under the rules on media administration and the parties fail to agree on the contents thereof, in case of an application in accordance with Article 172 (3). (2) If under this Act a legal dispute procedure may be instituted also in relation to the consideration for the media service distribution and the media service, the Media Council may prohibit the further application of the consideration and shall have the right to set the amount of the rightful price within the framework of this Act and may oblige the media service provider or the media service distributor to apply such a rightful price.

Proceedings Against a Media Content Provider Established in Another Member State

Article 176 (1) When the linear audiovisual media service of a media service provider established in another Member State is aimed only at the territory of

Hungary, the Media Council shall have the right to apply the legal sanctions defined in Article 187 (3) (c)-(d) regarding the media services distributed on the territory of Hungary, for the period of the infringement but up to one hundred eighty days at the most provided that the following conditions are met: a) the media service clearly and materially violates Article 17 (1), Article 19 (1) or Article 19 (4) of the Press Freedom Act or Article 9 or Article 10 (1)-(3) of this Act, b) the media service violated the provisions set forth under Paragraph (a) on at least two occasions within the twelve months prior to the decision to be issued by the Media Council under this Paragraph on the limitation of distribution; c) Hungary, at the initiative of the Media Council, notified in writing the media service provider involved and the European Commission of the instances of infringement as defined in Point (a) and the measures the Media Council intends to take in case of future infringement; and d) no agreement is made between Hungary and the Member State in which the media service provider is established within fifteen days from the notification defined in Point (c) on the basis of the consultations made with the Member State involved and the European Commission and the infringement described in Point (a) still exists or is committed repeatedly. (2) The Media Council shall send the decision defined under Paragraph (1) to the European Commission concurrently with the announcement thereof. (3)

If the European Commission obliges the Media Council to withdraw the decision passed under Paragraph (1) in a decision passed within two months of the notification defined under Paragraph (2), the Media Council shall proceed as provided for in the decision of the European Commission. Article 177 (1) When the on-demand audiovisual media service of a media service provider established in another Member State is aimed at the territory of Hungary or is distributed or published on the territory of Hungary, the Media Council shall have the right to apply the legal sanctions defined in Article 187 (3) (c)-(d) regarding the media services transmitted on the territory of Hungary, for the period of the infringement but up to one hundred eighty days at the most provided that the following conditions are met: a) the measures are necessary for the protection of public order, the prevention, investigation and prosecution of criminal acts, necessary on account of infringement of the prohibition of inciting hatred against communities, for the protection of minors, public health, public security, national security and consumers and investors; b) the measures are taken against a media service provider of an on-demand media service that violates or presents a serious risk on any of the interests defined in Point (a); and c) the measure is proportionate to the interests to be protected. (2) Prior to the institution of the proceedings intended for formulating the decision defined under Paragraph (1), the Media Council shall request the Member State under whose jurisdiction the media service provider rendering on-demand media services as defined under Paragraph (1) belongs to take appropriate measures. When the Member State fails to take, or improperly takes the measure within the reasonable time set forth in the request lodged by the Media Council, the Media Council shall send the draft version of the decision defined under Paragraph (1) to the European Commission and the particular Member State. If the European Commission obliges the Media Council to withdraw the draft decision, it shall proceed as provided for in the decision of the European Commission. (3) In cases of exceptional urgency, and with a view to protecting viewers' interests, in the case defined under Paragraph (1) the Media Council shall have the right to pass a temporary decision. The temporary decision shall be enforceable with immediate effect. The Media Council shall send the temporary decision to the European Commission and the Member State involved concurrently with the announcement thereof. The Media Council shall resolve as to whether to uphold or withdraw the temporary decision as provided for in the decision of the European Commission. Article 178 (1)

When the radio media service or the press product of a media content provider established in another Member State is aimed at, distributed or published on the territory of Hungary, the Media Council shall have the right to apply the legal sanction as defined in Article 187 (3) c) against the media service provider under its decision for the period of the infringement but up to one hundred eighty days, if the following conditions are met: a) the measures are necessary for the protection of public order, the prevention, investigation and prosecution of criminal acts, necessary on account of infringement of the prohibition of inciting hatred against communities, for the protection of minors, public health, public security, national security and consumers and investors; b) the measures are taken against a media content provider of radio media service or press product that violates or presents a serious risk on any of the interests defined in Point (a); and c) the measure is proportionate to the interests to be protected. (2) Prior to the institution of the proceedings intended for formulating the decision defined under Paragraph (1), the Media Council shall request the Member State under whose jurisdiction the media service provider rendering radio media services or the publisher of press product as defined under Paragraph (1) belongs to take appropriate measures. The Media Council may institute the proceedings defined under Paragraph (1) provided that the Member State fails to, or improperly takes the measure within the reasonable time set forth in the request lodged by the Media Council.

(3) In cases of exceptional urgency, and with a view to protecting listeners' and readers' interests, the Media Council shall have the right to pass an interim decision defined under Paragraph (1). The temporary decision shall be enforceable with immediate effect. The Media Council, concurrently with its

announcement, shall send the temporary decision to the Member State under whose jurisdiction the media service provider rendering radio media services or the publisher of a press product as defined under Paragraph (1) belongs and shall request such Member State to take appropriate measures. When the Member State takes the measures within the reasonable time set forth in the request, the Media Council shall resolve on the withdrawal of the temporary decision, while in case of failure, or improper delivery of the measures, it shall resolve on upholding the temporary decision.

Proceedings Against a Media Content Provider Established in Another Member State in Case of Circumvention of the Law

Article 179 (1) This Act and Articles 13-20 of the Press Freedom Act shall be applicable to the linear audiovisual media service of the media service provider established in another Member State, in accordance with the provisions of Paragraphs (2)-(5) of this Act, on condition that the media service provider established in another Member State aims the particular linear audiovisual media service for use in the territory of Hungary in its entirety or to a large extent and the media service provider was established outside the territory of Hungary with a view to avoid the applicability of more stringent rules thereon under this Act and the Press Freedom Act. (2) In its assessment as to whether the conditions defined under Paragraph (1) are met, the Media Council shall examine, among others, in which of the Member States the major sources of the advertisement and subscription revenues of the media service provider established in another Member State are to be found as regards its linear audiovisual media service, which is the primary language of the media service, in which Member State can the majority of its broadcast sites be found, and which Member State's audiences the programmes within the media services are addressed to. (3) When the conditions defined under Paragraph (1) are met, on infringement of the provisions of this Act and the Press Freedom Act, the Media Council shall request measures to be taken by the Member State under whose jurisdiction the media service provider rendering the media service defined under Paragraph (1) belongs. (4) The Media Council may apply the legal sanctions as defined in Article 187 (3) (b)-(d) against the media service provider defined under Paragraph (1) under its decision when it established that the Member State with jurisdiction as defined under Paragraph (3) failed to take the measures within two months, or improperly took such measures. (5) The Media Council shall send the draft decision defined under Paragraph (4) to the European Commission prior to the notification thereof. If the European Commission obliges the Media Council to withdraw the draft decision, it shall proceed as provided for in the decision of the European Commission.

Article 180 (1) This Act and Articles 13-20 of the Press Freedom Act shall be applicable to the radio media service and the press product of the media content provider established in another Member State in accordance with the provisions of Paragraphs (2)-(3) hereunder, on condition that the media service provider established in another Member State aims the particular radio media service or press product for use in the territory of Hungary in its entirety or to a large extent, and the media content provider was established outside the territory of Hungary with a view to avoid the applicability of more stringent rules thereon under this Act and the Press Freedom Act. (2) In its assessment as to whether the conditions defined under Paragraph (1) are met, the Media Council shall examine, among others, in which of the Member States the major sources of the advertisement and subscription revenues of the media content provider established in another

Member State are to be found as regards its radio media service or press product, which is the primary language of the media service or press product, in which Member State can the majority of its broadcast and report sites be found, and which Member State's audiences the programmes and other media content within the media services or press product are addressed to. (3) When the conditions defined under Paragraph (1) are met, the Media Council, on infringement of the provisions of this Act or the Press Freedom Act, shall request measures to be taken by the Member State under whose jurisdiction the media service provider rendering the media service or the publisher of the press product defined under Paragraph (1) belongs. (4) The Media Council may apply the legal sanctions as defined in Article 187 (3) (b)-(c) against the media service provider defined under Paragraph (1) under its decision when it established that the Member State with jurisdiction as defined under Paragraph (3) failed to take the measures within two months, or improperly took such measures.

Proceedings in Case of Infringement of the Obligation of Balanced Coverage

Article 181 (1) In case of infringement of the obligation of balanced coverage defined in Article 13 of the Press Freedom Act and Article 12 (2) of this Act, the holder of the viewpoint that was not expressed, or any viewer or listener (hereinafter for the purposes of Paragraphs (2)-(6): applicant) may initiate a regulatory procedure. The powers to assess a request concerning the media services rendered by media service providers with significant market power and the public media service provider shall be with the Media Council, while in case of other media services with the Office. The Authority shall not have the right to institute proceedings ex officio in case of infringement of the obligation of balanced coverage. (2) Prior to requesting regulatory procedure defined under Paragraph (1), the applicant shall resort to the media service provider with its objection. The applicant, within seventy-two hours from the broadcast of the contested information or, in case of re-broadcast, from the date of the last broadcast, shall have the right to request in writing that the media service provider broadcast the viewpoint required for a balanced coverage, properly, under circumstances similar to the contested information. The applicant may not exercise his/her right of challenge if another representative of the same viewpoint has already been given an opportunity to present the viewpoint not presented earlier, or if this opportunity has been given to the applicant but has failed to take advantage thereof. (3) The media service provider shall decide on the acceptance or refusal of the objection within forty-eight hours of the receipt thereof. The decision shall be communicated to the applicant in writing without delay. The applicant, within forty eight hours of the decision being notified, shall have the right to initiate at the Authority that a regulatory procedure be instituted, or, when the decision is not communicated, within ten days of the broadcast of the challenged or objected communication, together with the exact name of the challenged programme and the particular media service provider. A procedure may also be initiated at the Authority if the media service provider fails to comply with the contents of the objection in spite of its statement of acceptance. In this case, the regulatory procedure must be initiated at the Authority within forty-eight hours of the expiry of the deadline undertaken for complying with the objection. The statutory period of proceedings conducted by the Authority shall be fifteen days, which may be extended in justified cases on one occasion, by eight days at the most. (4) At the request of the Authority, the media service provider shall furnish the Authority with the recording of the challenged programme without delay. (5) Should the Authority, in its decision, establish that the media service provider has infringed the obligation of balanced coverage, the media service provider shall broadcast or publish the decision passed by the Authority or the notice defined in the decision, without any assessing comment thereon, as provided for in the decision of the Authority, in the manner and at the time specified by the Authority, or shall provide an opportunity for the applicant to present his/her viewpoint. In addition to the foregoing, the legal sanctions as defined in Articles 186-187 may not be applied against the breaching entity. (6) The procedure defined under Paragraphs (1)-(5) shall be exempt from dues and charges, and the applicant may not be obliged to pay administrative service fee either. (7) The provisions of Article 165 shall be applied respectively in terms of the legal remedy available against the decision of the Office passed within the framework of the regulatory procedure as per this Article, with the provision that a judicial review of the Media Council's decision of the second instance may be requested from the Budapest Administrative and Labour Court by the client and by any other participant in the proceeding as regards the provisions expressly applicable to him/her, within fifteen days of the decision's announcement, on the grounds of breach of law. The Media Council shall forward the statement of claim, together with the documents and representations of the case, to the Budapest Administrative and Labour Court within fifteen days of receipt thereof.

The court shall assess the statement of claim for a judicial review within sixty days from the submission of the statement of claim by the Media Council to the court and shall put down its decision in writing until the day of its announcement. No appeal may be lodged against the decision of the court and no retrial can be requested. The petition for review of the decision can be lodged within fifteen days from announcement of the decision, with the provision that the petition for review must be actually received by the Budapest Administrative and Labour Court within the time limit set for filing. If this deadline (limitation period) is missed, no petition for excuse will be accepted. The Curia shall assess the petition for review within forty five days and shall put down its decision in writing within this deadline. The Budapest Administrative and Labour Court and the Curia shall hold an accelerated procedure. (8) A judicial review of the decision of the Media Council passed within the framework of the regulatory procedure of the first instance as per this Article may be requested from the Budapest Administrative and Labour Court by the client and by any other participant in the proceeding as regards the provisions expressly applicable to him/her, within fifteen days of the decision's announcement, on the grounds of breach of law.

The Media Council shall forward the statement of claim, together with the documents and representations of the case, to the Budapest Administrative and Labour Court within fifteen days of receipt thereof. The court shall assess the statement of claim for a judicial review within sixty days from the submission of the statement of claim by the Media Council to the court and shall put down its decision in writing until the day of its announcement. No appeal may be lodged against the decision of the court and no retrial can be requested. The petition for review of the decision can be lodged within fifteen days from announcement of the decision, with the provision that the petition for review must be actually received by the Budapest Administrative and Labour Court within the time limit set for filing. If this deadline (limitation period) is missed, no petition for excuse will be accepted. The Curia shall assess the petition for review within forty five days and shall put down its decision in writing within this deadline. The Budapest Administrative and Labour Court and the Curia shall hold an accelerated procedure.

The Scope of Powers and Responsibilities of the Authority

Article 182 Acting in its regulatory powers, the Media Council, in accordance with Article 132, a) shall perform general regulatory supervision over public contracts concluded thereby; b) shall perform regulatory supervision regarding the following statutory provisions defined in this Act: ba) standards on the protection of children and minors; bb) standards on the broadcast of events of major importance;

bc) [not in effect] bd) provisions on extraordinary situations concerning media services; be) requirements on programme quotas; bf) requirements defined in Articles 23-25 on commercial communications; bg) provisions on product placement; bh) provisions on political advertisements, public service announcements and public service advertisements [except for the provisions of Article 32 (7)]; bi) requirements on advertisements and teleshopping as defined in Article 33; bj) must-carry obligation rules applicable to media service distributors; bk) obligations related to the offering of media services; bl) provisions on the diversity of media service distribution; bm) rules on the performance of tasks in public media service; c) shall supervise compliance with the requirements laid down in Article 14 and Articles 16-20 of the Press Freedom Act, d) shall exercise the regulatory powers in relation to infringements committed by media content providers established in another Member State; e) shall adopt a regulatory decision on the rating of a programme, at the request of a media service provider; f) shall conclude a public contract with the media service provider on exemption from the requirements on programme quotas; g) shall determine the amount of the media service provision basic fee; h) shall perform the tasks concerning the tendering of media service provision rights for radio and concerning media service provision rights granted for performing public duties; i) shall proceed in official matters related to the renewal of media service provision rights for analogue, linear media services; j) shall proceed in official matters related to media service public contracts; k) shall perform the tasks related to the connecting to the network by media service providers and extension of reception area; l) shall exercise the powers on the classification of media service provision as community media service provision, and shall supervise their operation; m) shall identify the media service providers with significant market power and shall define the obligations encumbering media service providers with significant market power; n) shall act in the context of fulfilment of obligations defined for media service providers with significant market power, excluding obligations defined in Article 39; o) shall perform the regulatory tasks related to control over market concentrations; p) shall conduct an inspection in the media market; q) shall conduct market surveillance procedure; r) shall act in legal disputes defined in this Act; s) shall perform the tasks related to public contracts on temporary media service provision; t) shall perform its tasks as a special authority in cases defined in this Act and the Act on the Prohibition of Unfair and Restrictive Market Practices; u) shall proceed in relation to complaints on imbalanced coverage that may arise in media services provided by media service providers with significant market power and by the public media service provider [under Article 13 of the Press Freedom Act and Article 12 of this Act]; v) [not in effect] x) shall determine under its regulatory decision the public service media services and community media services falling under a must carry obligation [Article 75 (3)]; y) shall perform regulatory tasks related to the proceedings and decisions of self-regulatory bodies; z) shall exercise other regulatory powers as defined by law.

Article 183 (1) Acting in its non-regulatory powers, the Media Council, in accordance with Article 132, a) shall elaborate the recommendations on classifications of media content prescribed for the protection of minors; b) shall elaborate the recommendations on requirements for the effective technical solution to enable access to media content for viewers or listeners over eighteen years of age only; c) may publish its recommendations on ensuring compliance of product placement and the relevant call with the provisions of this Act; d) shall provide information to the Parliament on the observance of the constitutional principle of the freedom of the press and the reasons and circumstances of exemptions from programme quotas granted to media service providers; e) shall decide on the reallocation of approved budgetary appropriations of expenditures; f) shall define and publish its rules of procedure; g) shall provide its opinion on draft legislation concerning spectrum management and communications; h) shall prepare positions and recommendations in certain media policy issues; i) shall formulate the concept of spectrum management effecting media service provision; j) shall prepare an annual report for the Parliament on the operation of the Media Council and the Office; k) shall manage the Fund, accept the subsidy policy, annual plan and report of the Fund, define and publish the detailed rules on the management of the Fund and approve the general conditions of tendering elaborated by the Fund; l) shall prepare a report for the European Commission on certain programme flow structure requirements; m) shall elaborate the rules concerning the utilization of assets handed over to the Public Service Foundation and asset management; n) shall cooperate with the media authorities of other Member States; o) shall supervise the operation of the Institute for Media Studies; p) shall perform the non-regulatory tasks related to the actions of self-regulatory bodies; q) shall prepare the list of events of major importance for society; r) shall perform other, non-regulatory, tasks defined by law. (2) The Media Council shall be responsible for implementing regulation 2006/2004/EC of the European Parliament and of the Council on cooperation between national authorities responsible for the enforcement of consumer protection laws in relation to intra-Community infringements of the laws of the Member States transposing Articles 19-26 of Directive 2010/13/EU of the European Parliament and of the Council on the coordination of certain provisions laid down by law, regulation or administrative action in Member States concerning the provision of audiovisual media services. In so doing, the Media Council shall proceed in the context of mutual assistance in accordance with Commission Directive 2007/76/EC. Article 184 (1) The Office, acting in its regulatory powers, shall a) maintain the official registers defined in this Act; b) determine the amount of the media service provision fee payable by media service providers having acquired the right for media service provision through registration; c) supervise observance of the following provisions of this Act: ca) the provisions of Article 32 (7) on political advertisements, public service announcements and public service advertisements; cb) regulations on advertisements published in public and community media service and public service announcements (Article 36); cc) regulations on programmes made accessible to people with a hearing disability (Article 39);

cd) regulations on changes in the ownership structure and other data of media service providers, publishers of press products and ancillary media service providers, the relevant reporting of such changes and the publication of certain data; ce) regulations on the ownership structure of the linear media service provider and ownership concentration of companies (Article 43); cf) provisions on media content with violence and suitable to raise disturbance and regulations on the protection of religious convictions (Article 14); cg) certain provisions on advertisement and teleshopping (Articles 34-35); ch) regulations on the sponsorship of media services and programmes (Articles 26-29); ci) the obligations to provide data set forth in Article 175 (12); d) perform the tasks related to the discontinuation and termination of media service provision right in the event of failure to commence service provision; e) act in the settlement of complaints involving the obligation to provide balanced information, excepting cases defined in Article 182 (u) (Article 13 of the Press Freedom Act and Article 12 of this Act); f) check observance of obligations on transmission of public media services (Article 74); g) check observance of the provisions on general contractual framework and conditions within the context of the obligation to offer media services (Article 79); h) exercise other powers vested with it as defined by law. (2) The Office, acting in its non-regulatory powers, shall a) perform the preparatory tasks in cases falling within the scope of powers and responsibilities of the Media Council; b) perform the preparatory tasks regarding the procedure for tendering media service provision rights, hold a public hearing; c) perform market analysis, assessment and other inquiry activities by the programme monitoring and analysis service; d) shall perform other non-regulatory tasks defined by law

LEGAL SANCTIONS APPLICABLE IN CASE OF INFRINGEMENT

Article 185 (1) The Media Council or the Office shall have the right to apply the legal sanction on parties infringing rules on media administration in accordance with the provisions of Articles 186-189. (2) In applying the legal sanction, the Media Council and the Office, under the principle of equal treatment, shall act in line with the principles of progressivity and proportionality; shall apply the legal sanction proportionately, in line with the gravity and rate of re-occurrence of the infringement, taking into account all circumstances of the case and the purpose of the legal sanction. Article 186 (1) When the infringement is of minor significance and no re-occurrence can be established, the Media Council or the Office, on noting and warning on the fact of the infringement, may request, setting a deadline of thirty days at the most, that the infringer discontinue its unlawful conduct, refrain from infringement in the future and act in a law-abiding manner and may also set the conditions thereof. (2) In the context of the request defined under Paragraph (1), the considerations defined in Article 187 (2) shall not be applicable. (3) When, considering all the circumstances of the case, the request may not be applicable or would prove inefficient to force compliance with the obligation to discontinue the infringement, the Media Council or the Office, without stating the reasons for dispensing with making a request, shall prohibit the unlawful conduct and/or may set obligations to ensure observance of the provisions of this Act and may apply legal sanctions. Article 187 (1) In case of repeated infringement, the Media Council and the Office shall have the right to impose a fine on the executive officer of the infringing entity in an amount not exceeding two million forints, in line with the gravity, nature of the infringement and the circumstances of the particular case. (2)

The Media Council and the Office shall impose the legal sanction, depending on the nature of the infringement, taking into account the gravity of the infringement, whether it was committed on one or more occasions, or on an ad hoc or continuous basis, its duration, the pecuniary benefits earned as a result of the infringement, the harm to interests caused by the infringement, the number of persons aggrieved or jeopardized by the harm to interests, the damage caused by the infringement, the violation of personality rights and the impact of the infringement on the market, and other considerations that may be taken into account in the particular case. (3) The Media Council and the Office, taking into account Paragraph (7), shall have the right to impose the following legal sanctions: a) it may exclude the infringer for a definite period of time from the opportunity to participate in the tenders of the Fund; b) it may impose a fine on the infringer in line with the following limits: ba) in case of infringement by a media service provider with significant market power and a media service provider affected by the regulations on the limitation of media market concentration, the fine shall be of an amount not exceeding two hundred million forints; bb) in case of infringement by a media service provider not covered under Point (ba), the fine shall be of an amount not exceeding fifty million forints; bc) in case of a daily newspaper of nationwide distribution, the fine shall be of an amount not exceeding twenty-five million forints; bd) in case of a weekly newspaper or periodical of nationwide distribution, the fine shall be of an amount not exceeding ten million forints; be) in case of other daily newspapers or weekly newspapers or periodicals, the fine shall be of an amount not exceeding five million forints; bf) in case of an online press product, the fine shall be of an amount not exceeding twenty-five million forints; bg) in case of a media service distributor, the fine shall be an amount not exceeding five million forints; bh) in case of an intermediary service provider, the fine shall be of an amount not exceeding three million forints; c) the infringer may be obliged to publish a notice or the decision on the opening page of its website, in a press product or a designated programme in the manner and for the period of time specified in the decision; d) it may suspend the exercise of the media service provision right for a specific period of time: da) the period of suspension may last from fifteen minutes up to twenty four hours; db) the period of suspension in case of serious violation of law may last from one hour up to forty eight hours; dc) the period of suspension in case of repeated and serious violation of law may last from three hours up to one week; e) it may delete the media service from the register as defined in Article 41 (4) in which the infringement was committed and may terminate the public contract on the media service provision right with immediate effect on repeated serious violation of law by the infringer. The media service deleted from the register may not be made accessible for the public once it has been deleted. (4) For the purposes of Paragraphs (1)-(3), the infringement shall be deemed as committed repeatedly when the infringer committed the unlawful conduct established in the final regulatory decision on the same legal basis and in breach of the same provisions of legislation, in the same subject, repeatedly within three hundred sixty-five days, not including minor offences. In the case of breach of Articles 20-21, 22 (2), 22 (3), 22 (5) and 22 (6), the infringement shall be considered as committed repeatedly if the infringer repeatedly commits the infringing conduct determined under the final and binding regulatory decision, on the same legal basis and in breach of the same provisions of legislation, within three years. (5) The legal sanctions defined under Paragraph (3) may also be imposed jointly.

(6) Media service provider of a linear media services may be subjected to the legal sanctions defined under Paragraph (3) (a)-(e), providers of on-demand or ancillary media services to the legal sanctions defined under Paragraph (3) (a)-(d), and publishers of press products to the legal sanctions defined under Paragraph (3) (b)-(c). (7) The power to apply legal sanction defined under Paragraph (3) (e) shall be with the Media Council. (8) In case of media service providers with broadcasting agreements the penalty defined in the contract and other legal sanctions may be enforced by the Media Council against the media service providers only by way of an administrative procedure.

Responsibility of Media Service Distributors and Intermediary Service Providers for Transmission of Media Services and Press Products Article 188 (1)

The media service distributor may be obliged to suspend or terminate the transmission of the media service specified, in accordance with Article 189, by virtue of the regulatory decision adopted by the Media Council, acting in its regulatory powers. (2) Intermediary service providers may be obliged to suspend the broadcasting of media services and online press products, in line with Article 189, by virtue of the regulatory decision adopted by the Media Council, acting in its regulatory powers. (3) The media service distributor shall not be responsible for the content of the programme flow of the broadcaster under the jurisdiction of a state party to the Agreement on the European Economic Area and European Convention on Transfrontier Television and in its supplementary Protocol signed in Strasbourg on 5 May 1989 and promulgated by Act XLIX of 1998. The media service distributor, however, may be obliged, by virtue of the regulatory decision adopted by the Media Council, acting in its regulatory powers, to suspend the distribution of the media service under Article 189, taking into account of the provisions of Articles 176-180. Article 189 (1) When the Media Council resorts to the legal sanction against the media service provider defined in Article 187 (3) (e), the media service distributor shall, on the basis of the regulatory decision issued in an ex officio regulatory procedure by the Media Council after the decision has become final, terminate the distribution of the media service constituting the subject of the decision containing the applicable legal sanctions. (2) When, in case of repeated infringement, the Media Council or the Office applies legal sanctions defined in Article 187 (3) (b)-(d) against the media service provider, and the media service provider fails to fulfil the terms of the final and executable decision containing legal sanctions at the request of the Media Council or the Office, the media service distributor may be obliged to suspend the distribution of the media service subject to the regulatory decision adopted in an ex officio regulatory procedure by the Media Council, and containing legal sanctions. (3) When, in case of on-demand or ancillary media services, the Media Council or the Office applies legal sanctions defined in Article 187 (3) (b)-(d) against the media service provider, and the media service provider fails to fulfil the terms of the final and executable decision containing legal sanctions at the request of the Media Council or the Office, the intermediary service provider may be obliged to suspend the broadcasting of the linear, on-demand or ancillary media service subject to the regulatory decision adopted in an ex officio regulatory procedure by the Media Council and containing legal sanctions. (4)

When, in case of online press products, the Media Council or the Office applies legal sanctions defined in Article 187 (3) (b)-(c) against the publisher of the press product, and the publisher fails to fulfil the terms of the final and executable decision containing legal sanctions at the request of the Media Council or the Office, the intermediary service provider may be obliged to suspend the transmission of the online press product subject to the regulatory decision adopted in an ex officio regulatory procedure by the Media Council and containing legal sanctions. (5) The decision mentioned in Paragraphs (1)-(4) shall contain the method, terms, performance deadline, and period of the termination or suspension, as well as the bearing and reimbursement of the costs associated with the termination or suspension of the distribution or broadcasting of the media service by the media service distributor and intermediary service provider, or with the suspension of the broadcasting of the press product. (6) The period of suspending the distribution or broadcasting set forth in Paragraphs (2)-(4) shall be proportionate to the weight and extent of the underlying legal sanction, and may not exceed the date of performance by the media service provider or by the publisher of the online press product – as set forth in the relevant final and enforceable decision – increased by the period necessary to terminate the suspension. The period of terminating the suspension by the media service distributor or intermediary service provider may not exceed fifteen days, including the notification of the media service distributor or intermediary service provider by the Media Council. (7) The costs incurred by the media service distributor or intermediary service provider in connection with the termination or suspension of media service distribution or broadcasting shall be borne by the condemned media service provider or publisher of the press product. (8) No appeal may be lodged against the decision of the Media Council as defined under Paragraphs (1)-(4). The client may seek review of the decision by claiming infringement of law, from the court proceeding in administrative cases within fifteen days of notification of the regulatory decision. The court will pass its decision, based on the hearing of the parties, if necessary, in out-of-court proceedings within fifteen days.

The submission of the application for out-of-court proceedings shall not have a suspensive effect on the enforcement of the decision. The court may not be requested to suspend the execution of the regulatory decision challenged by the application, and it may not be suspended by the court. The decision shall be enforceable immediately, irrespective of the filing of the application for an out-of-court proceeding. No appeal may be lodged against the order of the Budapest Administrative and Labour Court. (9) If the media service distributor or the intermediary service provider fails to comply with the provisions of the decision under Paragraphs (1)-(4), the Media Council shall launch a regulatory procedure against the media service distributor or the intermediary service provider and may apply the legal sanctions set forth in Article 187 (3) (bg) or (bh). (10) Thc provisions laid down in Article 188 and in this Article may not be applied until the decision of the court of first instance is adopted in the course of judicial review proceeding initiated on the suspension of the execution of the decision containing the legal sanction set forth in this Article, and may not be applied – until the final closure of the respective public administration lawsuit – if the court had suspended the execution of the decision containing the legal sanction.

CO-REGULATION IN MEDIA ADMINISTRATION

Article 190 (1) With a view to effective achievement of the objectives and principles set forth in this Act and the Press Freedom Act, facilitating voluntary observance of law and achieving a more flexible system for law enforcement on media administration, the Media Council shall cooperate with the professional self-regulatory bodies and alternative dispute resolution forums of media service providers, ancillary media service providers, publishers of press products, media service distributors and intermediary service providers (hereinafter for the purposes of this Chapter: self-regulatory bodies). (2) In the context of the cooperation defined under Paragraph (1), the Media Council shall have the right to conclude an administrative contract with a self-regulatory body established and operating in accordance with the pertaining legislation, with a view on the shared administration of cases falling within the regulatory powers expressly specified below, as defined in the present Chapter, and the cooperative performance of tasks, related to media administration and media policy, not defined as regulatory powers under legislation, but nevertheless compliant with the provisions of this Act. Article 191 (1)

Under the administrative contract defined in Article 195 (hereinafter as: administrative contract), the Media Council shall have the right to authorise the self-regulatory body to perform self-management tasks, as non-regulatory tasks, in relation to its registered members and media service providers, media service distributors, intermediary service providers or publishers of press products agreed to be bound by the terms of the Code of Conduct as defined in Article 194 (hereinafter jointly as: undertakings under the scope of the Code) in official matters specifically defined in Article 192 (2), within the powers vested with it under the administrative contract, prior to specific exercise of regulatory powers. (2)

The authorisation granted under Paragraph (1) shall not vest public administrative, executive and regulatory powers on the self-regulatory body, and the self-regulatory body shall not be deemed as an administrative authority, or a subject of the system of public administration under this authorisation. (3) The authorisation granted under the administrative contract shall not prejudice the powers of the Media Council under this Act, the Media Council shall have the right to act in official matters, irrespective of this authorisation, subject to the provisions of this Chapter. Article 192 (1) The Media Council shall conclude the administrative contract with the self-regulatory bodies fulfilling the conditions set forth in Article 190 (2), whose registered scope of activities covers or directly affects the official matter for which the authorisations was granted and that maintain a precise and verifiable register of the undertakings under the scope of the Code. (2) In the administrative contract, the Media Council shall have the right to grant authorisations to self-regulatory bodies to manage the following types of official matters as non-regulatory tasks, in relation to the undertakings under the scope of the Code: a) exercise supervision regarding compliance with Articles 14 and 16-20 of the Press Freedom Act or any of those provisions in relation to printed press products, b) exercise supervision regarding compliance with Articles 14 and 16-20 of the Press Freedom Act or any of those provisions in relation to online press products, c) exercise supervision regarding compliance with Articles 14 and 16-20 of the Press Freedom Act or any of those provisions in relation to on-demand media services, d) exercise supervision regarding compliance with Part Two, Chapter I of this Act or any of those provisions in relation to on-demand media services. (3) The authorisation granted to the self-regulatory body by the Media Council for the official matter type defined under Paragraph (2) shall cover: a) handling individual cases related to undertakings under the scope of the Code (including the procedure on applications and complaints involving the activities of the members); b) settlement of disagreements and legal disputes – involving the scope of the authorisation – between undertakings under the scope of the Code;) supervision of the operation and conduct of undertakings under the scope of the Code in relation to the authorisation. Article 193 (1) Under the administrative contract, the Media Council and the self-regulatory body may agree on joint performance of tasks, and implementing principles of activity and service development, programmes of public concern not regulated in legislation but closely linked to media administration and media policy, and any other objective related to media. (2) The rules on the tasks of the self-regulatory body, under an authorisation in an administrative contract, defined in this Chapter are laid down in detail in the administration contract. (3)

The Authority shall have the right to provide financing for the self-regulatory body to perform its tasks defined in this Chapter; the self-regulatory body shall give an account of its usage to the Authority each year by 31 May, on an item-by-item basis. Article 194 (1) The administrative contract concluded by the self-regulatory body and the Media Council shall include a professional code of conduct as a substantive part thereof, developed by the self-regulatory body, defining the self-regulatory performance of tasks as defined in this Chapter (hereinafter as: Code of Conduct). (2) The Code of Conduct shall be prepared by the self-regulatory body in the course of the conclusion of the administrative contract and shall be sent to the Media Council for consultation purposes. The Media Council shall examine the Code of Conduct as to whether it complies with relevant legislation. The condition for the validity of the conclusion of the public contract shall be that an agreement is reached by and between the Media Council and the self-regulatory body concerning the Code of Conduct. (3) The Code of Conduct shall specify in detail, within the scope of the authorisations granted in accordance with Article 192, the provisions on proceedings and guarantees related to the self-regulatory tasks to be performed by the self-regulatory body, the relevant rights and obligations of the members, the relationship between the members and the self-regulatory body, within the context of the authorisation, and the types, system and the legal impacts of decisions, within the discretion of the self-regulatory body. (4) In addition to the provisions of Paragraph (2), the substantive part of the Code of Conduct shall describe the rules, conditions and requirements concerning the activities, services and conduct designated by the scope of the authorisation. Article 195 (1)

The relationship between the Media Council and the self-regulatory body under this Chapter shall be regulated by the parties in detail in the administration contract. (2) The Media Council shall pass a decision in relation to the conclusion of the administrative contract. (3) The administrative contract may be concluded in writing only. (4) The Media Council, following the conclusion of the administrative contract, shall have the right to inspect the register maintained on the undertakings under the scope of the Code and may request that the self-regulatory body provide data from the register so that it may perform its tasks defined in this Chapter concerning the self-regulatory body. (5) In respect of administrative contracts, the general provisions of the Civil Code of Hungary shall apply, subject to the provisions of this Act. Article

196 (1) The Media Council shall have the right to terminate the administrative contract with immediate effect, in the event that the self-regulatory body: a) commits a grave or repeated breach of the provisions of the administrative contract; or b) performs its tasks defined in the administrative contract in deviation from the agreement terms or the terms of the Code of Conduct. (2) The administrative contract concluded for an indefinite period of time may be terminated by either of the parties with a thirty day notice.

Article 197 (1) The self-regulatory body shall act in official matters subject to the authorisations granted thereto in relation to its members as an entity performing the tasks within its own scope of competence and not as tasks under the regulatory powers of authorities, as provided for in this Chapter and the administrative contract. In so doing, its involvement shall have priority over and supplement the activities of the Media Council acting in its regulatory powers (hereinafter as: self-regulatory procedure). (2) In official case types defined in the administrative contract the Media Council shall have the right to proceed against the members of the self-regulatory body only if in its opinion the particular action of the self-regulatory body does not comply with relevant legislation or the provisions of the administrative contract concluded by the parties. (3) The self-regulatory procedure on the part of the self-regulatory body shall precede the regulatory procedure of the Media Council. (4) The self-regulatory body shall be responsible for elaborating, accepting and enforcing an internal regulation of procedure regarding its members that is capable of ensuring proper and effective performance of tasks defined in this Chapter and the appropriate observance of the rules contained in this Chapter. When due to failure to fulfil the provisions set forth above, the self-regulatory body is unable to properly perform its tasks defined in this Chapter and the administrative contract concluded with the Media Council, the Media Council shall have the right to terminate the administrative contract. Article 198 (1)

The self-regulatory body shall act upon an application requesting its self-regulatory procedure. Irrespective of the foregoing, the self-regulatory body shall also have the right to institute proceedings in cases falling within its scope of competence based on its own decision. (2) The statutory period for the self-regulatory procedure by a self-regulatory body shall be thirty days, which – in justified cases and with due heed to the complexity of the case and the difficulties that may arise in revealing the facts of the case – may be extended by fifteen days. A shorter period may also be provided for under the administrative contract. (3) When the Media Council receives an application in a subject falling within self-regulatory procedure, it shall forward the application to the self-regulatory body, considering the membership of the self-regulatory body and other associations subject to the Code of Conduct. When the case does not fall within the competence of the self-regulatory body after all, or the undertaking involved in the application is not subject to the Code of Conduct, the self-regulatory body shall forthwith return the application to the Media Council. When the self-regulatory body institutes its proceedings on the basis of the application forwarded by the Media Council, it shall refund to the applicant any dues and fees paid concurrently with the initiation of the proceedings of the Media Council. (4)

In the case defined under Paragraph (2), the application for the initiation of the proceedings of the Media Council shall not be deemed as an application giving rise to the obligation to institute proceedings as defined in the Act on the General Rules of Administrative Proceedings and Services, except when the application is returned by the self-regulatory body to the Media Council. In such cases, the regulatory procedure of the Media Council shall be commenced on the day that the application returned by the self-regulatory body arrives to the Media Council. (5) When the self-regulatory body receives an application that falls beyond the scope of its competence but is related to the powers of the Media Council, the self-regulatory body shall forthwith inform the applicant about the relevant powers of the Media Council, the opportunities to initiate proceeding and the rules thereof. Article 199 (1) The self-regulatory body shall assess the application in light of this Chapter, the administrative contract concluded with the Media Council and in particular the Code of Conduct constituting an integral part thereof and shall pass its decision in the case. The decision of the self-regulatory body has a binding force on the undertakings subject to the Code of Conduct and may set forth obligations. When the decision sets forth obligations, the self-regulatory body shall set an appropriate deadline to allow compliance therewith.

The self-regulatory body shall inform the Media Council of the decision containing obligations within ten days of the expiry of the deadline. The Media Council shall review the decisions containing obligations sent by the self-regulatory body. When the review of the self-regulatory body's decision is requested by the applicant or the party obliged under the decision, the Media Council shall review such decision within thirty days. (2) When the Media Council establishes that the decision of the self-regulatory body does not comply with the provisions of the administrative contract concluded with the self-regulatory body and in particular the provisions of the Code of Conduct, or when in its judgement the decision contradicts legislation, or when it establishes that the self-regulatory body is unable to have its decision properly observed, it will institute a regulatory procedure in the case covered by the application. In its procedure the Media Council shall not be bound by the procedure and decision of the self-regulatory body. Article 200 (1) The proper and effective performance of the tasks and activities falling beyond the scope of the regulatory powers of the Media Council but covered by the administrative contract concluded with the self-regulatory body shall be an independent task of the self-regulatory body, in line with practice formulated thereby. The Media Council shall cooperate with the self-regulatory body on a continuous basis, providing support and incentive for performing its tasks. (2) The parties shall notify one another on a continuous basis of their experiences regarding the performance of non-regulatory tasks defined under Paragraph (1) and the execution of other procedures. The self-regulatory body shall perform these tasks based on the administrative contract concluded with the Media Council and the Code of Conduct constituting an integral part thereof. To the extent possible, the Media Council shall take into account the experience earned in performing these tasks in exercising its regulatory powers, executing its regulatory procedures, performing market analysis, assessment and – in particular – drafting legislation.

Supervision over the Activities of the Self-regulatory Body

Provided for in this Chapter Article 201 (1) The Media Council shall exercise supervision over the activities of the self-regulatory body under the administrative contract. In so doing, the Media Council shall have the right to check fulfilment of the provisions of the administrative contract concluded with the Media Council on the part of the self-regulatory body on a continuous basis and their delivery in accordance with the contract. In the context of supervision, the Media Council shall have the right to familiarise itself with all the activities performed by the self-regulatory body in connection with the administrative contract, and to this end, may oblige the self-regulatory body to provide data. (2) To the extent deemed necessary, the Media Council shall monitor the procedures and decisions of the self-regulatory body defined in Articles 197-200 to comprehensive inspection. In so doing, the Media Council shall assess the decisions of the self-regulatory body, in terms of their compliance with the provisions of the administrative contract and the Code of Conduct constituting an integral part thereof on an individual and aggregate basis. (3) When, in the context of the supervision, the Media Council establishes that the self-regulatory body failed to act or acted improperly in cases subject to the authorisations granted under the administrative contract, in particular a) the self-regulatory body conducted the proceedings defined in Articles 197-200 in deviation from the provisions of the Code of Conduct; b) it assesses the applications in deviation from the provisions of the Code of Conduct; c) it passes its decisions with their content being in deviation from the provisions of the Code of Conduct; or d) it fails to check compliance with or observance of its decisions and/or fails to take measures to ensure that the provisions of its decisions are fulfilled; then the Media Council shall request that the self-regulatory body acts in accordance with the provisions of the administrative contract, setting an appropriate deadline. (4) When the self-regulatory body fails to fulfil the request defined under Paragraph (3) within the specified deadline, the Media Council shall have the right to terminate the administrative contract with immediate effect or with a period of notice defined in the contract. (5) When, on the basis of the inspection, the Media Council establishes that the proceedings and decision of the self-regulatory body contradict relevant legislation or the provisions of the administrative contract or the Code of Conduct that constitutes an integral part thereof, the Media Council, concurrently with establishing the fact of infringement, shall institute a regulatory procedure in the subject covered by the procedure and the decision. Article 202 The self-regulatory body shall prepare a report to the Media Council on its activities and tasks performed under the administrative contract on a continuous basis, but at least annually, while on the course, content, subjects of its self-regulatory proceedings, types, content and observance of its decisions at least every six months, in writing. The Media Council shall assess the report under its decision. Article 202/A The provisions stipulated in this Chapter, pertaining to co-regulation, shall neither affect nor restrict the right of media content providers to accept and apply self-regulatory initiatives, within the scope of their activities, by organising themselves, within the frameworks of this Act. The Media Council and the Authority shall support and respect these initiatives, in conformity with Article 8.

PART FIVE INTERPRETATION

Article 203 1. Founder shall mean the natural person, legal entity or organisation without legal personality that had determined the objective, purpose, nature and direction of the press product prior to publication of the first issue of the press product, and checks and controls these, and provides for the commencement of regular publication, and based on these, he has the right of disposition over the press product (notification of registration of the press product, notification or approval of deletion from the register, designation of the publisher); furthermore, the entity to which the founder's rights are transferred by the founder shall also be considered as a founder. 1a. Audiovisual media service shall mean media services offering programmes which contain moving images, still images with or without sound. 2. Transmission system shall mean the system of technical processes, electronic communications and other instruments ensuring the analogue or digital media service distribution of television or radio broadcast signals, which is connected to the transmission medium used for media service distribution, in particular the air and radio frequency, the vacuum, the coax cable, the stranded twin wire cable, the fibre optic cable. 3.

Qualifying holding shall mean: a) direct and indirect ownership in an undertaking, which – in aggregate – provides control in excess of twenty-five percent over the undertaking's assets or voting rights; the direct and indirect shareholding of close relatives shall be added together; b) a situation which ensures significant influence over the undertaking on the basis of a contract, the articles of association (statutes) or the preferred stock, through the appointment (removal) of the members of the decision-making or the supervisory bodies, or in any other way. 4. Surreptitious commercial communication shall mean any commercial communication, the publication of which deceives the audience about its nature. Communications serving the purposes of commercial communications may qualify as surreptitious commercial communications, even if no consideration is paid for their publication. 5. Documentary shall mean a non-fictional cinematographic work, the aim of which is to document reality. For example nature, scientific and educational films, historical documentaries, biographical and report films qualify as documentaries. 6. Electronic communications service shall mean services provided to another person, generally for consideration, which are entirely or predominantly composed of the transmission and – where applicable – the routing of signals through electronic communications networks; however it shall not include the services of providing content transmitted through the electronic communications networks and electronic communications services or the services of editorial control over such content; furthermore it shall not include services – defined in other laws – in connection with the information society, which not primarily consist of the transmission of signals through the electronic communications networks. 7. Electronic communications service provider shall mean the operator of an electronic communications network or a natural or legal person engaged in the provision of electronic communications services. 8.

Subscriber shall mean a natural or legal person or other organisation who or which is in a contractual relationship - concerning the use of the below services - with the provider of publicly accessible media services or electronic communications services or with the publisher of press products. 9. European work shall mean: (a) any Hungarian work; (b) any work originating in a member state of the European Union; (c) any work originating in a European state which is a party to the European Convention on Transfrontier Television, adopted in Strasbourg on 5 May 1989, promulgated by Act XLIX of 1998; (d) any work produced under the co-production of the production companies of a member state of the European Union and a state outside the European Union, provided that the majority of the total co-production costs is provided by the co-producers from a EU member state, and the production is not controlled by one or more producers who are established in a country other than an EU member state; or (e) any work produced in co-production, within the framework of an agreement concluded between the European Union and third countries concerning the audiovisual sector, and which complies with the conditions of the applicable agreements. The works mentioned in Points (b)-(c) are works which were produced by authors and with the contribution of professionals having their addresses in one or more states defined under points (b)-(c), provided that the given work meets one of the following three conditions: 1. it is the work of one or more producers established in one or more of the above-mentioned states; 2. its production is supervised and actually controlled by one or more producers established in one or more of the above-mentioned states; 3. the contribution of co-producers from the above-mentioned states to the total co-production costs is preponderant and the co-production is not controlled by one or more producers established outside the above-mentioned states. The works defined under Points (c) and (e) can qualify as European works if no discriminatory measures apply to the works originating from the members states in the given affected state outside the European Union. 10. User shall mean a natural or legal person or other organisation who or which uses or requests electronic communications services or media services. 11. Cinematographic works shall mean cinematographic works as defined in the Copyright Act, 122 excluding, amongst others, news and political programmes, programmes on current affairs and services, sports programmes or programmes broadcasting other events, game shows and quiz shows and commercial communications. Feature films, television films, television series, animation films and documentaries are in particular regarded as cinematographic works. 12. Independent production company shall mean a production company, in which neither the concerned media service provider nor the owner with a qualifying holding in such a media service provider has a direct or indirect shareholding; and neither any director, executive employee of the media service provider nor any of their close relatives is in a work-related relationship with or has an ownership share in such production company. 13. Connecting to the network shall mean the interconnection of two or more media service providers providing linear media services or of two or more linear media services, for the simultaneous or virtually simultaneous broadcasting of the same programme or programme flow. 14. Networked media service provider shall mean any media service provider providing linear media services, whose programme flow or programme is distributed in networked media services. 15. Local media services shall mean media services with a reception area covering the annual average population of maximum one hundred thousand people or maximum five hundred thousand people within a city. 16. Professional disaster management agency shall mean a law enforcement body participating in carrying out disaster management and executing administrative duties as well. 17.

News programme shall mean a programme which devotes at least ninety percent of its duration to cover the current events of Hungarian and international public affairs, not including traffic, weather and sports news programmes. 18. Information society service shall mean the services defined as such in the relevant act on certain issues concerning the information society services. 19. Game show shall mean a programme in which members of the audience or participants in the game show shall answer questions or solve problems in accordance with certain rules, generally for the purpose of winning the prize put up by the media service provider or a third party. Talent search programmes and telephone or interactive games qualifying as teleshopping or teleshopping windows shall not qualify as game shows. 20.

Commercial communication shall mean the media content aimed at promoting, directly or indirectly, the goods, services or image of a natural or legal person carrying out business activities. Such contents accompany or appear in media contents against payment or similar consideration or for the purpose of self-promotion. Forms of commercial communication shall include amongst others advertisements, the display of the name, the trademark, the image or the product of the sponsor, or teleshopping or product placement. 21. Noninteractive teletext shall mean any programme broadcasted in linear audiovisual media services that are used primarily to provide text-based information, and may also include still or moving images, sounds, or computer graphics. 21a. Publisher shall mean the natural person or legal entity that, for purpose of regularly publishing the press product, ensures the personnel and materials (means and equipment) required for publication under proper operational conditions, according to the agreement concluded with the founder if the founder and publisher of the press product are different persons or undertakings. 22. Publication shall mean: a) any book in a printed or an electronic format, on a disk, cassette or any other physical medium; online and downloadable book; b) any press product in a printed or an electronic format; online and downloadable periodical publication; c) any other printed material (address registers, name registers, publications containing graphics, drawings or photos, maps; flyers; printed postcards, greeting or similar cards; printed pictures, samples, photos; printed calendars; printed business advertisements, catalogues, brochures, poster ads and similar items; other textual publications) excluding printed stickers, postal-, excise duty-, duty-, etc. stamps; stamped papers, cheques, bank notes, share certificates, security papers, bonds, deeds and the like; d) any products of film-, video-, and television programme production (films intended for public showing on celluloid, video cassette, video disc, other physical medium; downloadable films, videos); e) any sound recordings (intended for public showing, recorded tapes, discs, downloadable sound content); f) any musical works (printed musical works, musical works in electronic format, downloadable musical works) 23. Ancillary media services shall mean all services – also containing content provision – which are transmitted through a media service distribution system and which qualify neither as media services nor as electronic communications services. For example, electronic programme guides are ancillary media services. 24. Small community media services shall mean – in the case of stereo reception – the local linear radio community media services operating in a reception area covering a geographical area corresponding to a circle with a maximum radius of one kilometre from the transmitting station. 25. Regional media services shall mean media services, whereof reception area exceeds that of the local media services, however less than half of the country's population resides within the reception area of such services. 26. Close relative shall mean spouses, registered partners, dependent relatives, adopted-, step- and foster children, adoptive-, step- and foster parents and siblings. 27. Public service announcement shall mean any announcement released without consideration, originating from an organization or a natural person fulfilling state or local governmental responsibilities or from a State financed or State managed institution, which provides specific information of public interest for the purpose of attracting the attention of the viewers or the audience, and does not qualify as political advertisement. 28. Audience share shall mean the ratio expressed in percentage points of the total time of viewing the programmes of the concerned linear audiovisual media services or listening to the programmes of the concerned linear radio media services to the total time of viewing all the linear audiovisual media services or listening to all the linear radio media services in the examined period. In the course of determining the audience share, the market of linear audiovisual media services and linear radio media services shall be examined separately within the territory of Hungary. 29. Indirect ownership shall mean the ownership share or the voting rights held by the owners of another undertaking (hereinafter as: intermediate undertaking), which has shareholding or voting rights in the undertaking. If there is any proportional difference between the ownership share and the voting rights, the greater one shall be taken into account. The ratio of indirect ownership shall be determined by multiplying the ownership share or voting rights held in the intermediate undertaking by the ownership share or voting rights held by the intermediate undertaking in the original undertaking. If the undertaking has majority ownership in the intermediate undertaking, it shall be considered as a whole. In the case of natural persons, the ownership shares and voting rights held or exercised by close relatives shall be added together. 30. Intermediary service provider shall mean the service provider providing information society services, which a) is engaged in the transmission of the information supplied by the recipient of services through telecommunications network or in providing access to such telecommunications network (simple data transfer and network access); b) is engaged in the transmission of the information supplied by the recipient of services through telecommunications network, and essentially serves the improvement of efficiency concerning the transmission of information initiated by other recipients of services (caching); c) is engaged in the storage of the information supplied by the recipient of services (hosting); d) is engaged in providing the recipient of services with tools to facilitate the finding of information (discovery services). 31. Public media service shall mean audiovisual or radio media services, news agency services or media contents made available via the Internet, provided by the public media service provider. 32. Public media service provider shall mean only and exclusively the media service provider described – with the purpose of achieving the objectives of public media services – in Article 84 (1) of this Act. 33. Public service media assets shall mean cinematographic and other audiovisual works, radio programmes, sound recordings and other documents ancillary to media services representing cultural values, copyrights and certain related rights of photographs or any other licenses of the aforementioned, and the physical media containing the aforementioned works (e.g. discs, tapes, cassettes, paper based documents, music scores) ordered by the public media service provider, its predecessors or the Fund, produced on any legal grounds, procured by way of a sale and purchase transaction, obtained or created in whole or in part by way of a licensing or any other agreement; furthermore costumes, props, film sets and other copyright materials, provided that the copyrights and certain related rights are owned or used to be owned by any of the predecessors of the public media service provider prior to the Act entering into force or by the Fund subsequent to the Act entering into force; and also those, over which any of the predecessors of the public media service provider obtained rights or over which the public media service provider itself obtains rights subsequent to this Act entering into force. 34. Publication shall mean posting on the bulletin board of the Authority or publishing on the website of the Authority. The effective date of the publication shall be the day of posting on the bulletin board. 35. On-demand media service shall mean the media services where, on the basis of a catalogue of programmes compiled by the media service provider, the user may, at his/her own request, watch or listen to the programmes at any time of his/her own choice. 36. Linear media services shall mean the media services provided by a media service provider that allow for the simultaneous watching or listening to programmes on the basis of a programme schedule. 37. Hungarian works shall mean: (a) works originally made in the Hungarian language in their entirety; (b) works originally made in several languages, but when considering their overall length, their parts originally made in Hungarian are longer than any of their other parts made in any other language; (c) works originally made in the languages of any of the nationalities recognised by Hungary, provided their subject matter concerns the life or culture of the given nationality in Hungary; (d) a music programme performed in Hungarian or performed in the language of any of the nationalities recognised by Hungary, provided its subject matter concerns the culture of the given nationality related to Hungary; (e) an instrumental music programme, which forms part of Hungarian culture or the Hungary-related culture of any of the nationalities recognised by Hungary. f) [not in effect] 38. Hungarian musical work shall mean a textual or instrumental musical work, which qualifies as a Hungarian work. 39. Rules on media administration shall mean this Act and Act CIV of 2010 on the Freedom of the Press and the Fundamental

Rules of Media Content, and any legislation issued in respect of the 125 implementation of the aforementioned acts; any directly applicable legal instruments of the European Union concerning media administration; any broadcasting agreement, any public contract entered into by and between the Media Council and the Office, and the regulatory decision issued by the Media Council and the Office. 40. Media service shall mean any independent service of a commercial nature, as defined in Articles 56 and 57 of the Treaty on the Functioning of the European Union, provided on a regular basis, for profit, by taking economic risks, for which the media service provider bears editorial responsibility, the primary aim of which is the delivery of programmes to the general public for informational, entertainment or educational purposes through an electronic communications network. 41. Media service provider shall mean the natural or legal person who or which has editorial responsibility over the composition of the media services and determines their contents. Editorial responsibility shall mean the responsibility for the actual control over the selection and composition of the media content and shall not necessarily result in legal responsibility in connection with the media service. 42. Media content shall mean any content offered in the course of media services and in press products. 43. Media content provider shall mean the media service provider or the provider of any media content. 44. Programme flow shall mean a series of radio or audiovisual programmes edited and publicly, continuously transmitted. 45. Preview shall mean any programme, which introduces, describes or promotes a programme or programmes the media service provider intends to transmit at a later time. 46. Transmission time shall mean the total time of the programmes continuously transmitted in the course of the media service during a specific period of time. 47. Programme shall mean the series of sounds or moving images or still images with or without sound, which form a separate unit in the programme schedule or the catalogue of programmes selected by the media service provider and the form and content of which is similar to that of radio or television media services. 48. Programme related products shall mean a product or service directly connected to the content of a programme and distributed by the media service provider, which enables the fuller enjoyment of the programme, for example by promoting the interactivity of the viewers or the listeners. 49. Broadcasting transmission shall mean the media service distribution in the course of which analogue or digital radio or audiovisual media services are transmitted to the subscriber or user, by means of a terrestrial transmission system that uses radio frequencies – other than frequencies allocated primarily for satellite services – and usually enabling one-way data transmission. Broadcasting transmission shall also include media service distribution implemented by using a digital broadcasting network or broadcasting station. 50. Media service distribution shall mean an electronic communications service implemented by using any type of transmission system, in the course of which the analogue or digital broadcasting signals generated by the media service provider are transmitted from the media service provider to the receiver of the subscriber or user, irrespective of the applied transmission system or technology. In particular, media service distribution includes broadcasting transmission, satellite media service distribution, media service distribution via a hybrid optical-coaxial transmission system, furthermore the transmission of media services using the Internet Protocol through certain transmission system, if the nature and circumstances of the service are identical to those of media service distribution or if it replaces media service distribution implemented in any other manner. Media service distribution shall also mean such media service distribution to which the subscriber receives access for a special fee or for a fee paid for a package that also contains the fee of some other electronic communications service. Signal transmission through a transmission system suitable for the connection of less than ten receivers shall not qualify as media service distribution. 51.

Media service distributor shall mean the provider of media service distribution, including the operator of a digital broadcasting network, if it provides the media service distribution itself. If the transmission network is not operated by the media service distributor, the service provider defining the conditions of the services provided to the subscriber or user and/or concluding the contract with the subscriber shall qualify as media service distributor. 51a. Media service distribution transmission platform shall mean the transmission system, typically analogue or digital, ensuring the transmission of signals of the same technology. 52. National media service shall mean the media services, in the reception area of which at least fifty percent of the population of Hungary resides. 53. Split screen advertisement shall mean an advertisement covering a particular portion of the screen displayed during a programme, not qualifying as a commercial communication in the course of audiovisual media service. 54. Composite programme shall mean a combination of several programmes bearing a single main title or other distinctive attribute. 55. Political advertisement shall mean any programme promoting or advocating support for a party, political movement, or the Government, or promoting the name, objectives, activities, slogan, or emblem of such entities, which appears and is transmitted in a manner similar to that of advertisements. 56. Political programme shall mean a programme, which devotes at least ninety percent of its duration to the analysis, coverage and evaluation of Hungarian or international political or current public affairs and to the exploration of the background of such affairs or events, which does not qualify as a news programme. 57. Programme package shall mean media services offered or provided by the media service distributor to the subscriber in one group. 58. Radio media services shall mean media services featuring programmes composed of the sequence of sounds. 59. Advertisement shall mean any communication, information or representation, qualifying as a programme, intended to promote the sale or other use of marketable tangible assets – including money, securities, financial instruments and natural resources that can be utilized as tangible assets – services, real estates or pecuniary rights or to increase, in connection with the above purposes, the public awareness of the name, designation or activities of an undertaking, or any merchandise or brand name. 60. Press products shall mean individual issues of daily newspapers or other periodical papers, online newspapers or news portals, which are offered as a business service, for the content of which a natural or legal person has editorial responsibility, and the primary purpose of which is to deliver textual or image content to the general public for information, entertainment or educational purposes, in a printed format or through any electronic communications network. Editorial responsibility shall mean the responsibility for the actual control over the selection and composition of the media content and shall not necessarily result in legal responsibility in connection with the press product. Business service shall mean any independent service of a commercial nature provided on a regular basis, for profit, by taking economic risks. 61.

Sports programme shall mean a programme broadcasting a sports event (simultaneously with the event, in a delayed or an edited format), excluding news reports on sports events and programmes containing discussions of sports related topics. 62. Member State shall mean a member state of the European Economic Area. 63. Sponsorship shall mean any contribution provided by an undertaking to finance a media service provider or a programme with the purpose of promoting its name, trade mark, image, activities or products. 127 64. Public service advertisement shall mean any communication or message with a public purpose, which does not qualify as a political advertisement, is not for profit and does not serve advertising purposes, is transmitted for or without consideration, and which aims to influence the viewer or the listener of the media service in order to achieve a goal of public interest. 65. Teleshopping shall mean an advertisement, which contains direct offers for the sale, purchase or other utilisation of goods, services, rights and obligations for payment or consideration, by way of establishing contact with the distributor or the service provider, including phone-ins operated as business undertakings transmitted in the media service. 66. Teleshopping window shall mean a teleshopping facility, the uninterrupted duration of which is at least fifteen minutes. 67. Thematic media service shall mean any media service, which broadcasts programmes of a similar theme in eighty percent of the daily transmission time in case of a linear media services and in eighty percent of the total time of all the programmes broadcasted in case of on-demand media services; such as the news or political programmes, programmes for minors, sports programmes, music programmes, educational programmes or programmes introducing a certain lifestyle. 68. Product placement shall mean any form of commercial communication, which contains products, services, the trademark of the above or any reference to them and appearing in a programme for payment or similar consideration. 69. Election campaign period shall mean the time period as defined in the Act on Electoral Procedures designated for pursuing the electoral campaign. 70.

Undertaking shall mean natural persons, private entrepreneurs, business associations, other legal persons. 71. Reception area: a) in case of media services provided through broadcasting transmission and media service distribution via satellites, accessible without the payment of a subscription fee, the number of the population residing in a geographically identifiable territory in which the level of the effective signals of the broadcasting transmission service transmitting the programme flow and the calculated level of interference protection reach the minimum values stipulated in the recommendations of the International Telecommunication Union; b) in case of media services provided through other transmission systems for media service distribution accessible without the payment of a subscription fee, the product of the number of households connected to the transmission system and the average number of persons living in a single household as defined by the Hungarian Central Statistical Office; or c) in case of media services accessible in return for a subscription fee, the product of the number of households subscribed to such media service or to the media service distribution containing such media service and the average number of persons living in a single household as defined by the Hungarian Central Statistical Office. 72. Virtual advertisement shall mean an advertisement inserted, digitally or by any other method, subsequently into the programme signal or the programme.

SHORT TITLE OF THE ACT

Article 205 This Act shall be referred to as the "Media Act" in other legislation.

Article 206 (1) The President of the National Media and Infocommunications Authority shall be authorised to establish by decree a) the frequency fees, the fees payable for the reservation and use of identifiers, as well as the supervisory fee for communications and postal service providers, the method and conditions of payment of these amounts, the rules of the related supervisions, b) the administrative service fee of the regulatory procedure related to the rating of programmes and classification of communications, c) the method and terms of the payment of the fees of the procedures conducted by the Authority and the Media Council as well as the amount and the rules of calculating such fees. (2) Until the decrees defined under Paragraph (1) are not adopted by the President of the National Media and Infocommunications Authority, the ministerial decrees governing the relevant issues shall remain in force. (3) The Government shall be authorised to regulate and define in a decree the suppliers of legal deposits, exemptions from the number of copies provided for by law, the method and deadline for providing legal deposits, the rules of implementation, the list of organisations entitled to receive legal deposits, the method of distribution, the rules of the storage and the use of legal deposits, as well as the procedural rules to be followed in case of failure to provide legal deposits. (3a) The Government is hereby authorized to determine in a decree the rules of payment of the programme fee, payable for that linear audiovisual media service of the linear audiovisual media service provider having significant market power, which has the highest average annual audience share. (4) The Minister responsible for culture shall be authorised to regulate by decree the detailed rules of providing the imprints of publications. (5) The Minister responsible for audiovisual policy shall be authorised to establish by decree the detailed rules governing the administrative service fee payable for the proceedings as special authority defined in Article 171, as well as the management, registration and reimbursement of such fees. (6) The Minister responsible for employment is hereby authorized to determine in a decree the posts of employment as per Article 108/B (1)

TRANSITIONAL PROVISIONS

Article 206/A Point (b) of Paragraph (1) of Article 42 and Paragraph (2a) of Article 42 of this Act, determined by Act LXXXV of 2012 on Simplification of certain family law and company law procedures, shall be applied regarding the applications submitted on or after 1 February 2013.

Transitional Arrangements for the Broadcasting Agreements

Article 207 (1) The analogue terrestrial broadcasting right defined in Act I of 1996 on Radio and Television Broadcasting (hereinafter as: Radio and Television Broadcasting Act) and the analogue linear media service provision right using state-owned limited resources as defined in this Act can only be exercised on the basis of the public contract concluded with the Media Council, with the exception of the media services of the public media service provider as per Paragraph 32 of Article 203. (2)-(5) [not in effect] (6) The linear audiovisual media service provider having significant market power is not entitled to request a programme fee for its linear audiovisual media service having the highest average annual audience share until the entry into force of the legislation issued on the basis of Article 206 (3a). (6a) The provision stipulated in Paragraph (6) shall also apply to that linear audiovisual media service having the highest average annual audience share of the linear audiovisual media service provider having significant market power which qualifies, at the time of entry into force of Act XXXIX of 2014 on the Amendment of certain acts related to budgetary planning and the more effective provision of money market and public utility services, as the linear audiovisual media service with highest average annual audience share of the linear audiovisual media service provider having significant market power, based on the Media Council's regulatory decision or public contract. (7) The broadcasting agreement may not be terminated if such agreement could not have been concluded due to a breach of law, however the media service provider is not solely responsible for such breach of law. (8) [not in effect] (9) Violations concerning subjects described in the broadcasting agreement and falling under the scope of the Press Freedom Act or of Chapter I of Part II of this Act shall be considered under the Press Freedom Act or the relevant provisions of this Act, instead of the provisions set forth in the broadcasting agreement.

Transitional Arrangements for the Requirement of Notification

Article 208 (1) Media services listed in the register kept by the National Media and Infocommunications Authority pursuant to the Radio and Television Broadcasting Act at the time of the entry into force of this Act shall provide the data specified in the rules on the notification procedure set out in this Act and not listed in the register, within thirty days, without the initiation of a new notification procedure. (2) Press products that are listed in the register kept by the National Office of Cultural Heritage (hereinafter as: National Office of Cultural Heritage) pursuant to Act II of 1986 on the Press (hereinafter as: Press Act) at the time of the entry into force of this Act, shall provide the data specified in the rules on the notification procedure set out in this Act and not listed in the register, within thirty days, without the initiation of a new notification procedure. (3) Until 1 January 2012, the National Office of Cultural Heritage shall be responsible for the regulatory tasks related to the registration of printed press products and the management of newspaper registration. As of 1 January 2012, the Authority shall perform the duties related to the registration of printed press products on the basis of this Act. (4)

Media services, online press products already operating at the time of the entry into force of this Act, however not registered by the Authority or the National Office of Cultural Heritage, shall be notified to the Authority by 30 June 2011 at the latest, while printed press products shall be notified to the National Office of Cultural Heritage by 30 June 2011 at the latest. (5) If the publisher of printed press products registered in the register kept by the National Office of Cultural Heritage at the time of entry into force of this Act, however not published during the three years preceding the entry into force of this Act, fails to re-launch regular publication of the press product by 31 December 2012, then the press product shall be deleted from the register. In other cases, the period specified in Article 46 (6) (c) subject to the deletion obligation, shall commence on the day of the entry into force of this Act. Articles 209-210 [not in effect]

Transitional Arrangements for the Members and Office Holders in the Bodies Defined by this Act

Article 211 (1) The entry into force of this Act shall not affect the mandate and the term of office of Presidents, Vice-Presidents, Deputy Presidents, Directors General, Deputy Directors General, CEOs, Deputy CEOs and members of the organisations and bodies specified in this Act. (2) Delegation to the Board of Public Services and the drawing of lots — set forth in Annex no. 1 — preceding such delegation shall be carried out by 31 March 2011. (3) If the President, the members of the new joint Supervisory Board, and the joint auditor of the public media service provider are not elected by the date of the entry into force of this Act, the term of office of the members, presidents of the previous supervisory boards and the auditors shall end when the new Supervisory Board and the auditor are elected. (4) Article 111/A (3) and Article 125 (5) of the Media Act, being established by Act XXXIII of 2013 on the Amendment of Act CIV of 2010 on the Freedom of the Press and the Fundamental Rules of Media Content and Act CLXXXV of 2010 on Media Services and Mass Media (hereinafter as: Amending Act), shall also be applied with respect to the President and the president of the Media Council being in office at the time of entry into force of the Amending Act. Entry into force of the Amending Act shall not affect the existence of the mandate of the President and the president and members of the Media Council being in office at the time of entry into force.

Transitional Arrangements for the Public Media Service Provider

Article 212 (1) The drafters of the Public Service Broadcasting Regulation drafted pursuant to the Radio and Television Broadcasting Act shall harmonise the Regulation with the Public Service Code or, in the absence thereof, shall repeal it. (1a) The provisions of the Code must be amended until 30 September 2015 in conformity with the provisions of Act CVII of 2014 on the amendment of certain laws regulating public media service and the media market. The rules regulating the adoption of the Code, as defined under Article 95 (2), shall be applied in respect of this amendment. (2) Regarding the term of employment of the persons having worked as public service employees at the Hungarian Radio, the Hungarian Television and the Hungarian News Agency prior to the establishment of Hungarian Radio Pte. Ltd., Hungarian Television Pte. Ltd., and Hungarian News Agency Pte. Ltd. and their employment having been uninterrupted at the same public media service provider ever since, the period spent as public service employees at the Hungarian Television, the Hungarian Radio and the Hungarian News Agency shall be considered as periods worked at the private companies limited by shares. (3) Notwithstanding Paragraph (2), in respect of the notice period and severance allowance, the term of employment at Hungarian Radio Ltd., Hungarian Television Ltd. and Hungarian News

Agency Ltd. shall be calculated from the date of the public service employment having been transformed into an employment relationship. The notice period and severance allowance based on the term of the previous public service employment in compliance with the relevant rules defined in the Act on the Legal Status of Public Service Employees effective at the time of the transformation of the status shall be added to the extent of the notice period and severance allowance. (4) Regarding claims arising from the public service employment and arising prior to the transformation of the legal status specified under Paragraph (2), the provisions of the Act on the Legal Status of Public Service Employees in effect at the time the claim arose shall apply, and the provisions of Act XXII of 1992 on the Labour Code shall apply to the procedure of enforcing such claims. Article 213 (1) In 2011, the Board of Trustees of the Public Service Foundation, the Fund and the public media service provider shall receive the sponsorships defined in the State Budget Act for 2011. The methods and amount of public service financing set out in this Act (public service contribution) shall be first applied for the year 2012. In 2011, the operational fee defined in the Radio and Television Broadcasting Act shall also form part of the Fund's financial resources. (2) Regarding the reduction of share capital of the company limited by shares required in relation to the assets transferred pursuant to the Parliamentary Decision no. 109/2010 (X. 28.), the rules set out in Articles 271-272 of Act IV of 2006 on Business Associations may not be applied. (3) The transfer of assets specified under Paragraph (2) shall be exempted from charges. The historical cost of the assets transferred free of charge to the Fund pursuant to Act C of 2000 on Accounting shall be equivalent to the book value of the assets recorded by the public media service provider at the time of transfer of such assets. (4) The public media service providers may transfer their rights and obligations arising from their contractual relations established prior to the entry into force of this provision to the Fund as a whole and on the same terms and subject to the same conditions. The change of the subject due to the transfer shall not affect the original rights and obligations of the contracting parties. Accordingly, in respect of the changes of the subject of contractual relations, the provisions defined in the Public Procurement Act pertaining to contract amendments shall not be applicable. The rights granted to and the obligations undertaken by the public media service provider as contracting authority in public procurement procedures initiated prior to the entry into force of this Act and still ongoing, are transferred to the Fund by the relevant declaration of the public media service provider aiming such transfer. (5)

In the course of the transfer of assets conducted pursuant to the Parliamentary Decision no. 109/2010 (X.28.), additional claims – to be borne by the public media service provides – which have not been barred by limitation and arising from agreements already performed and from obligations already fulfilled, shall continue to be borne by the public media service provider. Such claims shall not be enforceable vis-à-vis the Fund. (6) The state taxation authority may, on the basis of the application of the Fund and the public media service provider based on Paragraph (3) of Article 8 of Act CXXVII of 2007 on Value Added Tax, approve the group taxpayer status as of the date mutually specified by the Fund and the public media service providers. (7) Paragraph 6 of this Article and Article 108 (11) shall be applicable as of 1 January 2011. Article 214 (1) In order to enforce the provisions of this Act, media service distributors and the public media service providers may initiate with the other contracting party the review and amendment of media service distribution agreements concluded before 31 December 2010. None of the parties may refuse to negotiate the amendment of such agreements. (2) If the parties cannot reach an agreement within three months from the communication of the other party's offer regarding the review and amendment of the agreement, any of the parties may initiate a legal dispute procedure before the National Media and Infocommunications Authority

pursuant to the rules of the Electronic Communications Act. Article 215 In order to preserve artistic standards, the Fund shall be responsible for the maintenance and development of the artistic groups of Magyar Rádió Nonprofit Zrt. following the entry into force of this Act. The Minister responsible for culture and the Fund may conclude an agreement on changing the person responsible for maintaining the artistic groups. Article 215/A (1) The Hungarian Radio Non-Profit Private Limited Company, the Hungarian Television Non-Profit Private Limited Company and the National News Agency Non-Profit Private Limited Company, as public media service providers owned by the Public Service Foundation, shall be terminated as a result of the merger with Duna Television Non-Profit Private Limited Company. Deviating from Article 91 (b) of the Media Act, the Public Foundation shall be entitled and obliged to adopt the owner's decisions required for implementation of the merger until 31 March 2015 the latest. In connection with the merger, the Parliament shall be obliged to amend the Statutes of the Public Service Foundation. Subsequent to the merger, the name of Duna Television Non-Profit Private Limited Company shall be changed to Duna Media Service Provider Non-Profit Private Limited Company. (2) The Public Service Foundation shall adopt its decision on the merger at one of its meetings. The further measures required for the registration of the merger in the company register shall be taken by Duna Television Non-Profit Private Limited Company, in cooperation with the Public Service Foundation, the Fund and the other companies affected by the merger, in order to ensure that the date of the merger shall be 1 July 2015. (3) The provisions of Act V of 2013 on the Civil Code (hereinafter referred to as: the Civil Code), Act CLXXVI of 2013 on the transformation, merger and demerger of certain legal entities (hereinafter referred to as: the Transformation Act) and Act V of 2006 on Public Company Information, Company Registration and Voluntary Liquidation Proceedings (hereinafter referred to as: the Public Company Information Act) shall be applied in terms of the merger of the public media service provider companies limited by shares, subject to the following deviations: a) the rules stipulated under Articles 9, 10 (2)-(4) and 14 (5) of the Transformation Act, Article 3:40 of the Civil Code and Paragraphs (1a) and (5) of Article 57 and Section III.5 of Annex no. 1 of the Public Company Information Act shall not be applied; b) Paragraph (4) of Article 3:36 of the Civil Code shall be applied in such a way so that there shall be no suspension of execution of the order; c) Paragraph (1) of Article 57 of the Public Company Information Act shall be applied with the provision that the time limit for assessment of the application shall be ten working days. Article 215/B (1) Pursuant to this Act, the assets of the public media service provider, with the exception of the assets connected to a functional task, shall be transferred to the ownership of the State and the ownership rights over these assets shall be exercised by the Fund, without consideration.

Duna Media Service Provider Private Limited Company, created as of the merger, and the Fund shall enter into a handover agreement regarding the transfer of ownership and the execution of the related further tasks, wherein they shall agree on the transfer of the rights and obligations resulting from the legal relationships connected to the transferred assets as well. The change of the subject arising due to the transfer shall not affect the original rights and obligations of the contracting parties. Accordingly, in respect of the change of the subject of contractual relations, the provisions defined in the Public Procurement Act pertaining to contract amendments shall not be applicable. The rights granted to and the obligations undertaken by the public media service provider and its predecessors, as contracting authority, in public procurement procedures initiated prior to the entry into force of this Act and still ongoing, shall be transferred to the Fund by the respective declaration of the public media service provider. (2) For the purposes of Paragraph (1), the following assets shall qualify as assets connected to a functional task: the assets serving the corporate operations performed by the organizational units

created as a result of the internal division of tasks of the public media service provider, i.e. the institution operational and internal management tasks, hence in particular the means and equipment and technical conditions serving the human resource management, budgetary management, financial, legal, communications control and coordination tasks, furthermore the IT tasks serving the organisational operations of the public media service provider. The Public Foundation shall be entitled and obliged to determine the exact scope of these assets, based on the proposal of the public media service provider. (3) Pursuant to this Act, the ownership title of the concerned asset shall be transferred to the Hungarian State as of the day when the respective agreement is executed. The transfer of the assets shall be exempt from duties. The historical cost of the assets transferred free of charge to the State pursuant to Act C of 2000 on Accounting shall be equivalent to the book value of the assets recorded by the public media service provider at the time of transfer of such assets. (4) The Fund shall be liable, as a surety, for the claims arising prior to entry into force of Act CVII of 2014 on the amendment of certain laws regulating public media service and the media market, under a liquidation proceeding started within 3 years following the entry into force of the Act, up to the value of the assets taken over. Article 215/C The employment contracts of the concerned employees of the public media service provider and the Fund shall have to be amended to ensure their compliance with the requirements set forth under Article 108/B. The negotiations on the amendments have to be closed until 31 March 2015. In the event the parties are unable to agree concerning the amendment of the employment contracts until the above date, the provisions of Article 108/B shall be applied respectively regarding the employment contracts from 1 April 2015.

Transitional Arrangements for the Authority and its Procedure

Article 216 (1) Following the entry into force of this Act, the provisions specified in this Act — subject to the exception provided for in Paragraphs (2)-(5) — shall be applicable in the ongoing procedures before the Media Council or the Office and falling within the scope of this Act. (2) In tender procedures started before the entry into force of this Act, the Media Council and the Fund shall proceed in line with the rules of procedure effective at the time of the execution of the procedural action, as follows: a) in tender procedures where the Media Council selected the winner of the tender prior to the entry into force of this Act, the Media Council and the Fund shall conclude a public contract with the winning tenderer following the entry into force of this Act, proceeding in line with the provisions of this Act; b) in ongoing tender procedures where tenderers have already submitted their tenders, but the Media Council has not yet announced the winner or has not declared the tender procedure as unsuccessful, the Media Council shall, following the entry into force of this Act, proceed in line with the provisions of Act I of 1996 on Radio and Television Broadcasting pertaining to the general conditions of tendering and the invitation to tender, the examination, evaluation and assessment of tenders, with the proviso that its decisions are made in a regulatory procedure in accordance with the rules of procedure defined in this Act and that it concludes a public contract with the winning tenderer. These ongoing tender procedures shall, following the entry into force of this Act and pursuant thereto, qualify as official matters and legal relations of regulatory procedure; c) in tender procedures for the usage of analogue linear radio media service provision rights started prior to 6 September 2010, the Media Council may review and amend the draft invitation to tender and the wording of the invitation to tender accepted by the legal predecessor Board. If the Media Council decides to amend the draft invitation to tender or the invitation to tender, the Media Council shall publish the consolidated version of the text and hold a hearing as per Article 50. If the draft invitation to tender or the invitation to tender in the tender procedure has already been published, the Media Council shall notify the public on the reasons for the repeated publication and hearing in a notice posted on its bulletin board as per Article 50 (3) and on its website. (3) In case of breach of law committed prior to the entry into force of this Act, the provisions of substantive law shall apply, which were in force at the time the breach was committed. (4) The regulatory procedure specified in this Act may only be initiated after 1 July 2011, for breach of law committed after this date, against the media service provider of on-demand media services or publisher of press products in the event of violations of Articles 14 and 16-20 of the Press Freedom Act, and against the media service provider of on-demand media services in the event of violations of the provisions specified in Chapter I of Part Two of this Act. Media service providers and media service distributors shall comply with the obligations defined in Article 9 (3), Article 10 (1) (a), Article 72 (3) and Article 74 (3) of this Act following 1 April 2011.

Regulatory procedures for violation of the above obligations may only be initiated against them for breach of law committed after this date. (5) The stipulations set out in Article 171 shall also be applicable to ongoing procedures, with the proviso that no subsequent special authority fee will be charged. (6) In 2011, the financial management by the Authority and the Media Council shall be performed from the funds defined in Act CXLVI of 2010 on the 2011 Budget of the National Media and Infocommunications Authority and the Media Council of the National Media and Infocommunications Authority, in accordance with the provisions laid down in Article 134. The remaining uncommitted funds in the budgets of the National Media and Infocommunications Authority and the Media Council, as well as the legal predecessors thereof, accumulated in the course of 2009 and 2010 — including the uncommitted surplus accumulated in the Media Council's budget and the amount held by the National Communications Authority and blocked in 2010 pursuant to the Government's decision — shall be used to generate reserves for funding the public duties related to the implementation of the digital switchover, as well as the Fund's public service- and community media service-related activity. The committed remaining funds reserved until 31 December 2010 shall be used by the Authority in line with the legal statement forming the basis of the commitment. (7) For the purposes of the Act on the 2011 Budget of the Republic of Hungary, Act CXLVI of 2010 on the Budget of the National Media and Infocommunications Authority and the Media Council of the National Media and Infocommunications Authority, and the contractual obligations, the Broadcasting Support and Asset Management Fund referred to in these acts and in the contracts shall refer to the Media Service Support and Asset Management Fund. (8) In the case specified in Article 129 (1) (a), the date of termination of the mandate of the President and members of the Media Council shall be the commencement date of the mandate of the recently elected President and members. In the case specified in Article 113 (1) (a), the date of termination of the mandate of the President of the Authority shall be the commencement date of the mandate of the recently appointed President.

If the new President of the Authority is not elected as President of the Media Council by the Parliament within 30 days from his/her appointment, or, if such an appointment takes place outside the parliamentary session, within 15 days from the starting date of the forthcoming parliamentary session; the mandate of the former President of the Media Council shall continue until the election of the new President of the Media Council. If the Authority does not have an elected President, the powers and responsibilities of the President shall be performed by the President of the Media Council, or by the member of the Media Council in the case specified under Paragraph (2) of Article 131. Article 217 The provisions of this Act determined by Act LXVI of 2012 on amendment of certain acts related to media services and press products shall be applied to ongoing procedures as well, provided that the provisions of substantive law in force at the time the given offence was committed shall be applied regarding the offences committed prior to the entry into force of the above-mentioned provisions. Article 218

The management, maintenance and operation of the National Audiovisual Archive (hereinafter as: National Audiovisual Archive) shall be carried out by the Authority from 31 March 2011. The transfer of National Audiovisual Archive to the Authority shall be carried out by this date, including the transfer of the prorated part of the budgetary support granted for operation. Article 218/A The provisions of this Act determined by Act CXXI of 2013 on the Amendments of certain infocommunications related acts required to ensure the digital switchover of local and regional television channels shall be applied to ongoing procedures as well, provided that the provisions of substantive law in force at the time the given offence was committed shall be applied regarding the offences committed prior to the entry into force of the above mentioned provisions. Article 218/B The provisions of this Act determined by Act XXXIX of 2014 on the Amendment of certain acts related to budgetary planning and the more effective provision of money market and public utility services shall be applied to ongoing procedures as well, provided that the provisions of substantive law in force at the time the given offence was committed shall be applied regarding the offences committed prior to the entry into force of the above-mentioned provisions. Prior to entry into force of the provisions of this Act determined by Act XXXIX of 2014 on the Amendment of certain acts related to budgetary planning and the more effective provision of money market and public utility services, the Media Council shall send, in the ongoing proceedings started pursuant to Article 16 (2) of the Media Act, the draft list specified in Article 16 (2) to the European Commission, for approval, with the provision that the proceeding, following the entry into force of this Act, shall not qualify as a regulatory procedure as per the Act on Administrative Proceedings.

REFERENCES

1. Bartel, Diane. Putting on Appearances: Gender and Advertising. Temple University Press, 1988.
2. Examines the cultural meaning behind contemporary American advertising. The author shows how gender identities are emphasized and how advertising created a gendered relationship with the consumer.
3. Chapman, Simon. Great Expectorations: Advertising and the Tobacco Industry. London: Comedia, 1986.
4. The first major study to challenge the tobacco industry's claim that people are not affected by cigarette advertising.
5. Dyer, Gillian. Advertising as Communication. London: Methuen 1982.
6. Examines advertising as a form of communication in contemporary society and places it in its wider cultural and economic context.
7. Fox, Stephen. The Mirror Makers: A History of American Advertising and Its Creators. New York: Random, 1985.
8. Beginning with the origins of advertising in the nineteenth century, the book discusses the history of advertising to the present day.
9. Jhally, Sut. The Codes of Advertising: Fetishism and The Political Economy of Meaning in The Consumer Society. New York: Routledge, 1990.
10. Jhally argues that by watching commercial messages on TV, viewers actively create symbolic meaning and also generate profit for the media in return for the `wage' of entertainment.
11. Key, Wilson Bryan. Subliminal Seduction: Ad Media's Manipulation of A Not So Innocent America. New York: New American Library, 1981.
12. An exploration of the use of subliminal images in advertising.
13. Leiss, William et al. Social Communication in Advertising: Persons. Products and Images of Well-Being (Second Edition: Revised and Enlarged). New York: Routledge 1990.
14. The book looks at how advertising encompasses three influential domains of our lives: industrial technology, popular culture, and mass media.
15. Martin, David N. Romancing the Brand: The Power of Advertising and How to Use It. New York: AMACON, 1989.
16. An advertising professional tells how to use advertising to give brands the celebrity status they need for success in today's cluttered marketplace.
17. Moog, Carol. "Are They Selling Her Lips?" Advertising and Identity. New York: William Morrow, 1990.

18. Moog wants us to understand the psychological effects of advertising by putting the reader into an active dialogue with the creative process.: You will see what is behind the advertiser's message; what the ad is trying to say; what it is actually saying; and how you, as a consumer, interact with it.
19. Nelson, Joyce. Sultans of Sleeze: Public Relations and The Media. Toronto: Between The Lines Press, 1989.
20. Investigation of recent PR tactics for "the manufacture of consent". psychographic polling, advocacy ads, public affairs lobbying, and news management strategies that protect the status quo. Also looks at specific PR campaigns.
21. Ogilvy, David. Ogilvy on Advertising. Toronto: Jon Wiley, 1983.
22. Discussion of topics such as good and bad advertising campaigns and how to write successful copy.
23. Singer, Benjamin D. Advertising and Society. Don Mills: Addison-Wesley, 1987.
24. The book examines the present structure of advertising institutions, its explicit and explicit mechanism of social control, and control exerted over advertising.
25. Wernick, Andrew. Promotional Culture: Advertising. Ideology and Symbolic Expression. London: Sage, 1991.
26. A detailed analysis of advertisements as promotional texts showing how its impact on cultural formation has become increasingly fundamental with the spread of the market into every facet of social life.
27. Williamson, Judith. Decoding Advertisements: Ideology and Meaning in Advertising. London: Marion Boyars, 1978.
28. A detailed examination of advertisements attractiveness and appeal. And a discussion of the economic and ideological functions of advertising.
29. Ang, Ien. Desperately Seeking The Audience. London:Routledge, 1991.
30. Looking closely to American and European approaches to the TV audience, Ang gives us new insights into television culture, with the audience seen not as an object to be controlled, but as active social subjects, engaging with television in stubbornly contradictory ways.
31. Ball-Rokeach, Sandra J. and Cantor, Muriel G. (Editors).Media: Audience and Social Structure. London: Sage, 1986.
32. A sociological study of the media audience as active individuals who consumer media products in pursuit of their personal and social goals.
33. Barwise, Patrick and Ehrenberg, Andrew. Television and its Audience.

London: Sage, 1989.

34. The book looks at the nature of television starting from an audience perspective.
35. Bower, Robert T. The Changing Television Audience in America. New York: Columbia University Press, 1985.
36. Based on twenty years of research, the book looks at attitudes towards television.
37. Buckingham, David (Editor). Reading Audiences: Young People and The Media. Manchester: Manchester University Press, 1993.
38. Examines the diverse roles the media play in the family and peer group and also the complex ways in which young people make sense of what they watch and read.
39. Goodhardt, G.J., Ehrenberg, A.S.C., and Collins, M.A.Television Audience: Patterns of Viewing: An Update. London: Gower, 1987.
40. Summarizes much of what is known about how people watch television.
41. Jenkins, Henry. Textual Poachers: Television Fans and Participatory Culture. New York: Routledge, 1992.
42. An ethnographic account of the media fan community, its interpretive strategies, social institutions and cultural practices, and its troubled relationships to the mass mediaand consumer capitalism.
43. Lewis, Justin. The Ideological Octopus: An Exploration of Television and Its Audience. New York: Routledge, 1991.
44. Lewis suggests that the medium influences us in unpredictable ways, depending upon what we bring to the experience of watching television. He employs two major qualitative studies, one of TV news and the other of The Cosby show.
45. Lull, James. Inside Family Viewing: Ethnographic Research on Television's Audiences. New York: Routledge, 1990.
46. Working from an ethnographic perspective, Lull constructs a dialogue between the traditionally differing fields of quantitative and qualitative research in communications and cultural studies.
47. Seiter, Ellen et al. (Editors). Remote Control: Television. Audiences and Cultural Power. London: Routledge, 1989.
48. Essays investigating how viewers watch television and what they think about the programs they see.
49. Blum, Eleanor. Basic Books in The Mass Media (Second Edition). Chicago: University of Illinois Press, 1980

50. . An annotated selected book list covering general communications, book publishing, broadcasting, editorial journalism, film, magazines, and advertising.
51. Blum, Eleanor. Mass Media Biblionrahy: An Annotated Guide to Books and Journals for Research and Reference. Chicago: University of Illinois Press, 1990.
52. The successor to the 1972 and 1980 edtions of Basic Books in the Mass Media has been updated to 1987 and extensively revised and expanded.
53. Cooke, Liz (Editor). Media Studies Bibliography. London: BFI, 1984.
54. Intended primarily for teachers new to the field of Media Education and to complement the separate reading lists on film and television which are produced by the British Film Institute - Guide To Film Studies in secondary and Further Education and Television Studies: A Selected Book List.
55. Geretschlaeger, Ingrid. International Annotated Bibliography on Hedia Education. Paris: UNESCO, 1987.
56. Covering the period 1975-1985, this list draws from international sources in Australia, France, Great Britain, Norway, Switerland, India, Denmark,Germany, Italy and the USA.
57. Soukop, Paul A. Christian Communication: A Bibliographical Survey. New York: Greenwood Press, 1989.
58. Provides an introductory guide to the study of Christian communication by surveying and annotating a fairly representative cross section of literature in all areas of communication studies.
59. Buckingham, David. Children Talking Television: The Making of Television Literacy. London: The Falmer Press, 1993.
60. Discusses children's responses to television programs and analyses the role of television in family and peer group relationships.
61. Carlsson-Paige, Nancy and Levin, Diane E.. Who's Calling the Shots? How to Respond Effectively to Children's Fascination with War Play and War Toys. Philadelphia: New Society Publishers, 1990.
62. Examines the positive developmental needs served by dramatic play and contrasts them with the unimaginative, narrow -scripted play encouraged by today's merchandise-oriented children's tv and the accompanying specific war-related paraphernalia offered by the toy industry.
63. Davies, Maire Messenger. Television is Good For Your Kids. London: Hilary Shipman, 1989.
64. The book draws on recent research and first-hand evidence from children.

It shows how children bring their own resources of common sense, scepticism and creativity to bear on television; and that their lives and imaginations can be stimulated and enhanced by the use of television.

65. Dorr, Aimee. Television and Children: A Special Medium for a Special Audience. London: Sage, 1986.
66. The author emphasises the child's active role in making sense of television and determining its effect on him or her.
67. Gore, Tipper. Raising PG Children in an X-Rated Society. Nashville: Abingdon, 1985.
68. Written for parents who want to understand how to deal with the explicit messages on tv that bombard their children.
69. Greenfield, Patricia Marks. Mind and Media: The Effects of Television. Computers and Video Games. London: Fontana, 1984.
70. The author argues that the media can contribute to a child's development and that the ideal environment includes a multi-media approach to learning.
71. Gunter, Barrie and McAleer, Jill L. Children and Television: The One Eyed Monster? London: Routledge, 1990.
72. Examines how children use television, their response to it, and the effects it has on them, and concludes that children are far more selective and critical viewers than we give them credit for.
73. Hodge, Bob and Tripp, David. Children and Television: A Semiotic Approach. Cambridge: Polity Press, 1986.
74. An analysis of the messages of television cartoons and an examination of how children interpret these messages.
75. Kinder, Marsha. Playing With Power in Movies, Television and Video Games: From Muppet Babies to Teenage Mutant Ninja Turtles. Berkeley: University of California Press, 1991.
76. Traces the commercial and stylistic exchanges and interconnections among movies. videos, video games etc to show how they position today's youngster both as a passive consumer and as an interactive player.
77. Kline, Stephen. Out of The Garden: Toys and Children's Culture in the Age of TV Marketing. London: Verso, 1993.
78. Examiines the history of children's play, culture and toys. profiles the rise of children's mass media, reveals how the opportunity to reach children through tv was a pivotal point in developing new approaches to advertising. Examines how toy commercials provide a hots of sterotyped figures around which children can organize their imaginative experience.

79. Liebert, Robert M. and Sprafkin, Joyce. The Early Window: Effects of Television on Children and Youth (Third Edition). New York: Pergamon, 1988.

80. An updated account of the theory and research which has a direct bearing on television and children's attitudes, development and behaviour.

81. Livesley, Jack and Trotz, Frank. The Penguin Guide to Children's TV and Video. Toronto: Penguin, 1993.

82. Examines children's television shows from Saturday morning through to primetime, as well as reviews more than 400 specific programs and films for children of all ages.

83. Luke, Carmen. Television and Your Child: A Guide For Concerned Parents. Toronto: Kagan and Woo, 1988.

84. A practical guide for parents on how to teach children to watch television.

85. McDonnell, Kathleen. Kid Culture: Children & Adults & Popular Culture. Toronto: Second Story Press, 1994.

86. Examines why pop culture is an irresistable lure to kids and at the same time an adhesive which binds them together in a subculture of their own

87. Neuman, Susan B. Literacy in The Television Age: The Myth of the TV Age. Norwood, NJ: Ablex, 1991.

88. A review and synthesis ofthe major studies on how television influences children as well as a discussion of a new series of studies which analyze the relationship between media and literacy using both quantitative and qualitative measures

89. Palmer, Edward L. Television and America's Children: A Crisis of Neglect. New York: Oxford University Press, 1988.

90. The author focuses on the role of government, commercial television and public television in a search for a solution to the problem of American children's tv programming.

91. Palmer, Patricia. The Lively Audience: A Study of Children Around The TV Set. Sydney: Allen and Unwin, 1986.

92. The book reveals how children interact with television, how they incorporate it into their lives, and how television means very different things to different children.

93. Provenzo, Eugene F, Jr.. Video Kids: Making Sense Of Nintendo. Cambridge: Harvard University Press, 1991.

94. The author argues that from a social and cultural point of view, video games reflect and pass on the particular values of mainstream culture.

95. Schneider, Cy. Children's Television: The Art. The Business.and How It Works. Lincolnwood: NTC Business Books, 1989.
96. A guide for professional marketeers that looks at the forces that drive children's television, from programmers and advertisers to parents and children.
97. Schrag, Robert L. Taming The Wild Tube: A Family's Guide to Television and Video. Chapel Hill, NC: North Carolina University Press, 1990.
98. Written by a media professional and parent, the book proposed a genuinely constructive role for television in the lives of families and shows how to do this. Over 100 videotapes and programs are reviewed along with ways to influence network offerings.
99. Schwartz, Steven A. and Schwartz, Janet. Parent's Guide to Video Games: Essential Advice for Every Parent Whose Child Plays Video Games!. Rocklin, CA: Prima Publishing, 1994.
100. A ratings guide to the most popular video games, as well as discussion of how to make playing video games a family experience, how to choose the best system, how to manage the time children spend with video games and other topics.
101. Seiter, Ellen. Sold Separately: Parents and Children in Consumer Culture. New Brunswick,NJ: Rutgers University Press, 1993.
102. Argues that toys and television are culture and must be understood as cultures of childhood, of women's domestic labour, and as intersections of media and consumer goods.
103. Sheff, David. Game Over: How Nintendo Zapped an American Industry, Captured Your Dollars, and Enslaved Your Children. New York: Random House, 1993.
104. Traces the history of Nintendo, its marketing techniques and its plans.
105. Tuchscherer, Pamela. TV Interactive Toys: The New High Tech Threat to Children: Fight Back Without a Gun - Arm Your Child With Knowledge. Bend, OR: Pinaroo Publishing, 1988.
106. Describes the possible effects of interactive tv toys on children and also deals with how to help children become critical viewers of television.
107. Balio, Tino (Editor). Hollywood In The Age of Television. Boston: Unwin Hyman, 1990.
108. Essays tracing the history of the relationship between television and the movie industry from the 1940's to the present.
109. Bennett, Tony and Woollacott, Janet. Bond and Beyond: The Political Career of a Popular Hero. London: MacMillan, 1987.

110. Examines the image of Bond constructed in the novels and films and its reflection in a wide range of other media.
111. Boyum, Joy Gould. Double Exposure: Fiction into Film. New York: Mentor, 1985.
112. Refuting the view that film adaptations are inferior to the works on which they are based, Boyum contends that film is an art eminently capable of translating a novel, not only in plot and theme, but in style, technique and effect.
113. Bywater, Tim and Sobchack, Thomas. An Introduction to Film Criticism: Major Critical Approaches to Narrative Film. New York: Longman, 1989.
114. Examining seven principal techniques of criticism - journalistic, humanist, auteurist, genre, social science, historical, and ideological/theoretical - the text discusses the basic tenets, audiences, practitioners, and functions of each approach and gives a brief history of its development.
115. Clandfield, David. Canadian Film. Toronto: Oxford University Press, 1987.
116. A historical overview of film in both English and French Canada.
117. Ellis, Jack C. The Documentary Idea: A Critical History of English Language Documentary Film and Video. Englewood Cliffs: Prentice Hall, 1989.
118. Chronicles the main line of English language documentary in Great Britain, Canada, and the United States.
119. Fetherling, Douglas (Editor). Documents in Canadian Film. Peterborough: Broadview Press, 1988.
120. Drawn from official papers as well as from scholarly and popular periodicals, the book presents textual evidence of Canada's cinematic heritage and of the continuing struggle to enlarge film's place in the society.
121. Giannetti, Louis. Understanding Movies (Fourth Edition). Englewood Cliffs: Prentice-Hall, 1987.
122. Deals with such aspects of film as photography, editing, sound, acting, genre, and theory.
123. Hill, Geoffrey. Illuminating Shadows: The Mythic Power of Film. Boston: Shambhala, 1992.
124. In this study of film as a vehicle of mythology, the author asserts that the movie theatre is the modern equivalent of the tribal dreamhouse. His analysis of 17 films deals with timeless mythic themes and finds patterns unique to our own age.

125. Knelman, Martin. Home Movies: Tales From The Canadian Film World. Toronto: Key Porter, 1987.

126. A look at the financial, artistic and political complexities of Canadian film making over the past two decades.

127. Knight, Arthur. The Liveliest Art (Revised) New York: Mentor, 1979.

128. The classic history of world film.

129. Lewis, Jon. The Road to Romance and Ruin: Teen Films and Youth Culture. New York: Routledge, 1992.

130. Analysis of teen films as the medium best able to represent the chaotic and conflicting experiences of youth. Sees teen films as focused on the breakdown of traditional forms of authority - school, church, family.

131. Miller, Marc Crispin (Editor). Seeing Through Movies. New York: Pantheon, 1990.

132. Six essays explore the ways in which films have merged into our culture - how movies have come to exert a renewed influence on every aspect of contemporary life from consumerism to military policy.

133. Monaco, James. How To Read a Film. New York: Oxford University Press, 1977.

134. A classic study of the art, technology, language, history and theory of film and media.

135. Murray, Edward. Nine American Film Critics. New York: Frederick Ungar, 1975.

136. A rare critical examination of some of the best critics.

137. Nelson, Joyce. The Colonized Eye: Rethinking The Grierson Legend. Toronto: Between The Lines, 1988.

138. The author looks at the National Film Board of Canada's founder and his sponsorship formula for documentaries, the views expressed in his articles, and many of the films made under his tutelage.

139. O'Brien, Tom. The Screening of America: Movies and Values from Rocky to Rain Man. New York: Frederick Ungar, 1990.

140. An original investigation of how movies have reflected and helped shape the values of today's generation. O'Brien focuses on the key values (or their absence) found in American films over the past fifteen years in order to see more clearly what Americans really cherish in life, and how these values have evolved or change.

141. Philips, William H. Analyzing Films: A Practical Guide. Toronto: Holt, Rinehart and Winston, 1984.

142. Designed to give beginning students guidance in viewing, describing, and analyzing films, this is a splendid book for teachers.

143. Twitchell, James B. Dreadful Pleasures: An Anatomy of Modern Horror. New York: Oxford University Press, 1985.

144. An examination of the persistence of horror in our culture - art, literature, film - and our need for it.

145. Wyver, John. The Moving Image: An International History of Film. Television and Video. London: Basil Blackwell, 1989.

146. the story of the moving image from the prehistory and invention of cinema to video and beyond.

147. Sex Role Stereotyping in The Broadcast Media. Ottawa: Canadian Radio-Television and Telecommunications Commission, 1986.

148. A report on self-regulation by the broadcasting and television industry outlining the attempt to eliminate sex role stereotyping in the broadcast media.

149. Baehr, Helen (Editor). Women and the Media. Oxford: Pergamon Press, 1980.

150. Articles taken from "Women's Studies International Quarterly."

151. Baehr, Helen and Dyer, Gillian (Editors) Boxed In: Women and Television. New York: Pandora, 1987.

152. Essays looking at women's relationship with television - as performers, writers, program makers and viewers.

153. Banner, Louise. American Beauty. Chicago: University of Chicago Press, 1983.

154. Focusing on the ideals of female beauty as central expressions on American values, the book chronicles the social history of the perception of feminine beauty in America.

155. Brown, Mary Ellen (Editor). Television and Women's Culture: The Politics of the Popular. London: Sage, 1990.

156. Essays showing how and why different media such as game shows, police fiction and soap opera offer women opportunities for negotiation of their own meanings and their own aesthetic appreciation.

157. Brownmiller, Susan. Femininity. New York: Ballantine, 1984.

158. A study of those aspects of a woman's life which are embodied in the term femininity.

159. Burstyn, Varda. Women Against Censorship. Vancouver: Douglas and McIntyre, 1985.

160. A series of essays arguing that far from protecting women against violence, censorship will perpetuate those conditions which place them in danger.

161. Cohan, Steven and HArk, Ina Rae (Editors). Screening the Male: Exploring Masculinities in Hollywood Cinema. London: Routledge, 1993.

162. Demonstrates that Hollywood's representation of the male and his masculinity deserves the same kind of critical attention devoted to the problem posed by the female and her femininity.

163. Courtney, Alice and Whipple, Thomas U. Sex Stereotyping in Advertising. Toronto: DC Heath, 1983.

164. EXamines the results of sex stereotyping and questions its effectiveness as an advertising tool.

165. Coward, Rosalin. Female Desires: How They are Sought, Bought and Packaged. New York: Grove, 1985.

166. A study of female pleasure showing how society represents and misrepresents what is pleasurable to a woman.

167. Creedon, Pamela J. (Editor). Women In Mass Communication: Challenging Gender Values. London: Sage, 1989.

168. Essays on topics such as feminist perspectives on media law; minority women in mass communication; women in television, advertising, pr, newspapers and radio; and the effect of women communication teachers on their students.

169. de Laurentis, Teresa (Editor). Feminist Studies: Critical Studies. Bloomington: Indiana University Press, 1986.

170. Essays in the area of history, scientific discourse, literary criticism, and cultural theory.

171. Gentile, Mary C. Film Feminisms: Theory and Practice. Westport: Greenwood Press, 1985.

172. The focus of this book is the internalization of feminist film theory and its questions.

173. Goffman, Irving. Gender Advertisements. Toronto: Fitzhenry and Whiteside, 1979.

174. NB: Out of print. Though somewhat dated, the book is regarded as a seminal study of ways in which men and women are pictured in advertisements.

175. Gunter, Barry. Television and Sex Role Stereotyping. London: John Libbey, 1986.

176. A study of the portrayal of the sexes on television as well as the social effects of television and sex stereotyping.

177. Kaplan, E. Ann. Motherhood and Representation: The Mother inPopular Culture and Melodrama. London: Routledge, 1992.

178. Consideration of motherhood from three areas: the historical, the psycho-analytic, and the literary and the media.

179. Kay, Karyn and Peary, Gerald (Editors). Women and The Cinema: A Critical Anthology. New York: E.P. Dutton, 1977.

180. A collection of 45 essays on women and film.

181. Kramarae, Cheris (Editor). Technology and Women's Voices: Keeping in Touch. New York: Routledge & Kegan Paul, 1988.

182. Essays which focus upon gender to understand the social relations of technological processes and explores their effects on women's social interaction.

183. Kuhn, Annette. The Power of The Image: Essays on Representation and Sexuality. London: Routledge and Kegan Paul, 1985.

184. Combining semiotics and Marxist-feminist analysis, cultural studies and historical approaches the author investigates issues around representation and sexuality.

185. Kuhn, Annette. Women's Pictures: Feminism and The Cinema. London: Routledge and Kegan Paul, 1982.

186. A discussion of the issues, terms and alternatives for feminist film analysis and for feminist filmmakers.

187. Lakhoff, Robin and Scherr, Raquel. Face Value: The Politics Of Beauty. New York: Routledge, 1984.

188. Critiques the images of male and female beauty in our culture using a historical perspective.

189. Mattelart, Michele. Women, Media and Crisis: Femininity and Disorder. London: Comedia, 1986.

190. A look at the relationship between the present economic crisis of Western and Third World societies and the changing position of women in these societies.

191. Penley, Constance (Editor). Feminism and Film Theory. New York: Routledge, 1988.

192. Essays tracing the major issues in feminist film theory as they have evolved over the last decade.

193. Pribram, E. Deidre (Editor). Female Spectators: Looking at Film and

Television. London: Verso, 1988.

194. Essays providing a picture of feminist film criticism in the 1980's, readings of individual tv shows and films, and insights from women in the business today.

195. Root, Jane (Compiler). Women's Film List. London: BFI, 1985.

196. A list of films and television directed by women as well as a list of films of particular interest to women.

197. Spigel, Lynn and Mann, Denise (Editors). Private Screenings: Television and the Female Consumer. Minneapolis: University of Minnesota Press, 1992.

198. Essays exploring the ways television had inserted itself into women's lives, both at home and in the marketplace.

199. Szirom, Tricia. Teaching Gender? Sex Education and Sexual Stereotypes. Sydney: Allen and Unwin, 1988.

200. The book provides a perspective on the creation of gender and the way in which sex education programs in schools contribute to this.

201. Wolf, Naomi. The Beauty Myth. Toronto: Vintage, 1990.

202. Wolf exposes the beauty myth through the ages and its oppressive function today, in the home, at work, in literature, in the media and in relationship between men and women and between women and women.

203. Bonn, Thomas. Undercover: An Illustrated History of American Mass Market Paperbacks. London: Penguin, 1982.

204. An enjoyable history of mass market paperbacks from dime novels of the nineteenth century to the popular novels read today.

205. Draper, Robert. Rolling Stone Magazine: The Uncensored History. New York: Doubleday, 1990.

206. A complete, detailed, accurate, and inside account of the magazine's colourful history. Includes a portrait of founder Jann S. Wenner and his rise to press baron and power broker.

207. Jacoby, Jacob and Hoyer, Wayne D. The Comprehension and Miscomprehension of Print Communication: An Investigation of Mass Media Magazines. New York: The Advertising Educational Foundation, 1987.

208. A study done for practitioners and academics on how much comprehension readers actually have of what is presented them.

209. Jensen, Margaret Ann. Love's Sweet Return: The Harlequin Story. Toronto: The Women's Press, 1984.

210. An examination of the phenomenon of romance fiction, focusing specifically on one of the most successful book publishers in the world, the Canadian-based Harlequin Enterprises.Mogel, Leonard. The Magazine (Second Edition) Chester: Globe Pequot, 1988. A study of the magazine business for those considering entering this field.

211. Sampson, Robert. Deadly Excitement: Shadows and Phantoms. Bowling Green, Ohio: Bowling Green State University Popular Press, 1989.

212. Essays celebrating yesterday's pulp magazines and their heroes and heroines.

213. Sutherland, Fraser. The Monthly Epic: A History of Canadian Magazines. Markham: Fitzhenry & Whiteside, 1989.

214. The political, social and technological events that influenced Canada and the publishers, writers and editors who stamped their publications with their own vision and personal style are chronicled from 1978 to 1989.

215. Tebbel, John and Zuckerman, Mary Ellen. The Magazine in America: 1741 - 1990. New York: Oxford University Press, 1991.

216. A comprehensive one volume history of magazines.Wainwright, London. The Great American Magazine: An Inside History of Life. New York: Ballantine, 1986. A history of LIFE magazine.

217. News:Chancellor, John and Mears, Walter. The News Business. New York: Harper and Row, 1983.

218. A readable analysis of reporting in the press. The authors discuss style, slant, col our in news stories and they pass judgement on good and bad reporting.

219. Clurman, Richard M. Beyond Malice: The Media's Years of Reckoning. New Brunswick: Transaction Publishers, 1988.

220. A critical report of the news media in the 1980's.

221. Desbarats, Peter. Guide to Canadian News Media. Toronto: Harcourt, Brace, Jovanovich, Canada. 1990.

222. A concise overview of Canadian news media - their history, structure, method, personnel and impact on society - as well as a discussion of major issues in contemporary journalism.

223. Elliott, Deni (Editor). Responsible Journalism. London: Sage, 1986.

224. Essays dealing where journalistic responsibilities come from, how they fit in with legal and press theories, and how they play out in specific contexts.

225. Hartley, John. Understanding News. New York: Routledge, 1982.

226. A well written British book showing how news is constructed. Suggested questions and projects highlight the key issues.

227. Herman, Edward S. and Chomsky, Noam. Manufacturing Consent: The Political Economy of The Mass Media. New York: Pantheon, 1988.

228. The authors dissect the way in which the marketplace and the economics of publishing significantly shape the news.

229. MacLean, Eleanor. Between the Lines: How To Detect Bias and Propaganda in the News and Everyday Life. Montreal: Black Rose Books, 1981.

230. How to decode daily newspapers and radio and tv news.

231. Manoff, Robcrt Karl and Schudson, Michael (Editors). Readingthe News. New York: Pantheon, 1986.

232. Six essays on the who, what, when, where, why and how of journalism.

233. Stephens, Mitchell. A History of the News: From Drum to Satellite. New York: Viking, 1988.

234. The book introduces the history not just of journalism but of news.

235. Stewart, Walter. Canadian Newspapers: The Inside Story. Edmonton: Hurtig, 1980.

236. A critique of Canadian newspapers that has much useful inside information.

237. Strentz, Herbert. News Reporters and News Sources: Accomplices in Shaping and Misshaping the News (Second Edition). Ames: Iowa State University Press, 1989.

238. Focuses on what happens before a news story is written and considers the roles and responsibilities of reporters and sources in serving the news audience.

239. Vipond, Hary. The Mass Media In Canada. Toronto: James Lorimer, 1989.

240. Concentrates on daily papers, general interest magazines, movies, radio and television from their beginnings in Canada. Also deals with the attempts of the government to make the media serve national goals.

241. Walker, Tony, Golden, David and Fox, Brian. Behind The Headlines: A Toronto Star Media Literacy Program. Toronto: The Toronto Star, 1991.

242. A program designed to meet the needs of teachers and students in English, History, Business, Marketing, and Media Studies from middle school through to grade 12. The loose- leaf book is divided into 8 sections, each of which functions as a self-contained unit about various aspects

of producing a newspaper. There are questions and activities for each section.

243. Zwicker, Barrie and MacDonald, Dick (Editors). The News: Inside Canadian Media. Ottawa: Deneau, 1980.
244. An anthology of articles from CONTENT, Canada's national news media magazine.
245. Bain, George. Gotcha! How The Media Distort the News. Toronto: Key Porter Books, 1994.
246. Concrete examples of instances in which the media have served the Canadian public badly by yielding to political bias, ingrained negativity and intellectual laziness.
247. Gans, Herbert J. Deciding What's News: A Study of CBS Evening News, NBC Nightly News. Newsweek and Time. New York: Random House, 1980.
248. The comparison of the different media is especially interesting.
249. Parenti, Michael. Inventing Reality: The Politics of the Mass Media. New York: St. Martin's Press. 1986.
250. Concerns the way that public consciousness is shaped by the manipulation of the news.
251. Postman, Neil and Powers, Steve. How To Watch TV News. New York: Penguin, 1992.
252. Shows the difference between what TV news says it is presenting and what it actually delivers; points out the symbiotic relationship between TV news and advertising.
253. Robinson, John P. and Levy Mark R. The Main Source: Learning From Television News. London: Sage, 1986.
254. Discuss the "myth" that people learn about world events from television news.
255. Wallis, Roger and Baran, Stanley. The Known World of Broadcast News: International News and The Electronic Media. New York: Routledge, 1990.
256. An analysis of recent advancements in news broadcasting which have allowed events to be broadcast all over the world in a matter of hours, and the effect this has had on the integrity and un-biased nature of media broadcasting.
257. **Politics:**
258. Atkinson, Max. Our Masters' Voices: The Language and Body Language

of Politics. London: Methuen, 1984.

259. A review of how politicians use media to attempt to win our hearts and minds and votes.

260. Chilton, Paul. Orwellian Language and The Media. London: Pluto Press, 1989.

261. An analyses of the ideas of Orwell, Habermas, Chomsky and others to show how verbal messages transmitted by the media during and after the Falklands war expose the use of language as a political tool.

262. Chomsky, Noam. Necessary Illusions: Thought Control in Democratic Societies. Montreal: CBC Enterprises, 1989.

263. An inquiry into the nature of the media and the role of intellectuals in a democratic political situation.

264. Entman, Robert M. Democracy Without Citizens: Media and The Decay of American Politics. New York: Oxford University Press, 1989.

265. A discussion of the role and limitations of the press in advancing the democratic agenda.

266. Hollingsworth, Mark. The Press and Political Dissent: A Question of Censorship. London: Pluto, 1986.

267. The book looks at the way the British press has branded as treachery every view which differs from its own.

268. Kern, Montague. 30-Second Politics: Political Advertising in the Eiqhties. New York: Praeger, 1989.

269. In this age of the media campaign where television is the preferred source of candidate information, the author offers a scrutiny of political advertisements from 1972 to 1989.

270. Ryan, Michael and Kellner, Douglas. Camera Politica: The Politics and Ideology of Contemporary Hollywood Film. Bloomington: Indiana University Press, 1988.

271. Traces the major transitions in American society from the period of the New Left to that of the New Right and states that Hollywood film undermined liberalism and led to the rise of conservatism.

272. Angus, Ian and Jhally, Sut (Editors). Cultural Politics in Contemporary America. New York: Routledge, 1989.

273. Lays out the complex ways in which American media and American culture are powerfully interlocked.

274. Ekstrom, Reynolds R. Access Guide to Pop Culture. New Rochelle, NY: Don Bosco Multimedia, 1989.

275. Informative and critical commentaries on popular culture from a Christian perspective.

276. Finlayson, lain. Denim: An American Legend. New York: SImon and Schuster, 1990.

277. A record of the changing face of denim on the street, the screen, and in advertisement which examines the changing social and cultural implications of wearing blue jeans.

278. Fiske, John. Media Matters: Everyday Culture and Political Change. Minneapolis,MN: University of Minnesota Press, 1994.

279. Using examples of Murphy Brown, O.J. Simpson, Anita Hill, Rodney King and others, Fiske examines how people engaged in struggles over race, class, and gender have both been exploited and exploit the media.

280. Fiske, John. Power Plays Power Works. London: Verso, 1993.

281. Fiske argues that the consensus model has oulived its usefullness for everyone except those in control. He develops a theory of localizing powers to defend against the thrust of top-down power.

282. Fiske, John. Reading The Popular. Boston: Unwin Hyman, 1989.

283. An analysis of popular "texts" (shopping malls, popular music, television) which reveals both their explicit and implicit (and often opposite) meanings and uses, and the social and political dynamics they reflect.

284. Fiske, John. Understanding Popular Culture. Boston: Unwin Hyman, 1989.

285. Presentation of a radically different theory of what it means for culture to be popular: that is, literally, of the people. It is not imposed on them, it is created by them, and its pleasures and meanings reflect popular tastes and concerns.

286. Grossberg, Lawrence. We Gotta Get Out Of This Place: Popular Conservatism and Postmodern Culture. New York: Routledge, 1992.

287. A study of the power and importance of rock music in American history and the effect the new conservatism has on it.

288. Keen, Sam. Faces of the Enemy: Reflections of the Hostile Imagination. San Francisco: Harper and Row, 1988.

289. An analysis of propaganda posters, biased cartoons, and distorted images served up in print and on screen.

290. Kowinski, William Severini. The Malling of America: An Inside Look at The Great Consumer Paradise. New York: William Morrow & Company, 1985.

291. (NB: Out of print). A most thorough analysis making important connections between our experience of television and the shopping mall environment.

292. Real, Michael. Super Media: A Cultural Studies Approach. London: Sage, 1989.

293. An introduction and illustration of the newly emerging cultural studies approach to understanding the media in society.

294. Rushkoff, Douglas. Media Virus: Hidden Agendas in Popular Culture. New York: Ballantine, 1994.

295. Chronicles the adventures of the media-savvy culture jammers who have seized the media and turned it to their secretly anti-authoritarian ends.

296. Storey, John. An Introductory Guide to Cultural Theory and Popular Culture. Athens: Georgia: University of Georgia Press, 1993.

297. Charts the many problems encounteerd and the many solutions suggested in cultural theory's complex engagement with popular culture.

298. Scultze, Quentin J. et al. Dancing In The Dark: Youth. Popular Culture and the Electronic Media. Grand Rapids, Ml: William B. Eerdmans, 1991.

299. Critical examination of the role of the electronic media in packaging popular culture for youth consumption. The relationship is seen as a symbiotic one where the media need youth for exonomic survival and youth needs the guidance, nurture and constructed rality which media provides.

300. Twitchell, James B. Carnival Culture: The Trashing of America. New York: Columbia University Press, 1992.

301. Looks at the changes in publishing, movies and television since the 1960's that have affected changes on taste, particularly what is considered to be the vulgar.

302. Williamson, Judith. Consuming Passions: The Dynamics of Popular Culture. London: Marion Boyars. 1987.

303. The classic study that examines the forces of films, books, television, advertising etc which channel our tastes and structure our lives.

304. Blanchard, Tim et al. The Music Business: A Teaching Pack. London: Hodder & Stoughton, 1989.

305. A photocopiable pack - with audio cassette - which provides an introduction through active learning to all aspects of the music business.

306. Cooper, B. Lee. Popular Music Perspectives: Ideas, Themes, and Patterns in Contemporary Lyrics. Bowling Green, Ohio: Bowling Green State

University Popular Press, 1991.

307. Social change, human interaction, technology and intellectual development are the general points of departure for specific examinations of public education, railroads, deaths, cars, and rebels. These are the ideas and themes prominent in contemporary lyrics.
308. Frith, Simon (Editor). Facing the Music. New York: Pantheon, 1988.
309. Five excellent essays on pop music: the rationale behind Hit Radio; the meaning of black and white "crossover"; the packaging of pop as a commodity; how pop shapes teenage identity and sexuality; and an analysis of the pop industry in the age of video.
310. Frith, Simon. Music for Pleasure: Essays in the Sociology of Pop. New York: Routledge, 1988.
311. A wide ranging analysis of pop music and the entertainment industry in America and Britain.
312. Frith, Simon. Sound Effects: Youth. Leisure and the Politics of Rock `n' Roll. London: Constable, 1983.
313. A sociological perspective on the culture of rock with sections on production, consumption and ideology.
314. Frith, Simon and Goodwin, Andrew (Editors). On Record: Rock. Pop, and the Written Word. New York: Pantheon, 1990.
315. A comprehensive survey of critical approaches to popular music. Divided by theoretical categories, the book serves as a guide to the growing sophistication and shifting emphases in the field.
316. Frith Simon, Goodwin, Andrew and Grossberg, Lawrence (Editors). Sound and Vision: The Music Video Reader. London: Routledge, 1993.
317. A collection of classic and new articles on music videos.
318. Kaplan, E. Ann. Rocking Around the Clock: Music Television Postmodernism. and Consumer Culture. New York: Methuen, 1987.
319. An examination of the cultural context of Music Television and its relationship to the history of rock music.
320. Sexton, Adam (Editor). Desperately Seeking Madonna. New York: Delta, 1993.
321. Essays, cartoons, tabloid reports, academic essays trace the career of Madonna.
322. Shapiro, Harry. Waiting for The Man: The Story of Drugs and Popular Music. London: Quartet, 1988.
323. An examination of the association between drugs and popular music

giving case studies and the role of organized crime.

324. Shore, Michael. The Rolling Stone Book of Rock Video. New York: Quill, 1984.
325. Traces the history of visual music from the beginnings to 1984.
326. Shuker, Roy. Understanding Popular Music.
327. An introductory senior text which explores the history and meaning of rock and popular muisc.
328. Stambler, Irwin. The Encyclopedia of Pop. Rock and Soul revised Edition). London: Macmillan, 1989.
329. An alphabetical compilation guide to popular music.
330. Ward, Ed et al.. Rock of Ages: The Rolling Stone History of Rock and Roll. New York: Rolling Stone Press, 1986.

CITATION

CHAPTER 1

Elo Ibagere, The Mass Media, the Law and National Security: The Nigerian Perspective, J Soc Sci, 24(2): 121-128 (2010).

CHAPTER 2

Kim P. McCann, The Diversity Policy Model and Assessment of the Policy Debates and Challenges of (Media) Diversity, DOI: 10.1177/2158244013492780.

CHAPTER 3

Wayne W. L. Chan, The Open University of Hong Kong, Hong Kong, DOI: 10.1177/2158244015607935.

CHAPTER 4

El-Jardali F, Bou Karroum L, Bawab L, Kdouh O, El-Sayed F, Rachidi H, et al. (2015) Health Reporting in Print Media in Lebanon: Evidence, Quality and Role in Informing Policymaking. PLoS ONE 10(8): e0136435. doi:10.1371/journal.pone.0136435.

CHAPTER 5

Caterini, M. (2015) Criminal Risk, Media Representation and Role of the Criminal Law Culture. Beijing Law Review, 6, 55-68. doi: 10.4236/blr.2015.61008.

CHAPTER 6

Toole JL, Cha M, González MC (2012) Modeling the Adoption of Innovations in the Presence of Geographic and Media Influences. PLoS ONE 7(1): e29528. doi:10.1371/journal.pone.0029528.

INDEX

C

Civil Servant Cooperative (CSC) 56
Civil Society Organizations (CSOs) 55
Contemporary civil society 81
Criminal phenomenon 81, 82, 91, 94, 96, 97

D

Democracy 15, 16, 18, 19, 20, 21, 22, 26, 30, 31, 32, 33, 34, 35, 36, 37, 38, 39
Designated Market Area (DMA) 29
Diversity Index (DI) 27

E

Eastern Mediterranean Region (EMR) 55
Empirical demonstration 81
Equal Employment of Opportunity rules (EEO) 25

F

Federal Communications Commission's (FCC) 15

I

Independent Television (ITV) 9
Institutional Review Board (IRB) 60

J

Judicial nature 82

L

Lebanon is a Low and Middle Income Country (LMIC) 55

M

Micro-blogging platform 111, 112
Ministry of Public Health (MOPH) 56
Mobilization for Social and Economic Recovery (MAMSER) 4

N

National Social Security Fund (NSSF) 59
Nigerian Television Authority (NTA) 10

P

Peoples Democratic Party (PDP) 9

S

Social network structure 111
Spatial diffusion 112, 113, 125
Spatiotemporal adoption 111, 113, 125

State Security Services (SSS) 10
Susceptible - infected (SI) 112, 118

W

War against Indiscipline (WAI) 4